WOMEN'S RIGHTS IN THE UNITED STATES

WOMEN'S RIGHTS

IN THE

UNITED STATES

A DOCUMENTARY HISTORY

Edited by WINSTON E. LANGLEY
and VIVIAN C. FOX

Primary Documents in American History and Contemporary Issues

GREENWOOD PRESS
Westport, Connecticut • London

Library of Congress Cataloging-in-Publication Data

Women's rights in the United States : a documentary history / edited
by Winston E. Langley and Vivian C. Fox.
      p.   cm.—(Primary documents in American history and
contemporary issues, ISSN 1069–5605)
    Includes bibliographical references and index.
    ISBN 0–313–28755–4 (alk. paper)
      1. Women's rights—United States—History—Sources. 2. Women—
United States—History—Sources. 3. Women—Law and legislation—
United States—History—Sources. I. Langley, Winston. II. Fox,
Vivian C. III. Series.
HQ1236.5.U6W68 1994
305.42'0973—dc20   94–7429

British Library Cataloguing in Publication Data is available.

Library of Congress Catalog Card Number: 94–7429
ISBN: 0–313–28755–4
ISSN: 1069–5605

First published in 1994

Greenwood Press, 88 Post Road West, Westport, CT 06881
An imprint of Greenwood Publishing Group, Inc.

Printed in the United States of America

∞™

The paper used in this book complies with the
Permanent Paper Standard issued by the National
Information Standards Organization (Z39.48–1984).

10 9 8 7 6 5 4 3 2 1

Copyright Acknowledgments

The author and publisher gratefully acknowledge permission to reprint material from the following sources.

David Hall, *The Antinomian Controversy*, pp. 312–316. Duke University Press. Reprinted with permission from the publisher.

From *America's Working Women* by Rosalyn Baxandall, Linda Gordon and Susan Reverby. Copyright © 1976 by Rosalyn Baxandall, Linda Gordon and Susan Reverby. Reprinted by permission of Random House, Inc.

Hamilton—Great Lives Observed. Milton Cantor, Editor. 1971. Used by permission of the publisher, Prentice Hall/a Division of Simon & Schuster.

"Struggling with Words: The Bishops' Letter on Women," November 19, 1992, "Science vs. the Female Scientist," by Shirley M. Tilghman, January 25, 1993 (excerpt), and "Science vs. Women—A Radical Solution," by Shirley M. Tilghman, January 26, 1993. Copyright © 1992/93 by The New York Times Company. Reprinted by permission.

Reprinted from *The Feminine Mystique* by Betty Friedan, with the permission of Victor Gollancz and W.W. Norton & Company, Inc. Copyright © 1963, 1973, 1974, 1983 by Betty Friedan.

Feminism and Pornography by Ronald J. Berger, Patricia Searles, and Charles F. Cottle, pp. 33–43. Copyright © 1991 by Ronald J. Berger, Patricia Searles, and Charles F. Cottle, published by Praeger Publishers, an imprint of Greenwood Publishing Group, Inc., Westport, CT. Reprinted with permission.

Fathers to Daughters: The Legal Foundations of Female Emancipation by Peggy A. Rabkin, p. 184. Copyright © 1980 by Peggy A. Rabkin, published by Greenwood Press, an imprint of Greenwood Publishing Group, Inc., Westport, CT. Reprinted with permission.

The American Slave: A Composite Autobiography, edited by George P. Rawick, 5: Texas Narratives, part 4:174–178; Vol. 9: Arkansas Narratives, part 3:9; Vol. 2: South Carolina Narratives, part 2:12–13. Copyright © 1972 by George P. Rawick, published by Greenwood Press, an imprint of Greenwood Publishing Group, Inc., Westport, CT. Reprinted with permission.

Women at Work: The Transformation of Work and Community in Lowell, Massachusetts, 1826–1860 by Thomas Dublin, 1979. Copyright © Columbia University Press, New York. Reprinted with the permission of the publisher.

Schlesinger-Rockefeller Oral History Project. Francis Hand Ferguson, June, 1974. Interview with James W. Reed, p. 8–9.

Text excerpt from *The Dialectics of Sex* by Shulamith Firestone. Copyright © 1970 by Shulamith Firestone. By permission of William Morrow and Company, Inc., and Jonathan Cape, Ltd.

Jacqueline A. Goggin, "Challenging Sexual Discrimination in the Historical Profession: Women Historians and the American Historical Association, 1890–1940," *AHR*, vol. 97, no. 3 (June 1992), pp. 769–802.

Gerald E. Critoph, "The Flapper and Her Critics" in *Remember the Ladies: New Perspectives in Women in American History: Essays in Honor of Nelson Manfred Blake*, ed. Carol V. R. George (Syracuse: Syracuse University Press, 1975). Reprinted by permission of Syracuse University Press.

To Gregory, Diana, and Michael, whose lives have enriched my own with love. To Carmen and Sylvia, for whom service to others has been a central devotion.

Contents

Part IV: A Woman Is a Woman Is a Woman: The Struggle Continues, 1920–1963   **223**

Series Foreword

This series is designed to meet the research needs of high school and college students by making available in one volume the key primary documents on a given historical event or contemporary issue. Documents include speeches and letters, congressional testimony, Supreme Court and lower court decisions, government reports, biographical accounts, position papers, statutes, and news stories.

The purpose of the series is twofold: (1) to provide substantive and background material on an event or issue through the text of pivotal primary documents that shaped policy or law, raised controversy, or influenced the course of events; and (2) to trace the controversial aspects of the event or issue through documents that represent a variety of viewpoints. Documents for each volume have been selected by a recognized specialist in that subject with the advice of a board of other subject specialists, school librarians, and teachers.

To place the subject in historical perspective, the volume editor has prepared an introductory overview and a chronology of events. Documents are organized either chronologically or topically. The documents are full text or, if unusually long, have been excerpted by the volume editor. To facilitate understanding, each document is accompanied by an explanatory introduction. Suggestions for further reading follow the document or the chapter.

It is the hope of Greenwood Press that this series will enable students and other readers to use primary documents more easily in their research, to exercise critical thinking skills by examining the key documents in American history and public policy, and to critique the variety of viewpoints represented by this selection of documents.

Preface

Hope is the thing with feathers
that perches in the soul
And sings the tune without the words
And never stops at all.

Emily Dickinson

This book, a result of a collaborative process, was begun because of the writers' interest in the role women played in the field of human rights. Somewhere along the way we became infused with the fortitude, the intellectual grandness, the generosity of spirit, the vision, and the hope "that perches in the soul" of the women of America who struggled to give birth to their wholeness as human beings.

Our principal aim is to share with the reader the journeys of the women, and some men, who, armed with hope, challenged the status quo to achieve equal rights for women in America. Beginning with colonial times and ending in 1993, this book explores the nature, development, and significance of the women's movement in the hope that readers will also respond to the issues and spirit of the contributors to women's rights. We sought to maximize this experience through the use of as many original, representative documents as we could uncover—placed in context with their times and the formidable forces of opposition.

To provide a historical awareness of how long, how old, and how continuous the struggle for women's rights has been fulfills another goal of this book. Such an awareness liberates us from the current notion that the women's movement began in the 1960s and enlivens our imagination by encouraging us to ask a "what if" question. What if, for example, all the women—half the population—had been recognized as equal to men from the foundation of this country? What differences would the women, the country, the world have experienced? The nature of this question leads us to pose its converse: Why, for over 350 years, has there been such reluctance to accept intellectually able, socially confident, culturally creative women as participants in the public forum, from the condemned Anne Hutchinson in 1640 to Hillary Rodham Clinton in the 1990s? Indeed, fear of women playing a public role is so deeply embedded in our history that even the distinguished late Senator Sam Ervin found it acceptable to say, paraphrasing Christ's prayer of forgiveness on the cross, after failing in 1972 to convince his fellow senators to vote against the ERA, "Father, forgive us for we know not what we do." But "hope is the thing with feathers that . . . never stops at all."

In our research we were able to find new archival materials, but as the citations and the bibliography show, our book is also indebted to many who have written articles, biographies, documentaries, and other material. In addition, we would like to express our deep appreciation to Lu Houde of Worcester State College for her overflowing generosity, especially her secretarial contributions; to the Antiquarian Society in Worcester, Massachusetts; the Historical Society of Boston; the Widener and Lamont libraries of Harvard University; the valuable Schlesinger Library at Radcliffe; the Mugar Memorial; the theological and law libraries of Boston University; the Women's Library at Massachusetts Institute of Technology; the Boston Public Library; and Smith College for the help we received during our research. Always important, never absent, has been support from family and friends.

Introduction

The preparation of this volume has been, for the editors, inspiring, instructive, and disappointing—inspiring because, among other things, it catalogues the triumph, partial though it has been thus far, of a group that has faced overwhelming odds in its fight to escape stifling injustice and to gain social equality; instructive and disappointing because it clearly shows a United States that, despite its claimed commitment to human equality, has still not reconciled itself to granting equal dignity to over one-half of its population. That failure is particularly evident in certain recurring themes in the nation's history—from what we call "departures" to the "recognition of rights."

What kind of departures do we mean? Look at the Massachusetts of John Winthrop, the American Revolution, the Civil War, World War I and the postsuffrage era, and the Kennedy administration. Each purported to usher in profound changes that would represent a parting of company with the past. For Governor Winthrop, Massachusetts was to be "a city upon a hill"; for sponsors of the Revolution, the republic that they founded was to begin a new social order; and for those who led the nation out of the Civil War—the Radical Republicans—the new United States was to be defined by a reconstructed social system. World War I and the postsuffrage period would launch a "new day" for democracy; and Kennedy proposed a New Frontier. But for women in the United States, there was no departure, no parting of company with the past.

In every instance mentioned above, our leaders deliberately devised schemes to hold women "in their place," to see that they would not be part of any social and cultural departure. Governor Winthrop's scheme (see Documents 3 and 4) was to prevent women from sharing with men the public space or being seen as meriting the exercise of any authority in that space. John Adams (who can be said to have represented the Revolution) overlooked the intellectual and political abilities of women and emphasized their alleged "delicate nature." The Radical Republicans posed as champions of "the Negro hour" (advocates of rights for black men) to mask the continued and increased repression of women. World War I and the postsuffrage era as well as the New Frontier yielded little detectable difference in the nation's attitude toward the rights of women.

Despite the "new day" for democracy, opposition to women's rights coalesced in the 1920s attack on the Flapper—the "new woman" who dared to seek escape from the cultural restrictions imposed on her. The Kennedy administration, more sophisticated than its predecessors, created the Commission on the Status of Women, which actually helped the President sidestep pressure from women's groups for an Equal Rights Amendment (ERA).

Even moral heroes such as Thomas Paine and Abraham Lincoln have contributed to keeping women in their place. President Lincoln, for example, colluded in hiding from the public the fact that a woman, Anna Ella Carroll, devised the strategic plan that turned the military tide in favor of the Union forces during the Civil War (see Document 48).

Despite concerted effort to keep them in their place, many women have stubbornly refused to cooperate. They have done more; they have engaged in efforts to gain social, political, and economic standing equal to that of men. After each of these "departures," which left them no better off than in the past, they toiled anew, often with little or no help from the most enlightened men, for rights to which they were always morally and legally entitled. Such was the case after the Revolution, when Judith S. Murray laid much of the early intellectual foundation for what culminated in the 1848 Declaration of Sentiments (see Document 30). Such was the situation after the Civil War, when women's struggles climaxed in the 1920 adoption of the Nineteenth Amendment, granting them the right to vote. And such was the case—though in a quieter vein—with the activism that resulted in the 1961 creation of the Commission on the Status of Women. The struggle continued through the 1960s and 1970s, with the formation of the National Organization for Women (NOW); the 1973 Supreme Court decision in *Frontiero v. Richardson*, which made sex a suspect legal classification (see Document 109); and other achievements of the 1970s such as a woman's right to abortion. But these gains were offset by the defeat of the ERA in 1982, followed by efforts during the mid- and late 1980s to reverse them.

Although the history of the women's movement in the United States may lead one to conclude that there has been a gradual national acceptance of women's equality, the evidence does not support that conclusion. With few exceptions, women have gained rights less as a result of the nation's acceptance of the principle of equality than as its attempt to embrace the expedient. A look at the early efforts to educate women and to engage their labor outside the home, at the 1964 Civil Rights Act, and even at the 1993 Family and Medical Leave Act is instructive.

Benjamin Rush, whose influence on early American education was weighty, promoted the education of women not for their own development or because of their moral claim, but so that they could better manage their husbands' property, raise sons to serve the new republic, and train daughters who would replicate their own functions (see Document 15). (Hence the monumental task women faced and discharged in creating women's colleges, some of which came to rival the most celebrated men's colleges.) Founding Father Alexander Hamilton, chief architect of the economic development of the United States, supported women's labor outside the home not in concession to women's right to share the public economic space but because their plentiful and cheap labor would enable the United States to compete more effectively, economically and politically, with European states.

Expedience as an impetus to change was also central to the inclusion of women in the Civil Rights Act of 1964, perhaps the most important piece of federal legislation affecting women. The act was originally not intended to apply to women. Congressman Howard Smith of Virginia, knowing the opposition to equality for women, felt sure that the proposed law against discrimination based on race would be defeated if it also forbade sex discrimination. He miscalculated the strength and determination of those in favor of eliminating racial discrimination.

The same problem of expedience affects the 1993 Family Medical Leave Act. That statute allows all eligible employees up to twelve weeks unpaid leave for the birth or adoption of a child, or to care for a spouse or immediate family member. It confers no special rights on women, although, in the eyes of many, matters of birth, adoption, and care for the ill fall within the domain of "women's work." The act does not confer rights so much as it shapes social flexibility in an industrial economy that is based on a two-wage family.

With women increasingly "away at work," special accommodations for social care became mandatory. Were the rights of women truly considered in this piece of legislation, we would have had a law of an entirely different character—one that provides paid leave, especially in light of the escalating number of single mothers and women in poverty. Most important, it would provide a system of child care. Instituting such a system would in effect finally acknowledge that society as a whole shares the responsibility for child rearing.

We should not infer that the women's struggle did not exploit expedience, or that the achievements of that struggle are any less remarkable. On the contrary, those achievements are all the more distinguished by women's success in employing strategies to overcome the formidable obstacles arrayed against them. These strategies include using rhetoric, forming organizations to promote women's rights, and venturing into the areas of politics, education, scholarship, and the law.

Rhetoric can be defined as the art of argumentation and public discourse for the purpose of advancing, refuting, or establishing some order, cause, or proposition. Women have had to develop and employ rhetorical skills to protest the order that men have imposed on them. In trying to shape a new social order, women have pointed out the self-serving (expedient) grounds on which apparently neutral principles or institutions—the common law, the Bible, the Constitution, the family, and Republican ideology, for example—have rested. (See Documents 3, 11, 21, 35, 69, 105, 118, and 119 for instances of the rhetorical efforts of feminist leaders Anne Hutchinson, Judith Murray, Angelina Grimké, Paulina Davis, Elizabeth Cady Stanton, Shulamith Firestone, and Catherine MacKinnon.) This work offers examples of those efforts on issues ranging from the right to speak in public and women's education to matters of contraceptives, sexual harassment, and revolution.

After the Civil War, leaders of the women's movement encountered betrayal from male partners, including anti-abolitionists, in the struggle for *human rights*. They found out that in the eyes of many, they were not regarded as fully human. They discovered more: that sexism, in some respects, was more deeply etched in the nation's psychic underground than racism. The struggle over racism—regardless of what President Lincoln said about a house divided against itself—was *within* patriarchy, the dominant ideology; the women's struggle was both *within* and *against* patriarchy. That is why former allies such as Frederick Douglass suddenly found it possible to support rights for newly emancipated black men, but not for women. That is why, as Sojourner Truth so clearly understood, the very black man who had just been freed from bondage would join his former master to oppress women, including his newly freed mother, sister, and daughter. Faced with this ugly realization, the women's movement, which until then had included men in all aspects of its struggle, formed two independent national organizations in 1869, the American Woman Suffrage Association (AWSA) and the National Woman Suffrage Association (NWSA). Membership in the NWSA, led by Elizabeth Cady Stanton, was limited to women. This brings us to political strategy.

Discovering that, in pursuit of the expedient, the male political establishment would respond favorably if its power were threatened, women sought the right to vote. With the vote they could employ their numbers to influence those in power who could not bring themselves to do what, according to elementary legal and moral principles, was right. The task was arduous; women could not rely on the official media and other institutions to carry the message they had to deliver—at least, not in the form they sought. So they had to employ a variety of tactics, including traveling throughout the country to speak, preparing and distributing literature, organizing rallies and petitions, debating, writing articles, selecting delegates, succoring those persecuted for harboring the heresy of equal rights for women, establishing literary clubs, testifying before legislatures, and preparing select cases for court battles. Suffragist Alice Paul even led a political party, the Woman's Party (also called the National Woman's Party and the New Woman's Party).

Linked to but subsumed under political strategy were social efforts. Although women were always associated with social reform, their sensibilities became increasingly sharpened as they moved across the country and discovered the overwhelming numbers of battered, poor, unhoused, malnourished, unlettered, physically and emotionally ill, and sexually abused women. Many feminist leaders became increasingly involved in tending to the social concerns of the country—they championed the temperance movement, founded the Young Women's Christian Association, and established settlement houses. They created the National Consumers League, which by the turn of the century had taken up issues ranging from the quality of food to the working conditions under which goods were being manufactured. This care and concern stood the women's movement in good stead among many of the less fortunate and made the political strategy an even more powerful instrument than it might have been. By 1920 the women's movement had won enough support for women's suffrage among the states to make it expedient for the federal government to support it too. This documentary history aspires to give the reader an appreciation of this aspect of the women's rights struggle.

As early as the 1780s, Judith Murray proposed to put the lie to men's claim that women were intellectually inferior by urging that both women and men receive the same education. But men would have no such system of education. Even in the 1970s—almost two hundred years later—Nathan Pusey, President of Harvard, reacting to the adverse impact the draft was having on that university's graduate program, stated that conscription would leave Harvard with the "blind, the lame, and the women." And in the 1980s and 1990s, we find intellectually able women science students being asked to give their places to male students—all in support of the convenient fiction that women are "not good in science" (see Document 121). Leaders of the women's rights movement have always recognized the claim of women's intellectual inferiority as expedient. And beginning in 1837 with the founding of Mount Holyoke, women have sought to establish and maintain women's colleges to achieve both the full intellectual development of women and the defeat of the contrived excuses about their intellectual abilities. From the beginning of this century through World War II (when women took over men's jobs while men served in the armed forces), women developed opportunities to demonstrate their intellectual abilities. But excuses were quickly found, after the war, to "send women back to the kitchen," with the Fair Deal of President Truman presiding over the destruction of even the modest child care program that was introduced during the war.

Today, in spite of Title IX of the Civil Rights Act (1972) and the Equal Opportunities Act (1974)—two statutes that prohibit discrimination on the basis of sex in "any education program or activity" receiving federal funds—discrimination against women continues in education. (It should be understood that without equal educational chances, the equal employment opportunities provided in the Civil Rights Act of 1964 have no practical meaning.) The discrimination takes many forms and starts early. Teachers generally give preference to boys in class participation; females are urged to enter traditional fields such as education, nursing, and psychology, and to stay away from the sciences, although there have been significant improvements in the latter area, such as in the field of biology (see Document 121). We turn to scholarship.

Women have effectively used scholarship to promote the cause of women's rights. From Paulina Davis's "On the Education of Females" at the Worcester Convention (1851), Victoria Woodhull's testimony before Congress (1871), and Elizabeth Cady Stanton's *The Woman's Bible* (1895), to Charlotte Perkins Gilman's *Women and Economics* (1898), Carol Gilligan's *In a Different Voice* (1982), and Catherine MacKinnon's *Feminism Unmodified* (1987), one finds an unbroken chain of feminists seeking to reveal the subjective and self-serving categories (established by men and posing as neutral, objective truths) in law, economics, morals, philosophy, political theory, and science that have been used to oppress women.

To advance their rights, women have also used the law. After the Civil War, feminist leaders supported, instituted, or invited legal suits under the Fourteenth Amendment to the Constitution (1868). For a long time, however, they were frustrated, for the Supreme Court, contrary to the popular view of its commitment to judicial impartiality, became the most formidable supporter of the ideology of male superiority.

The Fourteenth Amendment prohibits a state from abridging "the privileges and immunities of citizens of the United States" and from denying to "any person within its jurisdiction the equal protection of the law." Certainly, as persons, women could seek equal protection with other persons—men. But in what is called the *Slaughterhouse Cases* (83 U.S. 36, 1873), the Supreme Court ruled that the equal protection principle would be applied to former slaves only. If that were so, what of black women? Feminists then turned to the privileges and immunities clause, claiming that as U.S. citizens, one of their privileges was their right to vote. The Court, however, in *Minor v. Happersat* (88 U.S. 162,

1874), ruled that the right to vote was not among those privileges; it went further, holding that states were not prevented by the Constitution from committing "that important trust (the right to vote) to men alone." A year earlier, in *Bradwell v. Illinois,* the same Supreme Court had ruled, in support of the state of Illinois, that the right to practice one's profession—in this case Myra Bradwell, a woman, had been refused a license by that state to practice law—was not a privilege and immunity of a U.S. citizen. As such, a state could refuse such a license to women.

This convenient, male-oriented interpretation of the Constitution continued from the 1921 *Adkins v. Children's Hospital* to the 1981 *Rostker v. Goldberg.* In the former, the Court, using the newly won right to suffrage as an excuse, bypassed an earlier ruling that protected women from substandard pay and danger to health from overwork, and struck down a District of Columbia minimum wage law. And what precisely was the excuse? Apart from the fact that the wage law was seen as but "one step" from feared socialism, the Court claimed that the suffrage amendment had emancipated women from "special protection." In *Goesaert v. Cleary* (1948), however, the Court saluted the extension of that type of "protection" to women because it then benefited men. So, too, with respect to *Rostker v. Goldberg*, where the Court differentially upheld a congressional policy that sought to "protect" women from combat status. In so doing, it decided that the governmental objective of protection—the very thing the District of Columbia was doing with the minimum wage—outweighed women's constitutional right to equality.

If the preceding examples, in emphasizing the difficult struggle American women have waged for their rights, give the impression that little has changed in the struggle for those rights, that impression is wrong. For example, women can engage in public speaking today, something they could not generally do in the 1640s. Indeed, this right to partake in the public space enabled the National American Woman Suffrage Association to gain 2 million members by 1917, to win the right to vote in thirty states by 1919, and to mobilize supportive suffrage organizations in thirty-six states by the same year. The right to partake in the public space compelled the adoption of the Nineteenth Amendment. Likewise, women today have a right to sit on juries, to equal employment opportunities, to privacy, to equal pay, to pursue almost any profession (see Document 123), to occupy any public office, and to equal educational opportunities. Most important, perhaps, the judicial system—especially the Supreme Court—has contributed to the recognition of those rights. In recent cases it has taken the position that classifications based on sex must be subject to the highest level of judicial scrutiny. This offers women a better legal chance to enjoy rights on equal terms with men. Indeed, in an affirmative vein, we can say that legislative and judicial actions from the mid-1960s to 1993 have been extremely significant for women's rights.

And yet, we have titled the section covering that period At the Cross-roads, because, despite these legislative and judicial decisions, the issue of expedience remains with us. As seen in the case of changes in the Married Women's Property Act of 1860 (see Document 47), acknowl-edged rights can easily be changed or otherwise undermined as long as doing so is deemed to be in the interest of the powerful. The fight for an Equal Rights Amendment has been motivated primarily to make equality for women an explicit part of the Constitution, one that cannot be changed by the ebb and flow of court decisions or legislative enact-ments (see Document 107). Its defeat is therefore troubling.

Today demographic changes caused by the influx of immigrants from traditions that are often less accommodating to women's equality, as well as the emergence of a global economy with transnational corporate own-ership, pose new challenges for women. In addition, feminists like bell hooks and Mary Ann Mason (see Documents 116 and 117) have ex-pressed doubts about the current goals, direction, and effectiveness of the women's movement. The Clinton presidency, although apparently committed to the cause of women in its New Covenant, cannot yet be properly evaluated. Finally, judicial and legislative commitments do not always translate into general cultural definitions of self. So, in the midst of these legal changes, we witness more abusive attitudes toward women in movies, novels, television, and magazines. And we find religious groups mobilizing to reverse the gains of the past.

We cannot close this introduction without discussing our approach to the book's preparation—its organization, content, and relationship to historical scholarship. We elected to observe a historically sequential or-ganization, with a few exceptions (for example, Document 14 fits more appropriately in the dominant themes of Part II). The book's historical periods roughly complement the traditional U.S. history curriculum, making it easy to integrate the materials in a course on American history. The chronological approach helps demonstrate some of the tensions and harmonies, continuities and discontinuties, of official U.S. history when seen from the standpoint of the women's rights movement. Finally, this organization gives the reader a useful way to assess the contributions of those who have struggled for women's rights.

We sought to include as many representative voices and as many im-portant issues affecting women's rights as was practical. The reader will find the experiences of American Indians, blacks, Chinese, Puerto Ricans, whites, mill workers, secretaries, middle- and upper-class women, con-servatives, socialists, anarchists, lesbians, Catholics, Quakers, Jews, Pu-ritans, slaves, former slaves, economists, students, writers, poets, legislators, judges, physicians, and scientists, among others. Documents were selected and many lengthy ones painstakingly edited to offer their authors' thought processes and reasoning as well as their conclusions.

Scholarship in women's history has undergone some significant changes. The question "Is there a women's history?" has been superseded by "What contributions, if any, have women made?" and "What are the character and compass of these contributions?" While it is not in the scope of this volume to answer the latter questions definitively, we can say that the contributions of the women's rights movement to the history of the United States are many and grand in scale. We can touch upon a few only, using themes such as liberty and the rule of law, development, the reach of rights, political theory, and social culture as examples.

Liberty and the rule of law are among the most prominent American values. Liberty is defined in institutional, political, and legal terms to mean democracy—a form of representative rule by a majority of citizens. The women's rights movement not only won women the right to vote in 1920; it enabled the nation, for the first time in its history, to redeem its pledge in 1776 to establish a political order of representative democracy. Women, in Rousseauan language, had forced the nation to be free. Unlike freedom from slavery, which was won by civil war, women won their rights (including the right to vote) by championing the spirit of the rule of law. Even the legal defeat of Susan B. Anthony, who was put on trial in 1873 for voting (see Document 59), was a moral and spiritual victory, because women used the judicial system to demonstrate that the manner in which the law was being interpreted and applied had nothing to do with justice.

Development is a complex term. It can denote progress and progression, a process of maturation, or an unfolding. In political terms, the women's rights movement developed from a group of women (at Seneca Falls in 1848) uncomfortable at even chairing their own meetings, to one that could, by 1919, mobilize millions of voters in thirty-six states to force a reluctant federal government to support suffrage. By 1993 that movement influenced a newly elected president to promise the appointment of women to high government positions in rough proportion to their percentage of the population. The women's movement has also evolved from a search for limitations on the power of males within the family, to an emphasis on equality with men, and finally to a demand for autonomy. Seen spiritually, the movement has given women an opportunity not only to fulfill themselves professionally but to experience the flowering of all their potentials. Associate Justice of the Supreme Court Ruth B. Ginsburg acknowledged her debt to the movement in her confirmation hearing.

In seeking to advance their cause, leaders of the women's rights movement did not confine their focus to women. With a few recent exceptions, they placed their emphasis on *human* rights. In declaring that "all men are created equal," the leaders of the 1776 Revolution also emphasized human rights. But their actions failed to match their rhetoric. It is to the women's movement that the nation owes the push for human rights. And it is not a matter of coincidence that Eleanor Roosevelt led so ably in shaping the Universal Declaration of Human Rights adopted by the United Nations in 1948.

Women's contribution to political theory is considerable. In Elizabeth Cady Stanton's "Solitude of Self" (see Document 67) are reflections that even the most refined existentialist philosopher would find enriching; and Charlotte Gilman's insight and originality in *Women and Economics* (see Document 72) exceed those of all but a few thinkers in the field. The women's movement has changed our thinking about public policy on social issues. Issues ranging from child care and reproductive rights to the quality of the food we eat and the health benefits we enjoy have become part of public policy because of the efforts of the women's movement. It is significant that a woman, Hillary Rodham Clinton, has led in shaping our complex national health care policy.

Finally, we are indebted to the women's movement for much of our social culture—from the public libraries and museums to women's colleges, coeducation, and paid vacations. To quote the Convention on the Elimination of All Forms of Discrimination Against Women, the future of the nation, "the welfare of the world and the cause of peace require the maximum participation of women on equal terms with men in all fields."

Significant Dates in the History of Women's Rights

1637	Trial of Anne Hutchinson
1776	Rejection of women as political participants in the coming "Republican Order"
1787	Benjamin Rush's "Thoughts on Female Education"
1790	Publication of "On the Equality of the Sexes" by Constantia
1790–91	Seneca women's property rights denied
1830	First American women's strike took place in Lowell, Massachusetts (March 1)
1836–37	*Letters on the Equality of the Sexes*
1837	Founding of Mt. Holyoke, the first women's college
1838	The upholding of women's right to petition government
1847	Admission of the first woman to medical school
1848	Passage of the Married Woman's Property Act in New York State
1848	Seneca Falls, the officially recognized beginning of the women's rights movement in the United States
1850	Definition of the women's movement by Paulina W. Davis at the first National Women's Rights Convention (Worcester)
1854	"Have We A Despotism Among Us!"
1855	Blackwell and Stone's marriage protest
1860	Amendments to the Married Women's Property Act of 1860

1863   Women's petition to Abraham Lincoln

1868   Fourteenth Amendment: The constitutional prohibition against
            women's right to vote

1869   In the territory of Wyoming, women's suffrage had its first
            victory

1873   The trial of Susan B. Anthony for voting

1873   *Bradwell v. State of Illinois*: The Supreme Court upheld the rights
            of states to deny women a license to practice law

1876   Declaration of Rights for Women

1881   Congressional recognition of Anna Ella Carroll's military con-
            tribution during the Civil War

1895   Publication of *The Woman's Bible*

1898   Publication of *Women and Economics*

1907   *Muller v. Oregon*: The Supreme Court upheld an Oregon law
            prohibiting employment of women in any mechanical estab-
            lishment, factory, or laundry

1910   Senate Report: *The History of Women in Industry in the United
            States*

1916   Formation of the National Women's Party

1920   The Nineteenth Amendment

1923   An Equal Rights Amendment first introduced in Congress

1942   Establishment of Planned Parenthood, successor to the Birth
            Control Federation of America

1961   *Hoyt v. Florida*: The Supreme Court upheld a Florida law that
            effectively exempted women from jury duty

1963   Publication of *The Feminine Mystique*

1963   The Equal Pay Act

1964   The Civil Rights Act, Title VII

1966   Establishment of the National Organization for Women

1972   Congressional passage of ERA

1973   *Roe v. Wade*: The Supreme Court recognized women's right to
            an abortion during the first trimester

1973   *Frontiero v. Richardson*: The Supreme Court recognized classi-
            fication based on sex as "suspect"

1991	The Civil Rights Act
1993	New policy on the assignment of women in the armed forces
1993	Family and Medical Leave Act

Part I

A Flavor of the Setting: Colonial Period to the Adoption of the Constitution

Few periods in the history of women's rights in the United States are more complex than the period covering the colonial experience, the Revolution, and the establishment of the federal constitution in 1789. It is from within the womb of this complexity that one can gain a more refined appreciation of the traditions, attitudes, and institutions, as well as the interpretations, arguments, opportunities, and obstacles that have defined the struggle for women's rights in the United States.

Migrants from Britain to the colonies brought various traditions with them, particularly the common law system (see Document 2 from Blackstone's *Commentaries on the Laws of England*). That system sought to negate the legal and social identity of women, leaving them to the care and supervision of their husbands and fathers. Another tradition is seen in the seventeenth century Quaker women's declaration, which sought to affirm and preserve the social and religious identity of women (see Document 5). But that Quaker tradition was contested. As manifested in St. Paul's Letter to the Ephesians ("Wives, be subject to your husbands. . . . For the husband is head of the wife as Christ is head of the church"), the weight of religious authority and tradition joined that of the common law. And that joining has proven to be one of the most formidable barriers to women's rights.

Few social institutions are as closely tied to the rights of women as the family and property. Many documents included in this collection confirm that their authors sought to confine women to the home or the domestic sphere. (Certainly they did not want women to share the public realm and its power.) It was, in part, the sphere from which Anne Hutchinson rebelled; to which Benjamin Franklin sought to consign his friend, Catherine Ray; and unto whose calling John Winthrop felt the wife of a Connecticut governor had not given sufficient attention, as a result of which, in his opinion, she became insane (see Documents 3, 7, and 4, respectively). The institution of property (see Part II) gave no brighter prospect for women's rights either.

John Adams, one of the leaders of the Revolution and the second president of the United States, understood the significance of property to the political and economic power of men. Likewise, he understood the disabilities faced by women who had no property. Yet, as may be seen from his letter to James Sullivan—written only about six weeks after his April 1776 letter to his wife, Abigail (see Document 9), he was not prepared to change a system that made women powerless and dependent on or subordinate to men. By linking the rights of property to the institution of the family, men assured their long-term social ascendency.

The husband was not only head of the family, but controller of marital property. He had ownership of his wife's personal property (moveables), including her wages; and he had control over her real property (land and other immoveables, including buildings), which, though he could not sell because it descended to her legal heirs, he could use as he judged appropriate. So ownership of property, which determined the right to vote (although single women with property could not vote) and was the most important source of personal autonomy, was effectively denied to wives. The legal fiction called "unity of the family" ensured the "civil death" of wives, leaving men—husbands and fathers—as the only legal persons. In the words of Blackstone (see Document 2): "By marriage, the husband and wife are one in law: that is, the very being or legal existence of the woman is suspended during the marriage, or at least is incorporated and consolidated into that of the husband; under whose wing, protection, and *cover*, she performs every thing."

The cultural patterns of Britain and western Europe were not the only ones to define the historical period under discussion. The American Indians made their contributions, including those features of culture related to property. Among Seneca Indians, for example, women were *owners of the land*. But that cultural expression was not allowed to invade the claims of Anglo-American common law. And where there were encounters between the two legal cultures, that of the Indians was either eliminated or made subordinate, ensuring the domination of property relationships that made women subordinate to men.

Attitudes, including expectations, have always played a role in the struggle for women's rights. During colonial times women believed themselves to be—and rightly so—central to the survival and success of colonial and postcolonial societies. Whether as hunters, soap makers, brewers, morticians, farmers, printers, bakers, preachers, counselors, or homemakers, their work was crucial to those societies' economic and social development. And during the period of political rebellion and revolution, they were "in no small measure responsible for enabling the colonies to withstand boycotts of English goods by their activities of spinning clothing, processing tea, and publicly encouraging others to buy only domestic products. As an integral part of the war effort, . . . women's groups assisted by producing much-needed ammunition, bandages, and clothes for soldiers, by shouldering the burden of farm work for men away from the front."[1]

It was this attitude of being central to the life of society that informed the letter of Abigail Adams to her husband entreating him to "remember the ladies," and "Sentiments of an American Woman" (see Documents 9 and 10), although neither of these documents purports to deal with that centrality. A revolution had been fought and won under the banner of the inalienable rights of men, who were said to be created equal. And women who had endured inferior status in society rightly expected that their demonstrated contributions and merit would invite a change in that status. As seen in Adams's letter to James Sullivan, however, such was not to be the case. The republican virtues of courage, self-sufficiency, and independence, which made men fit for the "hardy enterprises of war, as well as the arduous cares of state," were not to be found in women, whose "delicacy" and nature "made them fittest for domestic cares." Thomas Paine, that radical of the Revolution, understood—in part—the moral failing that was present in Franklin's and Adams's letters; but he did not see women as equals (see Document 8). Judith Murray was left to argue not only for women's equality but, perhaps, their superiority. Indeed, her arguments constitute an intellectual broadside has reverberated in almost every theme of the women's rights movement in the United States (see Document 11).

Everything seems to have been arranged to effect the oppression of women: religious doctrines as interpreted and practiced, the legal tradition as revered and taught, the institutions of family and property as promoted and nurtured, the republican ideology as understood and preached, and even popular sentiments as fostered and used for governing. So the efforts of the Quaker women, Anne Hutchinson, Judith Murray, Abigail Adams, and others did not succeed in changing the status of women. They did, however, lay some of the foundations on which their later sisters would build. And far from being caught in the "radical" or "conservative" theses about the meaning of the American Revolution, the women's rights struggle and movement were able to use the moral failings of that Revolution and like events—failings exhibited primarily in the gap between the claims of those events and the actual condition of women—to advance the moral and legal entitlements of women.

NOTE

1. Malvina Halberstam and Elizabeth Defeis, eds., *Women's Legal Rights* (New York: Transnational Publishers, 1987), 6.

DOCUMENT 1: Biblical Authority and Women's Rights

The people who left Europe in the early seventeenth century to colonize what is today the United States brought with them a number of cultural resources that were to shape their social and political communities. None of those resources was more important than their religion, which evolved from the Judeo-Christian tradition— a tradition that largely informed and reinforced a structure of male authority and claimed superiority.

While Document 1C suggests the equal standing of women and men (as will be urged by the Quakers in Document 5), Documents 1A and 1B preach the subordination of women and typically define the prevailing views of colonial and postcolonial society. Paul's Letter to Titus is somewhat vague, in that it allows women to teach— as will be argued by Anne Hutchinson in Document 3; at the same time, however, it *appears* that such women teachers should confine themselves to teaching other women and, further, that the content of that teaching should be women's subordination to men. The Letter to the Ephesians unmistakably teaches and upholds male authority. But how is one to understand the background from which Paul gave his instruction through those and other letters?

The answer to that question is, in part, to be found in the ideological position first presented in the book of Genesis in one of the creation stories and conveniently interpreted by Church Fathers, including St. Augustine (A.D. 354–430). The story contends that Eve, the first woman, was an afterthought in God's plan of creation; she was created out of the rib of the first man, Adam, in order to comfort and otherwise serve him; that she was subject to temptations, and so was the first sinner because of her weaker mind; and that she was possessed of the power of a temptress, as seen in her ensnaring Adam to violate the commands of God and endanger the relationship of all men with Him. Finally, after the Fall, Eve (and every subsequent woman) was made subject to man, as God is said to have stated in Genesis 3:16 ("To the woman he said, 'I will greatly multiply your pain in childbearing . . . yet your desire shall be for your husband, and he shall rule over you' "). In short, this ideology, claiming that the alleged nature of Eve is to be found in every woman, argued women's essential inequality to men. Paul's writings merely elaborated on that ideology.

A. PAUL'S LETTER TO THE EPHESIANS

Wives, be subject to your husbands, as to the Lord. For the husband is the head of the wife as Christ is the head of the church, his body, and is himself its Savior. As the church is subject to Christ, so let wives also be subject in everything to their husbands. . . .

Even so husbands should love their wives as their own bodies. He who loves his wife loves himself. For no man ever hates his own flesh, but nourishes and cherishes it, as Christ does the church, because we are members of his body. "For this reason a man shall leave his father and mother and be joined to his wife, and the two shall become one."

Source: Ephesians 5:22–31. All these references are from the Revised Standard Version of the Bible (New York: World, 1962).

B. PAUL'S LETTER TO TITUS

Bid the older women . . . to teach what is good, and so train the young women to love their husbands and children, to be sensible, chaste, domestic, kind and submissive to their husbands that the word of God may not be discredited.

Source: Titus 2:3–6.

C. ONE CREATION STORY IN GENESIS

So God created man in his own image, in the image of God he created him; male and female he created them.

And God blessed them, and God said to them, "Be fruitful and multiply, and fill the earth and subdue it; and have dominion over the fish of the sea and over the birds of the air and over every living thing that moves upon the earth."

Source: Genesis 1:27–28.

DOCUMENT 2: *Commentaries on the Laws of England* (William Blackstone, 1765)

English settlers brought with them to the American colonies the common law system. This body of custom, rules, principles, and shared expectations defined and embodied the images and norms of family and gender roles that constituted *coverture*—the legal concept of marital unity. From that concept flowed the status, position, obligations, and legal disabilities of a wife. The following document is from the *Commentaries* of William Blackstone, the greatest British authority on the laws of England; it became the legal Bible, the primary reference on women's position throughout the nineteenth century.

By marriage, the husband and wife are one person in law: that is, the very being or legal existence of the woman is suspended during the marriage, or at least is incorporated and consolidated into that of the husband; under whose wing, protection, and *cover*, she performs every thing; and is therefore called in our law-French a *feme-covert, foemina viro co-operta*; is said to be *covert-baron*, or under the protection and influence of her husband, her *baron*, or lord; and her condition during her marriage is called her *coverture*. Upon this principle, of a union of person in husband and wife, depend almost all the legal rights, duties, and disabilities, that either of them acquire by the marriage. I speak not at present of the rights of property, but of such as are merely *personal*. For this reason, a man cannot grant anything to his wife, or enter into covenant with her: for the grant would be to suppose her separate existence; and to covenant with her, would be only to covenant with himself: and therefore it is also generally true, that all compacts made between husband and wife, when single, are voided by the intermarriage. A woman indeed may be attorney for her husband; for that implies no separation from, but is rather a representation of, her lord. And a husband may also bequeath any thing to his wife by will; for that cannot take effect till the coverture is determined by his death. The husband is bound to provide his wife with necessaries by law, as much as himself; and, if she contracts debts for them, he is obliged to pay them; but for anything besides necessaries he is not chargeable. Also if a wife elopes, and lives with another man, the husband is not chargeable even for necessaries; at least if the person who furnishes them is sufficiently apprized of her elopement. If the wife be indebted before marriage, the husband is bound afterwards to pay the debt; for he has adopted her and her circumstances together. If the wife be injured in her person or her property, she can bring no action for redress without her husband's concurrence, and in his name, as well as her own: neither can she be sued without making the husband a defendant. There is indeed one case where the wife shall sue and be sued as a feme sole, viz. where the husband has abjured the realm, or is banished, for then he is dead in law; and the husband being thus disabled to sue for or defend the wife, it would be most unreasonable if she had no remedy, or could make no defence at all. In criminal prosecutions, it is true, the wife may be indicted and punished separately; for the union is only a civil union. But in trials of any sort they are not allowed to be evidence for, or against, each other: partly because it is impossible their testimony should be indifferent, but principally because of the union of person; and therefore, if they were admitted to be witness *for* each other, they would contradict one maxim of law, *"nemo in propria causa testis esse debet"*; and if *against* each other, they would contradict another maxim, *"nemo tenetur seipsum accusare."* But, where the offence is directly against the person of the wife, this rule has been usually dispensed with; and therefore, by statute 3 Hen. VII, c. 2, in case a woman be forcibly taken away, and married, she may be a witness against such her husband, in order to convict him of felony. For in this case she can with no propriety be reckoned his wife; because a main ingredient, her consent, was wanting to the contract: and also there is another maxim of law, that no man shall take advantage of his own wrong; which the ravisher here would do, if, by forcibly marrying a woman, he could prevent her from being a witness, who is perhaps the only witness to that very fact.

In the civil law the husband and the wife are considered as two distinct persons, and may have separate estates, contracts, debts, and injuries; and therefore in our ecclesiastical courts, a woman may sue and be sued without her husband.

But though our law in general considers man and wife as one person, yet there are some instances in which she is separately considered; as inferior to him, and acting by his compulsion. And therefore all deeds executed, and acts done, by her, during her coverture, are void; except it be a fine, or the like manner of record, in which case she must be solely and secretly examined, to learn if her act be voluntary. She cannot by will devise lands to her husband, unless under special circumstances; for at the time of making it she is supposed to be under his coercion. And in some felonies, and other inferior crimes, committed by her through constraint of her husband, the law excuses her: but this extends not to treason or murder.

The husband also, by the old law, might give his wife moderate correction. For, as he is to answer for her misbehaviour, the law thought it reasonable to intrust him with this power of restraining her, by domestic chastisement, in the same moderation that a man is allowed to correct his apprentices or children; for whom the master or parent is also liable in some cases to answer. But this power of correction was confined within reasonable bounds, and the husband was prohibited from using any violence to his wife, *aliter quam ad virum, ex causa regiminis et castigationis uxoris suae, licite et rationabiliter pertinet.* The civil law gave the husband the same, or a larger, authority over his wife: allowing him, for some misdemeanors, *flagellis et fustibus acriter verberare uxorem*; for others, only *modicam castigationem adhibere.* But with us, in the politer reign of Charles the second, this power of correction began to be doubted; and a wife may now have security of the peace against her husband; or, in return, a husband against his wife. Yet the lower rank of people, who were always fond of the old common law, still claim and exert their ancient privilege: and the courts of law will still permit a husband to restrain a wife of her liberty, in the case of any gross misbehaviour.

These are the chief legal effects of marriage during the coverture; upon which we may observe, that even the disabilities which the wife lies under are for the most part intended for her protection and benefit: so great a favourite is the female sex of the laws of England.

Source: William Blackstone, *Commentaries on the Laws of England*, vols. (1765), 1: 442–445.

DOCUMENT 3: The Examination of Mrs. Ann Hutchinson (1637)

Among the many remarkable women who challenged the ideology of male supremacy was Anne Hutchinson (1591–1643), who, with her husband, had migrated from England to Massachusetts Bay Colony in 1634. She became part of a theological controversy known as the Antinomian heresy, which threw the predominantly Puritan colony into social and political turmoil. Antinomianism (belief opposed to or against the law) opposed the teaching of religious obedience based on law or on works, and espoused the idea of salvation through faith and God's grace. It also contended, not unlike Quakerism (see Document 5), that individuals had direct access to divine revelation through the Holy Spirit. Since the relationship between church and state in Massachusetts was intimate, the challenge to orthodox Puritanism (which believed in salvation by works and the intervention of religious authority between God and the laity) became a challenge to the state as well.

Anne Hutchinson aired her criticism of local ministers at meetings in her home, where she analyzed their sermons. At first, these meetings were composed of women only, but later men who shared her views began to attend, and rumors of her criticism circulated. In November 1637 she was put on trial by the General Court of the colony and questioned by Governor John Winthrop and the other members of the legislature.

The real reason for the charge against Anne Hutchinson was not so much the religious view she held, however, as the meaning those views had for the status and role of women—and men. There was fear that her example of teaching men was subversive to the patriarchal order; that her claims to direct revelation would put the church hierarchy (and its control) in question; and, in general, that she disturbed the quietude of those who accepted the "natural" sphere of women as the home. She was excommunicated from the church and expelled from the colony. In 1643 she was killed by Indians in New York.

November 1637

The Examination of Mrs. Ann Hutchinson at the court at Newtown.

Mr. Winthrop, governor. Mrs. Hutchinson, you are called here as one of those that have troubled the peace of the commonwealth and the churches here; you are known to be a woman that hath had a great share in the promoting and divulging of those opinions that are causes of this trouble, and to be nearly joined not only in affinity and affection with some of those the court had taken notice of and passed censure upon, but you have spoken divers things as we have been informed very prejudicial to the honour of the churches and ministers thereof, and you have maintained a meeting and an assembly in your house that hath been condemned by the general assembly as a thing not tolerable nor comely in the sight of God nor fitting for your sex, and notwithstanding that was cried down you have continued the same, therefore we have thought good to send for you to understand how things are, that if you be in an erroneous way we may reduce you that so you may become a profitable member here among us, otherwise if you be obstinate in your course that then the court may take such course that you may trouble us no further, therefore I would intreat you to express whether you do not hold and assent in practice to those opinions and factions that have been handled in court already, that is to say, whether you do not justify Mr. Wheelwright's sermon and the petition.

Mrs. Hutchinson. I am called here to answer before you but I hear no things laid to my charge.

Gov. I have told you some already and more I can tell you. (*Mrs. H.*) Name one Sir.

Gov. Have I not named some already?

Mrs. H. What have I said or done?

Gov. Why for your doings, this you did harbour and countenance those that are parties in this faction that you have heard of. (*Mrs. H.*) That's matter of conscience, Sir.

Gov. Your conscience you must keep or it must be kept for you.

Mrs. H. Must not I then entertain the saints because I must keep my conscience.

Gov. Say that one brother should commit felony or treason and come to his other brother's house, if he knows him guilty and conceals him he is guilty of the same. It is his conscience to entertain him, but if his conscience comes into act in giving countenance and entertainment to him that hath broken the law he is guilty too. So if you do countenance those that are transgressors of the law you are in the same fact.

Mrs. H. What law do they trangress?

Gov. The law of God and of the state.

Mrs. H. In what particular?

Gov. Why in this among the rest, whereas the Lord doth say honour thy father and thy mother.

Mrs. H. Ey Sir in the Lord. (*Gov.*) This honour you have broke in giving countenance to them.

Mrs. H. In entertaining those did I entertain them against any act (for there is the thing) or what God hath appointed?

Gov. You knew that Mr. Wheelwright did preach this sermon and those that countenance him in this do break a law.

Mrs. H. What law have I broken?

Gov. Why the fifth commandment.

Mrs. H. I deny that for he saith in the Lord.

Gov. You have joined with them in the faction.

Mrs. H. In what faction have I joined with them?

Gov. In presenting the petition.

Mrs. H. Suppose I had set my hand to the petition what then? (*Gov.*) You saw that case tried before.

Mrs. H. But I had not my hand to the petition.

Gov. You have councelled them. (*Mrs. H.*) Wherein?

Gov. Why in entertaining them.

Mrs. H. What breach of law is that Sir?

Gov. Why dishonouring of parents.

Mrs. H. But put the case Sir that I do fear the Lord and my parents, may not I entertain them that fear the Lord because my parents will not give me leave?

Gov. If they be the fathers of the commonwealth, and they of another religion, if you entertain them then you dishonour your parents and are justly punishable.

Mrs. H. If I entertain them, as they have dishonoured their parents I do.

Gov. No but you by countenancing them above others put honour upon them.

Mrs. H. I may put honor upon them as the children of God and as they do honor the Lord.

Gov. We do not mean to discourse with those of your sex but only this; you do adhere unto them and do endeavour to set forward this faction and so you do dishonour us.

Mrs. H. I do acknowledge no such thing neither do I think that I ever put any dishonour upon you.

Gov. Why do you keep such a meeting at your house as you do every week upon a set day? . . .

Mrs. H. I conceive there lyes a clear rule in Titus, that the elder women should instruct the younger and then I must have a time wherein I must do it.

Gov. All this I grant you, I grant you a time for it, but what is this to the purpose that you Mrs. Hutchinson must call a company together from their callings to come to be taught of you?

Mrs. H. Will it please you to answer me this and to give me a rule for then I will willingly submit to any truth. If any come to my house to be instructed in the ways of God what rule have I to put them away?

Gov. But suppose that a hundred men come unto you to be instructed will you forbear to instruct them?

Mrs. H. As far as I conceive I cross a rule in it.

Gov. Very well and do you not so here?

Mrs. H. No Sir for my ground is they are men.

Gov. Men and women all is one for that, but suppose that a man should come and say Mrs. Hutchinson I hear that you are a woman that God hath given his grace unto and you have knowledge in the word of God I pray instruct me a little, ought you not to instruct this man?

Mrs. H. I think I may.—Do you think it not lawful for me to teach women and why do you call me to teach the court?

Gov. We do not call you to teach the court but to lay open yourself.

Mrs. H. I desire you that you would then set me down a rule by which I may put them away that come unto me and so have peace in so doing.

Gov. You must shew your rule to receive them.

Mrs. H. I have done it.

Gov. I deny it because I have brought more arguments than you have.

Mrs. H. I say, to me it is a rule.

Mr. Endicot. You say there are some rules unto you. I think there is a contradiction in your own words. What rule for your practice do you bring, only a custom in Boston.

Mrs. H. No Sir that was no rule to me but if you look upon the rule in Titus it is a rule to me. If you convince me that it is no rule I shall yield.

Gov. You know that there is no rule that crosses another, but this rule crosses that in the Corinthians. But you must take it in this sense that elder women must instruct the younger about their business, and to love their husbands and not to make them to clash.

Mrs. H. If you please to give me leave I shall give you the ground of what I know to be true. Being much troubled to see the falseness of the constitution of the church of England, I had like to have turned separatist; whereupon I kept a day of solemn humiliation and pondering of the thing; this scripture was brought unto me—he that denies Jesus Christ to be come in the flesh is antichrist—This I considered of and in considering found that the papists did not deny him to be come in the flesh, nor we did not deny him—who then was antichrist? Was the Turk antichrist only? The Lord knows that I could not open scripture; he must by his prophetical office open it unto me. So after that being unsatisfied in the thing, the Lord was pleased to bring this scripture out of the Hebrews. He that denies the testament denies the testator, and in this did open unto me and give me to see that those which did not teach the new covenant had the spirit of antichrist, and upon this he did discover the ministry unto me and ever since. I bless the Lord, he hath let me see which was the clear ministry and which the wrong. Since that time I confess I have been more choice and he hath let me to distinguish between the voice of my beloved and the voice of Moses, the voice of John Baptist and the voice of antichrist, for all those voices are spoken of in scripture. Now if you do condemn me for speaking what in my conscience I know to be truth I must commit myself unto the Lord.

Mr. Nowell. How do you know that that was the spirit?

Mrs. H. How did Abraham know that it was God that bid him offer his son, being a breach of the sixth commandment?

Dep. Gov. By an immediate voice.

Mrs. H. So to me by an immediate revelation.

Dep. Gov. How! an immediate revelation.

Mrs. H. By the voice of his own spirit to my soul. I will give you another scripture, Jer. 46. 27, 28—out of which the Lord shewed me what he would do for me and the rest of his servants.—But after he was pleased to reveal himself to me I did presently like Abraham run to Hagar. And after that he did let me see the atheism of my own heart, for which I begged of the Lord that it might not remain in my heart, and being thus, he did shew me this (a twelvemonth after) which I told you of before. Ever since that time I have been confident of what he hath revealed unto me.

Source: David Hall, ed., *The Antinomian Controversy, 1636–1638: A Documentary History* (Durham, N.C.: Duke University Press, 1990), 312–316, 336–337.

DOCUMENT 4: John Winthrop's View of a "Woman's Place" (1645)

John Winthrop (1588–1649), one of the original English settlers in New England, enjoyed considerable influence in Massachusetts Bay Colony, which he envisioned as a "city upon a hill"—a beacon of what a godly community should be like. He became governor of Massachusetts and presided over the trial of Anne Hutchinson (see Document 3). His journal reveals the reasoning behind his reaction to Hutchinson's efforts to share the public domain with men and his view of the likely consequences for women who forgot or deliberately neglected their "natural and socially appointed" sphere of home life—domesticity. It also suggests that men ought to exercise more care in helping women, particularly wives, to avoid those dire consequences.

(*April*) 13. Mr. Hopkins, the governor of Hartford upon Connecticut, came to Boston, and brought his wife with him, (a godly young woman, and of special parts,) who was fallen into a sad infirmity, the loss of her understanding and reason, which had been growing upon her divers years, by occasion of her giving herself wholly to reading and writing, and had written many books. Her husband, being very loving and tender of her, was loath to grieve her; but he saw his error, when it was too late. For if she had attended her household affairs, and such things as belong to women, and not gone out of her way and calling to meddle in such things as are proper for men, whose minds are stronger, etc., she had kept her wits, and might have improved them usefully and honorably in the place God had set her. He brought her to Boston, and left her with her brother, one Mr. Yale, a merchant, to try what means might be had here for her. But no help could be had.

Source: James Kendall Hosmer, ed., *Winthrop's Journal: History of New England, 1630–1649*, 2 vols. (New York: Barnes and Noble, 1908), 2: 225.

DOCUMENT 5: A Seventeenth Century Quaker Women's Declaration (1675)

This directive, estimated to have been published around 1675, became a standard followed by Quakers in the American colonies (as shown in the testimonies found in Document 6). It is significant in several respects. First, it focuses on a group of women who will exercise a dominant influence in the later struggle for women's rights. Second, it introduces the reader to a truly "peculiar" group of people—one whose self-perception differed fundamentally from that of the other colonial women who were shaped by the Judeo-Christian tradition. For example, they did not accept the "essential inequality" of women (see comments on Documents 1A, 1B, and 1C) based on original sin. Quakers believed that before original sin women and men were equal, and that after rebirth or conversion (those "who are baptized into Christ"), equality returns, with both women and men sharing "dominion and power" over creation. Because Quakers believe in direct inspiration, that one can experience—without any intermediary—the indwelling presence of Christ, they believe that any woman can have the equivalent spiritual experience of any man. So, in their lay ministries, women, like men, were public ministers. Because they participated in the governance of their religious community, taking a role in secular society as well presented no difficulty.

The self-image of the Quaker woman was not that of sinner, degenerate temptress, or source of impairment in the relationship between man and God. Rather, she saw herself as part of a "Royal offspring" and a "peculiar people" who wore some of the remarks of their peculiarity in their plain clothing, social concern, and assertiveness. Finally, this document should serve as a caution against generalizing about colonial women.

Dear Sisters,

In the blessed unity of the Spirit of grace our Souls Salute you who are sanctified in Christ Jesus, and called to be Saints, who are of the true and Royal offspring of Christ Jesus. . . . To you that are of the true seed of the promise of God in the beginning, that was to bruise the Serpent's head, and which is fullfilled in Christ Jesus of which we are made partakers, which is the seed the promise is to. . . . And that every particular of us, may be ready, and willing to answer what the lord requires of us;

in our several places and conditions; for as many of us as are baptized into Christ, have put on Christ; for we are all the children of God by faith in Christ Jesus, where there is neither male nor female etc. but are all one Christ Jesus. . . .

So here is the blessed Image of the living God, restored againe, in which he made them male and female in the beginning: and in his own Image God blessed them both and said unite them increase and multiply and replenish the earth . . . and have dominion over the fish of the sea . . . the fowles of the heavens . . . the beasts. . . . And in this dominion and power, the lord God is establishing his own seed, in male and female. . . .

Soe all Dear friends and sisters, make full proofe of the gift of God that is in you, and neglect it not, in this your day, and generation. . . .

And as the Apostle saith, let us press forward towards the marke, for the price of the high calling of God, in Christ Jesus. . . . And let us come into our practise, and into our possession of our portions, and inheritance, that we have of the lord. And let us stand faithfull, and true witnesses for him in our day, against all deceit, and wickedness.

And let us meet together, and keep our women's meetings, in the name and power, and fear of the lord Jesus, whose servants and handmaids we are, and in the good order of the Gospel. . . .

And also, to make inquiry . . . if there be any that walks disorderly. . . . Then send to them . . . to Admonish, and exhort them. . . .

And dear sisters it is duly Incumbent upon us to look into families, and to prevent our Children of running into the world for husbands, or for wives . . . for you know before the women's meetings were set up, Many have done so, which brought dishonour, both to God, and upon his truth and people. . . .

And also all friends . . . that they bring their Marriages twice to the womens meetings, and twice to the mens: the first time they are to come to the womens meetings that the women of the meeting, do examine both the man and the woman, that they are cleare and free from all other persons, and that they have their parents, and friends and Relations, Consent. . . .

And also all friends, in their womens monthly, and particular Meetings, that they take special care for the poore, and for those that stands in need. . . .

Also let Care be taken that every particular womens monthly meeting, have a booke to set down, and record their businesses and passages in, that is done and agreed upon . . . let the booke be read, the next monthly meeting, and see that business be performed, according to what was ordered. . . .

And also that the collections be set downe, in the booke: and that the Receipts, and disbursments of every particular meeting, be set down in their booke, and read at their womens monthly meeting, that every particular meeting may see and know, how their collection is disbursed. . . .

This is given for Information, Instruction, and Direction. . . .

Source: Milton D. Speizman and Jane C. Kronick, eds., "A Seventeenth Century Quaker Women's Declaration," *Signs: A Journal of Women in Culture and Society*, no. 1 (Autumn 1975): 235–245.

DOCUMENT 6: Interaction among Quaker Women: A Glimpse (1708–1726)

The statements below convey, in part, the range of interaction among Quaker women during the colonial period. We have evidence not only of their monthly and yearly meetings but of the fact that they depended on each other for advice and support in matters pertaining to marriage, mode of dress, decoration of the home, material sustenance, and even the affirmation of their standing with God.

MONTHLY MEETING OF WOMEN FRIENDS, CHESTER, PENNSYLVANIA, APRIL 26, 1714

The ffriends that carried the cloath to Mary Edwards for her Mother gave an account that she Read it kindly & is Loath to be troublesome to ffriends but if the Meeting is free to send her a litell money she shall take it in Love soe the Meeting hath ordered to be sent in Money further for her mothers use 20 shilling.

HANNAH HILL'S RECOMMENDATIONS FOR QUAKER DRESS AND CONDUCT, 1726

From Women ffriends at the Yearly Meeting held at Burlington [New Jersey], The 21st of the 7th. Month, 1726 [September 21].

Dear and Well-beloved Sisters:

A weighty Concern coming upon many ffaithful ffriends at this Meeting, in Relation to divers undue Liberties that are too frequently taken by some. . . . Tenderly to Caution & Advise ffriends against those things which we think Inconsistent with our Ancient Christian Testimony of Plainness. . . .

As first, That Immodest ffashion of hooped Pettycoats. . . .

And also That None of Sd ffriends Accustom themselves to wear their Gowns with Superfluous ffolds behind, but plain and Decent. Nor to go without Aprons. . . . Nor to wear their heads drest high. . . .

And that ffriends are careful to avoid Wearing of Stript Shoos, or Red or White heel'd Shoos. . . .

Likewise, That all ffriends be Careful to Avoid Superfluity of Furniture in their Houses. . . .

And also that no ffriends Use ye Irreverent practice of taking Snuff, or handing Snuff boxes one to Another in Meetings.

Also that ffriends Avoid ye Unnecessary use of ffans in Meetings. . . .

And also That ffriends do not Accustom themselves to go in bare Breasts or bare Necks.

There is Likewise a Tender Concern upon our minds to recommend unto all ffriends, the Constant use of ye plain Language. . . .

Dear Sisters, These Things we Solidly recommend. . . . That we might be unto ye Lord, a Chosen Generation, A Royal Priesthood, An Holy Nation, A Peculair People. . . .

Signed on behalf & by ord^r of ye sd meeting By

Hannah Hill

Source: Carol Ruth Berkin and Mary Beth Norton, eds., *Women of America: A History* (Boston: Houghton Mifflin, 1979), 134–136.

DOCUMENT 7: Letter to Catherine Ray (Benjamin Franklin, 1755)

Franklin exchanged letters with Catherine Ray Greene for thirty-four years—his longest running correspondence with a woman. Their friendship was expressed chiefly through letters, for they met only five times. He clearly relished the light pleasure afforded by this exchange, in marked contrast to his talk of politics with "the Grave ones," his male colleagues.

Philadelphia Oct. 16. 1755

Dear Katy

Your Favour of the 28th of June came to hand but the 28th of September, just 3 Months after it was written. I had, two Weeks before, wrote you a long Chat, and sent it to the Care of your Brother Ward. I hear you are now in Boston, gay and lovely as usual. Let me give you some fatherly Advice. Kill no more Pigeons than you can eat.—Be a good Girl, and don't forget your Catechise.—Go constantly to Meeting—or Church—till you get a good Husband;—then stay at home, & nurse the Children, and live like a Christian.—Spend your spare Hours, in sober Whisk, Prayers, or learning to cypher.—You must practise *Addition* to your Husband's Estate, by Industry & Frugality; *Subtraction* of all unnecessary Expences; *Multiplication* (I would gladly have taught you that myself, but you thought it was time enough & woud'n't learn) he will soon make you a Mistress of it. As to *Division*, I say with Brother Paul, *Let there be no Divisions among ye*. But as your good Sister Hubbard (my Love to her) is well acquainted with *The Rule of Two*, I hope you will become as expert in the *Rule of Three*; that when I have again the Pleasure of seeing you, I may find you like my Grape Vine, surrounded with Clusters, plump, juicy, blushing, pretty little rogues, like their Mama. Adieu. The Bell rings, and I must go among the Grave ones, and talk Politicks.

> Your affectionate Friend
> B. Franklin

Source: William G. Roelker, ed., *Benjamin Franklin and Catherine Ray Greene: Their Correspondence, 1775–1790* (Philadelphia: Memoirs of the American Philosophical Society, 1946), 20.

DOCUMENT 8: An Occasional Letter on the Female Sex (Thomas Paine, 1775)

Thomas Paine (1737–1809) is commonly regarded as one of the most radical of the opinion-shapers of the Revolution. His pamphlet, *Common Sense*, more than any other single work, incited revolutionary sentiments among the colonies. Indeed, many found him so radical that they wished him to leave the newly proclaimed nation. Yet he was wanting in his support of women's rights.

In the following document, one finds him accurately pointing to the oppression of women. And in his criticism one sees the moral failing of the Revolution insofar as the new order it claimed to launch pertained to the condition of women. But Paine was not seeking equality for women; he was not even seeking to uproot them from the domestic sphere. What he sought, rather, was due recognition of the importance of women's role in society. So he had women addressing men, in the former's search for justice, in the following manner: "Our duties are different from yours, but they are not therefore less difficult to fulfill, or of less consequence to society. They are the fountains of your felicity, and the sweeteners of life."

If we take a survey of ages and of countries, we shall find the women, almost—without exception—at all times, and in all places, adored and oppressed. Man, who has never neglected an opportunity of exerting his power, in paying homage to their beauty, has always availed himself of their weakness. He has been at once their tyrant and their slave. [He describes the condition of women in various parts of the world.] Even in countries where they may be esteemed most happy, constrained in their desires in the disposal of their goods, robbed of freedom of will by the laws, the slaves of opinion, which rules them with absolute sway, . . . surrounded on all sides by judges, who are at once tyrants and their seducers, and who, after having prepared their faults, punish every lapse with dishonor. . . . Who does not feel for the tender sex? Yet such, I am sorry to say, is the lot of women over the whole earth. . . . Over three-quarters of the globe Nature has placed them between contempt and misery. . . .

If a woman were to defend the cause of her sex, she might address [man] in the following manner:

'How great is your injustice? . . . Our duties are different from yours, but they are not therefore less difficult to fulfill, or of less consequence to society. They are the fountains of your felicity, and the sweeteners of life. We are wives and mothers. T'is we who form the union . . . of families. . . . Permit our names to be some time pronounced, beyond the narrow circle in which we live. . . . '

Source: Beth Millstein Kava and Jeanne Bodin, *We, the American Women* (Chicago: Science Research Associates, 1983), 48.

DOCUMENT 9: A Lack of Good Faith? (1776)

Abigail Adams (1744–1818) was one of the most self-confident women of her day. She belonged to the upper social crust of Massachusetts and knew those who helped to shape the Revolution and how they saw the tyrannical behavior of their British masters. She saw an analogy between the oppression in the British colonies that became the United States and male oppression of women in domestic life. Her letter to her husband, however, did not so much call for any broad-based liberation of women or even their representation in public life, as it did for limitations on the authority of men over women, as practiced then and sanctioned by common law.

John Adams (1735–1826) understood very well what his wife was saying, as his letters to her and to James Sullivan indicate. One even finds him lucidly pointing out the absurdity of excluding women from voting. Certainly he knew that many women, including his wife, had political judgment superior to that of many men; he also knew that some single women possessed property and should be allowed to vote; if non-possession of property were the only factor disqualifying women to vote. Although Adams was one of the "First among the Fathers," a group of leaders who sought to carry out a republican ideology that says all citizens are equal and that government derives its just powers from the governed, he turned his back on women. The "radical change" in principles, opinions, and sentiments which, for him, was to be "the real American Revolution" did not extend to women.

A. ABIGAIL ADAMS TO JOHN ADAMS

Braintree March 31 1776

I wish you would ever write me a Letter half as long as I write you; and tell me if you may where your Fleet are gone? What sort of Defence Virginia can make against our common Enemy? Whether it is so situated as to make an able Defence? Are not the Gentery Lords and the common people vassals, are they not like the uncivilized Natives Brittain represents us to be? I hope their Riffel Men who have shewen themselves very savage and even Blood thirsty; are not a specimen of the Generality of the people. . . .

I have sometimes been ready to think that the passion for Liberty cannot be Eaquelly Strong in the Breasts of those who have been accustomed to deprive their fellow Creatures of theirs. Of this I am certain that it is not founded upon that generous and christian principal of doing to others as we would that others should do unto us. . . .

—I long to hear that you have declared an independency—and by the way in the new Code of Laws which I suppose it will be necessary for you to make I desire you would Remember the Ladies, and be more generous and favourable to them than your ancestors. Do not put such unlimited power into the hands of the Husbands. Remember all Men would be tyrants if they could. If perticuliar care and attention is not paid to the Laidies we are determined to foment a Rebelion, and will not hold ourselves bound by any Laws in which we have no voice, or Representation.

That your Sex are Naturally Tyrannical is a Truth so thoroughly established as to admit of no dispute, but such of you as wish to be happy willingly give up the harsh title of Master for the more tender and endearing one of Friend. Why then, not put it out of the power of the vicious and the Lawless to use us with cruelty and indignity with impunity. Men of Sense in all Ages abhor those customs which treat us only as the vassals of your Sex. Regard us then as Beings placed by providence under your protection and in immitation of the Supreem Being make use of that power only for our happiness.

B. JOHN ADAMS TO ABIGAIL ADAMS

Ap. 14. 1776

You justly complain of my short Letters, but the critical State of Things and the Multiplicity of Avocations must plead my Excuse.—You ask where the Fleet is. The inclosed Papers will inform you. You ask what Sort of Defence Virginia can make. I believe they will make an able Defence. . . .

As to your extraordinary Code of Laws, I cannot but laugh. We have been told that our Struggle has loosened the bands of Government every where. That Children and Apprentices were disobedient—that schools and Colledges were grown turbulent—that Indians slighted their Guardians and Negroes grew insolent to their Masters. But your Letter was the first Intimation that another Tribe more numerous and powerfull than all the rest were grown discontented.—This is rather too coarse a Compliment but you are so saucy, I wont blot it out.

Depend upon it, We know better than to repeal our Masculine systems. Altho they are in full Force, you know they are little more than Theory. We dare not exert our Power in its full Latitude. We are obliged to go fair, and softly, and in Practice you know We are the subjects. We have only the Name of Masters, and rather than give up this, which would compleatly subject Us to the Despotism of the Peticoat, I hope General Washington, and all our brave Heroes would fight. I am sure every good Politician would plot, as long as he would against Despotism, Empire, Monarchy, Aristocracy, Oligarchy, or Ochlocracy.—A fine Story indeed. . . .

Source: Lyman H. Butterfield et al., eds., *The Adams Papers: Adams Family Correspondence*, vols. (Cambridge, Mass.: Harvard University Press, 1963), 1: 369–370.

C. JOHN ADAMS TO JAMES SULLIVAN

Philadelphia, 26 May, 1776.

Your favors of May 9th and 17th are now before me. . . .

Our worthy friend, Mr. Gerry, has put into my hands a letter from you, of the sixth of May, in which you consider the principles of representation and legislation, and give us hints of some alterations, which you seem to think necessary, in the qualification of voters.

I wish, Sir, I could possibly find time to accompany you, in your investigation of the principles upon which a representative assembly stands, and ought to stand, and in your examination whether the practice of our colony has been conformable to those principles. But, alas! Sir, my time is so incessantly engrossed by the business before me, that I cannot spare enough to go through so large a field; and as to books, it is not easy to obtain them here; nor could I find a moment to look into them, if I had them.

It is certain, in theory, that the only moral foundation of government is, the consent of the people. But to what an extent shall we carry this principle? Shall we say that every individual of the community, old and young, male and female, as well as rich and poor, must consent, expressly, to every act of legislation? No, you will say, this is impossible. How, then, does the right arise in the majority to govern the minority, against their will? Whence arises the right of the men to govern the women, without their consent? Whence the right of the old to bind the young, without theirs?

But let us first suppose that the whole community, of every age, rank, sex, and condition, has a right to vote. This community is assembled. A motion is made, and carried by a majority of one voice. The minority will not agree to this. Whence arises the right of the majority to govern, and the obligation of the minority to obey?

From necessity, you will say, because there can be no other rule.

But why exclude women?

You will say, because their delicacy renders them unfit for practice and experience in the great businesses of life, and the hardy enterprises of war, as well as the arduous cares of state. Besides, their attention is so much engaged with the necessary nurture of their children, that nature has made them fittest for domestic cares. And children have not judgment or will of their own. True. But will not these reasons apply to others? Is it not equally true, that men in general, in every society, who are wholly destitute of property, are also too little acquainted with public affairs to form a right judgment, and too dependent upon other men to have a will of their own? If this is a fact, if you give to every man who has no property, a vote, will you not make a fine encouraging provision for corruption, by your fundamental law? Such is the frailty of the human heart, that very few men who have no property, have any judgment of their own. They talk and vote as they are directed by some man of property, who has attached their minds to his interest.

Upon my word, Sir, I have long thought an army a piece of clock-work, and to be governed only by principles and maxims, as fixed as any in mechanics; and, by all that I have read in the history of mankind, and in authors who have speculated upon society and government, I am much inclined to think a government must manage a society in the same manner; and that this is machinery too.

Harrington has shown that power always follows property. This I believe to be as infallible a maxim in politics, as that action and reaction are equal, is in mechanics. Nay, I believe we may advance one step farther, and affirm that the balance of power in a society, accompanies the balance of property in land. The only possible way, then, of preserving the balance of power on the side of equal liberty and public virtue, is to make the acquisition of land easy to every member of society; to make a division of the land into small quantities, so that the multitude may be possessed of landed estates. If the multitude is possessed of the balance of real estate, the multitude will have the balance of power, and in that case the multitude will take care of the liberty, virtue, and interest of the multitude, in all acts of government.

I believe these principles have been felt, if not understood, in the Massachusetts Bay, from the beginning; and therefore I should think that wisdom and policy would dictate in these times to be very cautious of making alterations. Our people have never been very rigid in scrutinizing into the qualifications of voters, and I presume they will not now begin to be so. But I would not advise them to make any alteration in the laws, at present, respecting the qualifications of voters.

Your idea that those laws which affect the lives and personal liberty of all, or which inflict corporal punishment, affect those who are not qualified to vote, as well as those who are, is just. But so they do women, as well as men; children, as well as adults. What reason should there be for excluding a man of twenty years eleven months and twenty-seven days old, from a vote, when you admit one who is twenty-one? The reason is, you must fix upon some period in life, when the understanding and will of men in general, is fit to be trusted by the public. Will not the same reason justify the state in fixing upon some certain quantity of property, as a qualification?

The same reasoning which will induce you to admit all men who have no property, to vote, with those who have, for those laws which affect the person, will prove that you ought to admit women and children; for, generally speaking, women and children have as good judgments, and as independent minds, as those men who are wholly destitute of property; these last being to all intents and purposes as much dependent upon others, who will please to feed, clothe, and employ them, as women are upon their husbands, or children on their parents.

As to your idea of proportioning the votes of men, in money matters, to the property they hold, it is utterly impracticable. There is no possible way of ascertaining, at any one time, how much every man in a community is worth; and if there was, so fluctuating is trade and property, that this state of it would change in half an hour. The property of the whole community is shifting every hour, and no record can be kept of the changes.

Society can be governed only by general rules. Government cannot accommodate itself to every particular case as it happens, nor to the circumstances of particular persons. It must establish general comprehensive regulations for cases and persons. The only question is, which general rule will accommodate most cases and most persons.

Depend upon it, Sir, it is dangerous to open so fruitful a source of controversy and altercation as would be opened by attempting to alter the qualifications of voters; there will be no end of it. New claims will arise; women will demand a vote; lads from twelve to twenty-one will think their rights not enough attended to; and every man who has not a farthing, will demand an equal voice with any other, in all acts of state. It tends to confound and destroy all distinctions, and prostrate all ranks to one common level.

Source: Charles Adams, ed., *The Works of John Adams*, vols. (Boston: Little, Brown, 1854), 375–378.

DOCUMENT 10: Sentiments of an American Woman (1780)

This broadside is not only one of the more eloquent testimonies to the "pride and spirit" of American women during the Revolution but a forceful assertion of the historical role played by women in meeting the challenges that have confronted their respective societies. Circulated widely during the Revolution, it was used by ministers and others to generate political solidarity. It expresses, in

its own subtle way, a justification for further inclusion of women
in the political life of the state that was to represent a new order.

On the commencement of actual war, the Women of America manifested a firm resolution to contribute as much as could depend on them,
to the deliverance of their country. Animated by the purest patriotism,
they are sensible of sorrow at this day, in not offering more than barren
wishes for the success of so glorious a Revolution. They aspire to render
themselves more really useful, and this sentiment is universal from the
north to the south of the Thirteen United States. Our ambition is kindled
by the fame of those heroines of antiquity, who have rendered their sex
illustrious, and have proved to the universe, that, if the weakness of our
Constitution, if opinion and manners did not forbid us to march to glory
by the same paths as the Men, we should at least equal, and sometimes
surpass them in our love for the public good. I glory in all that which
my sex has done great and commendable. I call to mind with enthusiasm
and with admiration, all those acts of courage, of constancy and patriotism, which history has transmitted to us. . . .

Born of liberty, disdaining to bear the irons of a tyrannic Government,
we associate ourselves to the grandeur of those Sovereigns, cherished
and revered, who have held with so much splendour the scepter of the
greatest States, The Batildas, the Elizabeths, the Maries, the Catharines,
who have extended the empire of liberty, and contented to reign by
sweetness and justice, have broken the chains of slavery, forged by tyrants in the times of ignorance and barbarity. . . .

But I must limit myself to the recollection of this small number of
achievements. Who knows if persons disposed to censure, and sometimes too severely with regard to us, may not disapprove our appearing
acquainted even with the actions of which our sex boasts? We are at
least certain, that he cannot be a good citizen who will not applaud our
efforts for the relief of the armies which defend our lives, our possessions, our liberty? The situation of our soldiery has been represented to
me; the evils inseparable from war, and the firm and generous spirit
which has enabled them to support these. But it has been said, that they
may apprehend, that, in the course of a long war, the view of their
distresses may be lost, and their services be forgotten. Forgotten! never;
I can answer in the name of all my sex. Brave Americans, your disinter-
estedness, your courage, and your constancy will always be dear to
America, as long as she shall preserve her virtue.

We know that at a distance from the theatre of war, if we enjoy any
tranquility, it is the fruit of your watchings, your labours, your dangers.
If I live happy in the midst of my family; if my husband cultivates his
field, and reaps his harvest in peace; if, surrounded with my children, I
myself nourish the youngest, and press it to my bosom, without being

afraid of feeling myself separated from it, by a ferocious enemy; if the house in which we dwell; if our barns, our orchards are safe at the present time from the hands of those incendiaries, it is to you that we owe it. And shall we hesitate to evidence to you our gratitude? Shall we hestitate to wear a cloathing more simple; hair dressed less elegant, while at the price of this small privation, we shall deserve your benedictions. Who, amongst us, will not renounce with the highest pleasure, those vain ornaments, when she shall consider that the valiant defenders of America will be able to draw some advantage from the money which she may have laid out in these; that they will be better defended from the rigours of the seasons, that after their painful toils, they will receive some extraordinary and unexpected relief; that these presents will perhaps be valued by them at a greater price, when they will have it in their power to say: This is the offering of the Ladies. . . . Let us not lose a moment; let us be engaged to offer the homage of our gratitude at the altar of military valour, and you, our brave deliverers, while mercenary slaves combat to cause you to share with them, the irons with which they are loaded, receive with a free hand our offering, the purest which can be presented to your virtue.

By An AMERICAN WOMAN

Source: *American Broadsides*, No. 15, selected and introduced by Georgia B. Bumgardner (Barre, Mass.: Imprint Society, 1971).

DOCUMENT 11: "On the Equality of the Sexes" (Constantia, 1790)

Constantia was the pen name used by Judith Sargent Murray (1751–1820) of Gloucester, Massachusetts. The oldest of four surviving children of Judith and Winthrop Sargent (he was a successful shipowner and merchant), Judith exhibited a strong intellectual bent at an early age. Her most significant educational experience was being allowed to share in the lessons of a brother as he prepared with a tutor to enter Harvard University. Twice married and the mother of two children, she was able—despite difficulties caused by the financial problems of her husbands—to write a number of essays, plays, and poems. Her most celebrated writings are contained in a three-volume work entitled *The Gleaner*, which was published in 1798 and is today regarded as a minor classic in the literature of the young republic.

We include a document of more than average length from her, despite the difficulty in reading it at intervals, for reasons that should become evident to readers: (1) she raised themes that remain with the struggle for women's rights today; (2) she was among the first to argue not only for women's claim to equality but for their potential superiority; (3) unlike Abigail Adams and others who would accept an incrementally improved place for women within the emerging republican ideology, she confronted the assumptions of that ideology; (4) different portions of the document contribute in varying ways—note the sophisticated argumentation she employed, for example, in reversing the traditional thinking about Adam and Eve and the temptation of the serpent; and (5) although the articles constituting the document were not published until 1790, they were written around 1779, over a decade before the 1792 appearance of *Vindication of the Rights of Woman* by the British Mary Wollstonecraft—a date from which it is often claimed that the modern women's rights movement began.

Is it upon mature consideration we adopt the idea, that nature is thus partial in its distributions? Is it indeed a fact that she hath yielded to one half of the human species so unquestionable a mental superiority? I know that to both sexes elevated understanding, and reverie, are common. But suffer me to ask, in what the minds of females are so notoriously deficient, or unequal. May not the intellectual powers be ranged under these four heads—imagination, reason, memory, and judgment. The province of imagination hath long since been surrendered up to us, and we have been crowned undoubted sovereigns of the regions of fancy. Invention is perhaps the most arduous effort of the mind; this branch of imagination hath been particularly ceded to us, and we have been time out of mind invested with that creative faculty. Observe the variety of fashions (here I bar the contemptuous smile) which distinguish and adorn the female world; how continually they [are] changing, insomuch that they almost render the wise man's assertion problematical, and we are ready to say, *there is something new under the sun*. Now what a playfulness, what an exuberance of fancy, what strength of inventive imagination, doth this continual variation discover? Again, it hath been observed, that if the turpitude of the conduct of our sex, hath been ever so enormous, so extremely ready are we, that the very first thought presents us with an apology, so plausible, as to produce our actions even in an amiable light. Another instance of our creative powers, is our talent for slander; how ingenious are we at inventive scandal? what a formidable story can we in a moment fabricate merely from the force of a prolific imagination? how many reputations, in the fertile brain of a female, have been utterly despoiled? how industrious are we at improving a hint? suspicion how easily do we convert into conviction, and conviction, embellished by the power of eloquence, stalks abroad to the surprise and confusion of unsuspecting innocence. Perhaps it will be asked if I furnish these facts as instances of excellency in our sex. Certainly not; but as proofs of a creative faculty, of a lively imagination. Assuredly great activity of mind is thereby discovered, and was this activity properly directed, what beneficial effects would follow. Is the needle and kitchen sufficient to employ the operations of a soul thus organized? I should conceive not. Nay, it is a truth that those very departments leave the intelligent principle vacant, and at liberty for speculation. Are we deficient in reason? we can only reason from what we know, and if an opportunity of acquiring knowledge hath been denied us, the inferiority of our sex cannot fairly be deduced from thence. Memory, I believe, will be allowed us in common, since every one's experience must testify, that a loquacious old woman is as frequently met with, as a communicative old man; their subjects are alike drawn from the fund of other times, and the transactions of their youth, or of maturer life, entertain, or perhaps fatigue you, in the evening of their lives. "But our judgment is not so strong—we do not distinguish so well."—Yet it may be questioned, from what doth this superiority, in this determining faculty of the soul, proceed. May we not trace its source in the difference of education, and continued advantages? Will it be said that the judgment of a male of two years old, is more sage than that of a female of the same age? I believe the reverse is generally observed to be true. But from that period what partiality! how is the one exalted, and the other depressed, by the contrary modes of education which are adopted! the one is taught to aspire, and the other is early confined and limited. As their years increase, the sister must be wholly domesticated, while the brother is led by the hand through all the flowery paths of science. Grant that their minds are by nature equal, yet who shall wonder at the *apparent* superiority, if indeed custom becomes *second nature*; nay if it taketh the place of nature, and that it doth the experience of each day will evince. At length arrived at womanhood, the uncultivated fair one feels a void, which the employments allotted her are by no means capable of filling. What can she do? to books she may not apply; or if she doth, *to those only of the novel kind*, lest she merit the appellation of a *learned lady*; and what ideas have been affixed to this term, the observation of many can testify. Fashion, scandal, and sometimes what is still more reprehensible, are then called in to her relief; and who can say to what lengths the liberties she takes may proceed. Meantime she herself is most unhappy; she feels the want of a cultivated mind. Is she single, she in vain seeks to fill up time from sexual employments or amusements. Is she united to a person whose soul nature made equal to her own, education hath set him so far above her, that in those entertainments which are productive of such rational felicity, she is not qualified to accompany him. She experiences a mortifying consciousness of inferiority, which embitters every enjoyment. Doth the person to whom her adverse fate hath consigned her, possess a mind incapable of improvement, she is equally wretched, in being so closely connected with an individual whom she cannot but despise. Now, was she permitted the same instructors as her brother (with an eye however to their particular departments) for the employment of a rational mind an ample field would be opened. . . .

Will it be urged that those acquirements would supersede our domestick duties. I answer that every requisite in female economy is easily attained; and, with truth I can add, that when once attained, they require no further *mental attention*. Nay, while we are pursuing the needle, or the superintendency of the family, I repeat, that our minds are at full liberty for reflection; that imagination may exert itself in full vigor; and that if a just foundation is early laid, our ideas will then be worthy of rational beings. If we were industrious we might easily find time to arrange them upon paper, or should avocations press too hard for such an indulgence, the hours allotted for conversation would at least become more refined and rational. Should it still be vociferated, "Your domestick employments are sufficient"—I would calmly ask, is it reasonable, that a candidate for immortality, for the joys of heaven, an intelligent being, who is to spend an eternity in contemplating the works of Deity, should at present be so degraded, as to be allowed no other ideas, than those which are suggested by the mechanism of a pudding, or the sewing the seams of a garment? Pity that all such censurers of female improvement do not go one step further, and deny their future existence; to be consistent they surely ought.

Yes, ye lordly, ye haughty sex, our souls are by nature *equal* to yours; the same breath of God animates, enlivens, and invigorates us; and that we are not fallen lower than yourselves, let those witness who have greatly towered above the various discouragements by which they have been so heavily oppressed; and though I am unacquainted with the list of celebrated characters on either side, yet from the observations I have made in the contracted circle in which I have moved, I dare confidently believe, that from the commencement of time to the present day, there hath been as many females, as males, who, by the *mere force of natural powers*, have merited the crown of applause; who, *thus unassisted*, have seized the wreath of fame. I know there are those who assert, that as the animal powers of the one sex are superiour, of course their mental faculties also must be stronger; thus attributing strength of mind to the transient organization of this earth born tenement. But if this reasoning is just, man must be content to yield the palm to many of the brute creation, since by not a few of his brethren of the field, he is far surpassed in bodily strength. Moreover, was this argument admitted, it would prove too much, for occular demonstration evinceth, that there are many robust masculine ladies, and effeminate gentlemen. Yet I fancy that Mr. Pope, though clogged with an enervated body, and distinguished by a diminutive stature, could nevertheless lay claim to greatness of soul; and perhaps there are many other instances which might be adduced to combat so unphilosophical an opinion. Do we not often see, that when the clay built tabernacle is well nigh dissolved, when it is just ready to mingle with the parent soil, the immortal inhabitant aspires to, and even attaineth heights the most sublime, and which were before wholly unexplored. Besides, were we to grant that animal strength proved any thing, taking into consideration the accustomed impartiality of nature, we should be induced to imagine, that she had invested the female mind with superiour strength as an equivalent for the bodily powers of man. But wa[i]ving this however palpable advantage, for *equality only*, we wish to contend.

I am aware that there are many passages in the sacred oracles which seem to give the advantage to the other sex; but I consider all these as wholly metaphorical. Thus David was a man after God's own heart, yet see him enervated by his licentious passions! beyond him following Uriah to the death, and shew me wherein could consist the immaculate Being's complacency. Listen to the curses which Job bestoweth upon the day of his nativity, and tell me where is his perfection, where his patience—*literally* it existed not. David and Job were types of him who was to come; and the superiority of man, as exhibited in scripture, being also emblematical, all arguments deduced from thence, of course fall to the ground. The exquisite delicacy of the female mind proclaimeth the exactness of its texture, while its nice sense of honour announceth its innate, its native grandeur. And indeed, in one respect, the preeminence seems to be tacitly allowed us, for after an education which limits and confines, and employments and recreations which naturally tend to enervate the body, and debilitate the mind; after we have from early youth been adorned with ribbons, and other gewgaws, dressed out like the ancient victims previous to a sacrifice, being taught by the care of our parents in collecting the most showy materials that the ornamenting our exteriour ought to be the principal object of our attention; after, I say, fifteen years thus spent, we are introduced into the world, amid the united adulation of every beholder. Praise is sweet to the soul; we are immediately intoxicated by large draughts of flattery, which being plentifully administered, is to the pride of our hearts the most acceptable incense. It is expected that with the other sex we should commence immediate war, and that we should triumph over the machinations of the most artful. We must be constantly upon our guard; prudence and discretion must be our characsticks; and we must rise superiour to, and obtain a complete victory over those who have been long adding to the native strength of their minds, by an unremitted study of men and books, and who have, moreover, conceived from the loose characters which they have seen portrayed in the extensive variety of their reading, a most contemptible opinion of the sex. Thus unequal, we are, notwithstanding forced to the combat, and the infamy which is consequent upon the smallest deviation in our conduct, proclaims the high idea which was formed of our native strength; and thus, indirectly at least, is the preference acknowledged to be our due. And if we are allowed an equality of acquirements, let serious studies equally employ our minds, and we will bid our souls arise to equal strength. We will meet upon even ground, the despot man; we will rush with alacrity to the combat, and, crowned by success, we shall then answer the exalted expectations which are formed. Though sensibility, soft compassion, and gentle commiseration, are inmates in the female bosom, yet against every deep laid art, altogether fearless of the event, we will set them in array; for assuredly the wreath of victory will encircle the spotless brow. If we meet an equal, a sensible friend, we will reward him with the hand of amity, and through life we will be assiduous to promote his happiness; but from every deep laid scheme for our rule, retiring into ourselves, amid the flowery paths of science, we will indulge in all the refined and sentimental pleasures of contemplation. And should it still be urged, that the studies thus insisted upon would interfere with our more peculiar department, I must further reply, that *early hours*, and close application, will do wonders; and to her who is from the first dawn of reason taught to fill up time rationally, both the requisites will be easy. I grant that niggard fortune is too generally unfriendly to the mind, and that much of that valuable treasure, time, is necessarily expended upon the wants of the body; but it should be remembered, that in embarrassed circumstances our companions have as little leisure for literary improvement, as is afforded to us; for most certainly their provident care is at least as requisite as our exertions. . . .

CONSTANTIA

By way of Supplement to the foregoing pages, I subjoin the following extract from a letter, wrote to a friend in the December of 1780.

. . . The superiority of your sex hath, I grant, been time out of mind esteemed a truth incontrovertible; in consequence of which persuasion, every plan of education hath been calculated to establish this favourite tenet. Not long since, weak and presuming as I was, I amused myself with selecting some arguments from nature, reason, and experience, against this so generally received idea. I confess that to sacred testimonies I had not recourse. I held them to be merely metaphorical, and thus regarding them, I could not persuade myself that there was any propriety in bringing them to decide in this *very important debate*. However, as

you, sir, confine yourself entirely to the sacred oracles, I mean to bend
the whole of my artillery against those supposed proofs, which you have
from thence provided, and from which you have formed an intrench-
ment *apparently* so invulnerable. And first, to begin with our great pro-
genitors; but here, suffer me to premise, that it is for mental strength I
mean to contend, for with respect to animal powers, I yield them undisputed to that sex, which enjoys them in common with the lion, the tyger,
and many other beasts of prey; therefore your observations respecting
the *rib, under the arm, at a distance from the head*, &c. &c. in no sort militate
against my view. Well, but the woman was first in the transgression.
Strange how blind *self love* renders you men; were you not wholly absorbed in a partial admiration of your own abilities, you would long
since have acknowledged the force of what I am now going to say. It is
true some ignoramuses have absurdly enough informed us, that the
beauteous fair of paradise, was seduced from her obedience, by a malignant demon, *in the guise of a baleful serpent*; but we, who are better informed, know that the fallen spirit presented himself to her view, *a
shining angel still*; for thus, saith the criticks in the Hebrew tongue, ought
the word to be rendered. Let us examine her motive—Hark! the seraph
declares that she shall attain a perfection of knowledge; for is there aught
which is not comprehended under one or other of the terms *good* and
evil. It doth not appear that she was governed by any sensual appetite;
but merely by a desire of adorning her mind; a laudable ambition fired
her soul, and a thirst for knowledge impelled the predilection so fatal in
its consequences. Adam could not plead the same deception; assuredly
he was not deceived; nor ought we to admire his superiour strength, or
wonder at his sagacity, when we so often confess that example is much
more influential than precept. His gentle partner stood before him, a
melancholy instance of the direful effects of disobedience; he saw her
not possessed of that wisdom which she had fondly hoped to obtain,
but he beheld the once blooming female, disrobed of that innocence,
which had heretofore rendered her so lovely. To him then deception
became impossible, as he had proof positive of the fallacy of the argument, which the deceiver had suggested. What then could be his in-
ducement to burst the barriers, and to fly directly in the face of that
command, which *immediately* from the mouth of deity *he* had received,
since, I say, he could not plead that fascinating stimulous, the accumulation of knowledge, as indisputable conviction was so visibly portrayed
before him. What mighty cause impelled him to sacrifice myriads of
beings yet unborn, and by one impious act, which *he saw* would be productive of such fatal effects, entail undistinguished ruin upon a race of
beings, which he was yet to produce. Blush, ye vaunters of fortitude; ye
boasters of resolution; ye haughty lords of the creation; blush when ye
remember, that he was influenced by no other motive than a bare pu-

sillanimous attachment to a woman! by sentiments so exquisitely soft, that all his sons have, from that period, when they have designed to degrade them, described as highly feminine. Thus it should seem, that at the arts of the grand deceiver (since means adequate to the purpose are, I conceive, invariably pursued) were requisite to mislead our general mother, while the father of mankind forfeited his own, and relinquished the happiness of posterity, merely in compliance with the blandishments of a female. . . .

Source: Constantia, "On the Equality of the Sexes," *Massachusetts Magazine* 2 (March 1790): 132–135; and 2 (April 1790): 223–226.

DOCUMENT 12: The Rights of Seneca Women (1790–1791)

Although common law placed women—especially married women—in an economically subordinate position to men and, by so doing, deprived them of the social and political power associated with ownership of property, common law was not the only legal tradition in America. American Indians had their own tradition. The following document concerns the property and political rights of women from the Seneca nation. They had appeared before the lodge of Colonel Procter, General Washington's representative to the Seneca nation, who was in peace negotiations with a number of Seneca chiefs. Faced with unprecedented disruption of their society since 1780—disruption caused by war with the white man and by disease—the women wanted peace and sought to tell Procter so, after they had considered his proposals.

You ought to hear and listen to what we, women, shall speak, as well as to the sachems; for we are the owners of the land,—and it is ours. It is we that plant it for our and their use. Hear us, therefore, for we speak of things that concern us while our men shall say more to you; for we have told them.

Source: Katherine Kish and Thomas Dublin, eds., *Women and Power in American History*, vols. (Englewood Cliffs, N.J.: Prentice-Hall, 1991), 1: 12.

DOCUMENT 13: Did Women Gain from the Revolution? (1790–1791)

Over the years historians have debated whether the American Revolution was conservative or radical. In looking at the Revolution from that perspective, one rarely—if ever—confronted the relationship between the status of women and the changes the Revolution is supposed to have forged. Below is a debate on that relationship. First we look at the position of Elizabeth Fox-Genovese, Eleanore Raoul Professor of Humanistic Studies at Emory University, followed by that of Forrest McDonald, Distinguished Research Fellow at the University of Alabama.

ELIZABETH FOX-GENOVESE

Was the American Revolution, whether conservative or radical for men, a revolution at all for women? . . .

When Abigail Adams wrote to her husband that he should "remember the ladies," she was asking that the domestic powers of husbands be reduced and, above all, that they cease behaving like tyrants within the household. But she was not asking that women be allowed to participate in government. During the second half of the eighteenth century advanced advocates of women's rights were insisting on women's capacity for an essentially female excellence, not asking that women be recognized as functionally interchangeable with men.

In effect, the American Revolution strengthened gender as a form of social classification. Previously women had been able to relate to the polity, or at least the public area, as delegates of families on occasion when family and class membership superseded gender membership. After the Revolution they related to the polity as women first and members of families or classes second. This intensification of gender as a form of social classification has led historians to argue that women actually lost opportunities as a result of the Revolution. Other contend that women gained through their heightened identification with other women, through the emergence of a recognizable "woman's sphere" within which they forged tight bonds of sisterhood. But the question remains: if the Revolution did not result in women's inclusion in the polity, if the new republic did not welcome women as citizens, what did the revolutionary times specifically offer women?

The change amounted to an improvement in the view of women specifically as women: the view of what it meant to be a woman. Earlier seen as potentially dangerous and deviant, as possible witches or probable shrews, women were suddenly seen as the mothers of citizens of the republic. Previously obliged to labor under the direction of the male heads of their households, they now were granted governance of the home. The ties that bound women to their gender tightened, but their gender gained status. The belief that women had a particular feminine sensibility legitimated their demands for education, though an education different from that for men. The conviction that they were capable of superior moral purity and had special insights into the human condition legitimated their concern with social problems, as long as they did not take those concerns into the political sphere. The respect and self-respect that they had won legitimated their quest for excellence within their own sphere. . . .

FORREST MCDONALD

The Revolution was even more an all-male phenomenon than Professor Fox-Genovese describes it. The principles of republican theory were familiar even to the common man in the new nation, and Americans fashioned their state constitutions upon those principles. What does all this have to do with the role of women in the Revolution? Republicanism totally and expressly excluded them.

The word "republic" derives from the Latin *res publica*, meaning the public thing or that which is of concern to the public: "Public," in turn, comes from the same Latin root as *pubic*, meaning maturity or manhood. Women were necessarily excluded, as were children, slaves, and the propertyless; for all these people were dependent, which was regarded as incompatible with the full status of manhood. (Unlike "public," "people" and "popular" were terms that included everybody.)

It was universally agreed that the activating principle of a republic was and must be virtue. This did not mean benevolence, kindness, or any of the other attributes associated with the idea of Christian charity. Rather, "virtue" stemmed from the Latin *virtus*, meaning manliness: it connoted courage, strength, virility, self-sufficiency. To say that public virtue must activate the republic, then, is almost to be redundant: it means that manly men must attend to those matters that are of concern to men. The opposite of virtue, in eighteenth-century usage, was "effeminacy," which was used interchangeably with "vice" and "luxury."

John Adams had a great deal to say on the subject. When the principles of a republic were pure, he wrote, it was "productive of everything, which is great and excellent among Men." But "there must be a positive Passion for the public good, the public interest, Honor, Power, and Glory." This public passion "must be Superior to all private Passions. Men must be ready, they must pride themselves, and be happy to sacrifice their private Pleasures, Passions, and Interests, nay, their private Friendships and dearest Connections, when they stand in Competition with the Rights of Society." As for women, "their delicacy renders them unfit for practice and experience in the great business of life, and the hardy enterprise of war, as well as the arduous cares of state."

A less rigorous form of republican theory, popular among Americans outside of New England, also had little place for women. Agrarian republicanism, formulated by the seventeenth-century English political theorist James Harrington, held that ownership and cultivation of the land breeds independence and manly virtue, and contended that if most of the people own and cultivate their own land the supply of public virtue will always be adequate for the support of the republic. The great mass of the white adult males in the former British North American colonies were in fact owners and cultivators of the soil, but the consequence for women was to deprive them of part of the limited role that Professor Fox-Genovese depicts them as having had in the early republic. They could be mothers of the sons of the republic, it is true, but they could not have the dominant role in child rearing. Not for another generation, when increasing numbers of men began to go into manufacturing, commerce, and other urban pursuits that kept them away from home all day, did women begin to take over the rearing of their sons.

Source: Virginia Bernhard et al., *Firsthand America*, vols. (New York: Brandywine Press, 1992), 1: 192–193.

Part II

The Republican Order and the Cracks in Its Design, 1790–1865

The period 1790–1865 brought great changes not only to the nation as a whole but to women. During the nineteenth century the United States shifted from an agricultural society to an industrial one. Simultaneously, religious ferment and reform stirred the land. The period closed with a brutal, destructive civil war, which freed all slaves but enfranchised only the men. The documents presented here examine the effect of the tumultuous events of this period on women's rights.

Early feminists challenged the prevailing ideology of "separate spheres"—that is, roles and functions—for men and women based on sexual differences. They presented a radical counterimage to that ideology; instead of acknowledging biological difference as the sole determiner of gender roles, early feminists focused on the characteristics that were common to both men and women. Documents in this section illustrate how the traditional forces of society objected to, fought against, and felt threatened by the campaign for women's rights.

In the post-revolutionary period Americans instrumental in establishing the republic were concerned about whether it would succeed. What factors, what conditions of society, and what behavior, they asked, would ensure that the American republican experiment would endure? The answer was an active, well-educated citizenry that was willing to defend the country. But, they reasoned, men could not do it alone: they required the assistance of women. The authors of the first three documents in Part II believed that if women remained within the traditional framework established by religion and common law, their talents would enhance the civic virtues needed by males in a republic. Thus, the Reverend James

Fordyce (Document 14) as early as 1770 noted that society benefited when women adhered to their pure and pious nature, while Benjamin Rush (Document 15) advised a concerned public that women's contribution, as their husbands' helpmates and as mothers who trained their sons and daughters to serve the republic, required special "female" education. That the education of girls and boys be distinct was not unusual, for it reflected the long-held view that the nature of males and females differed, and that this difference, when nurtured through specialized training, would enhance society. The new feature here is the significance Rush attached to the instrumental role played by post-revolutionary American women. Indeed, before the Revolution mothers educated their sons only until the age of seven, when their fathers or tutors assumed their instruction, while in England servants supplemented a wife's or mother's work. Uniquely, an American republican mother with the kind of education proposed by Rush was deemed competent to continue educating her son for citizenship even after he reached the age of seven, and she could, in addition, tend to her husband's affairs.

We find another role assigned to women of the new republic by Alexander Hamilton (Document 16) who believed that working-class American women, like their English counterparts, could contribute to a new manufacturing economy by working outside the home, in factories, which would allow the republic to compete favorably with Europe. Thus, in each of these ways women's talents were considered valuable to the new country's prosperity.

The development of commerce and industry drew more and more men to jobs outside the home, while women remained there. The "ideology of separate spheres" seemed to confirm reality and served to promote women's domestic autonomy, a status unknown when their husbands were at home to rule the household. Did this separate domestic status have an effect on women's rights? Perhaps in an intangible social sense, but not legally during these early republican years, for most married women had limited civil and property rights, and were still expected to exhibit the characteristics of passivity, purity, and docility.

Nevertheless, historical perspective reveals the emergence of a counterideology that began to undermine the construct of the republican-antebellum gendered world. The most important of these undermining elements was the increase in educational opportunities for women, welcomed by Rush but rejected by others for fear that women would acquire masculine characteristics. Women such as Priscilla Mason (Document 17), who as early as 1793 protested in a public forum against the constraints imposed on her gender not by God but by male society, embodied those fears. Mason had the opportunity for special, private education, but the majority of the white, northern female population had to wait until the mid-nineteenth century to receive an adequate education. They rarely received advanced instruction in science and mathematics until after the Civil War.

Arguments in favor of the education of women were also advanced by Catherine Beecher (Document 21), who took the conservative position that when you educate a woman you educate a family and that an educated woman offers her husband effective companionship which enhances the marital relationship. A middle ground was presented by Emma Willard and Mary Lyon (Document 19), who claimed that educated women could fill the country's need for teachers, a profession that would allow them to express their natural, nurturing qualities and provide the unmarried with an income. The most radical proposed that women should be educated no differently from men, because they shared the same *human* qualities (Documents 17, 23, 32, 35, and 39). At variance in the extreme with the republican, antebellum gendered world order, this nineteenth century human rights perspective rejected sexual differences as determinative in all areas except those of physical strength and woman's fulfillment of her duties as wife and mother, and maintained that females should be granted equal opportunities and equal rights with males. And when some women succeeded in male professions, as did, for example, Elizabeth Blackwell in medicine (Document 28) and Antoinette Brown Blackwell in the ministry (Document 36), their peers, proud of their accomplishments, held them up as role models and as evidence of women's capacity to perform equally with men (Document 40).

The Quakers continued to advocate equal education (see Part I, Document 5). Their participation in antislavery organizations also served to undermine the system of separate spheres. Nothing could demonstrate this better than the activities of two Quaker-educated sisters, Angelina and Sarah Grimké, whose public protest against slavery (Documents 21 and 23) led the Massachusetts Congregational Church to censure their behavior, claiming that their public addresses are injurious to female character (Document 22). The religious establishment's position was upheld and expanded by the Presbyterian preacher Jonathan F. Stearns (Document 25), who maintained that any activity outside the female sphere was to be regarded as dangerous to the well-being of society. Subtle methods of persuasion, including that of instilling guilt, were applied to keep women docile and subordinate. No doubt this helped to silence many, but not the sisters Grimké, who remained adamant in

their belief in human rights while simultaneously becoming increasingly aware of how the oppression of women was analogous
to that of the slave. Other women responded similarly. Antislavery
activity influenced the women's rights beliefs of Elizabeth Cady
Stanton. She and the articulate Quaker Lucretia Mott organized a
historic meeting for women at Seneca Falls in 1848 (Document 30),
which, in Stanton's words, required a Declaration of Sentiments of
women's rights. Using the format of the Declaration of Independence, their declaration echoed the language of the Enlightenment
by proclaiming that the inequality of women was in opposition to
the intention of the Creator, for "all men and women are created
equal."

After Seneca Falls, feminists organized national women's rights
conventions, at which they demanded the right to suffrage (Document 30), equality as human beings (Document 34), equal education
(Document 35), reform in the common law (Document 29), and
much more. In addition, feminists petitioned political conventions
held in Ohio (Document 33) and in Massachusetts (Document 38),
demanding the right to vote.

They poured their ideas, beliefs, hopes, and sentiments into petitions, their only officially recognized political tool. They used
them to declare their entitlement to suffrage (Document 38), to
press for passage of the Married Women's Property Act (Document
29), and to express their opposition to the extension of slavery (Document 31). In their petitions, speeches, and writings, these activists
rejected society's characterizations of women as weak, submissive,
and lacking in intellect. And through these activities they demonstrated the unfairness of excluding them from the public arena and
forbidding them to control their own property on the basis of traits
arbitrarily assigned to their sex.

The issue of temperance agitated and consequently activated
more women than any other (Document 37), for it underscored
their helplessness against alcohol, emphasized their lack of control
over husbands who were under its sway, and demonstrated society's double standard, which required purity of them but permitted
men liberty of behavior. The effects of intemperance were a primary
motivation for Stanton to recommend to the New York State legislators that the divorce laws be liberalized (Document 46). The
temperance movement also helped white middle-class women to
empathize with their black female slave sisters (Document 45).
Some feminists protested against the subjugation of married
women by exchanging marriage vows that reflected principles of
equality (Document 42).

The women's rights movement developed in the workplace as

well. At the Lowell factories in Massachusetts, women workers jeopardized their wages and even their jobs when they went out on strike to protest wage cuts and excessively long hours (Document 18).

Women also formed unions to protest substandard working conditions and to fight for their rights as workers. However, many were discouraged from joining male unions.

Despite these elements of "subversion," the ideology of separate spheres for men and women remained largely undamaged, entrenched in the power establishment of government and culture. Most women overwhelmingly accepted its propaganda, believing that marriage and motherhood should define their lives. Few had the leisure or education to study the issues presented by the feminists. In addition, the continuing strength of the patriarchal–common law tradition remained. Despite evidence of physical and sexual abuse, women seeking divorce were hardly ever granted one (Documents 27 and 46), and the courts still allowed the husband the sole choice of domicile (Document 45).

Two important episodes at the end of this period showed the continuing vitality of the separate sphere ideology. The first was the silence that surrounded Anna Ella Carroll's important contributions to the Union victory (Document 48). Withheld from the public for more than a decade because of her gender, and still largely ignored in American history textbooks, the strategy she devised was of such significance that had she been a man her name would sit alongside those of Grant and Lee. The second episode came at the end of the Civil War when feminists heard that their long-standing desire for the right to suffrage was to be denied. Once again they poured their energies into writing a petition, this time to the Senate and the House of Representatives, in the vain hope of persuading male legislators not to exclude them (Document 49).

What, then, can we say about how this period affected the rights of women? In substantive legal areas, the rights they gained were meager. But a significant barrier to patriarchy was broken with passage of the married women's property acts (see Document 29), which ended the legal myth of the unity of husband and wife. (Many men endorsed this legislation for their own personal economic gain. And judicial interpretation of these laws largely confirmed the common law interpretation of property ownership.) Further legislation kept chipping away at the common law, and despite some regression during the time of the Civil War, in the areas of property rights, divorce (which was in theory more acceptable), and child custody, women were somewhat better off than they had been in the early part of the nineteenth century (Document 50). Most important, feminists brought a new perspective to the image of women. No longer were they ideationally restricted to the domestic sphere, for feminists emphasized and demonstrated that women could contribute to the outside world as well as to the home. This counterimage of women continued to inspire the feminists of the future.

DOCUMENT 14: Religion, Virtue and the Behavior of Women (1770)

In this document the Reverend James Fordyce (1720–1796) preached a view widely held at the time, that by nature women were more inclined toward religion than men. Beginning in the 1690s the clergy claimed that female experiences in childbirth, motherhood, and housewifery shaped such characteristics as tenderness, piety, and purity. Thus, they claimed, women found an expression for their spiritually oriented natures in the church. The distinctions between the sexes had become so encrusted in eighteenth century values that Fordyce was able to warn female "infidels" that their popularity, and, by implication, their marriage prospects, might suffer should they not demonstrate these "feminine" characteristics.

A bigoted woman every man of sense will carefully shun, as a most disagreeable, and even dangerous companion. But the secret reverence, which that majestic form Religion imprints on the hearts of all, is such, that even they who will not submit to its dictates themselves, do yet wish it to be regarded by those with whom they are connected in the nearest relation. The veriest infidel of them all, I am apt to believe, would be sorry to find his sister, daughter, or wife, under no restraint from religious principle. Thus it is, that even the greatest libertines are forced to pay, at the same instant, a kind of implicit respect to the two main objects of their profligate satire. Piety and Women: while they consider these as formed for each other, and tacitly acknowledge that the first is the only effectual means of insuring the good behaviour of the last. Let them talk as long, and as contemptuously as they will, about that easy credulity, and those superstitious terrors, which they pretend to be the foundation of your religion; something within will always give them the lie, so long as they perceive that your religion renders you more steadily virtuous, and more *truly* lovely . . . .

To attempt the conviction of female infidels falls not within my present design. Indeed I fear it were a hopeless undertaking. The preposterous vanity, together with the open or secret profligacy, by which they have been warped into scepticism, would in all likelihood baffle any endeavours of mine. If they be not however so far gone in that unhappy system, as to be resolved against all sober inquiry, I would earnestly recommend to their perusal a few of the many excellent writings, which this age and country have produced in favour of religion both natural and revealed. At the same time I would just remind them, that the daring and disputatious spirit of unbelief is utterly repugnant to female softness, and to that sweet docility which, in their sex, is so peculiarly pleasing to ours: not to mention, that from an infidel partner a man can have no prospect of consolation in those hours of distress, when the hopes of futurity can alone administer relief.—To you, my christian hearers, I was going to observe, that the stedfast and serious belief of immortality, as pointed out in your frame, and brought to light by the gospel, will excite such a mighty concern to secure its grand interests, such a high sense of your internal dignity, such a predominant ambition of being acceptable in his sight, who can make you happy or wretched forever, as must necessarily lessen in your esteem every external and perishing advantage.

Source: Reverend James Fordyce, *Sermons to Young Women* (1740), in Rosemary Radford Ruether and Rosemary Skinner Keller, eds., *Women and Religion in America. The Nineteenth Century: A Documentary History*, vols. (San Francisco: Harper and Row, 1981), 1: 14–15.

DOCUMENT 15: *Thoughts upon Female Education* (Benjamin Rush, 1787)

Although Cotton Mather sermonized in 1692 that "education would enable a woman to better serve her husband and family," it was not until the end of the eighteenth century that education for women became a significant issue for public debate.

Benjamin Rush's essay, perhaps the most famous on the subject during this time, echoes Mather's belief that the purpose of a woman's education was to enable her to assist her family. But Rush was addressing a republican, not a colonial, audience. As American republican wives and mothers, he argued, they would need to know how to help mange their husbands' property, how to raise sons to serve the new republic, and how to raise daughters who would replicate their mothers' functions. Rush clearly believed that the future of the republic depended upon such specialized training. He rejected the view that educating women masculinized them as "the prejudice of little minds."

GENTLEMEN,

I have yielded with diffidence to the solicitations of the Principal of the Academy, in undertaking to express my regard for the prosperity of this seminary of learning by submitting to your candor a few thoughts upon female education.

The first remark that I shall make upon this subject is that female education should be accommodated to the state of society, manners, and government of the country in which it is conducted.

This remark leads me at once to add that the education of young ladies in this country should be conducted upon principles very different from what it is in Great Britain and in some respects different from what it was when we were a part of a monarchical empire.

There are several circumstances in the situation, employments, and duties of women in America which require a peculiar mode of education.

I. The early marriages of our women, by contracting the time allowed for education, renders it necessary to contract its plan and to confine it chiefly to the more useful branches of literature.

II. The state of property in America renders it necessary for the greatest part of our citizens to employ themselves in different occupations for the advancement of their fortunes. This cannot be done without the assistance of the female members of the community. They must be the stewards and guardians of their husbands' property. That education, therefore, will be most proper for our women which teaches them to discharge the duties of those offices with the most success and reputation.

III. From the numerous avocations to which a professional life exposes gentlemen in America from their families, a principal share of the instruction of children naturally devolves upon the women. It becomes us there to prepare them, by a suitable education, for the discharge of this most important duty of mothers.

IV. The equal share that every citizen has in the liberty and the possible share he may have in the government of our country make it necessary that our ladies should be qualified to a certain degree, by a peculiar and suitable education, to concur in instructing their sons in the principles of liberty and government.

V. In Great Britain the business of servants is a regular occupation, but in America this humble station is the usual retreat of unexpected indigence; hence the servants in this country possess less knowledge and subordination than are required from them; and hence our ladies are obliged to attend more to the private affairs of their families than ladies generally do of the same rank in Great Britain. "They are good servants," said an American lady of distinguished merit in a letter to a favorite daughter, "who will do well with good looking after." This circumstance should have great influence upon the nature and extent of female education in America.

The branches of literature most essential for a young lady in this country appear to be:

I. A knowledge of the English language. She should not only read but speak and spell it correctly. . . .

II. Pleasure and interest conspire to make the writing of a fair and legible hand a necessary branch of female education. . . .

III. Some knowledge of figures and bookkeeping is absolutely necessary to qualify a young lady for the duties which await her in this country. There are certain occupations in which she may assist her husband with this knowledge, and should she survive him and agreeably to the custom of our country be the executrix of his will, she cannot fail of deriving immense advantages from it.

IV. An acquaintance with geography and some instruction in chronology will enable a young lady to read history, biography, and travels, with advantage, and thereby qualify her not only for a general intercourse with the world but to be an agreeable companion for a sensible man. To these branches of knowledge may be added, in some instances, a general acquaintance with the first principles of astronomy and natural philosophy, particularly with such parts of them as are calculated to prevent superstition, by explaining the causes or obviating the effects of natural evil. . . .

VI. Dancing is by no means an improper branch of education for an American lady. It promotes health and renders the figure and motions of the body easy and agreeable. I anticipate the time when the resources of conversation shall be so far multiplied that the amusement of dancing shall be wholly confined to children. But in our present state of society and knowledge, I conceive it to be an agreeable substitute for the ignoble pleasures of drinking and gaming in our assemblies of grown people.

VII. The attention of our young ladies should be directed as soon as they are prepared for it to the reading of history, travels, poetry, and moral essays. . . .

VIII. It will be necessary to connect all these branches of education with regular instruction in the Christian religion. For this purpose the principles of the different sects of Christians should be taught and explained, and our pupils should early be furnished with some of the most simple arguments in favor of the truth of Christianity. . . . A clergyman of long experience in the instruction of youth informed me that he always found children acquired religious knowledge more easily than knowledge upon other subjects, and that young girls acquired this kind of knowledge more readily than boys. The female breast is the natural soil of Christianity.

IX. If the measures that have been recommended for inspiring our pupils with a sense of religious and moral obligation be adopted, the government of them will be easy and agreeable. I shall only remark under this head that *strictness* of discipline will always render *severity* unnecessary and that there will be the most instruction in that school where there is the most order.

I have said nothing in favor of instrumental music as a branch of female education because I conceive it is by no means accommodated to the present state of society and manners in America. The price of musical instruments and the extravagant fees demanded by the teachers of instrumental music form but a small part of my objections to it.

To perform well upon a musical instrument requires much time and long practice. . . .

I beg leave further to bear a testimony against the practice of making the French language a part of female education in America. In Britain, where company and pleasure are the principal business of ladies, where the nursery and the kitchen form no part of their care, and where a daily intercourse is maintained with Frenchmen and other foreigners who speak the French language, a knowledge of it is absolutely necessary. But the case is widely different in this country. . . .

To be the mistress of a family is one of the great ends of a woman's being, and while the peculiar state of society in America imposes this station so early and renders the duties of it so numerous and difficult, I conceive that little time can be spared for the acquisition of this elegant accomplishment. . . . To you, therefore, YOUNG LADIES, an important problem is committed for solution; and that is, whether our present plan of education be a wise one and whether it be calculated to prepare you for the duties of social and domestic life. I know that the elevation of the female mind, by means of moral, physical, and religious truth, is considered by some men as unfriendly to the domestic character of a woman. But this is the prejudice of little minds and springs from the same spirit which opposes the general diffusion of knowledge among the citizens of our republics. If men believe that ignorance is favorable to the government of the female sex, they are certainly deceived, for a weak and ignorant woman will always be governed with the greatest difficulty.

I have sometimes been led to ascribe the invention of ridiculous and expensive fashions in female dress entirely to the gentlemen in order to divert the ladies from improving their minds and thereby to secure a more arbitrary and unlimited authority over them. It will be in your power, LADIES, to correct the mistakes and practice of our sex upon these subjects by demonstrating that the female temper can only be governed by reason and that the cultivation of reason in women is alike friendly to the order of nature and to private as well as public happiness.

Source: Benjamin Rush, "Thoughts upon Female Education, Accommodated to the Present State of Society, Manners, and Government in the United States of

America" (Boston, 1787), in *Essays on Education in the Early Republic*, ed. Frederick Rudolph (Cambridge, Mass.: Harvard University Press, 1965), 27–40.

DOCUMENT 16: Report on Manufactures (Alexander Hamilton, 1791)

Alexander Hamilton (1755–1804), the first secretary of the treasury, wrote this report prior to the onset of the Industrial Revolution in the United States. In it he was prescient to regard manufacturing as the necessary factor by which America would gain its independence from Europe. He enumerated the requirements that would foster manufacturing, one of which was hiring women and children to work in factories, where, he argued, they would become "more useful . . . than they would otherwise be." Although Hamilton expected a different "class" of women to work in the factories than Rush hoped to educate, by the end of the eighteenth century the role of women expanded to include working outside the home.

The secretary of the Treasury, in obedience to the order of ye House of Representatives, of the 15th day of January, 1790, has applied his attention, at as early a period as his other duties would permit, to the subject of Manufactures; and particularly to the means of promoting such as will tend to render the United States, independent on foreign nations for military and other essential supplies. . . .

It is . . . proper to . . . enumerate the principal circumstances, from which it may be inferred—that manufacturing establishments not only occasion a positive augmentation of the Produce and Revenue of the Society, but that they contribute essentially to rendering them greater than they could possibly be, without such establishments. These circumstances are—

1. The division of labour.
2. An extension of the use of Machinery.
3. Additional employment to classes of the community not ordinarily engaged in the business.
4. The promoting of emigration from foreign Countries.
5. The furnishing greater scope for the diversity of talents and dispositions which discriminate men from each other.
6. The affording a more ample and various field for enterprize.

7. The creating in some instances a new, and securing in all, a more certain and steady demand for the surplus produce of the soil. . . .

The employment of Machinery forms an item of great importance in the general mass of national industry. 'Tis an artificial force brought in aid of the natural force of man; and, to all the purposes of labour, is an increase of hands; an accession of strength, *unencumbered too by the expense of maintaining the laborer*. May it not therefore be fairly inferred, that those occupations, which give greatest scope to the use of this auxiliary, contribute most to the general Stock of industrious effort, and, in consequence, to the general product of industry? . . .

The Cotton Mill, invented in England, within the last twenty years, is a signal illustration of the general proposition, which has been just advanced. In consequence of it, all the different processes for spinning Cotton are performed by means of Machines, which are put in motion by water, and attended chiefly by women and Children; and by a smaller number of persons, in the whole, than are requisite in the ordinary mode of spinning. . . .

In places where those . . . manufacturing . . . institutions prevail, besides the persons regularly engaged in them, they afford occasional and extra employment to industrious individuals and families, who are willing to devote the leisure resulting from the intermissions of their ordinary pursuits to collateral labours, as a resource for multiplying their acquisitions or their enjoyments. The husbandman himself experiences a new source of profit and support from the increased industry of his wife and daughters; invited and stimulated by the demands of the neighboring manufactories. . . .

It is worthy of particular remarks, that, in general, women and Children are rendered more useful, and the latter more early useful by manufacturing establishments, than they would otherwise be. . . .

Source: Milton Cantor, ed., *Hamilton* (Englewood Cliffs, N.J.: Prentice-Hall, 1971), 77–83.

DOCUMENT 17: The Valedictory and Salutatory Orations of Women at The Young Ladies Academy of Philadelphia (1792 and 1793)

At this academy, established in 1787, girls were able to obtain an unusually excellent education. As part of the educational process competitions were held and prizes were awarded to the winners. As a part of the victory celebration the girls delivered public orations, quite extraordinary for the times, and occasionally their speeches were published.

In 1792 Molly Wallace delivered the valedictory oration, and in 1793 Priscilla Mason gave the salutatory oration. Both addressed the topic of females speaking in public, but their approaches differed. While Wallace questioned the fairness of denying women the intellectual privileges granted to males, she did so softly, that is, without losing her "feminine" composure. Mason, however, exhibited less constraint. Unequivocally rejecting the intellectual reins placed on her gender by men, she declared them to restrain the development of women's humanness and to retard the achievement of the divinity of their souls.

A. VALEDICTORY ORATION BY MOLLY WALLACE, 1792

The silent and solemn attention of a respectable audience, has often, at the beginning of discourses intimidated, even veterans, in the art of public elocution. What then must my situation be, when my sex, my youth and inexperience all conspire to make me tremble at the talk which I have undertaken? But the friendly encouragement, which I behold in almost every countenance, enables me to overcome difficulties, that would otherwise be insurmountable. . . .

. . . After all, we do not expect women should become perfect orators. Why then should they be taught to speak in public? This question may possibly be answered by asking several others.

Why is a boy diligently and carefully taught the Latin, the Greek, or the Hebrew language, in which he will seldom have occasion, either to write or converse? Why is he taught to demonstrate the propositions of Euclid, when during his whole life, he will not perhaps make use of one of them? Are we taught to dance merely for the sake of becoming dancers? No, certainly. These things are commonly studied, more on account of the habits, which the learning of them establishes, than on account of any important advantages which the mere knowledge of them can afford. So a young lady, from the exercise of speaking before a properly selected audience, may acquire some valuable habits, which, otherwise she can obtain from no examples, and that no precept can give. But, this exercise can with propriety be performed only before a select audience: a promiscuous and indiscriminate one, for obvious reasons, would be absolutely unsuitable, and should always be carefully avoided. . . .

My dear School mates;

Before I bid you adieu, you will claim my particular attention; that I should endeavour to animate you in the prosecution of your studies; and that I should offer you my advice in a manner; which, at any other time, might be deemed arrogant, but which, the solemnity of the occasion may possibly justify.—We must be sensible, that we are favoured with opportunities of improvements, of which thousands of our sex are denied. This ought surely to inspire us with gratitude to the Author of the Universe, who hath distinguished us in a manner so singular, and with reverence and affection toward our parents and guardians, who, in many instances, have given us the advantage of instruction superior to that, which they themselves have enjoyed. We ought doubtless to emulate their virtues.— But, shall we equal them? If we do not, ignominy and reproach will inevitably be our portion. It is our duty then nobly to exert ourselves, and to shew, that the labour and care which have been bestowed upon us have not been bestowed in vain; and to prove that the female mind will reward the most assiduous culture. Our utmost efforts, however, will give us but a small allowances, which an awkward and uncouth mode of elocution would necessarily require. But yet it may be asked, what, has a female character to do with declamation? That she should harangue at the head of an Army, in the Senate, or before a popular Assembly, is not pretended, neither is it requested that she ought to be an adept in the stormy and contentious eloquence of the bar, or in the abstract and subtle reasoning of the Senate;—we look not for a female Pitt, Cicero, or Demosthenes.

There are more humble and milder scenes than those which I have mentioned, in which a woman may display her elocution. There are numerous topics, on which she may discourse without impropriety, in the discussion of which, she may instruct and please others, and in which she may exercise and improve her own understanding.

B. SALUTATORY ORATION BY PRISCILLA MASON, 1793

A female, young and experienced, addressing a promiscuous assembly, is a novelty which requires an apology, as some may suppose. I therefore, with submission, beg leave to offer a few thoughts in vindication of female eloquence.

I mean not at this early day, to become an advocate for that species of female eloquence, of which husbands so much, and so justly, stand in awe,—a species of which the famous Grecian orator, Xantippe, was an illustrious example. Although the free exercise of this natural talent, is a part of the rights of woman, and must be allowed by the courtesy of Europe and America too; yet it is rather to be *tolerated* than *established*;

and should rest like the sword in the scabbard, to be used only when occasion requires.—Leaving my sex in full possession of this prerogative, I claim for them the further right of being heard on more proper occasions—of addressing the reason as well as the fears of the other sex.

Our right to instruct and persuade cannot be disputed, if it shall appear, that we possess the talents of the orator—and have opportunities for the exercise of those talents. Is a power of speech, and volubility of expression, one of the talents of the orator? Our sex possess it in an eminent degree.

Do personal attractions give charms to eloquence, and force to the orator's arguments? There is some truth mixed with the flattery we receive on this head. Do tender passions enable the orator to speak in a moving and forcible manner? This talent of the orator is confessedly ours. In all these respects the female orator stands on equal,—nay, on *superior* ground.

If therefore she should fail in the capacity for mathematical studies, or metaphysical profoundities, she has, on the whole, equal pretensions to the palm of eloquence. Granted it is, that a perfect knowledge of the subject is essential to the accomplish'd Orator. But seldom does it happen, that the abstruse sciences, become the subject of eloquence. And, as to that knowledge which is popular and practical,—that knowledge which alone is useful to the orator; who will say that the female mind is incapable?

Our high and mighty Lords (thanks to their arbitrary constitutions) have denied us the means of knowledge, and then reproached us for the want of it. Being the stronger party, they early seized the sceptre and the sword; with these they gave laws to society; they denied women the advantage of a liberal education; forbid them to exercise their talents on those great occasions, which would serve to improve them. They doom'd the sex to servile or frivolous employments, on purpose to degrade their minds, that they themselves might hold unrivall'd, the power and preeminence they had usurped. Happily, a more liberal way of thinking begins to prevail. The sources of knowledge are gradually opening to our sex. Some have already availed themselves of the privilege so far, as to wipe off our reproach in some measure. . . .

But supposing now that we posses'd all the talents of the orator, in the highest perfection; where shall we find a theatre for the display of them? The Church, the Bar, and the Senate are shut against us. Who shut them? *Man*; despotic man, first made us incapable of the duty, and then forbid us the exercise. Let us by suitable education, qualify ourselves for those high departments—they will open before us. They *will*, did I say? They have done it already. Besides several Churches of less importance, a most numerous respectable Society, has display'd its impartiality.—I had almost said gallantry in this respect. With *others*, women forsooth, are complimented with the wall, the right hand, the head of the table,—with a kind of mock pre-eminence in small matters; but on great occasions the sycophant changes his tune, and says, "Sit down at my feet and learn." Not so the members of the enlightened and liberal Church. They regard not the anatomical formation of the body. They look to the soul, and allow all to teach who are capable of it, be they male or female.

But Paul forbids it! Contemptible little body! The girls laughed at the deformed creature. To be revenged, he declares war against the whole sex: advises men not to marry them; and has the insolence to order them to keep silence in the Church—: afraid, I suppose, that they would say something against celibacy, or ridicule the old bachelor.

With respect to the bar, citizens of either sex have an undoubted right to plead their own cause there. Instances could be given of females being admitted to plead the cause of a friend, a husband, a son; and they have done it with energy and effect. I am assured that there is nothing in our laws or constitution, to prohibit the licensure of female Attornies; and sure our judges have too much gallantry, to urge *prescription* in bar of their claim. In regard to the senate, prescription is clearly in our favour. We have one or two cases exactly in point.

Heliogabalus, the Roman Emperor, of blessed memory, made his grandmother a Senator of Rome. He also established a senate of women; appointed his mother President; and committed to them the important business of regulating dress and fashions. And truly methinks the dress of our country, at this day, would admit of some regulation, for it is subject to no rules at all—It would be worthy the wisdom of Congress, to consider whether a similar institution, established at the seat of our Federal Government, would not be a public benefit. We cannot be independent, while we receive our fashions from other countries, nor act properly, while we imitate the manners of governments not congenial to our own. Such a Senate, composed of women most noted for wisdom, learning and taste, delegated from every part of the Union, would give dignity, and independence to our manners; uniformity, and even authority to our fashions.

It would fire the female breast with the most generous ambition, prompting to illustrious actions. It would furnish the most noble Theatre for the display, the exercise and improvement of every faculty. It would call forth all that is human—all that is *divine* in the soul of woman; and having proved them equally capable with the other sex, would lead to their equal participation of honor and office.

Source: Carol Ruth Berkin and Mary Beth Norton, eds., *Women of America: A History* (Boston: Houghton Mifflin, 1979), 87–91.

DOCUMENT 18: Women as Industrial Workers, Organizers, and Strikers in the 1830s and 1840s

From the late 1820s, the Lowell factory mills attracted as workers girls and women, most of whom came from New England farms. In their correspondence to family members, the Lowell "girls" (Document 18A) discussed the new freedoms and sense of control they experienced by being able to earn wages on their own. Yet they objected to working under conditions they believed unfair, and were even willing to strike to rectify the injustice.

The strike or "turn-out" originated in the Lowell mills in 1830 when agents reduced wages because of a sluggish market. The "girls" claimed this action to be unjust and demeaning to their status as daughters of freemen (Document 18B). The male agents, however, demonstrated resentment when the women refused their offer. Overturning the prescribed social code, the daughters of free-men called for the formation of a union (Document 18C).

By 1845 the Lowell Female Labor Reform Association (LFLRA) was formed, with Sarah Bagley as its president. Important goals of the LFLRA were the attainment of a ten-hour workday and the maximization of educational and professional development (Document 18D). At a number of meetings they aired their complaints, among which were the various constraints imposed on their "sphere" (Document 18E) and the extensive control men exercised over the mechanisms of power (Document 18F). In a span of fifteen years these female workers altered their personas: in 1830 they protested as daughters of freemen, whereas in 1845 they identified themselves solely as workers who were members of LFLRA.

A. REASONS FOR LEAVING HOME

Mary Paul, of Barnard, Vermont, began work in the Lowell mills at 15 or 16, in November 1845. Before going to the mills she had worked briefly as a domestic servant and then lived with relatives a short distance from her home; at that time she wrote seeking her father's permission to go to Lowell. In this letter she revealed the basic motivation that prompted her request: "I think it would be much better for me [in Lowell] than to stay about here.... I am in need of clothes which I cannot get about here and for that reason I want to go to Lowell or some other place." ...

Sally Rice of Somerset, Vermont, left her home in 1838 at the age of 17 to take her first job "working out." Her work and her travels took her to Union Village, New York, where she supported herself on farm work, and led eventually to Thompson, Connecticut, where she found employment in a textile factory. That she was working for her own personal support and not to assist her family is evident in a poignant letter she wrote to her parents from Union Village in 1839 rejecting her familial home:

I can never be happy there among so many mountains. . . . I feel as though I have worn out shoes and strength enough riding and walking over the mountains. I think it would be more consistent to save my strength to raise my boys. I shall need all I have got and as for marrying and settling in that wilderness, I wont. If a person ever expects to take comfort it is while they are young. I feel so. . . . I have got so that by next summer if I could stay I could begin to lay up something. . . . I am most 19 years old. I must of course have something of my own before many more years have passed over my head. And where is that something coming from if I go home and earn nothing. . . . You may think me unkind but how can you blame me for wanting to stay here. I have but one life to live and I want to enjoy myself as well as I can while I live.

One Lucy Ann had her sights set on using her wages to attend Oberlin College. In a letter to a cousin she wrote: "I have earned enough to school me awhile, & have not I a right to do so, or must I go home like a dutiful girl, place the money in father's hands, & then there goes all my hard earnings." If she had to turn her wages over to her family she would consider them a "dead loss" and all her efforts would have been "spent in vain." Clearly mill employment could be turned to individualistic purposes. As Lucy Ann summed up her thinking: "I merely wish to go [to Oberlin] because I think it the best way of spending the money I have worked so hard to earn."

B. GRIEVANCES

We the undersigned considering ourselves wronged and our privileges invaded by the unjust and unreasonable oblidgment of our wages, do hereby mutually and cheerfully engage not to enter the Factory on the first of March, nor after for the purpose of work, unless the paper which causes our dissatisfaction be removed and another signed . . . purport[in]g that our wages shall be after the same rate as previous to the first of March.

... In all, about a sixth of all women workers in Lowell turned out. The Boston *Evening Transcript* reported the procession and the mass outdoor rally that followed:

> The number soon increased to nearly *eight hundred*. A procession was formed and they marched about town. ... We are told that one of the leaders mounted a pump and made a flaming Mary Woolstonecroft [sic] speech on the rights of women and the iniquities of the "*monied* aristocracy," which produced a powerful effect on her auditors, and they determined "to have their own way if they died for it."

At the rally operatives endorsed a petition calling on fellow workers to "discontinue their labors until terms of reconciliation are made." The petition concluded:

> Resolved, That we will not go back into the mills to work unless our wages are continued ... as they have been.
> Resolved, That none of us will go back, unless they receive us all as one.
> Resolved, That if any have not money enough to carry them home they shall be supplied.

C. UNION IS POWER

Our present object is to have union and exertion, and we remain in possession of our unquestionable rights. We circulate this paper wishing to obtain the names of all who imbibe the spirit of our Patriotic Ancestors, who preferred privation to bondage, and parted with all that renders life desirable and even life itself to procure independence for their children. The oppressing hand of avarice would enslave us, and to gain their object, they gravely tell us of the pressure of the times, this we are already sensible of, and deplore it. If any are in want, the Ladies will be compassionate and assist them; but we prefer to have the disposing of our charities in our own hands; and as we are free, we would remain in possession of what kind Providence has bestowed upon us, and remain daughters of freemen still.

D. FEMALE LABOR ASSOCIATION AND INDUSTRIAL REFORM LYCEUM

The Female Labor Reform Association was the heart of the Ten Hour Movement in Lowell. The existence of this relatively permanent female labor organization, surviving though in modified form for at least three years, is an important distinguishing element of the period and sets it off from the earlier years. From the start the LFLRA was part of the larger movement for labor reform. Organized in conjunction with the male Mechanics and Laborers' Association in December 1844, the LFLRA used that association's reading room for its first meetings. *The Operative*, a labor paper published in Lowell, welcomed its formation. "Let the work go on," the paper noted. "We greatly need the cooperation of the females in the cause. Their influence is potent and powerful, and with their aid shall we not succeed."

The activities of the association went beyond these gala social events. From the start they met weekly to promote labor reform. A newspaper notice advertised meetings every Tuesday evening in the reading room of the Mechanics and Laborers' Association, "All females interested in the reform of the present system of labor . . . respectfully invited to attend." These meetings were supplemented in 1846 with an Industrial Reform Lyceum, a lecture series aimed at countering the traditional, apolitical lyceum lectures. The first series of six lectures, with an admission price of 25 cents for the set, featured such well-known reformers as William H. Channing, Robert Rantoul, William Lloyd Garrison, George Ripley, William White, and Horace Greeley.

E. THE SELF-SUPPORTED AND THE SUPPORTED

In following the traditional ideal that everyone should work and contribute to self-support, Lowell women found themselves in conflict with the newer notion that women should be "supported" by men, that economic dependence and subordination were hallmarks of "true womanhood." When they saw these ideals being used against them under the guise of "protection" and paternalism, they expressed opposition to these standards as well as to their proponents. Thus they saw the sphere of home and family as being too limited and accused men of fostering confining definitions of womanhood.

"An Operative" wrote similarly that men determined the customs, laws, and opinions that defined women. She went on to complain of the narrowness of this perspective:

Woman is never thought to be out of her *sphere*, at home; in the nursery, in the kitchen, over a hot stove cooking from morning till evening—over a wash-tub, or toiling in a cotton factory 14 hours per day. But let her once step out, plead the cause of right and humanity, plead the wrongs of her slave sister of the South or of the operative of the North, or even attempt to teach the science of Physiology, and a cry is raised against her, "*of out of her sphere.*"

F. SOME SEMINAL QUESTIONS

Some made a less direct attack on the cult, carrying its precepts to their logical conclusions and thereby demanding more power for women than the cult's advocates had ever intended. One writer gently poked fun at the assertion that women had a peculiar capacity for instructing the young:

But if woman is well adapted to teach, so beautifully calculated and gifted by the author of her existence, to instruct the youthful mind, as has been represented—qualified to impress the great lessons of truth and morality, and give a right tone to sentiments—in short, capable of making man a noble being, but a little below the angels, I wish to inquire why in the name of common sense she is not permitted to finish the work she may have begun? Why are all the offices in public institutions of learning filled by men? Why is the child taken from under the maternal care and placed under the teachings of man? Why is every professorship usurped by man? Why not confer them upon woman, and permit her to go on with the good work?

Source: Thomas Dublin, *Women at Work: The Transformation of Work and Community in Lowell, Massachusetts, 1826–1860* (New York: Columbia University Press, 1979), 36–129.

DOCUMENT 19: To the Friends of Christian Education (1835)

Beginning in the 1820s, a number of women, among them Emma Willard, Catherine Beecher, and Mary Lyon, promoted secondary education for women. Lyon made this speech to raise money to establish Mount Holyoke. In her appeal she emphasized three points to her female audience: (1) the religious nature of the seminary, a very important factor during the time of evangelical Protestantism; (2) that women could help to remedy the teacher shortage; and (3) that better female education would improve their sex and thus ultimately the country.

After much deliberation, prayer, and correspondence, the friends of the Redeemer have determined to erect a school for the daughters of the church, the object of which shall be to fit them for the highest degree of usefulness. The justly celebrated school at Ipswich embraces the principal features which we wish this to possess. We will state the outlines of our plan.

1. The seminary is designed to be permanent: to be under the guardianship of those who are awake to all the interests of the church. It will not, under God, depend upon the health or the life of a particular teacher, but, like our colleges, be a permanent blessing to our children, and to our children's children.

2. It is to be based entirely on Christian principles; and while it is to be furnished with teachers of the highest character and experience, and to have every advantage which the state of female education in this country will allow, its brightest feature will be, that it is a school for Christ.

3. It is located at South Hadley, Massachusetts, on the banks of the Connecticut, at the foot of Mount Holyoke, in the centre of New England, easy of access from all quarters, and amid the most lovely scenery. In selecting the location, the committee had in view centrality, retirement, and economy, morality, and natural scenery.

4. The buildings are to be adequate to receive and board two hundred young ladies.

5. It is designed to cultivate the missionary spirit among its pupils; the feeling that they should live for God, and do something as teachers, or in such other ways as Providence may direct.

6. The seminary is to have a library and apparatus equal to its wants; to have its internal arrangements such that its pupils may continue to practise such habits of domestic economy as are appropriate to the sex, and without which all other parts of education are purchased at too dear a rate.

7. The seminary is to be placed on such a foundation by the Christian public, if they sustain our views, that all the advantages of the institution may be afforded so low, as to be within the reach of those who are in the middle walks of life. Indeed, it is for this class principally, who are the bone and sinew and the glory of our nation, that we have engaged in this undertaking. The wealthy can provide for themselves; and though we expect to offer advantages which even they cannot now command, yet it is not for their sakes that we erect this Christian seminary, and thus ask the funds of the church. In regard to this, we hope and expect that it will be like our colleges, so valuable that the rich will be glad to avail themselves of its benefits, and so economical that people in very moderate circumstances may be equally and as fully accommodated. We expect that distinctions founded on such incidental circumstances as wealth will not find a new place within its walls, any more than they do at the table of Jesus Christ.

8. In order to establish such a seminary, the committee believe that the Christian public must be invited to contribute a sum not less than

thirty thousand dollars. While every thing is to be done on a scale as economical as possible, yet the committee feel that the materials and work should all be the first of their kind. Of this sum, the village of South Hadley has contributed eight thousand dollars, which, with the subscriptions of the few who, in addition, have been invited to contribute, makes the sum already raised about one third of the amount specified.

Source: David Hitchcock, *The Power of Christian Benevolence Illustrated in the Life and Labors of Mary Lyon* (Northampton, Mass.: Hopkins, Bridgeman, 1851): 212–213.

DOCUMENT 20: Dissertation on the Characteristic Differences Between the Sexes (Thomas R. Drew, 1835)

Thomas R. Drew, a teacher at the College of William and Mary, drew clear, polar distinctions between the sexes. Basing his claim on the "biological" natures of men and women rather than on the usual biblical sources, an important departure, Drew postulated that the well-being of society required the maintenance of these differences, for each in its own way provided value to the community.

Women exhibited such characteristics as "grace, modesty and loveliness . . . calculated to win over to her side the proud lord of creation," while men acted with the courage of lions to protect women. All of this, according to Drew, was in the nature of things.

The relative position of the sexes in the social and political world, may certainly be looked upon as the result of organization. The greater physical strength of man, enables him to occupy the foreground in the picture. He leaves the domestic scenes; he plunges into the turmoil and bustle of an active, selfish world; in his journey through life, he has to encounter innumerable difficulties, hardships and labors which constantly beset him. His mind must be nerved against them. Hence courage and boldness are his attributes. It is his province, undismayed, to stand against the rude shocks of the world; to meet with a lion's heart, the dangers which threaten him. He is the shield of woman, destined by nature to guard and protect her. Her inferior strength and sedentary habits confine her within the domestic circle; she is kept aloof from the bustle and storm of active life; she is not familiarized to the out of door dangers and hardships of a cold and scuffling world: timidity and modesty are her attributes. In the great strife which is constantly going forward around her, there are powers engaged which her inferior physical strength prevents her from encountering. She must rely upon the strength of others; man must be engaged in her cause. How is he to be drawn over to her side? Not by menace—not by force; for weakness cannot, by such means, be expected to triumph over might. No! It must be by conformity to that character which circumstances demand for the sphere in which she moves; by the exhibition of those qualities which delight and fascinate— which are calculated to win over to her side the proud lord of creation, and to make him an humble suppliant at her shrine. Grace, modesty and loveliness are the charms which constitute her power. By these, she creates the magic spell that subdues to her will the more mighty physical powers by which she is surrounded. Her attributes are rather of a passive than active character. Her power is more emblematical of that of divinity: it subdues without an effort, and almost creates by mere volition; whilst man must wind his way through the difficult and intricate mazes of philosophy; with pain and toil, tracing effects to their causes, and unraveling the deep mysteries of nature—storing his mind with useful knowledge, and exercising, training and perfecting his intellectual powers, whilst he cultivates his strength and hardens and matures his courage; all with a view of enabling him to assert his rights, and exercise a greater sway over those around him.

Source: Thomas R. Drew, "Dissertation on the Characteristic Differences Between the Sexes," *Southern Literary Messenger* (Richmond, Virginia) 1 (May 1835): 439–512.

DOCUMENT 21: *Letters to Catherine Beecher* (Angelina Grimké, 1838)

Angelina Grimké (1805–1879) and her older sister Sarah Moore Grimké were born to a slave-holding family in South Carolina. They left the South, converted to the Quaker faith, and became articulate agitators on behalf of the abolition of slavery. Their antislavery work led them to regard the condition of American women as analogous to that of slaves.

The letter below is addressed to Catherine Beecher, a famous reformer on behalf of women's education. Beecher promoted teaching as a career for women, claiming that it utilized women's "natural" nurturing talent. Unlike Grimké, Beecher rejected the notion that the sexes should have equal rights, advocating instead that women pursue careers within their own sphere. Grimké starkly and eloquently protested that when it came to rights, the only consideration was being human, and that differences in sex or race were irrelevant.

LETTER XII [1836]

The investigation of the rights of the slave has led me to a better understanding of my own. I have found the Anti-Slavery cause to be the high school of morals in our land—the school in which *human rights* are more fully investigated, and better understood and taught, than in any other. Here a great fundamental principle is uplifted and illuminated, and from this central light, rays innumerable stream all around. Human beings have *rights*, because they are *moral* beings: the rights of *all* men grow out of their moral nature; and as all men have the same moral nature, they have essentially the same rights. These rights may be wrested from the slave, but they cannot be alienated: his title to himself is as perfect *now*, as is that of Lyman Beecher: it is stamped on his moral being, and is, like it, imperishable. Now if rights are founded in the nature of our moral being, then the *mere circumstance of sex* does not give to man higher rights and responsibilities, than to woman. To suppose that it does, would be to deny the self-evident truth, that the "physical constitution is the mere instrument of the moral nature." To suppose that it does, would be to break up utterly the relations, of the two natures, and to reverse their functions, exalting the animal nature into a monarch, and humbling the moral into a slave; making the former a proprietor, and the latter its property. When human beings are regarded as *moral beings, sex,* instead of being enthroned upon the summit, administering upon rights and responsibilities, sinks into insignificance and nothingness. . . .

This regulation of duty by the mere circumstance of sex, rather than by the fundamental principle of moral being, has led to all that multifarious train of evils flowing out of the anti-christian doctrine of masculine and feminine virtues. By this doctrine, man has been converted into the warrior, and clothed with sternness, and those other kindred qualities, which in common estimation belong to his character as a *man*; whilst woman has been taught to lean upon an arm of flesh, to sit as a doll arrayed in "gold, and pearls, and costly array," to be admired for her personal charms, and caressed and humored like a spoiled child, or converted into a mere drudge to suit the convenience of her lord and master. . . .

... I recognize no rights but *human* rights—I know nothing of men's rights and women's rights; for in Christ Jesus, there is neither male nor female. It is my solemn conviction, that, until this principle of equality is recognised and embodied in practice, the church can do nothing effectual for the permanent reformation of the world. Woman was the first transgressor, and the first victim of power. In all heathen nations, she has been the slave of man, and Christian nations have never acknowledged her rights. Nay more, no Christian denomination or Society has ever acknowledged them on the broad basis of humanity. I know that in some denominations, she is permitted to preach the gospel; not from a conviction of her rights, nor upon the ground of her equality as a *human being,* but of her equality in spiritual gifts—for we find that woman, even in these Societies, is allowed no voice in framing the Discipline by which she is to be governed. Now, I believe it is woman's right to have a voice in all the laws and regulations by which she is to be *governed,* whether in Church or State; and that the present arrangements of society, on these points, are *a violation of human rights, a rank usurpation of power,* a violent seizure and confiscation of what is sacredly and inalienably hers—thus inflicting upon woman outrageous wrongs, working mischief incalculable in the social circle, and in its influence on the world producing only evil, and that continually. *If* Ecclesiastical and Civil governments are ordained of God, *then* I contend that woman has just as much right to sit in solemn counsel in Conventions, Conferences, Associations and General Assemblies, as man—just as much right to sit upon the throne of England, or in the Presidential chair of the United States.

Source: Angelina Emily Grimké, *Letters to Catherine Beecher: In Reply to an Essay on Slavery and Abolitionism, Addressed to A. E. Grimké, Revised by the Author* (Boston: I. Knapp, 1838), 103–121.

DOCUMENT 22: Pastoral Letter of the General Association of Massachusetts (Orthodox) to the Churches under Their Care (1837)

This letter was written by the Congregational Church leaders in response to the public antislavery addresses of Angelina and Sarah Grimké in Massachusetts. It was required reading from the pulpit by every Congregational minister in the state.

Strongly condemnatory, it referred to the Grimké speeches as "promiscuous conversation" since men were also present, and warned that should this activity persist and scriptural injunction continue to be trespassed, the female character would suffer "permanent injury." This pastoral letter, written almost two hundred years after Anne Hutchinson was expelled from Massachusetts, shows that little had changed in clerical thinking since that time. (See Document 3.)

... We invite your attention to the dangers which at present seem to threaten the female character with wide-spread and permanent injury.

The appropriate duties and influence of woman are clearly stated in the New Testament. Those duties and that influence are unobtrusive and private, but the source of mighty power. When the mild, dependent, softening influence of woman upon the sternness of man's opinions is fully exercised, society feels the effects of it in a thousand forms. The power of woman is in her dependence, flowing from the consciousness of that weakness which God has given her for her protection, and which keeps her in those departments of life that form the character of individuals and of the nation. There are social influences which females use in promoting piety and the great objects of Christian benevolence which we cannot too highly commend. We appreciate the unostentatious prayers and efforts of woman in advancing the cause of religion at home and abroad; in Sabbath-schools; in leading religious inquirers to the pastors for instruction; and in all such associated effort as becomes the modesty of her sex; and earnestly hope that she may abound more and more in these labors of piety and love.

But when she assumes the place and tone of man as a public reformer, our care and protection of her seem unnecessary; we put ourselves in self-defence against her; she yields the power which God has given her for protection, and her character becomes unnatural. If the vine, whose strength and beauty is to lean upon the trellis-work and half conceal its clusters, thinks to assume the independence and the overshadowing nature of the elm, it will not only cease to bear fruit, but fall in shame and dishonor into the dust. We cannot, therefore, but regret the mistaken conduct of those who encourage females, to bear an obtrusive and ostentatious part in measures of reform, and countenance any of that sex who so far forget themselves as to itinerate in the character of public lecturers and teachers.—We especially deplore the intimate acquaintance and promiscuous conversation of females with regard to things "which ought not to be named"; by which that modesty and delicacy which is the charm of domestic life, and which constitutes the true influence of woman in society, is consumed, and the way opened, as we apprehend, for degeneracy and ruin.

We say these things not to discourage proper influences against sin, but to secure such reformation (!) as we believe is Scriptural, and will be permanent.

Source: Elizabeth Cady Stanton, Susan B. Anthony, and Matilda Joslyn Gage, *History of Woman Suffrage* (hereafter cited as *HWS*), vols. (New York: Fowler and Wells, 1881), 1:81–82. Reprint. Salem: Ayer Co., 1985. Future references will be to the 1881 edition.

DOCUMENT 23: *Letters on the Equality of the Sexes and the Condition of Women* (Sarah Grimké, 1837)

In the following letters, Sarah Grimké depicts the condition of women in America during the 1830s as limited and superficial, immoral and unequal. She rests the blame for this deplorable state on society's belief that there are basic differences between the sexes. As a result, women are used—willingly in the fashionable world— as men's play objects, and—unwillingly in the world of slavery— to satisfy the lust of masters.

In addition, this stress on sexual differences has relegated females almost solely to domestic affairs and precluded equal education with men. While church officials forbid women to preach, they hypocritically allow women to teach Sunday school. Grimké finds that these false, socially constructed distinctions harm society.

LETTER VIII

. . . I shall now proceed to make a few remarks on the condition of women in my own country. . . .

They seldom think that men will be allured by intellectual acquirements, because they find, that where any mental superiority exists, a woman is generally shunned and regarded as stepping out of her "appropriate sphere," which, in their view, is to dress, to dance, to set out to the best possible advantage her person, to read the novels which inundate the press, and which do more to destroy her character as a rational creature, than any thing else. Fashionable women regard themselves, and are regarded by men, as pretty toys or as mere instruments of pleasure; and the vacuity of mind, the heartlessness, the frivolity which is the necessary result of this false and debasing estimate of women, can only be fully understood by those who have mingled in the folly and wickedness of fashionable life.

LETTER XV

To perform our duties, we must comprehend our rights and responsibilities; and it is because we do not understand, that we now fall so far short in the discharge of our obligations. Unaccustomed to think for ourselves, and to search the sacred volume, to see how far we are living up to the design of Jehovah in our creation, we have rested satisfied with the sphere marked out for us by man, never detecting the fallacy of that reasoning which forbids women to exercise some of her noblest faculties, and stamps with the reproach of indelicacy those actions by which women were formerly dignified and exalted in the church.

I should not mention this subject again, if it were not to point out to my sisters what seems to me an irresistible conclusion from the literal interpretation of St. Paul, without reference to the context, and the peculiar circumstances and abuses which drew forth the expressions, "I suffer not a woman to teach"—"Let your women keep silence in the church," i.e. congregation. It is manifest, that if the apostle meant what his words imply, when taken in the strictest sense, then women have no right to *teach* Sabbath or day schools, or to open their lips to sing in the assemblies of the people; yet young and delicate women are engaged in all these offices; they are expressly trained to exhibit themselves, and raise their voices to a high pitch in the choirs of our places of worship. I do not intend to sit in judgment on my sisters for doing these things; I only want them to see, that they are as really infringing a *supposed* divine command, by instructing their pupils in the Sabbath or day schools, and by singing in the congregation, as if they were engaged in preaching the unsearchable riches of Christ to a lost and perishing world. Why, then, are we permitted to break this injunction in some points, and so sedu[l]ously warned not to overstep the bounds set for us by our *brethren* in another? Simply, as I believe, because in the one case we subserve *their* views and *their* interests, and act *in subordination to them*; whilst in the other, we come in contact with their interests, and claim to be on an equality with them in the highest and most important trust ever committed to man, namely, the ministry of the word. It is manifest, that if women were permitted to be ministers of the gospel, as they unquestionably were in the primative ages of the Christian church, it would interfere materially with the present organized system of spiritual power and ecclesiastical authority, which is now vested solely in the hands of men. It would either show that all the paraphernalia of theological seminaries, &c. &c. to prepare men to become evangelists, is wholly unnecessary, or it would create a necessity for similar institutions in order to prepare women for the same office; and this would be an encroachment on that learning, which our kind brethren have so ungenerously monopolized. I do not ask any one to believe my statements, or adopt my conclusions, because they are mine; but I do earnestly entreat my sisters to lay aside their prejudices, and examine these subjects *for themselves*, regardless of the "traditions of men," because they are intimately connected with their duty and their usefulness in the present important crisis.

All who know any thing of the present system of benevolent and religious operations, know that women are performing an important part in them, in *subserviency to men*, who guide our labors, and are often the recipients of those benefits of education we toil to confer, and which we rejoice they can enjoy, although it is their mandate which deprives us of the same advantages. Now, whether our brethren have defrauded us intentionally, or unintentionally, the wrong we suffer is equally the same. . . .

There is another and much more numerous class in this country, who are withdrawn by education or circumstances from the circle of fashionable amusements, but who are brought up with the dangerous and absurd idea, that *marriage* is a kind of preferment; and that to be able to keep their husband's house, and render his situation comfortable, is the end of her being. Much that she does and says and thinks is done in reference to this situation; and to be married is too often held up to the view of girls as the sine qua non of human happiness and human existence. For this purpose more than for any other, I verily believe the majority of girls are trained. This is demonstrated by the imperfect education which is bestowed upon them, and the little pains taken to cultivate their minds, after they leave school, by the little time allowed them for reading, and by the idea being constantly inculcated, that although all household concerns should be attended to with scrupulous punctuality at particular seasons, the improvement of their intellectual capacities is only a secondary consideration, and may serve as an occupation to fill up the odds and ends of time. In most families, it is considered a matter of far more consequence to call a girl off from making a pie, or a pudding, than to interrupt her whilst engaged in her studies. This mode of training necessarily exalts, in their view, the animal above the intellectual and spiritual nature, and teaches women to regard themselves as a kind of machinery, necessary to keep the domestic engine in order, but of little value as the *intelligent* companions of men.

Let no one think, from these remarks, that I regard a knowledge of housewifery as beneath the acquisition of women. Far from it: I believe that a complete knowledge of household affairs is an indispensable requisite in a woman's education,—that by the mistress of a family, whether married or single, doing her duty thoroughly and *understandingly*, the happiness of the family is increased to an incalculable degree, as well as a vast amount of time and money saved. All I complain of is, that our education consists so almost exclusively in culinary and other manual operations. I do long to see the time, when it will no longer be necessary for women to expend so many precious hours in furnishing "a well spread table," but that their husbands will forego some of their accustomed indulgences in this way, and encourage their wives to devote some portion of their time to mental cultivation, even at the expense of having to dine sometimes on baked potatoes, or bread and butter. . . .

There is another way in which the general opinion, that women are inferior to men, is manifested, that bears with tremendous effect on the laboring class, and indeed on almost all who are obliged to earn a subsistence, whether it be by mental or physical exertion—I allude to the disproportionate value set on the time and labor of men and of women. A man who is engaged in teaching, can always, I believe, command a higher price for tuition than a woman—even when he teaches the same branches, and is not in any respect superior to the woman. This I know is the case in boarding and other schools with which I have been acquainted, and it is so in every occupation in which the sexes engage indiscriminately.

Source: Sarah Grimké, *Letters on the Equality of the Sexes and the Condition of Women Addressed to Mary S. Parker* (Boston: I. Knapp, 1838), 46–55, 115–128.

DOCUMENT 24: "The Times that Try Men's Souls" (Maria Weston Chapman, 1837)

One response to the pastoral letter was this poem by Maria Weston Chapman (1806–1885), who lived in Boston, the seat of much antislavery activity. Chapman was well educated and in 1828 became the first woman principal in a young ladies' high school. After her marriage she was instrumental in the formation of the Boston Female Anti-Slavery Society, where she met the Grimké sisters.

Although she pursued many untraditional roles and devoted herself to the antislavery cause, Chapman's own sense of inadequacy prevented her from speaking publicly. Yet, as the poem demonstrates, she was an ardent advocate for those women capable of withstanding public ridicule. Indeed, she maintained that women's "unquestioned submission is quite out of date."

Confusion has seized us, and all things go wrong,
    The women have leaped from "their spheres,"
And, instead of fixed stars, shoot as comets along,
    And are setting the world by the ears!
In courses erratic they're wheeling through space,
In brainless confusion and meaningless chase.

In vain do our knowing ones try to compute
    Their return to the orbit designed;
They're glanced at a moment, then onward they shoot,
    And are neither "to hold nor to bind";
So freely they move in their chosen ellipse,
The "Lords of Creation" do fear an eclipse.

They've taken a notion to speak for themselves,
    And are wielding the tongue and the pen;
They've mounted the rostrum; the termagant elves,
    And—oh horrid!—are talking to men!
With faces unblanched in our presence they come
To harangue us, they say, in behalf of the dumb.

They insist on their right to petition and pray,
    That St. Paul, in Corinthians, has given them rules
For appearing in public; despite what those say
    Whom we've trained to instruct them in schools;
But vain such instructions, if women may scan
And quote texts of Scripture to favor their plan.

Our grandmothers' learning consisted of yore
    In spreading their generous boards;
In twisting the distaff, or mopping the floor,
    And *obeying the will of their lords*.
Now, misses may reason, and think, and debate,
Till unquestioned submission is quite out of date.

Our clergy have preached on the sin and the shame
    Of woman, when out of "her sphere,"
And labored *divinely* to ruin her fame,
    And shorten this horrid career;
But for spiritual guidance no longer they look
To Fulsom, or Winslow, or learned Parson Cook.

Our wise men have tried to exorcise in vain
    The turbulent spirits abroad;
As well might we deal with the fetterless main,
    Or conquer ethereal essence with sword;

Like the devils of Milton, they rise from each blow,
With spirit unbroken insulting the foe.

Our patriot fathers, of eloquent fame,
    Waged war against tangible forms;
Aye, *their* foes were men—and if ours were the same,
    We might speedily quiet their storms;
But, ah! their descendants enjoy not such bliss—
The assumptions of Britain were nothing to this.

Could we but array all our force in the field,
    We'd teach these usurpers of power
That their bodily safety demands they should yield,
    And in the presence of manhood should cower;
But, alas! for our tethered and impotent state,
Chained by notions of knighthood—we can but debate.

Oh! shade of the prophet Mahomet, arise!
    Place woman again in "her sphere,"
And teach that her soul was not born for the skies,
    But to flutter a brief moment here.
This doctrine of Jesus, as preached up by Paul,
If embraced in its spirit, will ruin us all.

Source: Stanton, Anthony, and Gage, *HWS*, 1: 82–83.

DOCUMENT 25: Discourse on Female Influence (Jonathan Stearns, 1837)

Jonathan F. Stearns (1808–1889) preached this sermon to his Presbyterian congregation in Newburyport, Massachusetts, on July 30, 1837. In it he upheld the traditional clerical stance regarding the special and distinctive contribution of women to the well-being of society. However, Stearns acknowledged the threat posed by the budding feminist movement. He based his disapproval of public speaking by women not on their inferiority, but rather on moral grounds.

He declared that women who debated publicly were indecent, that is, they behaved without Christian propriety. Furthermore, he noted that women have achieved much progress under Christianity, for which they should feel grateful, and that departing from their traditional role would harm society.

The influence of woman in forming the character of her relatives, gentle and unobserved as it is, is one which can never be adequately appreciated, till the great day of revelation shall disclose the secret springs of human action and feeling. We all know, by experience, what a charm there is in the word HOME, and how powerful are the influences of domestic life upon the character. It is the province of woman to make home, *whatever it is*. If she makes that delightful and salutary—the abode of order and purity, though she may never herself step beyond the threshold, she may yet send forth from her humble dwelling, a power that will be felt round the globe. She may at least save some souls that are dear to her from disgrace and punishment, present some precious ornaments to her country and the church, and polish some jewels, to shine brightly in the Saviour's crown. . . .

But the influence of woman is not limited to the domestic circle. *Society* is her empire, which she governs almost at will. . . . It is her province to *adorn* social life, to throw a *charm* over the intercourse of the world, by making it lovely and attractive, pure and improving. . . .

Much dispute has arisen in modern times in regard to the comparative intellectual ability of the sexes. . . . Now the whole debate, as it seems to me, proceeds from a mistake. The truth is, there is a natural *difference*, in the mental as well as physical constitution of the two classes—a difference which implies not *inferiority* on the one part, but only *adaptation to a different sphere*. Cultivate as highly as you will the mind of a female, and you do not deprive it of its distinguishing peculiarities. On the other hand, deprive man of his advantages, keep him in ignorance and intellectual depression, and you make him a kind of *brute beast*, but you do not approximate his character to the character of a woman. . . .

That there are ladies who are capable of public debate, who could make their voice heard from end to end of the church and the senate house, that there are those who might bear a favorable comparison with others as eloquent orators, and who might speak to better edification than most of those on whom the office has hitherto devolved, I am not disposed to deny. The question is not in regard to *ability*, but to *decency*, to order, to christian *propriety*. . . .

On you, ladies, depends, in a most important degree, the destiny of our country. In this day of disorder and turmoil, when the foundations of the great deep seem fast breaking up, and the flood of desolation threatening to roll over the whole face of society, it peculiarly devolves upon you to say what shall be the result. Yours it is to determine, whether the beautiful order of society . . . shall continue as it has been, to be a source of blessings to the world; or whether, despising all forms and distinctions, all boundaries and rules, society shall break up and become a chaos of disjointed and unsightly elements. Yours it is to decide, under God, whether we shall be a nation of refined and high minded Christians, or whether, rejecting the civilities of life, and throwing off the restraints of morality and piety, we shall become a fierce race of semi-barbarians, before whom neither order, nor honor, nor chastity can stand.

Source: Jonathan Stearns, *Female Influence and the True Christian Mode of Its Exercise: A Discourse Delivered in the First Presbyterian Church in Newburyport, July 30, 1837*. (Newburyport, 1837): 8–12.

DOCUMENT 26: The Right of the People, Men and Women, to Petition (1838)

This document concerns some of the discussion in the House of Representatives regarding the question of women's right to petition. Since women could not vote, the petition was one of the few means open to them by which to influence public policy. They used this instrument over and over again to protest against slavery and to enlarge their rights in the public sphere.

Women from the Massachusetts district represented by John Quincy Adams, ex-President and now member of the House, wrote petitions against the extension of slavery in Texas. Mr. Howard, chairman of the Committee of Foreign Affairs, maintained that even the petition should be declared out of bounds for women; their proper sphere was the domestic one. Adams, however, believed otherwise. In his refutation of Howard, he brought to bear evidence from the Bible, from history, and from the Constitution, which supported women's right to petition.

... When I last addressed the House I was engaged in discussing the principle asserted by the chairman of the Committee on Foreign Affairs; the practical effect of which must be to deprive one half the population of these United States of the right of petition before this House. I say it goes to deprive the entire female sex of all right of petition here. The principle was not an abstract principle. It is stated abstractedly, in the report of his remarks, which I have once read to the House. I will read it again; it is highly important, and well deserving of the attention of this House, and its solemn decision. It referred to all petitions on the subject of the annexation of Texas to this Union which come from women.

Many of these petitions were signed by women. He always felt regret when petitions thus signed were presented to the House relating to political matters. He thought that these females could have a sufficient field for the exercise of their influence in the discharge of their duties to their fathers, their husbands, or their children, cheering the domestic circle, and shedding over it the mild radiance of the social virtues, instead of rushing into the fierce struggles of political life. He felt sorrow at this departure from their proper sphere, in which there was abundant room for the practice of the most extensive benevolence and philanthropy, because he considered it discreditable, not only to their own particular section of the country, but also to the national character, and thus giving him a right to express this opinion. . . .

Why does it follow that women are fitted for nothing but the cares of domestic life? for bearing children, and cooking the food of a family? devoting all their time to the domestic circle—to promoting the immediate personal comfort of their husbands, brothers, and sons? Observe, sir, the point of departure between the chairman of the committee and myself. I admit that it is their duty to attend to these things. I subscribe, fully, to the elegant compliment passed by him upon those members of the female sex who devote their time to these duties. But I say that the correct principle is, that women are not only justified, but exhibit the most exalted virtue when they do depart from the domestic circle, and enter on the concerns of their country, of humanity, and of their God. The mere departure of woman from the duties of the domestic circle, far from being a reproach to her, is a virtue of the highest order, when it is done from purity of motive, by appropriate means, and towards a virtuous purpose.

Now, I aver, further, that in the instance to which his observation refers, viz: in the act of petitioning against the annexation of Texas to this Union, the motive was pure, the means appropriate, and the purpose virtuous, in the highest degree. As an evident proof of this, I recur to the particular petition from which this debate took its rise, viz: to the first petition I presented here against the annexation—a petition consisting of three lines, and signed by 238 women of Plymouth, a principal town in my own district. Their words are:

The undersigned, women of Plymouth, (Mass.,) thoroughly aware of the sinfulness of slavery, and the consequent impolicy and disastrous tendency of its extension in our country, do most respectfully remonstrate, with all our souls, against the annexation of Texas to the United States, as a slaveholding territory.

Those are the words of their memorial. And I say that, in presenting it here, their motive was pure, and of the highest order of purity. They petitioned under a conviction that the consequence of the annexation would be the advancement of that which is sin in the sight of God, viz: slavery. I say, further, that the means were appropriate, because it is Congress who must decide on the question; and, therefore, it is proper that they should petition Congress if they wish to prevent the annexation. And I say, in the third place, that the end was virtuous, pure, and of the most exalted character, viz: to prevent the perpetuation and spread of slavery through America. I say, moreover, that I subscribe, in my own person, to every word the petition contains. . . .

Source: John Quincy Adams, *The Right of the People, Men and Women, to Petition: On the Freedom of Speech and of Debate* (Washington, D.C.: Gales and Seaton, 1838), 67–68.

DOCUMENT 27: *Shaw v. Shaw* (1845)

The state of Connecticut recognized "intolerable cruelty" as grounds for divorce. The case of *Shaw v. Shaw* gives a fairly standard example of the terrifying circumstances women had to face in order to satisfy the requirement of intolerable cruelty. In this case the requirement was not satisfied. In face of what two judges of the lower court found to be "torture inflicted upon" Mrs. Shaw, the supreme court of the state rejected her plea for divorce and upheld what it considered the authority of the husband in the home.

A decree of divorce, on the ground of intolerable cruelty, will not be granted, unless the acts complained of are in fact intolerable, and as cruel at least as those for which, under the head of extreme cruelty, the courts in Great Britain and elsewhere divorce a mensa et thoro.

Vulgar, obscene and harsh language, with epithets suited deeply to wound the feelings and excite the passions, but not accompanied with any act or menace indicating violence to the person, does not constitute such cruelty. The unreasonable exercise of the husband's authority in regard to his wife's social intercourse with her relatives and friends, excluding them from his house and forbidding her to visit them, does not constitute such cruelty.

Where it was found, that the husband repeatedly compelled his wife, against her wishes and remonstrances, to occupy the same bed with himself, when, in consequence of her ill health, it was indelicate, improper, unreasonable and injurious to her health so to do, and was calculated to endanger, and did in fact endanger her health; though this effect was not in fact intended or forseen by him; it was held, that such conduct of the husband did not constitute intolerable cruelty, within the statutes.

And where it was further found, that though she had no reason to fear from him personal violence of any other character; yet she had just reason to fear, that he would again compel her to occupy the same bed with him, regardless of the consequences to her health; it was held, that this fact, neither by itself, nor in connection with the other facts in the case, entitled her to a decree of divorce. [One judge dissenting]

Source: *Shaw v. Shaw*, 17 Conn. 189 (1845).

DOCUMENT 28: The Admission of the First Woman to a Male Medical College (Steven Smith, M.D., 1847)

Steven Smith relates the circumstances under which Elizabeth Blackwell (1821–1910) was accepted to Geneva College for medical studies after having been turned down by twenty-nine other medical schools. Smith, a student at the college, was particularly struck by the transformation in the male students' behavior, previously noisy and unruly, they became well mannered and quiet after Blackwell joined their classes.

Elizabeth Blackwell came from a family that strongly valued women's rights. Determined to succeed despite the discomfort of her situation at the medical school and the hostility of the rural townspeople, she graduated at the head of her class on January 23, 1847. She founded the New York Infirmary for Women and Children in 1857 and the Women's Infirmary Medical School in 1868. As a result she became a significant role model for women.

Medical circles were recently entertained by a symposium of prominent physicians discussing the propriety of the medical co-education of the sexes. All of the writers were opposed to the suggestion; some, notably Dr. Weir Mitchell, of Philadelphia, expressed the utmost disgust at the proposition. It happened to me to have witnessed the first instance of the co-education of medical students of both sexes in this country, and the results quite upset the theories of these gentlemen.

The first course of medical lectures which I attended was in a medical college in the interior of this State in 1847–48. The class, numbering about 150 students, was composed largely of young men from the neighbouring towns. They were rude, boisterous, and riotous beyond comparison. On several occasions the residents of the neighbourhood sent written protests to the faculty, threatening to have the college indicted as a nuisance if the disturbance did not cease. During lectures it was often almost impossible to hear the professors, owing to the confusion.

Some weeks after the course began the dean appeared before the class with a letter in his hand, which he craved the indulgence of the students to be allowed to read. Anticipation was extreme when he announced that it contained the most extraordinary request which had ever been made to the faculty. The letter was written by a physician of Philadelphia, who requested the faculty to admit as a student a lady who was studying medicine in his office. He stated that she had been refused admission by several medical colleges, but, as this institution was in the country, he thought it more likely to be free from prejudice against a woman medical student. The dean stated that the faculty had taken action on the communication and directed him to report their conclusion to the class. The faculty decided to leave the matter in the hands of the class, with this understanding—that if any single student objected to her admission, a negative reply would be returned. It subsequently appeared that the faculty did not intend to admit her, but wished to escape direct refusal by referring the question to the class, with a proviso which, it was believed, would necessarily exclude her.

But the whole affair assumed the most ludicrous aspect to the class, and the announcement was received with the most uproarious demonstrations of favour. A meeting was called for the evening, which was attended by every member. The resolution approving the admission of the lady was sustained by a number of the most extravagant speeches which were enthusiastically cheered. The vote was finally taken, with what seemed to be one unanimous yell, 'Yea!' When the negative vote was called, a single voice was heard uttering a timid 'No.'

The scene that followed passes description. A general rush was made for the corner of the room which emitted the voice, and the recalcitrant member was only too glad to acknowledge his error and record his vote in the affirmative. The faculty received the decision of the class with evident disfavour, and returned an answer admitting the lady student. Two weeks or more elapsed, and as the lady student did not appear, the incident of her application was quite forgotten, and the class continued in its riotous career. One morning, all unexpectedly, a lady entered the lecture-room with the professor; she was quite small of stature, plainly dressed, appeared diffident and retiring, but had a firm and determined expression of face. Her entrance into that Bedlam of confusion acted like magic upon every student. Each hurriedly sought his seat, and the most absolute silence prevailed. For the first time a lecture was given without the slightest interruption, and every word could be heard as distinctly as it would if there had been but a single person in the room. The sudden transformation of this class from a band of lawless desperadoes to gentlemen, by the mere presence of a lady, proved to be permanent in its effects. A more orderly class of medical students was never seen than this, and it continued to be to the close of the term.

The real test of the influence of a woman upon the conduct and character of a man in co-education was developed when the Professor of Anatomy came to that part of his course which required demonstrations that he believed should be witnessed only by men. The professor was a rollicking, jovial man, who constantly interspersed his lectures with witty remarks and funny anecdotes. Nor did he study to have his language chaste, or the moral of his stories pure and elevating. In fact, vulgarity and profanity formed a large part of his ordinary lectures; and especially was this true of the lectures on the branch of anatomy above mentioned. On this account, chiefly, he was exceedingly popular with his class; and during his lectures stamping, clapping, and cheering were the principal employments of the students.

One morning our lady student was missed at the lecture on anatomy, and the professor entered the room evidently labouring under great excitement. He stated that he had a communication to make to the class which demanded the most serious consideration. He then explained that he had thought it highly improper that the lady student should attend certain lectures specially adapted for men, and as he was approaching that subject he had frankly advised her to absent herself, in a letter which he read. He dwelt upon the indelicacy of the subject, the embarrassment under which he should labour if a lady were present, and the injustice which would be done to the class by the imperfect manner in which he should be obliged to demonstrate the subject. He closed by offering her abundant private opportunities for study and dissection. He then read her reply. It was gracefully written, and showed a full appreciation of his embarrassing position, when viewed from the low standpoint of impure and unchaste sentiments. But she could not conceive of a medical man whose mind was not so elevated and purified by the study of the science of anatomy that such sentiments would for a moment influence him. Coming to the practical question of her attendance upon these lectures, she stated that if the professor would really be embarrassed by the presence of a lady on the first tier of seats, she would take her seat on the upper tier; and she trusted that his interest in this subject would lead him to entirely forget the presence of student No. 130—her registered number. At the close of the letter the professor acknowledged the justice of the rebuke which he had received and declared that a lady who was animated by such elevated views of her profession was entitled to every possible encouragement which the class or faculty could give. He then opened the door and she entered, only to receive an ovation of the most overwhelming character. The lectures on anatomy proceeded in regular order to their conclusion; and it was the universal testimony of the oldest students that they had never listened to such a complete and thorough course.

At the close of the term our lady student came up for examination for graduation, and took rank with the best students of the class. As this was the first instance of the granting of a medical diploma to a woman in this country, so far as the faculty had information, there was at first some hesitation about conferring the degree. But it was finally determined to take the novel step, and in the honour list of the roll of graduates for that year appears the name Dr. Elizabeth Blackwell.

Church Union

Source: Elizabeth Blackwell, *Pioneer Work in Opening the Medical Profession to Women: Autobiographical Sketches* (London: Longman, Green, 1895), 255–259.

DOCUMENT 29: Married Women's Property Acts, New York (1848–1849)

Colonization and revolution in America did not fundamentally alter the English common law tradition of the legal identity of a husband and wife. Although each colony, then state, enacted its own laws on property and inheritance rights, in principle the position of married women fit Blackstone's description that "husband and wife are one in law" (see Document 2)

This meant that a wife could not enter into a contract, be sued or sue, or make a will. All her personal property belonged to her husband, including clothes, jewels, furniture, and wages, which he could dispense with as he saw fit. He was constrained by having to obtain his wife's permission to sell her real property, but he had the right to manage it and to derive the benefits from it. Finally, coverture allowed the husband to chastise his wife and to appoint guardians other than her for their children in the case of his death. Some married couples rejected the legal impairments placed on the wife (Document 42). Modifications also existed in some states with equity rules and in the frontier regions.

By the 1830s and 1840s the legal fiction of marital unity began to undergo modification through the enactment of married women's property acts, which allowed married women to keep their property in their own name. The married women's property acts, passed by New York State, became a model for other states. By the end of the Civil War period some twenty-nine states had passed such acts.

Much research has been devoted to these acts, especially the New York State acts, since it recorded its legislative proceedings. Scholars have debated their origins and impact, some subscribing to the view that they were part of the post-revolutionary process whereby the colonies asserted their identity as an independent nation, and that these acts acted as stimuli for further reforms.

Others argue, however, that post-revolutionary conditions were unfriendly to women and that, notwithstanding these acts, they remained in "procedural limbo," since their other civil disabilities remained intact, while courts used a common law mentality when interpreting the married women's property statutes.

AN ACT *for the more effectual protection of the property of married women.*
Passed April 7, 1848.
The People of the State of New York, represented in Senate and Assembly, do enact as follows:

§1. The real and personal property of any female who may hereafter marry, and which she shall own at the time of marriage, and the rents issues and profits thereof shall not be subject to the disposal of her husband, nor be liable for his debts, and shall continue her sole and separate property, as if she were a single female.

§2. The real and personal property, and the rents issues and profits thereof of any female now married shall not be subject to the disposal of her husband; but shall be her sole and separate property as if she were a single female except so far as the same may be liable for the debts of her husband heretofore contracted.

§3. It shall be lawful for any married female to receive, by gift, grant devise or bequest, from any person other than her husband and hold to her sole and separate use, as if she were a single female, real and personal property, and the rents, issues and profits thereof, and the same shall not be subject to the disposal of her husband, nor be liable for his debts.

§4. All contracts made between persons in contemplation of marriage shall remain in full force after such marriage takes place.

AN ACT *to amend an act entitled "An act for the more effectual protection of the property of married women," passed April 7, 1848.*
Passed April 11, 1849.
The People of the State of New York, represented in Senate and Assembly, do enact as follows:

§1. The third section of the act entitled "An act for the more effectual protection of the property of married women," is hereby amended so as to read as follows:

§3. Any married female may take by inheritance or by gift, grant, devise or bequest, from any person other than her husband and hold to her sole and separate use and convey and devise real and personal property, and any interest of estate therein, and the rents, issues and profits thereof in the same manner and with like effect as if she were unmarried, and the same shall not be subjec[t] to the disposal of her husband nor be liable for his debts.

§2. Any person who may hold or who may hereafter hold as trustee for any married woman, any real or personal estate or other property under any deed of conveyance or otherwise, on the written request of such married woman accompanied by a certificate of a justice of the supreme court that he has examined the condition and situation of the property, and made due enquiry into the capacity of such married woman to manage and control the same, may convey such married woman by deed or otherwise, all or any portion of such property, or the rents issues or profits thereof, for her sole and separate use and benefit.

§3. All contracts made between persons in contemplation of marriage shall remain in full force after such marriage takes place.

Source: Peggy A. Rabkin, *Fathers to Daughters: The Legal Foundations of Female Emancipation* (Westport, Conn.: Greenwood Press, 1980), 184.

DOCUMENT 30: Declaration of Sentiments (1848)

Seneca Falls and the Declaration of Sentiments marked the official beginning of the women's rights movement in America, one of the most influential of its kind in the world. The convention was organized by five women, all of whom were married and had children. Four were Quakers and abolitionists: Lucretia Mott, Jane Hunt, Martha Coffin Wright, and Mary Ann McClintock. The fifth, Elizabeth Cady Stanton, was Presbyterian and an abolitionist, wrote the Declaration of Sentiments, a title borrowed from the American Anti-Slavery Association. The Declaration of Sentiments was nurtured in the theory of natural rights and modeled after the Declaration of Independence. It eloquently asserted the belief that women were entitled to the same inalienable rights as men.

When, in the course of human events, it becomes necessary for one portion of the family to man to assume among the people of the earth a position different from that which they have hitherto occupied, but one to which the laws of nature and of nature's God entitle them, a decent respect to the opinions of mankind requires that they should declare the causes that impel them to such a course.

We hold these truths to be self-evident: that all men and women are created equal; that they are endowed by their Creator with certain inalienable rights, that among these are life, liberty, and the pursuit of happiness; that to secure these rights governments are instituted, deriving their just powers from the consent of the governed. Whenever any form of government becomes destructive of these ends, it is the right of those who suffer from it to refuse allegiance to it, and to insist upon the institution of a new government, laying its foundation on such principles, and organizing its powers in such form as to them shall seem most likely to effect their safety and happiness. Prudence, indeed, will dictate that governments long established should not be changed for light and transient causes; and accordingly, all experience hath shown that mankind are more disposed to suffer, while evils are sufferable, than to right themselves by abolishing the forms to which they were accustomed. But when a long train of abuses and usurpations, pursuing invariably the same object evinces a design to reduce them under absolute despotism, it is their duty to throw off such government, and to provide new guards for their future security. Such has been the patient sufferance of the women under this government, and such is now the necessity which constrains them to demand the equal station to which they are entitled.

The history of mankind is a history of repeated injuries and usurpations on the part of man toward woman, having in direct object the establishment of an absolute tyranny over her. To prove this, let facts be submitted to a candid world.

He has never permitted her to exercise her inalienable right to the elective franchise.

He has compelled her to submit to laws, in the formation of which she had no voice.

He has withheld from her rights which are given to the most ignorant and degraded men—both natives and foreigners.

Having deprived her of this first right of a citizen, the elective franchise, thereby leaving her without representation in the halls of legislation, he has oppressed her on all sides.

He has made her, if married, in the eye of the law, civilly dead.

He has taken from her all right in property, even to the wages she earns.

He has made her, morally, an irresponsible being, as she can commit many crimes with impunity, provided they be done in the presence of her husband. In the covenant of marriage, she is compelled to promise obedience to her husband, he becoming, to all intents and purposes, her master—the law giving him power to deprive her of her liberty, and to administer chastisement.

He has so framed the laws of divorce, as to what shall be the proper causes of divorce; in case of separation, to whom the guardianship of the children shall be given; as to be wholly regardless of the happiness of women—the law, in all cases, going upon a false supposition of the supremacy of man, and giving all power into his hands.

After depriving her of all rights as a married woman, if single and the owner of property, he has taxed her to support a government which recognizes her only when her property can be made profitable to it.

He has monopolized nearly all the profitable employments, and from those she is permitted to follow, she receives but a scanty remuneration.

He closes against her all the avenues to wealth and distinction, which he considers most honorable to himself. As a teacher of theology, medicine, or law, she is not known.

He has denied her the facilities for obtaining a thorough education—all colleges being closed against her.

He allows her in Church, as well as State, but a subordinate position, claiming Apostolic authority for her exclusion from the ministry, and, with some exceptions, from any public participation in the affairs of the Church.

He has created a false public sentiment, by giving to the world a different code of morals for men and women, by which moral delinquencies which exclude women from society, are not only tolerated but deemed of little account in man.

He has usurped the prerogative of Jehovah himself, claiming it as his right to assign for her a sphere of action, when that belongs to her conscience and to her God.

He has endeavored, in every way that he could, to destroy her confidence in her own powers, to lessen her self-respect, and to make her willing to lead a dependent and abject life.

Now, in view of this entire disfranchisement of one-half the people of this country, their social and religious degradation,—in view of the unjust laws above mentioned, and because women do feel themselves aggrieved, oppressed, and fraudulently deprived of their most sacred rights, we insist that they have immediate admission to all the rights and privileges which belong to them as citizens of the United States.

In entering upon the great work before us, we anticipate no small amount of misconception, misrepresentation, and ridicule; but we shall use every instrumentality within our power to effect our object. We shall employ agents, circulate tracts, petition the state and national legislatures, and endeavor to enlist the pulpit and the press in our behalf. We hope this Convention will be followed by a series of Conventions, embracing every part of the country.

Firmly relying upon the final triumph of the Right and the True, we do this day affix our signatures to this declaration.

Source: *Proceedings of the Woman's Rights Conventions Held at Seneca Falls and Rochester, N.Y.* (New York: Robert J. Johnston, 1870), 5–7. Reprint. Arno Press (1969).

DOCUMENT 31: The Rights of Women: A Reaction to Seneca Falls (Frederick Douglass, 1848)

Frederick Douglass, a free black from Rochester, New York, attended the Seneca Falls convention. He published this editorial in support of equal rights for men and women in his newspaper, the *North Star*.

THE RIGHTS OF WOMEN.—One of the most interesting events of the past week, was the holding of what is technically styled a Woman's Rights Convention at Seneca Falls. The speaking, addresses, and resolutions of this extraordinary meeting were almost wholly conducted by women; and although they evidently felt themselves in a novel position, it is but simple justice to say that their whole proceedings were characterized by marked ability and dignity. No one present, we think, however much he might be disposed to differ from the views advanced by the leading speakers on that occasion, will fail to give them credit for brilliant talents and excellent dispositions. In this meeting, as in other deliberative assemblies, there were frequent differences of opinion and animated discussion; but in no case was there the slightest absence of good feeling and decorum. Several interesting documents setting forth the rights as well as grievances of women were read. Among these was a Declaration of Sentiments, to be regarded as the basis of a grand movement for attaining the civil, social, political, and religious rights of women. We should not do justice to our own convictions, or to the excellent persons connected with this infant movement, if we did not in this connection offer a few remarks on the general subject which the Convention met to consider and the objects they seek to attain. In doing so, we are not insensible that the bare mention of this truly important subject in any other than terms of contemptuous ridicule and scornful disfavor, is likely to excite against us the fury of bigotry and the folly of prejudice. A discussion of the rights of animals would be regarded with far more complacency by many of what are called the *wise* and the *good* of our land, than would be a discussion of the rights of women. It is, in their estimation, to be guilty of evil thoughts, to think that woman is entitled to equal rights with man. Many who have at last made the discovery that the negroes have some rights as well as other members of the human family, have yet to be convinced that women are entitled to any. Eight years ago a number of persons of this description actually abandoned the anti-slavery cause, lest by giving their influence in that direction they might possibly be giving countenance to the dangerous heresy that woman, in respect to rights, stands on an equal footing with man. In the judgment of such persons the American slave system, with all its concomitant horrors, is less to be deplored than this *wicked* idea. It is perhaps needless to say, that we cherish little sympathy for such sentiments or respect for such prejudices. Standing as we do upon the watch-tower of human freedom, we can not be deterred from an expression of our approbation of any movement, however humble, to improve and elevate the character of any members of the human family. While it is impossible for us to go into this subject at length, and dispose of the various objections which are often urged against such a doctrine as that of female equality, we are free to say that in respect to political rights, we hold woman to be justly entitled to all we claim for man. We go farther, and express our conviction that all political rights which it is expedient for man to exercise, it is equally so for woman.

Source: Stanton, Anthony, and Gage, *HWS*, 1: 74–75.

DOCUMENT 32: Paulina W. Davis's Definition of the Women's Movement (1850)

Paulina W. Davis delivered this inspiring statement on October 28, 1850, to the first national women's rights convention, held at Worcester. She defined the women's rights movement as both radical and universal, having justice as its core claim. Davis, a woman of uncommon spirit, intelligence, and talent, was active in the abolitionist movement in the 1830s and a public lecturer on physiology and women's health during the 1840s. In the 1850s she chaired a number of women's rights conventions. She became the editor of *UNA*, the Rhode Island women's rights newspaper, in February 1853.

The reformation we propose in its utmost scope is radical and universal. It is not the mere perfecting of a reform already in motion, a detail of some established plan, but it is an epochal movement—the emancipation of a class, the redemption of half the world, and a conforming reorganization of all social, political, and industrial interests and institutions. Moreover, it is a movement without example among the enterprises of associated reformations, for it has no purpose of arming the oppressed against the oppressor, or of separating the parties, or of setting up independence, or of severing the relations of either.

Its intended changes are to be wrought in the intimate texture of all societary organizations, without violence or any form of antagonism. It seeks to replace the worn-out with the living and the beautiful, so as to reconstruct without overturning, and to regenerate without destroying.

Our claim must rest on its justice, and conquer by its power of truth. We take the ground that whatever has been achieved for the race belongs to it, and must not be usurped by any class or caste. The rights and liberties of one human being can not be made the property of another, though they were redeemed for him or her by the life of that other; for rights can not be forfeited by way of salvage, and they are, in their nature, unpurchasable and inalienable. We claim for woman a full and generous investiture of all the blessings which the other sex has solely, or by her aid, achieved for itself. We appeal from man's injustice and selfishness to his principles and affections.

Source: Stanton, Anthony, and Gage, *HWS*, 1: 222–223.

DOCUMENT 33: Memorial (Women's Efforts to Influence the Ohio Constitutional Convention, 1850)

In 1850, the state of Ohio held a convention to amend its constitution. Advocates of women's rights sought changes that would remove the common law disabilities to which women were subject. This "Memorial," by Mariana Johnson, was one effort to persuade delegates to the convention (all of them male) to give women rights equal to those of men.

MEMORIAL

We believe the whole theory of the Common Law in relation to woman is unjust and degrading, tending to reduce her to a level with the salve, depriving her of political existence, and forming a positive exception to the great doctrine of equality as set forth in the Declaration of Independence. In the language of Prof. Walker, in his "Introduction to American

Law": "Women have no part or lot in the foundation or administration of the government. They can not vote or hold office. They are required to contribute their share, by way of taxes, to the support of the Government, but are allowed no voice in its direction. They are amenable to the laws, but are allowed no share in making them. This language, when applied to males, would be the exact definition of political slavery." Is it just or wise that woman, in the largest and professedly the freest and most enlightened republic on the globe, in the middle of the nineteenth century, should be thus degraded?

We would especially direct the attention of the Convention to the legal condition of married women. Not being represented in those bodies from which emanate the laws, to which they are obliged to submit, they are protected neither in person nor property. . . .

Woman by being thus subject to the control, and dependent on the will of man, loses her self-dependence; and no human being can be deprived of this without a sense of degradation. The law should sustain and protect all who come under its sway, and not create a state of dependence and depression in any human being. The laws should not make woman a mere pensioner on the bounty of her husband, thus enslaving her will and degrading her to a condition of absolute dependence.

Believing that woman does not suffer alone when subject to oppressive and unequal laws, but that whatever affects injuriously her interests, is subversive of the highest good of the race, we earnestly request that in the New Constitution you are about to form for the State of Ohio, women shall be secured, not only the right of suffrage, but all the political and legal rights that are guaranteed to men.

Source: Stanton, Anthony, and Gage, *HWS*, 1: 105.

DOCUMENT 34: "Ain't I a Woman?" (Sojourner Truth, 1851)

Born a slave in 1795 and freed in 1827 when New York State abolished slavery, Isabella became Sojourner Truth when she began her travels throughout the country to speak about the crimes against her people.

In 1850 she joined the women's movement and was the only black to attend the first National Women's Rights Convention in Worcester. The document below reflects the power her innocent yet stirring candor must have had on her audience. Delivered in 1851 to a women's rights convention in Akron, Ohio, it was a spur of the moment response to views expressed by men of the cloth.

Well, children, where there is so much racket there must be something out of kilter. I think that 'twixt the negroes of the South and the women at the North, all talking about rights, the white men will be in a fix pretty soon. But what's all this here talking about?

That man over there says that women need to be helped into carriages, and lifted over ditches, and to have the best place everywhere. Nobody ever helps me into carriages, or over mud-puddles, or gives me any best place! And ain't I a woman? Look at me! Look at my arm! I have ploughed and planted, and gathered into barns, and no man could head me! And ain't I a woman? I could work as much and eat as much as a man—when I could get it—and bear the lash as well! And ain't I a woman? I have borne thirteen children, and seen them most all sold off to slavery, and when I cried out with my mother's grief, none but Jesus heard me! And ain't I a woman?

Then they talk about this thing in the head; what's this they call it? [Intellect, someone whispers.] That's it, honey. What's that got to do with women's rights or negro's rights? If my cup won't hold but a pint, and yours holds a quart, wouldn't you be mean not to let me have my little half-measure full?

Then that little man in black there, he says women can't have as much rights as men, 'cause Christ wasn't a woman! Where did your Christ come from? Where did your Christ come from? From God and a woman! Man had nothing to do with Him.

If the first woman God ever made was strong enough to turn the world upside down all alone, these women together ought to be able to turn it back, and get it right side up again! And now they is asking to do it, the men better let them.

Obliged to you for hearing me, and now old Sojourner ain't got nothing more to say.

Source: Stanton, Anthony, and Gage, *HWS*, 1: 116.

DOCUMENT 35: "On the Education of Females" (Paulina W. Davis, 1851)

Throughout these years questions were raised over and over again about differences between the sexes and their consequences.

Paulina W. Davis (Document 32) tackled such questions from the point of view of education. Her approach was epistemological if not rhetorical. First, she asked, Should differences, if there be any, determine how the sexes are educated? How do differences between the sexes determine talent, since each person is unique and talent is dependent upon the entire person, not one variable such as sex? Second, upon what philosophic principle can one quantify sexual differences? None that she could determine. Finally, she maintained that if sexual differences should determine which professions the sexes should pursue, then by generally accepted belief women's superior talent in the home should grant them exclusive control there, and their propensity for religion should lead to their monopoly in that profession. All this Davis believed to be nonsense. The well-being of society depended on allowing the talents of each individual to flourish with proper education, regardless of gender.

By Equality, we do not mean either identity or likeness; in general or in particulars, of the two sexes; but, equivalence of dignity, necessity and use; admitting all differences and modifications which shall not affect a just claim to equal liberty in development and action.

In the respective sexes, the faculties having the same general use, character, and name, may differ greatly in force or in acuteness, in some quality of substance or of action, without being thereby divorced from each other in their drift toward the same objects, and without affecting the whole method and movement of either of them, so as to throw it out of harmony with the other. Indeed, Nature seems never to repeat herself, and no individual is equal in fact and form with any other in the universe; and it is quite consonant with this principle of creation that sex should impress still a different *kind* of variety upon all faculties, feelings and vital forces, than those of measure and degree, simply. And if it be so, it should, rather than any other sort of difference, be exempted from the degradation of relative inferiority. The wise and the less wise, the strong and the weak of the same sex, may more justly be ranked and valued against each other; for they are sufficiently alike in texture, quality, and mode of action, to admit of comparison and relative estimate; but the essential difference of sex refuses any logical basis for measurement, as by weight and scale. There is no philosophy in balancing light against heat, love against knowledge, force against agility, or mathematics against imagination, and driving thence a short of feudal subordination among the subjects of the sciences of chemistry, mental philosophy, and social and civil government.

The differences which we admit are, on the contrary, reciprocal, and really adjust the sexes to each other, and establish mutuality where otherwise there would be but an aggregation of like to like, without relief to monotony or increase in efficiency. It is only in materialism that addition of similars adds to their value: a fool is no help to a wise man in thinking, nor a coward to a brave one in daring and enduring. In physical life there is this broad provision, that all difference in kind is available, and not *less or more* only is the measure of increase, but all variety is riches. Differences in moral and intellectual things, if regarded as antagonism to the extent of the unlikeness, would render any consistent system of organization impossible.—Thus: Woman, from her conceded superiority in the family affections, would be entitled to exclusive control in the domestic function; her higher and more susceptible religious constitution would give her the monopoly of the *priestly* office; and her eminent moral endowments fit her for the rule of *social life* and *manners*, including all those municipal laws which regulate the relations of men to each other in civil society. So that the professions of Law, Theology, and Medicine, in nearly all its branches, would belong to her by right of special fitness, and men, by the same rule, would be wholly excluded. This principle of distribution would leave—what would it leave to the sole administration of men? Nothing but the ordering of those affairs, and the cultivation of those sciences, for which their ruder strength of muscle, greater bluntness of nerve, and firmer quality of logical reasoning, if they have all these, or either of them, qualify them. In general terms, the cultivation of those physical sciences which direct in the use of mechanical forces, and those coarser competitions and ruder conflicts of men, which foreign commerce and destructive wars require, would fall to the province of the sterner sex.

When the argument for restraint is rested upon Woman's alleged *incapacities*, we might triumphantly answer, that where an actual and obvious incapability is seen and known among men, their eligibility is not therefore taken away, but that incapacity is found in itself a sufficient bar to great abuses, and a sufficient protection of the interests to be affected; at least, no other is adopted. Certain men, ay, multitudes of them, are unfit for lawyers, physicians, governors, and military officers; yet, the chance and hope are left freely open to all these as well as to the most capable without mischief, and the world gets along as well as it deserves, and as well as it wishes, notwithstanding. Incompetency, in all these cases, (and they are myriads) is not excluded from office, rank, and honorably remunerated service by legal impediments, or the force of custom and opinion, which are quite as rigorous and absolute in their rule. Justice and consistency alike demand that the avenues of hope and life shall be opened as fairly and freely to the excluded sex as to the notoriously incompetent of the other, and there can be no doubt that it may be done in every department of human affairs as safely, to say the least. The common sense of the world will be as able to protect itself in the one case as in the other; and besides, the Providence of Heaven is responsible for the safe working of all the forces which He has provided for the conduct of human life.—If women really cannot practice medicine, law, and theology, well and safely, the sick, the suitors, and the suffering sinners will discover the fact, and there is nothing specially put in danger by the trial except the illiberal opinion which refuses it. But this objection is in itself so weak and unwarranted, that it may be justly set down as merely arrogant and selfish. Medical schools, for instance, are really not closed against women because they *cannot* acquire the knowledge of the profession and practice it successfully, but because they *can* do both, and threaten very seriously to wrest the business from the hands which have so long usurped it. And, surely, there is no likelihood that the "weaker sex" would betray the science into greater confusion and disgrace than the dozen or twenty conflicting systems have done, which now divide and distract the world about their rival merits. No, no, gentlemen; theory and practice are not so well established in medicine as to prove the sole capability of the sex which has appropriated its authority and delivered its oracles for the last few centuries of modern history. The world has lost its respect for the pompous mystery of the craft, and the chaos you have created where we looked for light and certainty, disproves your proud pretension of exclusive fitness in the sex which bears the responsibility. Beards and wigs have gone so nearly into bankruptcy in this business, that they cannot refuse the fresh partners and increased capital that are wanting to repair their failing fortunes! . . .

This may seen over-bold and direct, and wanting in reverence, if not in sober earnestness; but it may as well be said here as elsewhere, that the best intelligence and integrity of the age, feel the faults we censure, and are almost hopeless of a thorough remedy, while the administration continues in the hands of those who are, by their education, made perpetual successors to the evil inheritance and devoted to its continuance. The democratic method, which is reversing as fast as it can, all the precedents of antiquity in this matter of office and civil and social trusts, is nothing else than a protest against the claim of exclusive qualification by the old incumbents and their legitimate disciples. This rising idea *we* push forward to the full truth which there is in it. To the popular cry, *Admit the People* to the temples of their own religion, to the bench of their own Courts, to the halls of their own Legislatures, to the doctorate of the learned professions, and the throne of their own sovereignty, we add, *Admit the* WHOLE *People*, if ye would be true to your own idea, and worthy of your own liberty. . . .

Source: *UNA* (Providence, R.I.), November 1854.

DOCUMENT 36: Syracuse National Woman's Rights Convention (1852)

Religion was such a significant force in the lives of Americans that the clergy's views on women were discussed continually, even at the women's rights convention held at Syracuse in 1852.

As we have seen in Parts I and II, most Christian churches taught that women should be subordinate to men. Many religious women's rights activists found this teaching intolerable. Three contributions to the discussion of women's status and role in the church follow. Abby Price praised the egalitarian principles of Christianity but accused the church of being false for those principles. Antoinette Brown was the first American female ordained as a minister. In that capacity she rejected the church's traditional interpretation of the Bible, which placed women below men, and supported the position, similar to that held by the Quakers, that the Bible recognized that men and women were created equal. Ernestine Rose, a proponent of the married women's property acts, dismissed all authority, religious or otherwise, as the basis for women's rights. She presented a resolution asking for women's rights not as "a gift of charity, but as an act of justice."

Abby Price, of Hopedale, said: I shall briefly consider woman's religious position, her relation to the Church, and show that by its restrictions she has suffered great injustice; that alike under all forms of religion she has been degraded and oppressed, the Church has proscribed her, and denied the exercise of her inalienable rights, and in this the Church is false to the plainest principles of Christianity. "There is neither Jew nor Greek; there is neither bond nor free; there is neither male nor female: for ye all are one in Christ Jesus." Gal., chap. iii., v. 28. "So God created man in his *own* image; in the image of God created He him; male and *female* created He *them*, and said unto *them*: have dominion over the fish of the sea, and over the fowl of the air; over every living thing that moveth upon the earth." Genesis i., v. 27, 28. Notwithstanding these explicit declarations of equality, even in the Godhead, the Church claiming to be "Christian" denies woman's right of free speech. The priesthood, from Paul down, say gravely: "It is not permitted for woman to speak in the churches." Some denominations have gravely debated whether she should be allowed in the service, or chants, to respond Amen! . . .

Antoinette L. Brown offered the following resolution, and made a few good points on the Bible argument:

Resolved, That the Bible recognizes the rights, duties, and privileges of woman as a public teacher, as every way equal with those of man; that it enjoins upon her no subjection that is not enjoined upon him; and that it truly and practically recognizes neither male nor female in Christ Jesus.

God created the first human pair equal in rights, possessions, and authority. He bequeathed the earth to them as a joint inheritance; gave them joint dominion over the irrational creation; but none over each other. (Gen. i. 28). They sinned. God announced to them the results of sin. One of these results was the rule which man would exercise over women. (Gen. iii, 16). This rule was no more approved, endorsed, or sanctioned by God, than was the twin-born prophecy, "thou (Satan) shalt bruise his (Christ's) heel." God could not, from His nature, command Satan to injure Christ, or any other of the seed of woman. What particle of evidence is there then for supposing that in the parallel announcement He commanded man to rule over woman? Both passages should have been translated will, instead of shall. Either auxiliary is used indifferently according to the sense, in rendering that form of the Hebrew verb into English. . . .

Ernestine L. Rose: For my part, I see no need to appeal to any written authority, particularly when it is so obscure and indefinite as to admit of different interpretations. When the inhabitants of Boston converted their harbor into a teapot rather than submit to unjust taxes, they did not go to the Bible for their authority; for if they had, they would have been told from the same authority to "give unto Caesar what belonged to Caesar." Had the people, when they rose in the might of their right to throw off the British yoke, appealed to the Bible for authority, it would have answered them, "Submit to the powers that be, for they are from God." No! on Human Rights and Freedom, on a subject that is as self-evident as that two and two make four, there is no need of any written authority. But this is not what I intended to speak upon. I wish to introduce a resolution, and leave it to the action of the Convention:

Resolved, That we ask not for our rights as a gift of charity, but as an act of justice. For it is in accordance with the principles of republicanism that, as woman has to pay taxes to maintain government, she has a right to participate in the formation and administration of it. That as she is amenable to the laws of her country, she is entitled to a voice in their enactment, and to all the protective advantages they can bestow; and as she is as liable as man to all the vicissitudes of life, she ought to enjoy the same social rights and privileges. And any difference, therefore, in political, civil, and social rights, on account of sex, is in direct violation of the principles of justice and humanity, and as such ought to be held up to the contempt and derision of every lover of human freedom. . . .

Source: Stanton, Anthony, and Gage, *HWS*, 1: 535–537.

DOCUMENT 37: New York State Temperance Convention, Rochester (1852)

In 1852 Susan B. Anthony (1820–1906) and other women's rights reformers were denied a platform at the New York Temperance Convention, so they organized one of their own. Anthony, a major advocate of women's rights, came from a long line of Quakers. The second of eight children she helped to support her family by working as a teacher in Rochester, New York; paid one-quarter of what her male counterparts earned, Anthony was attracted to women's reform groups. Her connection to the women's movement was cemented when she met Elizabeth Cady Stanton in 1851; their friendship was to last fifty years. The letters that follow, by Frances Gage and Mrs. C.I.H. Nichols to the 1852 convention, show why temperance became a women's rights issue and why Anthony was so attracted to it. Reformers such as Stanton desired liberalized divorce laws, while others advocated enacting temperance laws.

A. LETTER FROM FRANCES DANA GAGE

McConnellsville, O., April 5, 1852.

My Dear Miss Anthony:—Yours of March 22d, asking of me words of counsel and encouragement for the friends of temperance, who are to meet at Rochester on the 20th inst., is before me. . . .

If we examine the statistics of crime in the United States, we shall find that a very large proportion of the criminals of our land are the victims of intemperance. The records of poverty, shame, and degradation furnish the same evidence against the traffic and use of ardent spirits. Examine those same statistics, and another great truth stares us in the face—that nine-tenths of all the manufacturers of ardent spirits, of all the drinkers of ardent spirits, and of all the criminals made by ardent spirits, are men. But we find, too, in our search, a fact equally interesting to us, that the greatest sufferers from all this crime and shame and wrong, are women. Is it not meet, then, that women should lay aside the dependent inactivity which has hitherto held them powerless, and give their strength to the cause of reform which is now agitating the minds of the people?

What is woman? The answer is returned to me in tones that shake my very soul. She is the mother of mankind! The living providence, under

God, who gives to every human being its mental, moral, and physical organism—who stamps upon every human heart her seal for good or for evil! Who then, but she, should cry aloud, and spare not, when the children she has borne—forgetting their allegiance to her and their duty to themselves, have assumed the power to rule over her, shutting her out from their counsels, and surrounding her, without her own consent, with circumstances which lead to misery and death; and, in their pride and strength, trampling upon justice, love, and mercy, withering her heart by violence and oppression, and yet compelling her, in her dependence as a wife, to perpetuate in her offspring their own depraved appetites and disorganized faculties?

It will not be denied that woman in all past ages has been made, by both law and custom, the inferior of her own children. Man has assumed to himself the power of being "lord of creation": yet what has be done for his kind? Look at the present state of society and receive your answer! He has filled the world with madness, with oppression and wrong; he has allowed snares to be laid at every turn, to entangle the feet of our children, and lead them away into vice and crime. He has legalized the causes which fill the jails, the penitentiaries, the houses of correction, the poorhouses, and asylums with the blood of our hearts, even our children, and our children's children. There is not a drunkard in the land, not a criminal that has been made by strong drink, but is the child of a woman. Yet not one woman's vote has ever been given to legalize the sale of ardent spirits, that have maddened the brain of her child. No woman's vote ever sanctioned the rum-seller's bar, at which her husband has bartered away his manhood, and made himself more vile than the brutes that perish. . . .

B. LETTER FROM MRS. C.I.H. NICHOLS

Brattleboro, Vt., April 13, 1852.

Sisters and Friends of Temperance:—In resorting to the pen as a medium of communication with your Convention, I feel, most sensibly, its inferiority to a *vis-à-vis* talk—it tells so little, and that so meagerly! But, remembering that a single just thought or vital truth, communicated to intelligent minds and willing hearts, is an investment sure of increase, I will bless God for the pen, and ask of Him to make it a tongue for humanity.

The limits of a written communication will forbid me to say much, and I would address myself to a single point broached in your Albany Convention, and a point that seems to me of the first importance; because a mistake in morals, a wrong perpetrated in the home relations, is the greatest of all wrongs to humanity. And married, indeed, would be your triumph, if, in preventing the repeal of one unjust statute, you sanction the enactment of another. So true it is that one injustice becomes the source of another, I fear to contemplate the enactment of a trifling encroachment even upon inalienable rights or divinely sanctioned pursuits. . . .

Source: Stanton, Anthony, and Gage, *HWS*, 1: 845–847.

DOCUMENT 38: Constitutional Convention of Massachusetts (July 1853)

When it was decided that a convention would be held to consider reforming the Massachusetts Constitution, women sent petitions with 2,000 signatures to the Committee on Qualification of Voters, requesting, among other things, that the word "male" be removed in regard to voting, that women be allowed to vote on amendments to the constitution, and that women be granted suffrage.

The response of the chairman of the committee, Amasa Walker, was in the form of an explanation as to why the requests of the women were denied. Declaring the principle enunciated by the Declaration of Independence, that "all governments derive their just powers from the consent of the governed," he went on to explain that the 2,000 signatures did not constitute a majority of the women of Massachusetts, consequently the requests did not constitute "consent of the governed."

IN CONVENTION, July 1, 1853.

The Committee on Qualification of Voters, to whom were referred the petitions of Francis Jackson and others, that the word 'male' may be stricken from the Constitution, and also of Abby B. Alcott and other women of Massachusetts, that they may be allowed to vote on the amendments that may be made to the Constitution. . . .

REPORT:

. . . At the request of the petitioners, a hearing was granted them at two different sittings of the Committee, and patient attention given to the arguments presented by persons of learning and ability of both sexes, who appeared in their behalf.—These persons maintained the following propositions:

1. That women are human beings, and therefore have human rights, one of which is, that of having a voice in the government under

which they live, and in the enactment of laws they are bound to obey.

2. That women have interests and rights which are not, in fact, and never will be, sufficiently guarded by governments in which they are not allowed any political influence.

3. That they are taxed, and therefore, since taxation and the right of representation are admitted to be inseparable, they have a right to be represented.

4. That so far as education and general intelligence is concerned, they are as well qualified to exercise the elective franchise as many who now enjoy that right.

5. That in mental capacity and moral endowments, they are not inferior to many who now participate in the affairs of government.

6. That there is nothing in their peculiar position, or appropriate duties, which prevents them from taking a part in political affairs.

Of the truth or fallacy of these several positions the Committee do not feel called upon to decide.

All questions involving the rights and interests of any part of the human family, should ever be determined by some well-established and generally recognized principle or fundamental maxim of government; otherwise, it cannot be expected that such decision will be regarded as reasonable or satisfactory.

Upon what principle, then, shall the present question be decided?

The Declaration of Independence asserts, that 'all governments derive their just powers from the consent of the governed.' By the 'consent of the governed,' the Committee understand the consent, either express or implied, of the persons concerned. At the present time, there are within the State of Massachusetts, not far from 200,000 women over twenty-one years of age. Of these, less than 2,000 have asked to be admitted to the right of suffrage. From this fact, the Committee have a right to infer, and also from their personal knowledge of the views and feelings of the class of persons referred to, that a great majority of the women of Massachusetts do willingly consent that the government of the State should be, as it hitherto has been, in the hands of their fathers, husbands, brothers and sons. Of the correctness of this conclusion, the Committee entertain no doubts.

It may be said, in reply to this, that it cannot be justly inferred from the silence of the women of Massachusetts, that they do consent to the present limitations of the right of suffrage. But the Committee do so infer, because they know that the women aforesaid do now, and always have enjoyed the right of petition, to the fullest extent, and have often exercised that right in behalf of the unfortunate and oppressed, and in aid of many noble and philanthropic objects of legislation. In one case, it is believed, that more than 50,000 women petitioned the General Court, for the enactment of a law for the suppression of the sale of intoxicating drinks.

It may be further urged, that by the same course of reasoning, it might be shown that those who are held in bondage consent to the laws under which they live. But this is not true. Slaves have no right to petition. They cannot make known their wants to the government. They are speechless and helpless. Their whole existence is a stern and living protest against the wrongs they suffer, and they are kept in subjection only by the strong arm of power.

In view of these indisputable facts in relation to the right of petition, in this Commonwealth, enjoyed by all its inhabitants of both sexes, the Committee feel justified in deciding that a vast proportion of the women of Massachusetts do consent to their political condition, and, therefore, that the powers exercised by the government of this Commonwealth, over that class of its population, are 'just powers,' and it is inexpedient for this Convention to take any action in relation thereto.

Amasa Walker, *Chairman*.

Source: UNA (Providence, R.I.), August 1853.

DOCUMENT 39: Women's Rights Convention, New York (August 1853)

At this women's rights convention two speakers asked the same question: What changes have occurred as a result of the women's rights movement?

Lucy Stone found that women had made progress since the 1848 Seneca Falls Convention (see Document 30). Stone noted that women presided over meetings, spoke more freely in public, entered professions such as medicine and the ministry, and were even to be found among the merchant class. Implicitly, therefore, Stone believed that women were making progress.

William Lloyd Garrison represented another view. He observed that the major sources of power, such as the church, the state, and the press, had forged a campaign to prevent women from obtaining their rights, including suffrage. The forces opposed to granting women's rights were as old as mankind, controverting the principle enunciated in the Declaration of Independence that governments derive "their just power from the consent of the governed." By denying women the vote, the government denied them representation. Garrison advocated revolution if change was not forthcoming.

Miss Lucy Stone said that she had now time only to offer a few remarks, and would probably speak more fully before the Convention broke up. We may, she continued, congratulate ourselves on our progress. Five years ago we had a meeting of a handful of persons in Central New York, and scarcely any one heard of it. It was presided over by Mrs. Mott. [Mrs. Mott corrected; it was presided over by her husband. At that time women did not go so far as to think of presiding over meetings.] Miss Stone—That also shows our progress. We now see that a woman can fill the chair, and well. I look over the past five years, and find many arguments supplied to us in that time. We have now authority. It was said women could not be doctors. Well, Harriet Hunt has proved by practice that a woman can be, and is, a successful physician. You have now two women in your city who are able medical practitioners. We have Female Medical Colleges with classes. Thus one point is gained. We could not be merchants! I know a woman in Lowell who is a successful merchant. Mrs. Tindale has for many years conducted a shoe-store there, and grown rich by her trade. In the Ministry we are also represented. The sermon of Antoinette Brown, at Metropolitan Hall, is enough to show that. [A hiss.] Some men hiss whose mothers taught them no better; but there are men in New York who know they can hear the words of God from a woman as well as from a man, and they have called her to be their minister, and she is to be ordained this month. Some of the reporters stated that she was a Unitarian, but she is orthodox as the best, and so is her Church. We have also more fully than before established woman's right to address an audience. I have spoken in an assembly of men without announcing my intention, and when I came from the platform a lady said to me, "My blood ran cold to see you." "Why?" I asked, "were they not good men I was among?" "Oh, yes, my husband was one of them, but it was terrible." Last fall (that is six or seven years after) the same woman was chosen to preside over a meeting of men and women in Columbus, Ohio, and she took the Chair without objection. In Chicago a woman is cashier of a Bank. Two editors of papers (women) set near me.

The race, more than individuals, will be benefitted by the development we claim.

Wm. Lloyd Garrison

This question of Woman's Rights was a world question, and as old as the human race. In all ages, woman has been regarded by man as an inferior, and had been robbed of the rights, with which God had endowed her, in common with every human being.

But woman had been aroused. What would be the result. The land was convulsed; the opposition to this movement was assuming a malignant, a Satanic character. The pulput and the press, the Church and the State had arrayed themselves to extinguish a movement in behalf of justice to one half of the human race. The Bible had been used by pulpit interpreters to aid the cause of the foes in the human rights—of justice. Infidelity had been charged on us, in order that public sentiment might be arrayed against our cause. There was nothing strange in all this. We were passing a world crisis; we were merely abused as all reformers of all ages had been abused. At first all are accused of irreligion.

The question of Woman's Rights was a governmental question. Our Government, by endorsing the Declaration of Independence—which declared that all governments derived their just power from the consent of the governed—had conceded the justice of their claims. Women in our country were not represented—therefore, unless Government granted Woman's Rights, and thereby carried the maxim, alluded to into practice, it should be overturned.

Source: UNA (Providence, R.I.), September 1853.

DOCUMENT 40: Changes in Women's Economic Conditions (1853)

The following editorial by Paulina W. Davis expressed the view that women have lost their economic function and possess only the "mission" of marriage and genteel dependency. To Davis this reflected a decline in their status.

In order to change their spiritually vacuous and economically impoverished state of existence, Davis advocated that women find new functions within industry and the professions. She believed that "poverty is essentially slavery" and that freedom for women would come only with economic independence.

The changes of the times have robbed womanhood of its *function* and given her instead, a *mission*, which is our reproach with the undiscerning.

Agriculture, with all its labors, cares, and concerns, passed from her hands, first, into hands better fitted to the earlier labor saving instruments, and is now rapidly becoming a matter of machinery and brute and chemical power merely. Manufactures, in like manner, have departed from the fireside and the homestead, and installed themselves in vast workshops, where science directs, and steam accomplishes, the work of fabricating the food and clothing of the community. Machinery has not only snatched the distaff, and the loom from her hands, but the needle, also, in all its ordinary uses is fast following the wool cards and the knitting pins. In the middle ages she was the surgeon and doctress, also, as well as the nurse of the sick. The learned profession of Leech-craft has taken these from her too, even to the branch that most concerns her own dignity and delicacy; until stripped at last of all her reliances and uses, by which her worth might be proved, or her independence secured, her wages have sunk to the starvation point; her industry has ceased to be a virtue, having ceased to be a service or a support, and, in the broadest sense of the word we may say, her "occupation's gone." The factory and the school room at *slave wages* remain to her, but every one incapable of these, and every one forbidden by position to enter them, is put aside from the uses of life, and thrown upon the charity and indulgence of the industry that supports the welfare of the world. . . .

But there is instruction for ourselves, and direction in valuable for our own use, in the facts of our past and present condition. History teaches us something in this wise. The masses of our modern societies have been emancipated from serfdom by the power that there is in usefulness, and the inherent force that there is in available capability.

With the rise of productive industry to greater control over the elements which support life, and those things which enlighten and refine societary existence, the agents, actually employed in the liberalizing work, have been carried up with it until, in our freer communities, every man of full age has a voice in his own government, and, to that extent, a control over the distribution and appropriation of his own products. Liberty is seldom achieved by victory in arms, but it is always acquired by the might of arms in useful industry. . . .

Here then we stand amid the wreck of our fortunes, amid the ruins which the years have wrought, and cry for redress. We ask that the avocations which progress and improvement have substituted for all that we have lost be fairly opened to us. We appeal to the age which has deprived us of our functions and fortunes for restitution. You have taken away all that was ours of the old world. Give us therefore the positions which belongs to us in the new. In the days of Soloman we bought wool and flax and manufactured them into cloth and "our husbands had need of no other *spoil*" that our industry supplied. You have swallowed up a thousand household workshops in every great factory, and we demand our place at the power loom with wages up to the full value of our services. We reclaim also our right of merchandize and its profits as of yore. In the middle ages we practised surgery, medicine and obstetrics.

The healing art was ours by prescription. Restore it to us. In the middle ages, copying manuscripts was a profession providing employment for thousands of women. Give us our place at the press that has displaced the lost art. For the ruder labor, from which we have been taken and from which the world is now forever delivered, give us the use of those arts of modern birth to which we are so much better adapted than the usurping sex. Dentistry, daguerreotyping, designing, telegraphing, clerking in record offices, and a thousand other engagements which ask neither larger bones nor stronger sinews, and which touch neither the delicacy nor the retirement, that you harp upon as the propriety of our sex.

For shame! Surrender these to us, or, at least, open them fairly to our even handed competition. The sovereignty of free citizens, even in this republic, is denied to us; but of this I do not speak, for it is not within the range of the present subject. I am now urging only our first claim to the privileges and facilities for earnest and useful recompensing and self-supporting work.

Poverty is essentially slavery, if not legal, yet actual. The women of the time—the women worthy of the time—must understand this, and they must *go to work*. They must press into every avenue, every open door, that custom and law leave unguarded, aye, and themselves withdraw the bolts and bars from others still closed against them, that they may enter and take possession. They *must* purchase themselves out of bondage.

Add not the unblushing selfishness of a refusal of this to the insincere considerateness, that you profess in despoiling us of our inherent right of self-government. Your Anglo-Saxon common law—the glory of modern freedom—took away our legal existence, merging it in that of our husbands when we have any, to absorb our property and receive our earnings, and suspending the civil rights of maidenhood and widowhood when we had none. Your arts and sciences have taken away that which supplied our animal existences, and gave us position and power in the community, and now, are we not justified at least in demanding useful occupations and the blessings which belong to them? The civil subjection of the past was bad enough, but it was mitigated by our social, domestic, and industrial consequence. All this is gone, or going, and you offer us only the chance of genteel pauperism and dependence, under pretty names, that do not even conceal your own contempt, much less, our shame.

The occupations now generally accepted to us are essentially menial. We must take the character of servants to enter most of them, and then, in the language of this progressive and calculating age, they "don't pay."

We must take the reputation which courtesy gives the sex in our hands and put it at risk, while we put the prejudice and selfishness that restrains us to the question.

In a word we must endeavor to establish our *personal* independence, and we must no longer be content with the position and the limits which opinion assigns us. It needs but to set a good example in every promising department of self-supporting industry, to carry our point and effect our emancipation. . . .

Source: *UNA* (Providence, R.I.), September 1853, 137–138.

DOCUMENT 41: Have We A Despotism Among Us! (1854)

The anonymous woman who wrote this article, published in the *UNA*, believed that it was justifiable to describe as despotism the circumstances under which women were living in the American republic.

She cites as evidence for this conclusion the recently proposed revision of the Massachusetts Constitution (see Document 38). Women's privileges include "obeying laws made without [their] assistance, and which neglect [their] rights; sending petitions to bodies which scornfully reject them; being tried for both moral and legal offences, by a judge and jury in which [they have] no peer; and paying taxes to support a government in which [they] are totally unrepresented." Her conclusion? The despotism women experience makes ludicrous the contention that America is a republic.

It has become an interesting question lately, in circles where thought has superseded gossip, what is woman in a political sense? In Turkey or Egypt this question is easily answered—legally she is nobody—none of her rights are respected, she is utterly subject to the will of her master—who is father—husband—Sultan, as the case may be. In European countries, where the Salic law does not prevail, she has an occasional value as a queen. Even in other monarchies, as a wife to kings and princes, she can occasionally be useful in a political speculation, or even act as regent during a minority. But in republican America we are curious to know what her position actually is. Miss Bremer thinks she has all the advantages she desires, and every fourth of July orator, or pulpit declaimer, congratulates her on the religion and civilisation which have elevated her to her present exalted position. We were specially led to these thoughts by a perusal of the new constitution proposed for Massachusetts, which we had the audacity to read, and try to understand, notwithstanding our incapacity to write upon it. Although this constitution was not adopted, yet as we have not the old one at hand, and as this certainly represents the liberal side in politics, and there was no discussion about woman's position, involved in it, for neither the conscientious divine who so manfully opposed his friends by rejecting it, his companion, the son of that man who so bravely contended all his life for the rights of the minority, and the power of petitioning, the whole conservative Whig party, or the conscientious Free Soilers, objected to this constitution as utterly neglecting the right and petition of woman to be reinstated in her true legal position, I shall take it as the groundwork of my present remarks.

The first section says:—"The end of the institution, maintenance, and administration of government, is to secure the existence of the body politic; to protect it, and to furnish the *individuals* who compose it, with the power of enjoying it in safety and tranquility, their natural rights and the blessings of life, &c."

Individuals are the first class named. Are women individuals? Let us see further.

"The body *politic* is formed by a voluntary association of individuals; it is a social compact, by which the whole people covenants with each *citizen*, and each citizen with the whole people, that all shall be governed by certain laws for the common good. It is the duty of the *people*, therefore, in framing a constitution of government, to provide for an equitable mode of making laws, as well as for an impartial interpretation, and a faithful execution of them; that every *man* may, at all times, find his security in them."

Here we have the *body politic*, *citizen*, *people*, *man* named. Does woman belong to the *body politic*, is she a *citizen*, one of the *people*? Is she a *man*?

The next paragraph settles it that she is not one of the *people*, for

"We, therefore, the *people* of Massachusetts, acknowledge with gratified hearts the goodness of the great Legislator of the Universe, in affording us, in the course of his providence, an opportunity, deliberately and peaceably, without fraud, violence or surprise, of entering into an *original*, explicit, and solemn compact with each other, &c."

Now, certainly, no woman had this opportunity provided for her, and had she attempted to make it, I think, considerable surprise, and to judge from experience, no little violence would have been manifested towards her. One point is settled, we are not of "the people." Let us look at the "declaration of the rights of the inhabitants of the commonwealth of Massachusetts." Is woman an inhabitant?

Art. 1. Says "All *men* are born free and equal, and have a certain natural, essential, and inalienable rights, &c."

Art. 2. Concerns the rights of all *men* to protection in public religious worship.

Remember it is not yet shown whether women are or are not men.

Art. 3. Treats of religious persons, and says: "All *persons* belonging to any religious society, shall be taken and held to be members."

Now, as two thirds of the members of religious societies are often women, we must conclude that women are persons, unless we read to the contrary.

Art. 4. "The people of this Commonwealth have the sole and exclusive right of governing, &c."

Women are not the people then.

Art. 9. "All elections ought to be free, and all the *inhabitants* of this Commonwealth having such qualifications as they (i.e. the *inhabitants*) shall establish by their frame of government, have an equal right to elect officers, and to be elected for public employments."

Poor woman is not an inhabitant, for she has framed no government, yet cannot elect or be elected to public offices.

Art. 10. Is so involved that it is hard to analyze it. "Each *individual* of the society has a right to be protected by it in the enjoyment of his life, liberty and property, according to standing laws. He is obliged, consequently, to contribute his share to the expense of this protection, to give his personal service, or an equivalent when necessary; but no part of the property of any *individual* can with justice, be taken from him, or applied to public uses, without his own consent, or that of the representative body of the *people*, &c."

Now, as women are certainly taxed, yet as they are not the people, and have no part in the representative body of the people, we must conclude either that an individual is without justice taxed, or that she is not an individual. Let us be too charitable to suspect injustice, but rather favor the latter idea, which the exclusive use of the masculine pronoun in a document not at all chary of words seems to favor, and set it down that woman is not an *individual.*

Art. 11. Here we have a new word. "Every *subject* of the Commonwealth ought to find a certain remedy, by having recourse to the laws &c.;" and,

Art. 13. "No subject shall be held to answer any offence, &c."

Art. 15. "Every *subject* has a right to be secure from all unwarrantable searches and seizures of his person, &c." And again:

So far it would seem as if we had found an appellation for woman—as a *subject* of the State she has the power of being punished, and of causing the punishment of others—but let us see.

Passing over the Chapters touching the duties of magistrates &c., we come to Chapter 11, on the qualifications of voters and elections.

Art. 1: "Every male citizen, of twenty-one years of age and upwards, (excepting paupers and persons under guardianship) who shall have resided &c., &c., * * shall have a right to vote, * * and no other person shall have such right." It seems very clear that women are among those other persons. She is no *individual* no *citizen*, does not belong to the *public*, is not even an inhabitant, but is an *"other* person," and a *subject* of the *State*. We thought this last word appropriate to monarchies and despotisms; that kings and emperors, sultans and czars had subjects, but in a *free* commonwealth it seems to us an inappropriate term.

You are not, then, my fellow subjects, idiots, if you were you would be educated to the extent of your capacity, which you are not now, by the State; you are not paupers, or you would have a free home provided for you; you are not insane or special guardians would be appointed for you; but you are subjects of the State. Your privileges are obeying laws made without your assistance, and which neglect your rights; sending petitions to bodies which scornfully reject them; being tried for both moral and legal offenses, by a judge and jury in which you have no peer; and paying taxes to support a government in which you are totally unrepresented.

It is curious to see how carefully the word woman is left out of this instrument; the obnoxious "slave" is not more skillfully avoided in the constitution. One would suppose it a little difficult in a document purporting to cover the whole subject of social and political government, entirely to ignore one half, and in Massachusetts more than half of the human beings in the State; but except in one single paragraph, relating to "marriage" divorce, and alimony," we have been unable to find one word acknowledging her existence.

We rejoice with our Whig friends, with whom we seldom can rejoice, that this constitution was defeated, though doubtless better than the old one, it is yet unworthy of the age, and the people for whom it was framed. We must have reform, but it must be far more thorough and radical. We trust to live to see the day when the constitution of Massachusetts will be made for all, and not for half.

X.

Source: UNA (Providence, R.I.), January 1854, 206–207.

DOCUMENT 42: Marriage under Protest (Henry Blackwell and Elizabeth Stone, 1855)

Lucy Stone (1818–1893) was a woman ready for a change in her status. A graduate of Oberlin College, imbued with feminist ideas of egalitarianism and human rights, this abolitionist and women's rights reformer met Henry Blackwell, of the prominent Blackwell family (see Document 28), who shared her views on slavery and women's rights. Blackwell, seven years her junior, courted Stone, who was reluctant to give up her independence, for five years, promising her "perfect equality" in a marriage he believed would follow the principle of progression and improve over time.

In their marriage vows, printed below, Stone and Blackwell joined a number of other feminist couples who protested against the institution of marriage as it then existed and who strove for a spiritual marriage informed by justice and love.

While acknowledging our mutual affection by publicly assuming the relationship of husband and wife, yet in justice to ourselves and a great principle, we deem it a duty to declare that this act on our part implies no sanction of, nor promise of voluntary obedience to such of the present laws of marriage, as refuse to recognize the wife as an independent, rational being, while they confer upon the husband an injurious and unnatural superiority, investing him with legal powers which no honorable man would exercize, and which no man should possess. We protest especially against the laws which give to the husband:

1. The custody of the wife's person.
2. The exclusive control and guardianship of their children.
3. The sole ownership of her personal, and use of her real estate, unless previously settled upon her, or placed in the hands of trustees, as in the case of minors, lunatics, and idiots.
4. The absolute right to the product of her industry.
5. Also against laws which give to the widower so much larger and more permanent an interest in the property of his deceased wife, than they give to the widow in that of the deceased husband.
6. Finally, against the whole system by which "the legal existence of the wife is suspended during marriage," so that in most States, she neither has a legal part in the choice of her residence, nor can she make a will, nor sue or be sued in her own name, nor inherit property.

We believe that personal independence and equal human rights can never be forfeited, except for crime; that marriage should be an equal and permanent partnership, and so recognized by law; that until it is so recognized, married partners should provide against the radical injustice of present laws, by every means in their power.

We believe that where domestic difficulties arise, no appeals should be made to legal tribunals under existing laws, but that all difficulties should be submitted to the equitable adjustment of arbitrators mutually chosen.

Thus reverencing law, we enter our protest against rules and customs which are unworthy of the name, since they violate justice, the essence of law.

(Signed), Henry B. Blackwell,
Lucy Stone.

Source: Stanton, Anthony, and Gage, *HWS*, 1: 260–261.

DOCUMENT 43: Condition of Black Women Before the Civil War (mid-1850s)

During the antebellum period black female slaves experienced the greatest deprivation of freedom and therefore of control over their lives and that of their families. The recollections of former slaves in the documents below attest to the various forms of degradation they experienced.

Rose Williams, for example, recalled how a "relatively" kind master forced her to live with a man she detested because of the kind of offspring he hoped they would produce. Mary Gaines remembered how her frightened mother wanted to escape from a master because of the punishment inflicted on pregnant women by his overseer. Finally, Susan Hamlin recounted how some masters separated children from their mothers despite the despair expressed by both.

Such experiences were not lost on white women in the abolitionists movement. It led many of them to view their own condition as analogous to slavery.

A. ROSE WILLIAMS

What I say am de facts. If I's one day old, I's way over 90, and I's born in Bell County, right here in Texas, and am owned by Massa William Black. He owns mammy and pappy, too. Massa Black has a big plantation but he has more niggers dan he need for work on dat place, 'cause he am a nigger trader. He trade and buy and sell all de time.

Massa Black am awful cruel and he whip de cullud folks and works 'em hard and feed dem poorly. We'uns have for rations de cornmeal and milk and 'lasses and some beans and peas and meat once a week. We'uns have to work in de field every day from daylight till dark and on Sunday we'uns do us washin'. Church? Shucks, we'uns don't know what dat mean.

I has de correct mem'randum of when de war start. Massa Black sold we'uns right den. Mammy and pappy powerful glad to git sold, and dey and I is put on de block with 'bout ten other niggers. When we'uns gits to de tradin' block, dere lots of white folks dere what come to look us over. One man shows de intres' in pappy. Him named Hawkins. He talk to pappy and pappy talk to him and say, "Dem my woman and chiles. Please buy all of us and have mercy on we'uns." Massa Hawkins say, "Dat gal am a likely lookin' nigger, she am portly and strong, but three am more dan I wants, I guesses."

De sale start and 'fore long pappy am put on de block. Massa Hawkins wins de bid for pappy and when mammy am put on de block, he wins de bid for her. Den dere am three or four other niggers sold befo' my time comes. Den Massa Black calls me to de block and de auction man says, "What am I offer for dis portly, strong young wench. She's never been 'bused and will made de good breeder."

I wants to hear Massa Hawkins bid, but him say nothin'. Two other men am biddin' 'gainst each other and I sho' has de worryment. Dere am tears comin' down my cheeks 'cause I's bein' sold to some man dat would make sep'ration from my mammy. One man bids $500.00 and de auction man ask, "Do I hear more? She am gwine at $500.00." Den someone say, $525.00 and de auction man say, "She am sold for $525.00 to Massa Hawkins." Am I glad an' 'cited! Why, I's quiverin' all over.

Massa Hawkins takes we'uns to his place and it am a nice plantation. Lots better am dat place dan Massa Black's. Dere is 'bout 50 niggers what is growed and lots of chillen. De first thing massa do when we'uns gits home am give we'uns rations and a cabin. You mus' believe dis nigger when I says dem rations a feast for us. Dere plenty meat and tea and coffee and white flour. I's never tasted white flour and coffee and mammy fix some biscuits and coffee. Well, de biscuits was yum, yum, yum to me, but de coffee I doesn't like.

De quarters am purty good. Dere am twelve cabins all made from logs and a table and some benches and bunks for sleepin' and a fireplace for cookin' and de heat. Dere am no floor, jus' de ground.

Massa Hawkins am good to he niggers and not force 'em work too hard. Dere am as much diff'erence 'tween him and old Massa Black in de way of treatment as 'twixt de Lawd and de devil. Massa Hawkins 'lows he niggers have reason'ble parties and go fishin', but we'uns am never tooken to church and has no books for larnin'. Dere am no education for de niggers.

Dere am one thing Massa Hawkins does to me that I can't shunt from my mind. I knows he don't do it for meanness, but I allus holds it 'gainst him. What he done am force me to live with dat nigger, Rufus, 'gainst my wants.

After I been at he place 'bout a near, de massa come to me and say, "You gwine live with Rufus in dat cabin over yonder. Go fix it for livin'." I's 'bout sixteen years old and has no larnin', and I's just igno'nus chile. I's thought dat him mean for me to tend de cabin for Rufus and some other niggers. Well, dat am start de pestigation for me.

I's took charge of de cabin after work am done and fixes supper. Now, I don't like dat Rufus, 'cause he a bully. He am big and 'cause he so, he think everybody do what him say. We'uns has supper, den I goes here and dere talkin', till I's ready for sleep and den I gits in de bunk. After I's in, dat nigger come and crawl in de bunk with me 'fore I knows it. I says, "What you means, you fool nigger?" He say for me to hush de mouth. "Dis am my bunk, too," he say.

"You's teched in de head. Git out," I's told him, and I puts de feet 'gainst him and give him a shove and out he go on de floor 'fore he know what I's doin'. Dat nigger jump up and he mad. He look like de wild bear. He starts for de bunk and I jumps quick for de poker. It am 'bout three foot long and when he comes at me I lets him have it over de head. Did dat nigger stop in he tracks? I's say he did. He looks at me steady for a minute and you's could tell he thinkin' hard. Den he go and set on de bench and say, "Jus' wait. You thinks it am smart, but you's am foolish in de dead. Dey's gwine larn you somethin'."

"Hush yous big mouth and stay 'way from dis nigger, dat all I wants," I say, and jus' sets and hold dat poker in de hand. He jus' sets, lookin' like de bull. Dere we'uns sets and sets for 'bout an hour and den he go out and I bars de door.

De nex' day I goes to de missy and tells her what Rufus wants and missy say dat am de massa's wishes. She say, "Yous am de portly gal and Rufus am de portly man. De massa wants you'uns for to bring forth portly chillen."

I's thinkin' 'bout what de missy say, but say to myse'f, "I's not gwine live with dat Rufus." Dat night when him come in de cabin, I grabs de poker and sits on de bench and says, "Git 'way from me, nigger, 'fore I busts yous brains out and stomp on dem." He say nothin' and git out.

De nex' day de massa call me and tell me, "Woman, I's pay big money for you and I's done dat for de cause I ants yous to raise me chillens. I's put yous to live with Rufus for data purpose. Now, if you doesn't want whippin' at de stake, yous do what I wants."

I thinks 'bout massa buyin' me offen de bloc and savin' me from bein' sep'rated from my folks and 'bout bein' whipped at de stake. Dere it am. What am I's to do? So I 'cides to do as de massa wish and so I yields.

When we'uns am given freedom, Massa Hawkins tells us we can stay and work for wages or share crop de land. Some stays and some goes. My folks and me stays. We works de land on shares for three years, den moved to other land near by. I stay with my folks till they dies.

If my mem'randum am correct, it am 'bout thirty year since I come to Fort Worth. Here I cooks for white folks till I goes blind 'bout ten year ago.

I never marries, 'cause one 'sperience am 'nough for dis nigger. After what I does for de massa, I's never wants no truck with any man. De Lawd forgive dis cullud woman, but he have to 'scuse me and look for some others for to 'plenish de earth.

B. MARY GAINES

One reason mother said she wanted to get away from their new master, he have a hole dug out with a hoe and put pregnant women on their stomach. The overseers beat their back with cowhide and them strapped down. She said 'cause they didn't keep up work in the field or they didn't want to work. She didn't know why. They didn't stay there very long. She didn't want to go back there.

C. SUSAN HAMLIN

Lots of wickedness gone on in dem days, just as it do now, some good, some mean, black and white, it just dere nature, if dey good dey going to be kind to everybody, if dey mean dey going to be mean to everybody. Sometimes chillen was sold away from dey parents. De Mausa would come and say "Where Jennie," tell um to put clothes on dat baby, I want um. He sell de baby and de ma scream and holler, you know how dey carry on. Geneally (generally) dey sold it when de ma wan't dere.

Source: George P. Rawick, ed., *The American Slave: A Composite Autobiography*, Vol. 5: *Texas Narratives* (Westport, Conn.: Greenwood Press, 1972), part 4: 174–178; Vol. 9: *Arkansas Narratives*, part 3: 9; Vol. 2: *South Carolina Narratives*, part 2: 12–13.

DOCUMENT 44: *Commonwealth v. Patrick Fogerty* (1857)

Few issues affect the lives of women as intimately as the right to their bodies. The right to the integrity of one's body has generally been recognized. The law has attempted to reinforce that right by making unconsented sexual intercourse a crime—the crime of rape. However, a husband, even if he engaged in sexual intercourse with his wife "against her will," could not be held guilty of rape. The case that follows represents an attempt to exploit that exception in an indictment (a written statement formally charging one with a crime). Although the court disagreed with the complaining party, it did affirm that during a trial (as distinct from a mere statement charging one with a crime), a man would have a valid defense to the charge of rape by proving that he was the husband of the victim.

G. M. Stearns, for the defendants.

1. In order to constitute this offence, the carnal knowledge must be had "by force" as well as "against the will" of the woman. . . .
It is therefore necessary to allege the act in the words of the statute, or in equivalent words. . . .
The words "with force and arms" in the indictment, if they could be applied to the allegation of ravishment, (which they cannot, as it is a separate traversable allegation,) would only show that force was a concomitant, not that it was the means of accomplishment of the act. An act may be done "violently," and yet not accomplished "by force."

2. A man cannot commit a rape on his own wife. . . . It is therefore necessary to allege, as in the case of adultery, that the woman was not the wife of the defendant; because the facts alleged may be true, and yet no crime committed. . . .

Bigelow, J. The indictment in the present case is in conformity with well established precedents. It sufficiently sets forth all the elements necessary to constitute the offence of rape. It alleges that the carnal knowledge was had "violently," which means by violence, and was against the consent of the prosecutrix. The word ravished—*"rapuit"*—of itself imports the use of force, and, when coupled with the allegation that the act was done against the consent of the woman, technically charges the crime of rape, which is the carnal knowledge of a woman by force and against her will. . . .

Of course, it would always be competent for a party indicted to show, in defence of a charge of rape alleged to be actually committed by him-self, that the woman on whom it was charged to have been committed was his wife. But it is not necessary to negative the fact in the indictment. *Exceptions overruled.*

Source: Commonwealth v. Fogerty, 74 Mass. 489 (1857).

DOCUMENT 45: *Hair v. Hair* (1858)

One area of discrimination faced by married women concerned the right to determine where they would live. The husband had the right to decide the domicile of the family, and the wife was obliged to comply with his decision. Even where the husband and wife had made an explicit agreement to the contrary, as in *Hair v. Hair*, the court ruled that such an agreement bore no weight in face of the superior right of the husband.

The opinion of the Court was delivered by

DARGAN, CH. The plaintiff charges in her bill that her husband, the defendant ... before the solemnization of their nuptials, entered into a solemn engagement, that if she would marry him, he would never re-move her, without her consent, from the neighborhood of her mother, or to a place where she could not enjoy her mother's society, and that of her friends. On this condition she married him, as she says. Her mother (Mrs. Matheney,) also obtained from him (as it is charged) a similar promise, as the condition of her assent to the marriage. The mar-riage was celebrated on the 13th October, 1853. From that time the young pair lived with the plaintiff's mother until the 9th December, 1854, dur-ing which period, the plaintiff bore to her husband a daughter, who is the only issue of the marriage. At the last mentioned date, the defendant, with his wife and child, went to live at a place which he had bought, about a half mile distant from that of his mother-in-law, where, as the plaintiff herself says, they "lived in comfort, peace, and harmony, up to the twenty-seventh day of September, 1857." This statement appears to be in strict conformity with the truth, except as relates to some immor-alities on his part which had come to her knowledge, and which were condoned on her part by their subsequent cohabitation. After the plaintiff and defendant had gone to live at their own home, he became restless and dissatisfied, and anxious to remove to Louisiana, to which State some of his near relatives had emigrated. His land was poor, and he wished, as he says in his answer, to better his condition, by moving to a country where lands were fertile and cheap. But his wife was unwilling to go, positively refused, and pleaded his solemn engagement and promise made previous to their marriage.... They had frequent and intemperate altercations on the subject, he insisting that she should accompany him in his move to the west, and she pertinaciously refusing and declaring that she never would leave the place near her mother's, where she then lived. Perceiving that he could make no impression upon her mind, nor effect any change of her will, he announced to her his determination to go without her, unless she should choose to accompany him. She said he might go and leave her, provided he would leave her the negroes (three in number, the only ones he had, which he had acquired by his marriage with her.) She says in her bill that he consented to this arrangement about leaving the negroes. In his answer he denies it, and there is no further proof. Under these circumstances, and at this stage of the controversy, he commenced making preparations for his departure. He rented his land, sold his crop in the field, some hogs, &c., with the view of raising the necessary funds. Whether his preparations were made secretly, as charged in the bill, or not, he did not communicate to *her* the fact that he was making his preparation, nor his design *then* to go. She had no reason to believe that he was going at that particular time. It took her by surprise. In fact, it would seem that she did not believe that he would go at all, unless she consented to accompany him. Having completed his preparations, on Sunday, the 27th September, 1857, about the hour of midnight, he called his two negro women to the field, under the pretence of driving out the hogs, but, in fact, with the view of securing and carrying them off. He seized them both. They made a great outcry, which reached the ear of the plaintiff at the house. The negroes were unwilling to go; one of them (Hager) made her escape, the other one (Ann) he tied, went to the house and got her young child. He put them both in a conveyance which he had ready, carried them to Blackville, where he put them on the cars that same night, and carried them off to Louisiana, where they yet remain. The plaintiff continued to reside, and still resides, at the same house.... On the eleventh day after the defendant's departure, the plaintiff filed this bill, setting forth the facts that have been recited, and praying an injunction to restrain him from disturbing her in the possession of the property in her possession, or from selling or disposing of the same, until some adequate provision shall be made by the defendant, under the order of this Court, for the support of the plaintiff and her child.

The defendant, on learning that his wife had filed a bill against him for alimony, immediately returned to South Carolina, filed his answer, and has submitted himself to the judgment of the Court. On his return the defendant visited his wife, and made earnest overtures to her to accompany him to his new home in the Parish of Bienville, in Louisiana, promising to treat her with the kindness and affection due to her as his wife. These overtures were rejected by her with firmness and with passionate disdain.... She intimated that she would live with him if he would come back to the place which he had left. She said she would not go with him to the west to save his life, and that she intended to live and die where she was. The defendant, in his answer, iterates his proposals to take his wife and child with him to his home in the west, and to provide for them to the best of his ability.

These are the undisputed facts of the case, and the question for the court to decide is, whether under these circumstances, the plaintiff is entitled to a decree for alimony. The circuit decree allowed her claim for alimony, and ordered a reference. But we are of opinion, that the decree cannot be sustained upon the principles which prevail in this Court on the subject....

... In ... South Carolina, alimony is granted for bodily injury inflicted or threatened and impending....

Alimony is also granted in South Carolina for the desertion of the wife by the husband. To these may be added a third class of cases, in which, though the husband has inflicted or threatened no bodily injury upon the wife, yet practices such obscene and revolting indecencies in the family circle, and so outrages all the sentiments of delicacy and refinement characteristic of the sex, that a modest and pure minded woman would find these grievances more dreadful and intolerable to be borne, than the most cruel inflictions upon her person, she would be held justifiable in fleeing from the polluting presence of that monster, with whom in an evil hour she had united her destinies....

Except in cases embraced within the three classes above commented on, I am not aware that a suit for alimony has been sustained in South Carolina. The plaintiff has sought to bring her case within the principles of the second class. She charges desertion....

The question is, whether the plaintiff has made out a case of desertion. That the defendant left her and removed to another State, is beyond controversy, and not denied. But did he leave her in an unjustifiable manner? Her own declarations in her bill shew that he most earnestly solicited her for years, to accompany him. His solicitations amounted to importunity. At length, upon her persistent, I may well say, obstinate refusal, he went alone—without his wife and child. Certainly the husband, by our laws, is lord of his own household, and sole arbiter on the question as to where himself and family shall reside. But she complains that before the marriage he entered into a solemn engagement, without which, the marriage would never have been solemnized, that he would not take her away from the immediate neighborhood of her mother without her consent. This promise, she says, was also made to her mother, without which, *her* assent would have been withheld. The defendant, in his answer, denies these allegations. But the evidence brings the charges home to him. My opinion is that he made the promises in the manner charged in the bill. But they created a moral obligation only. . . . The contract of matrimony has its well understood and its well defined legal duties, relations and obligations, and it is not competent for the parties to interpolate into the marriage compact any condition in abridgment of the husband's lawful authority over her person, or his claim to her obedience. . . .

Stripped of all extraneous matters, the simple question is, did the defendant desert his wife, the plaintiff? It must be a legal desertion. It is not every withdrawal of himself by the husband from the society of the wife that constitutes desertion in legal contemplation. The conduct of the wife must be blameless. If she elopes, or commits adultery, or violates or omits to discharge any of the important hymeneal obligations which she has assumed upon herself, the husband may abandon her without providing for her support; and this Court would sustain him in such a course of conduct.

The husband has the right, without the consent of the wife, to establish his domicil in any part of the world, and it is the legal duty of the wife to follow his fortunes, wheresoever he may go. The defendant, in the exercise of his undoubted prerogative, had determined to make his domicil in the Parish of Bienville, in the State of Louisiana, and wished his wife to accompany him. *She*, preferring the society of her mother and her relatives, refused to go—in opposition to his wishes, his importunate solicitations, his earnest entreaties. Considering the relative duties and obligations of husband and wife, as defined by the law, who, under these circumstances, is guilty of desertion? The wife, assuredly.

What I have said would constitute a sufficient ground for refusing the prayer of the bill. Yet, there is another additional and sufficient ground of defence on the part of the husband. Within a very short period after the filing of the bill, he returned to the State, for the purpose, I must believe of inviting his wife to his new home, which he had established in the west. He twice visited her for this purpose. To these invitations, she gave a stern, angry, and insulting refusal. To the Court, in his answer, he renews these overtures, and offers to receive his wife in his new home, and to treat her with conjugal affection and tenderness. Under these circumstances the Court could not give alimony, even if he was wrong in the beginning. Though alimony has been decreed, if the husband makes a *bona fide* offer to take back the wife whom he has deserted, and to treat her with conjugal kindness and affection, and the wife refuses, on application by the husband, the Court will, if satisfied of the sincerity of the husband's offers, rescind the decree for alimony. . . .

It is ordered and decreed, that the Circuit decree be reversed, and that the bill [for alimony] be dismissed.

Source: 10 Rich (S.C.) 163 (1858).

DOCUMENT 46: Address on Behalf of the New York Divorce Bill (Elizabeth Cady Stanton, 1861)

In about 1852 Elizabeth Cady Stanton (1815–1902), along with Susan B. Anthony and Lucy Stone, came to the conclusion that marriages that degrade women should be allowed to end. But antebellum America was scandalized by divorce, believing that it would ruin family life, promote free love, and encourage social chaos.

Stanton, the fourth of six children, read most of her father's law books. She also studied Greek, Latin, and mathematics, subjects unusual for women. Initially attracted to reform by her husband, who was a professional speaker for the antislavery campaign, she became committed to the question of women's rights when she met Lucretia Mott, a Quaker reformer and a prominent advocate for women's rights. Indeed, Stanton became the architect of much feminist theory during the years she devoted to being a wife and a mother. Of a radical turn of mind, she claimed early in her reform career that "the existing public sentiment of any age is wrong." It is not surprising, therefore, that she recognized the inconsistency between a wife's elevated social status and the humiliation she experienced in marriage. When New York State introduced a divorce bill in 1860 similar to the one passed in Indiana in 1859, which expanded the grounds for divorce to include habitual drunkenness, Stanton spoke on its behalf, addressing her remarks to the Judiciary Committee of the New York Senate on February 8, 1861.

Gentlemen of the Judiciary—In speaking to you, gentlemen, on such delicate subjects as marriage and divorce, in the revision of laws which are found in your statute books, I must use the language I find there.

May I not, without the charge of indelicacy, speak in a mixed assembly of Christian men and women, of wrongs which my daughter may tomorrow suffer in your courts, where there is no woman's heart to pity, and no woman's presence to protect?

I come not before you, gentlemen, at this time, to plead simply the importance of divorce in cases specified in your bill, but the justice of an entire revision of your whole code of laws on marriage and divorce. ... If civilly and politically man must stand supreme, let us at least be equals in our nearest and most sacred relations. ...

The contract of marriage is by no means equal. From Coke down to Kent, who can cite one law under the marriage contract where woman has the advantage? The law permits the girl to marry at twelve years of age, while it requires several more years of experience on the part of the boy. In entering this compact, the *man* gives up nothing that he before possessed; he is a *man* still: while the legal existence of the woman is suspended during marriage and is known but in and through the husband. She is nameless, purseless, childless; though a woman, an heiress, and a mother. ...

The laws on divorce are quite as unequal as those on marriage; yes, far more so. The advantages seem to be all on one side, and the penalties on the other. In case of divorce, if the husband be the guilty party he still retains a greater part of the property! If the wife be the guilty party she goes out of the partnership penniless. ... In New York and some other states the wife of the guilty husband can now sue for a divorce in her own name, and the costs come out of the husband's estate; but in a majority of the states she is still compelled to sue in the name of another, as she has no means of paying costs, even though she may have brought her thousands into the partnership. ... Many jurists, ... "are of opinion that the adultery of the husband ought not be noticed or made subject to the same animadversions as that of the wife, because it is not evidence of such entire depravity, nor equally injurious in its effects upon the morals and good order and happiness of domestic life." ...

There can be no heaven without love; and nothing is sacred in the family and home, but just so far as it is built up and anchored in purity and peace. Our newspapers teem with startling accounts of husbands and wives having shot or poisoned each other, or committed suicide, choosing death rather than the indissoluble tie, and still worse, the living death of faithless men and women, from the first families in the land, dragged from the privacy of home into the public prints and courts, with all the painful details of sad, false lives.

Now, do you believe, honorable gentlemen, that all these wretched matches were made in heaven? That all these sad, miserable people are bound together by God? But, say you, does not separation cover all these difficulties? No one objects to separation, when parties are so disposed. ... Now, if a noble girl of seventeen marries, and is unfortunate in her choice, because the cruelty of her husband compels separation, in her dreary isolation, would you drive her to a nunnery, and shall she be a nun indeed? She, innocent child, perchance the victim of a father's pride, or a mother's ambition. ... Henceforth, do you doom this fair young being ... to a joyless, loveless, solitude? By your present laws you say, though separated, she is married still; indissolubly bound to one she never loved; by whom she was never wooed or won; but by false guardians sold. And now, no matter though in the coming time her soul should for the first time wake to love, and one of God's own noblemen should echo back her choice, the gushing fountains of her young affections must be stayed. Because some man still lives who once called her wife, no other man may give her his love; and if she love not the tyrant to whom she is legally bound, she shall not love at all. ...

What do our present divorce laws amount to? Those who wish to evade them have only to go into another state to accomplish what they desire. If any of our innocent children trembling with fear fly to the corners and dark places of the house, to hide from the wrath of drunken, brutal fathers, but forgetting their past sufferings rush out again at their mother's frantic screams, "Help! oh, help!" Beyond the agonies of those young hearts as they see the only being on earth they love, dragged about the room by the hair of her head, kicked and pounded and left half dead and bleeding on the floor! Call that sacred, where fathers like these have the power and legal right to hand down their natures to other beings, to curse other generations with such moral deformity and death! ...

Fathers! do you say, let your daughters pay a life-long penalty for one unfortunate step? How could they, on the threshold of life, full of joy and hope, believing all things to be as they seemed on the surface, judge of the dark windings of the human soul? How could they foresee that the young man, today so noble, so generous, would in a few short years be transformed into a cowardly, mean tyrant or a foul-mouthed, bloated drunkard? What father could rest at his home by night, knowing that his lovely daughter was at the mercy of a strong man, drunk with wine and passion, and that, do what he might, he was backed up by law and public sentiment? The best interests of the individual, the family, the state, the nation, cry out against these legalized marriages of force and endurance.

Say you, these are but the opinions of men? On what else, I ask, are the hundreds of women depending who this hour demand in our courts a release from burdensome contracts? Are not these delicate matters left wholly to the discretion of the courts? Are not young women, from our first families, dragged into your public courts—into assemblies of men exclusively? The judges all men, the jurors all men! No true woman there to shield them by her presence from gross and impertinent questionings, to pity their misfortunes or to protect against their wrongs! The administration of justice depends far more on the opinions of eminent jurists than on law alone, for law is powerless when at variance with public sentiments. ...

If marriage is a human institution, about which man may legislate, it seems but just that he should treat this branch of his legislation with the same common sense that he applies to all others. If it is a mere legal contract, then it should be subject to the restraints and privileges of all other contracts. A contract, to be valid in law, must be formed between parties of mature age, with an honest intention in said parties to do what they agree. The least concealment, fraud or intention to deceive, if proved, annuls the contract. . . . But in marriage, no matter how much fraud and deception are practiced, nor how cruelly one or both parties have been misled; no matter how young or inexperienced or thoughtless the parties, nor how unequal their condition and position in life, the contract cannot be annulled. Think of a husband telling a young and trusting girl, but one short month his wife, that he married her for her money; that those letters, so precious to her, that she read and re-read, and kissed and cherished, were written by another; that their splendid home, of which, on their wedding day, her father gave to him the deed, is already in the hands of his creditors; that she must give up the elegance and luxury that now surround her, unless she can draw fresh supplies of money to meet their wants. . . .

Thus far, we have had the man-marriage, and nothing more. From the beginning, man has had the whole and sole regulation of the matter. He has spoken in Scripture, and he has spoken in law. As an individual, he has decided the time and cause for putting away a wife; and as a judge and legislator he still holds the entire control.

Source: Address of Elizabeth Cady Stanton on the Divorce Bill Before the Judiciary Committee of the New York State Senate in the Assembly Chamber, February 8, 1861 (Albany, 1861).

DOCUMENT 47: Changes in the Married Women's Property Act of 1860, New York, and Some Reactions to Them

The years 1857 and 1860 saw amendments passed to New York's Married Woman's Property Act of 1848 (see Document 29), enlarging the rights of married women.

In the amendments of 1860, for example, married women were granted the right to hold their real and personal property without spousal interference, to keep their wages, to trade, to sue and be sued, to buy and sell, to contract without the consent of their husbands, to have equal rights of inheritance with their children in the event of their husbands' death, and to be joint guardians of their children with their husbands.

In the document below, Stanton, Anthony, and Gage reveal how some of these acquired rights were eroded during the Civil War, initiating a period of regression in women's rights.

In 1861 came "the war of the rebellion," the great conflict between the North and the South, the final struggle between freedom and slavery. The women who had so perseveringly labored for their own enfranchisement now gave all their time and thought to the nation's life; their patriotism was alike spontaneous and enduring. In the sanitary movement, in the hospitals, on the battlefield, gathering in the harvests on the far-off prairies—all that heroic women dared and suffered through those long dark years of anxiety and death, should have made "justice to woman" the spontaneous cry on the lips of our rulers, as we welcomed the return of the first glad days of peace. All specific work for her own rights she willingly thrust aside. No Conventions were held for five years; no petitions circulated for her civil and political rights; the action of State Legislatures was wholly forgotten. In their stead, Loyal Leagues were formed, and petitions by the hundred thousand for the emancipation of the slaves rolled up and sent to Congress—a measure which with speech and pen they pressed on the nation's heart, seeing clearly as they did that this was the pivotal point of the great conflict.

Thus left unwatched, the Legislature of New York amended the law of 1860, taking from the mother the lately guaranteed right to the equal guardianship of her children, replacing it by a species of veto power, which did not allow the father to bind out or will away a child without the mother's consent in writing. The law guaranteeing the widow the control of the property, which the husband should leave at death, for the care and protection of minor children, was also repealed. This cowardly act of the Legislature of 1862 is the strongest possible proof of woman's need of the ballot in her own hand for protection. Had she possessed the power to make and unmake legislators, no State Assembly would have dared thus to rob the mother of her natural rights. But without the suffrage she was helpless. While, in her loyalty to the Government and her love to humanity, she was encouraging the "boys in blue" to fight for the freedom of the black mothers of the South, these dastardly law-makers, filled with the spirit of slaveholders, were stealing the children and the property of the white mothers in the Empire State!

When Susan B. Anthony heard of the repeal of 1862, she was filled with astonishment, and wrote thus to Miss Lydia Mott:

Dear Lydia:—Your startling letter is before me. I knew some weeks ago that that abominable thing was on the calendar, with some six or eight hundred bills *before it*, and hence felt sure it would not come up this winter, and that in the meantime we should sound the alarm. Well, well; while the other guard sleep the young "devils" are wide-awake, and we deserve to suffer for our confidence in "man's sense of justice," and to have all we have gained thus snatched from us. But nothing short of this can rouse our women again to action. All our reformers seem suddenly to have grown politic. All alike say, "Have no conventions at this crisis"! Garrison, Phillips, Mrs. Mott, Mrs. Wright, Mrs. Stanton, etc., say, "Wait until the war excitement abates"; which is to say, "Ask our opponents if they think we had better speak, or rather, if they do not think we had better remain silent." I am sick at heart, but I can not carry the world against the wish and the will of our best friends. But what can we do now, when even the motion to retain the mother's joint guardianship is voted, down! Twenty thousand petitions rolled up for that—a hard year's work!—the law secured!—the echoes of our words of gratitude in the capitol have scarce died away, and now all is lost!

Source: Stanton, Anthony, and Gage, *HWS*, 1: 747–749.

DOCUMENT 48: Recognition of Anna Ella Carroll's Military Contribution to the Civil War (1881)

Anna Ella Carroll, a resident of the state of Maryland who freed her slaves, was a military genius whose advice was indispensable to the Union victory in the Civil War.

In the fall of 1861 a plan of action deemed necessary to the success of the North was abandoned as unworkable. This decision was the result of a long memorandum by Anna Ella Carroll addressed to, among others, Assistant Secretary of War Thomas A. Scott, pointing out the defects of the Union plan and suggesting an alternative strategy. Carroll contended that the military operations directed toward the Mississippi River were unworkable and should be shifted to the Tennessee River, making it possible to cut the Confederacy in two. Fortunately, Scott recognized the significance of the plan and informed the President. The strategy succeeded, and some military historians consider it one of the crucial events in military history.

For many years the identity of the author of the plan was kept secret. Fearing backlash because she was a civilian and a woman, government officials persuaded her to keep silent. Even today few American history books acknowledge her contribution. But the testimony below, before the Committee on Military Affairs in the

House of Representatives in 1881, finally revealed her authorship and its importance to the Union victory. A quote from *The History of Woman Suffrage* places her contribution in perspective:

That assumption of man that a feud is the origin of all laws: that as woman does not fight she shall not vote, that her rights are to be forever held in obeyance to his wishes, was forever silenced by the military genius of Anna Ella Carroll in planning this brilliant campaign. Proving, too, that as right is of no sex, so genius is of no sex.

The Committee on Military Affairs, to whom the memorial of Anna Ella Carroll was referred, asking national recognition and reward for services rendered the United States during the war between the States, after careful consideration of the same, submit the following:

In the autumn of 1861 the great question as to whether the Union could be saved, or whether it was hopelessly subverted, depended on the ability of the Government to open the Mississippi and deliver a fatal blow upon the resources of the Confederate power. The original plan was to reduce the formidable fortifications by descending this river, aided by the gun-boat fleet, then in preparation for that object.

President Lincoln had reserved to himself the special direction of this expedition, but before it was prepared to move he became convinced that the obstacles to be encountered were too grave and serious for the success which the exigencies of the crisis demanded, and the plan was then abandoned, and the armies diverted up the Tennessee River, and thence southward to the center of the Confederate power.

The evidence before this Committee completely establishes that Miss Anna Ella Carroll was the author of this change of plan, which involved a transfer of the National forces to their new base in North Mississippi and Alabama, in command of the Memphis and Charleston Railroad; that she devoted time and money in the autumn of 1861 to the investigation of this feasibility is established by the sworn testimony of L. D. Evans, Chief-Justice of the Supreme Court of Texas, to the Military Committee of the United States Senate in the 42nd Congress . . . ; that after that investigation she submitted her plan in writing to the War Department at Washington, placing it in the hands of Thomas A. Scott, Assistant Secretary of War, as is confirmed by his statement, . . . also confirmed by the statement of Hon. B. F. Wade, Chairman of the Committee on the Conduct of the War, made to the same Committee, . . . and of President Lincoln and Secretary Stanton. . . .

That the campaign defeated National bankruptcy, then imminent, and opened the way for the system of finance to defend the Federal cause, is shown by the debates of the period in both Houses of Congress. . . .

The effect of this campaign upon the country and the anxiety to find out and reward the author are evidenced by the resolution of Mr. Roscoe Conkling, in the House of Representatives 24th of February, 1862. . . . But it was deemed prudent to make no public claim as to authorship while the war lasted. . . .

The wisdom of the plan was proven, not only by the absolute advantages which resulted, giving the mastery of the conflict to the National arms and evermore assuring their success even against the powers of all Europe should they have combined, but it was likewise proven by the failures to open the Mississippi or win any decided success on the plan first devised by the Government.

It is further conclusively shown that no plan, order, letter, telegram, or suggestion of the Tennessee River as the line of invasion has ever produced, except in the paper submitted by Miss Carroll on the 30th of November 1861, and her subsequent letters to the Government as the campaign progressed. . . .

In view of all the facts, this Committee believe that the thanks of the nation are due Miss Carroll, and that they are fully justified in recommending that she be placed on the pension rolls of the Government, as a partial measure of recognition for her public service, and report herewith a bill for such purpose and recommend its passage. . . .

Source: Stanton, Anthony, and Gage, *HWS*, 2: 863–864.

DOCUMENT 49: The Loyal Women of the Country to Abraham Lincoln (1863)

In this brief but eloquent statement of loyalty and commendation for the Emancipation Proclamation, Elizabeth Cady Stanton, on behalf of the Women's National Loyal League, appeals to President Lincoln to "finish the work by declaring . . . justice and protection" for all women in the country. The request no doubt would include those rights for women found in the resolutions to the national women's rights conventions held prior to the war. Inspired by the Emancipation Proclamation, the appeal reflects the optimism of this group of women who labored during the antebellum period not only for themselves but for the rights of blacks.

We come not to criticise or complain. Not for ourselves or our friends do we ask redress of specific grievances, or posts of honor or emolument. We speak from no considerations of mere material gain; but, inspired by true patriotism, in this dark hour of our nation's destiny, we come to pledge the loyal women of the Republic to freedom and our country. We come to strengthen you with earnest words of sympathy and encouragement. We come to thank you for your proclamation, in which the nineteenth century seems to echo back the Declaration of Seventy-six. Our fathers had a vision of the sublime idea of liberty, equality, and fraternity; but they failed to climb the heights that with anointed eyes they saw. To us, their children, belongs the work to build up the living reality of what they conceived and uttered.

It is not our mission to criticise the past. Nations, like individuals, must blunder and repent. It is not wise to waste one energy in vain regret, but from each failure rise up with renewed conscience and courage for nobler action. The follies and faults of yesterday we cast aside as the old garments we have outgrown. Born anew to freedom, slave creeds and codes and constitutions must now all pass away. "For men do not put new wine into old bottles, else the bottles break, and the wine runneth out, and the bottles perish; but they put new wine into new bottles, and both are preserved."

Our special thanks are due to you, that by your Proclamation two millions of women are freed from the foulest bondage humanity ever suffered. Slavery for man is bad enough, but the refinements of cruelty must ever fall on the mothers of the oppressed race, defrauded of all the rights of the family relation, and violated in the most holy instincts of their nature. A mother's life is bound up in that of her child. There center all her hopes and ambition. But the slave-mother, in her degradation, rejoices not in the future promise of her daughter, for she knows by experience what her sad fate must be. No pen can describe the unutterable agony of that mother whose past, present, and future are all wrapped in darkness; who knows the crown of thorns she wears must press her daughter's brow; who knows that the wine-press she now treads, unwatched, those tender feet must read alone. For, by the law of slavery, "the child follows the condition of the mother."

By your act, the family, that great conservator of national virtue and strength, has been restored to millions of humble homes, around whose altars coming generations shall magnify and bless the name of Abraham Lincoln. By a mere stroke of the pen you have emancipated millions from a condition of wholesale concubinage. We now ask you to finish the work by declaring that nowhere under our national flag shall the motherhood of any race plead in vain for justice and protection. . . .

Source: Stanton, Anthony, and Gage, *HWS*, 2: 67–68.

DOCUMENT 50: Petition to the Senate and House of Representatives and Editorial by Theodore Tilton of the *New York Independent*, Regarding Women's Suffrage and the Fourteenth Amendment (1865)

When women suffragists learned that the proposed Fourteenth Amendment to the U.S. Constitution not only failed to grant women the vote, but for the first time identified suffrage solely with the male gender, they felt outraged, betrayed, and frightened. Outraged, because, having devoted so much time and energy to human rights issues, they were excluded from the fruits of their labor. Betrayed, because many former supporters, such as Frederick Douglass and Gerrit Smith, justified excluding women because this was "the Negro's hour." Frightened, because, as Stanton predicted, the amendment would set back women's suffrage for a generation. As it turned out, it was sixty years before passage of the Nineteenth Amendment secured women the right to vote in every state.

In the petition reproduced here, signed by Stanton, Anthony, Stone, and others, they once more demanded suffrage, once more drew attention to the proposition that, constitutionally, they were regarded as "free people," and once more proclaimed their qualifications to vote. And they did not stand alone. The editorial response to the proposed Fourteenth Amendment by Theodore Tilton expressed the bitterness of their male feminist supporters. At the same time, however, Tilton refused to accept defeat, challenging members of Congress to live up to the republican form of government by not denying half of the citizens equal rights.

A. WOMEN'S PETITION TO CONGRESS

FORM OF PETITION.—*To the Senate and House of Representatives:*—The undersigned women of the United States, respectfully ask an amendment of the Constitution that shall prohibit the several States from disfranchising any of their citizens on the ground of sex.

In making our demand for Suffrage, we would call your attention to the fact that we represent fifteen million people—one-half the entire population of the country—intelligent, virtuous, native-born American citizens; and yet stand outside the pale of political recognition. The Constitution classes us as "free people," and counts us *whole* persons in the basis of representation: and yet are we governed without our consent, compelled to pay taxes without appeal, and punished for violations of law without choice of judge or juror. The experience of all ages, the Declarations of the Fathers, the Statute Laws of our own day, and the fearful revolution through which we have just passed, all prove the uncertain tenure of life, liberty, and property so long as the ballot—the only weapon of self-protection—is not in the hand of every citizen.

Therefore, as you are now amending the Constitution, and, in harmony with advancing civilization, placing new safeguards round the individual rights of four millions of emancipated slaves, we ask that you extend the right of Suffrage to Woman—the only remaining class of disfranchised citizens—and thus fulfill your constitutional obligation "to guarantee to every State in the Union a Republican form of Government." As all partial application of Republican principles must ever breed a complicated legislation as well as a discontented people, we would pray your Honorable Body, in order to simplify the machinery of Government and ensure domestic tranquility, that you legislate hereafter for persons, citizens, tax-payers, and not for class or caste. For justice and equality your petitioners will ever pray.

Source: Stanton, Anthony, and Gage, *HWS*, 2: 91.

B. A LAW AGAINST WOMEN

The spider-crab walks backward. Borrowing this creature's mossy legs, two or three gentlemen in Washington are seeking to fix these upon the Federal Constitution, to make that instrument walk backward in like style. For instance, the Constitution has never laid any legal disabilities upon woman. Whatever denials of rights it formerly made to our slaves, it denied nothing to our wives and daughters. The legal rights of an American woman—for instance, her right to her own property, as against a squandering husband; or her right to her own children, as against a malicious father—have grown, year by year, into a more generous and just statement in American laws. This beautiful result is owing in great measure to the persistent efforts of many noble women who, for years past, both publicly and privately, both by pen and speech, have appealed to legislative committees, and to the whole community, for an enlargement of the legal and civil status of their fellow-country women. Signal, honorable, and beneficent have been the works and words of Lucretia Mott, Lydia Maria Child, Paulina W. Davis, Abby Kelly Foster, Frances D. Gage, Lucy Stone, Caroline H. Dall, Antoinette Brown Blackwell, Susan B. Anthony, Elizabeth Cady Stanton, and many others. Not in all the land lives a poor woman, or a widow, who does not owe some portion of her present safety under the law to the brave exertions of these faithful laborers in a good cause.

Now, all forward-looking minds know that, sooner or later, the chief public question in this country will be woman's claim to the ballot. The Federal Constitution, as it now stands, leaves this question an open one for the several States to settle as they choose. Two bills, however, now lie before Congress proposing to array the fundamental law of the land against the multitude of American women by ordaining a denial of the political rights of a whole sex. To this injustice we object totally! Such an amendment is a snap judgment before discussion; it is an obstacle to future progress; it is a gratuitous bruise inflicted upon the most tender and humane sentiment that has ever entered into American politics. If the present Congress is not called to legislate *for* the rights of women, let it not legislate *against* them.

But Americans now live who shall not go down into the grave till they have left behind them a Republican Government; and no republic is Republican which denies to half its citizens those rights which the Declaration of Independence, and which a true Christian Democracy make equal to all. Meanwhile, let us break the legs of the spider-crab!

Source: Theodore Tilton, "A Law Against Women" (editorial), *New York Independent*, reprinted in Stanton, Anthony, and Gage, *HWS*, 2: 93.

Part III

The Suffrage Issue: One among Many, 1866–1920

Women's issues came to the forefront during the post–Civil War period. The women's movement became institutionalized (see Document 82), and feminists raised the issues of access to the professions, educational opportunities, control of women's bodies and limits to family size, social welfare, women's role in society, and women's contribution to culture as a whole. But the single issue that dominated this period was women's suffrage.

Despite the Seneca Falls meeting in 1848 (See Document 30), the women's rights movement before the Civil War was constrained by Abigail Adams's "remember the ladies" attitude (see Document 9A), which relied on men to do the "right thing" for women. Women had suspended their drive for voting rights during the war, believing that when peace came, the country, led by a Radical Republican Congress, would thankfully concede them the right to vote. They were to be disappointed.

Defeat came not only from conservatives, who saw in women's suffrage the seeds of destruction of the family and society, but from their putative 'friends" in Congress. Later that betrayal was continued by liberals (see Document 65), socialists (see Document 63), and former abolitionist allies (see Document 54), as well as by the Equal Rights Association, which was formed after the war to fight for the rights of women and blacks but whose predominantly male leadership did not fulfill its promises to women (see Documents 52 and 54).

Stung by the betrayal of the Equal Rights Association, and fueled by the need to be self-sufficient, to promote a women's suffrage amendment to the Constitution, and to institutionalize the women's movement, feminist leaders broke with the Equal Rights Association. But they were not united among themselves. One group, led by Elizabeth Cady Stanton and Susan B. Anthony, formed the National Woman Suffrage Association (NWSA) in 1869, whose membership was open to women only. The same year, Lucy Stone and Julia Ward Howe formed the American Woman Suffrage Association (AWSA).

Both organizations were committed to women's suffrage, but the AWSA initially contented itself with concentrating on the franchise, bypassing other controversial issues, like divorce, that could impair the potential support of influential groups. The NWSA, however, sought to embrace almost every issue affecting women. Some of the NWSA's tactics, which included demonstrations and legal challenges to the Fourteenth Amendment (see Document 59), were calculated not only to disrupt the political process, but to gain publicity and secure additional members. The established political order understood those tactics, and a contest of wills was joined. The behavior of the judge who presided at the trial of Susan B. Anthony for voting, for example, was designed to break the will of women by saying to them: Judicial policy on women's suffrage is settled—you cannot have it; the Fourteenth Amendment does not support it; and the harmony of the nation is not going to be further disturbed. Those who do not or cannot accept this "fact" will have to contend with jail.

Additional areas of difference between the two major suffrage organizations included the willingness of the AWSA to admit male members. Like the NWSA, however, it was determined to keep out those who were not fully committed to the cause of women's rights. At the 1869 convention that sponsored its founding, only representatives from recognized suffrage organizations were seated, reversing a policy that had allowed anyone who so desired to participate in women's conventions.

In the area of access to professions, the struggle for women's rights was formidable. And so it had to be, given the definition of "profession" as a public calling requiring specialized knowledge and often intensive academic preparation. It was that definition women had in mind when, in the Declaration of Sentiments adopted at Seneca Falls in 1848 (see Document 30), they noted the absence of women in theology, medicine, pharmacology, and law. If women were to gain specialized knowledge, engage in long, intensive academic preparation, and follow a public calling, they could not be restricted to the home. Most men and the institutions they represented knew this. So opposition to women in professions, including their exclusion from institutions of professional training and the refusal of state and professional associations to certify them, followed. The experience of Myra Bradwell is instructive. Having completed a law degree, she applied to the Supreme Court of the state of Illinois for a license to practice law; she was refused, and that decision was affirmed by the Supreme Court of the United States (see Document 60).

By the first decade of the twentieth century, thanks to the women's movement, significant numbers of women were graduating annually from accredited colleges. In 1910 alone, over eight thousand women graduated, some of whom moved on to professional schools.

Unless there is a strong commitment to educational excellence, access to professions can never be assured. The pursuit of that excellence for women during this period was often undermined not only by some of the previously mentioned obstacles to professional training but by the ideology, judicially affirmed in *Muller v. Oregon* (see Document 73), that women were intellectually inferior; that their physiognomy limited their potential for contributing to society; and that too rigorous mental exertion in the pursuit of academic excellence would impair their reproductive capacity, thus threatening society, which can only duplicate and extend itself through them.

The reaction of women? They followed a variety of strategies. Those who felt that women would receive the best education by pursuing the same curriculum as men urged coeducation, along with fellowships and other supports for women. And a number of academic institutions such as Boston University (1869), Cornell (1874), and the University of Pennsylvania (1876) adopted coeducation. (Antioch and Oberlin had earlier become coeducational.) Some, like Swarthmore (1869), were founded as coeducational colleges. But there was much skepticism about this route, in face of women's continuing difficulty in gaining acceptance to college, and the absence of a socially and academically nurturing environment when they were accepted. Equally important were questions about the values on which instruction would be grounded. This skepticism found expression in the drive to found colleges that ministered exclusively to the academic needs of women.

The founding of women's colleges predated the Civil War (see Part II). Mount Holyoke was opened in 1837; it did not offer instruction consonant with collegiate standards, however, until much later. Vassar, the first *bona fide* women's college, was founded in 1865. But it was not until about the time of the founding of Wellesley and Smith (1875) that women's colleges could boast equality with men's colleges in the quality of instruction, curricular offerings, and admission standards. By the beginning of the twentieth century, the "seven sisters" (Barnard, Bryn Mawr, Mount Holyoke, Radcliffe, Smith, Vassar, and Wellesley) had become a powerful influence in American society.

Except at Oberlin, black women, who had the farthest to "lift themselves," did not find many seats in colleges to which middle-class white women had access. Coming out of slavery, these largely unlettered women often had to return to the domestic work they did during slavery. Fortunately, predominantly black colleges such as Howard and Atlanta were coeducational and a number of black women were gradually able to gain access to the professions. Finally, both black and white women were able to achieve a certain level of educational excellence through land grant colleges, especially those in the Midwest.

At the end of the nineteenth century and the beginning of the twentieth, American society underwent more rapid and radical socioeconomic changes than at any time in its history. The industrialization of the country brought with it changes in every sphere of life—changes which, at times, appeared to threaten "civilization" as people then knew it. In the midst of those changes, the family and home—the woman's sphere—became a refuge from the moral, social, and cultural compromises of the world. But if the home were to remain that haven, it would mean that women would have to continue to play the role traditionally assigned to them. That continuity is exactly what the feminists opposed. And birth control, perhaps more than any other issue, symbolized that opposition.

Before the advent of dependable birth control measures, women could not reliably set limits on reproduction. Most repeated the cycle of conception, gestation, childbirth, and postpartum recovery until death or loss of the capacity to reproduce. As America moved from an agricultural to an industrial society and men's livelihood took them out of the home and into the factory, women were left to care for the children alone and to deal with problems associated with reproduction. The cost in lives, time, physical and emotional energy, and lost opportunities informed Elizabeth Cady Stanton's statements on self-sovereignty (see Document 67), forged powerful bonds among women, and set fire to the movement for birth control.

Antifeminists believed that birth control would destroy the family, nurture the "selfish impulse" of women who sought higher social status, encourage moral laxity, disrupt the "natural order" of things, legitimize abortion (which they believed was murder), and threaten "racial suicide," since many women who sought birth control were from the upper and middle classes. (There was a fear that the population of the "decent" classes would decrease while that of the "rabble" who had recently migrated from eastern and southern Europe would increase.) Hence, antifeminists waged a vigorous effort to limit dissemination of birth control information, to encourage the passage of laws that criminalized this dissemination, and, most important, to make the definition of this "criminal" action vague enough to permit arbitrary arrest and punishment (see Document 58).

Feminists saw birth control as a means to mitigate the social problems of drunkenness, child and wife abuse, and women's dependency on men. Most important, they sought to restore to women control of their bodies—a first and indispensable step toward self-determination, self-respect, and personal fulfillment. The battle soon was joined. Margaret Sanger, the founder of the birth control movement in the United States, gives us a sense of that battle and the stakes involved (see Document 81).

Feminists realized that political equality would only be realized by addressing social problems such as illiteracy, homelessness, low wages, inhumane working conditions, alcoholism, and prostitution. Because these problems weighed most heavily on women, feminists felt that they could not be addressed without effective organizations. During this period women founded a number of organizations: the Young Women's Christian Association in the 1860s, the Woman's Christian Temperance Union (WCTU) in 1874, the Consumers League in 1889, and the National Women's Trade Union League in 1903.

The WCTU led by Frances Willard, was the largest women's organization in the United States in the nineteenth century. It focused its considerable power on issues ranging from physical culture and hygiene, prisons, and kindergarten education to alcoholism, suffrage, and prostitution. The Consumers League, targeting issues from the minimum wage and paid vacations to child labor and workers' safety, became the representative of the buying public's interest. It was largely as a result of pressure from the National Women's Trade Union League, led by Mary Kenny and others, that Congress sponsored and financed a comprehensive investigation into the condition of women workers (see Document 76).

In many of these social welfare efforts, linkages developed between middle-class (and sometimes upper-class) and working-class women that forged an important common force for other social and economic struggles. Equally significant, in taking on and defeating powerful groups, the women's rights movement gained increased confidence. But it did more: it taught the public that effective address of social problems could not be left to public opinion, as the laissez faire social philosophy of the day argued, but required the direct involvement of government. The action of the women's rights movement laid the foundation for important social legislation on what today we call social rights.

Centrally connected to women's rights are the broader issues of the validity of women's experience, contribution to social culture, and role in society. To exclude the experience of one-half of the population from public culture is to stifle their identity and to distort the common memory that is passed on to future generations. Anna G. Spencer (see Document 79) asked whether male-dominated educational institutions would continue to exclude women's experiences and contributions by denying them faculty appointments. Women's colleges, with a critical mass of women professors, ensured the inclusion of women's experiences in their education. This validation of women's experience was certainly part of the focus of Elizabeth Cady Stanton's efforts to publish *The Woman's Bible* (see Document 69).

Another issue was the role that women should play in society. Traditionally, women had been assigned roles; they were not permitted to choose them. During this period women increasingly questioned their traditional assigned roles and insisted on their right to reshape social culture. It is within this context that one should view the work of Emma Goldman (see Document 77) and Charlotte Gilman (see Document 72).

Suffrage was finally won in 1920 (see Document 82). This was the feminists' most important goal during this period. But the road to victory was associated with defeats as well as triumphs. Divisions had to be healed along the way. The differences between the NWSA and the ASWA were overcome in 1890, when these organizations merged to form the National American Woman Suffrage Association (NAWSA). Divisions remained, however, between other groups, such as NAWSA and the National Federation of Afro-American Women—despite the efforts of the federation's leaders, Ida Wells and Josephine Ruffin—but both organizations worked in parallel in the fight for suffrage. Defeats, which were painful and many, included the failure to gain the right to vote through the courts (see Documents 59 and 60) and the Congress (see Document 57). But a few triumphs gave some solace.

In 1869 the Territory of Wyoming granted full suffrage to women. Wyoming was followed by Colorado in 1893, Utah in 1894, Washington in 1910, California in 1911, and Montana and Nevada in 1914—all western states. By way of contrast, in 1915 New York, New Jersey, Pennsylvania, and Massachusetts, bastions of liberalism, voted against suffrage. (There were also a number of defeats the previous year in other areas—the Dakotas, Ohio, Nebraska, and Missouri.)

Yet, in part, the defeats were partial victories. Women mobilized and became politically educated. Despite the efforts of some to discredit women's suffrage by pointing out that states in which they had the right to vote had not markedly improved morally (see Document 78), it was clear that many of the fears about women's suffrage were misplaced. Most important were the fruits from previous efforts: the many organizations that women had created in the areas of settlement houses, birth control, consumer protection, labor, temperance, education, and culture provided a groundswell for suffrage that could not be arrested. Indeed, Carrie Chapman Catt (see Document 74) best typified the fruits of those efforts. Recognized for her organizational genius during the lost suffrage campaign in New York, she was recruited to lead the NAWSA and the national campaign for suffrage. Victory was largely due to her extraordinary abilities.

DOCUMENT 51: Congressional Debate on Women's Suffrage (1866)

Despite the counterimages that women had succeeded in creating of themselves during the pre–Civil War period, the attitudes of most men, including public officials, changed little. Document 51A presents the opinions of Senator George H. Williams of Oregon on the suffrage issue. He would support women's right to vote if they were soldiers and sailors, trade or business persons. But how were they to be soldiers and sailors if, by nature, according to him, they belonged in the home? The position of Senator Frederick T. Frelinghuysen of New Jersey was similar. These statements, which typified the 1866 debate in Congress about women's suffrage, suggest no awareness that approximately four hundred women actually saw some duty as soldiers during the Civil War.

A. SENATOR GEORGE H. WILLIAMS

Mr. President, to extend the right of suffrage to the negroes in this country I think is necessary for their protection; but to extend the right of suffrage to women, in my judgment, is not necessary for their protection. . . .

When women ask Congress to extend to them the right of suffrage it will be proper to consider their claims. Not one in a thousand of them at this time wants any such thing, and would not exercise the power if it was granted to them. Some few who are seeking notoriety make a feeble clamor for the right of suffrage, but they do not represent the sex to which they belong. . . .

Sir, it has been said that, "the hand that rocks the cradle rules the world;" and there is truth as well as beauty in that expression. Women in this country by their elevated social position can exercise more influence upon public affairs than they could coerce by the use of the ballot. When God married our first parents in the garden according to that ordinance they were made "bone of one bone and flesh of one flesh;" and the whole theory of government and society proceeds upon the assumption that their interests are one, that their relations are so intimate and tender that whatever is for the benefit of the one is for the benefit of the other; whatever works to the injury of the one works to the injury of the other.

I say, sir, that the more identical and inseparable these interests and relations can be made, the better for all concerned; and the woman who undertakes to put her sex in an adversary position to man, who undertakes by the use of some independent political power to contend and fight against man, displays a spirit which would, if able, convert all the now harmonious elements of society into a state of war, and make every home a hell upon earth.

Women do not bear their proportion and share, they cannot bear their proportion and share, of the public burdens. Men represent them in the Army and in the Navy; men represent them at the polls and in the affairs of the Government; and though it be true that individual women do own property that is taxed, yet nine tenths of the property and the business from which the revenues of the Government are derived are in the hands and belong to and are controlled by the men. Sir, when the women of this country come to be sailors and soldiers; when they come to navigate the ocean and to follow the plow; when they love to be jostled and crowded by all sorts of men in the thoroughfares of trade and business; when they love the treachery and the turmoil of politics; when they love the dissoluteness of the camp and the smoke and the thunder and the blood of battle better than they love the affections and enjoyments of home and family, then it will be time to talk about making the women voters; but until that time, the question is not fairly before the country.
. . .

B. SENATOR FREDERICK T. FRELINGHUYSEN

Sir, I confess a little surprise at the remark which has been so frequently made in the Senate, that there is no difference between granting suffrage to colored citizens and extending it to the women of America. The difference, to my mind, is as wide as the earth. As I understand it, we legislate for classes, and the women of America as a class do vote now, though there are exceptions from the peculiar circumstances of individuals. Do not the American people vote in this Senate to-day on this question? Do they not vote in the House of Representatives? So the women of America vote by faithful and true representatives, their husbands, their brothers, their sons; and no true man will go to the polls, and deposit his ballot without remembering the true and loving constituency that he has at home. . . .

But, Mr. President, besides that, the women of America are not called upon to serve the Government as the men of America are. They do not bear the bayonet, and have not that reason why they should be entitled to the ballot; and it seems to me as if the God of our race has stamped upon them a milder, gentler nature, which not only makes them shrink from, but disqualifies them for the turmoil and battle of public life. They have a higher and a holier mission. It is retiracy, to make the character of coming men. Their mission is at home, by their blandishments and their love to assuage the passions of men as they come in from the battle of life, and not themselves by joining in the contest to add fuel to the very flames. . . .

Mr. President, it seems to me that the Christian religion, which has elevated woman to her true position as a peer by the side of man, from which she was taken; that religion which is a part of the common law of this land, in its very spirit and declarations recognizes man as the representative of woman. The very structure of that religion which for centuries has been being built recognizes that principle, and it is written on its very door-posts. The woman, it is true, was first tempted; but it was in Adam that we all died. The angel, it is true, appeared to Mary; but it is in the God-man that we are all made alive. . . .

Source: *Congressional Globe*, December 11, 1866, 56, 65.

DOCUMENT 52: "Keep the Thing Going while Things Are Stirring" (Sojourner Truth, 1867)

The immediate post–Civil War period was one of utter frustration for the women's rights movement. Women had made considerable contributions to that war, by raising funds, nursing the wounded, and even suggesting military strategy (see Part II). In defense of the union they had suspended activities on behalf of the rights they sought. In support of abolition, they had gathered hundreds of thousands of petitions. Yet Congress betrayed them, for the proposed Fourteenth Amendment gave suffrage to former black male slaves but not to women. The American Equal Rights Association, formed at the end of the Civil War to further the rights of both blacks and women, elected to support the proposed amendment. And during a very important referendum campaign in Kansas in 1867 over removing the word "male" from voting requirements, the eastern liberal newspapers, which were widely read in the state, were all but silent. Faced with the call of "the Negro's hour," an angry Susan B. Anthony asserted that she would rather "cut off [her] right arm" than work "for or demand

the ballot for the Negro and not the woman." Elizabeth Cady
Stanton was not as charitable.

In the midst of a widening division between those who supported the suffrage of black men and those who sought the equivalent for women (some thought primarily and even exclusively of
white women), Sojourner Truth (see Document 34) took up the
cause of the forgotten black woman and urged women generally
to keep up the fight for their rights.

My friends, I am rejoiced that you are glad, but I don't know how you
will feel when I get through. I come from another field—the country of
the slave. They have got their liberty—so much good luck to have slavery partly destroyed; not entirely. I want it root and branch destroyed.
Then we will all be free indeed. I feel that if I have to answer for the
deeds done in my body just as much as a man, I have a right to have
just as much as a man. There is a great stir about colored men getting
their rights, but not a word about the colored women; and if colored
men get their rights, and not colored women theirs, you see the colored
men will be masters over the women, and it will be just as bad as it was
before. So I am for keeping the thing going while things are stirring;
because if we wait till it is still, it will take a great while to get it going
again. White women are a great deal smarter, and know more than colored women, while colored women do not know scarcely anything. They
go out washing, which is about as high as a colored woman gets, and
their men go about idle, strutting up and down; and when the women
come home, they ask for their money and take it all, and then scold
because there is no food. I want you to consider on that, chil'n. I call
you chil'n; you are somebody's chil'n, and I am old enough to be mother
of all that is here. I want women to have their rights. In the courts women
have no right, no voice; nobody speaks for them. I wish woman to have
her voice there among the pettifoggers. If it is not a fit place for women,
it is unfit for men to be there.

I am above eighty years old; it is about time for me to be going. I have
been forty years a slave and forty years free, and would be here forty
years more to have equal rights for all. I suppose I am kept here because
something remains for me to do; I suppose I am yet to help to break the
chain. I have done a great deal of work; as much as a man, but did not
get so much pay. I used to work in the field and bind grain, keeping up
the cradler; but men doing no more, got twice as much pay; so with the
German women. They work in the field and do as much work, but do
not get the pay. We do as much, we eat as much, we want as much. I
suppose I am about the only colored woman that goes about to speak
for the rights of the colored women. I want to keep the thing stirring,
now that the ice is cracked. What we want is a little money. You men

know that you get as much again as women when you write, or for what you do. When we get our rights we shall not have to come to you for money, and may be you will ask us for money. But help us now until we get it. It is a good consolation to know that when we have got this battle once fought we shall not be coming to you any more. You have been having our rights so long, that you think, like a slave-holder, that you own us. I know that it is hard for one who has held the reins for so long to give up; it cuts like a knife. It will feel all the better when it closes up again. I have been in Washington about three years, seeing about these colored people. Now colored men have the right to vote. There ought to be equal rights now more than ever, since colored people have got their freedom. I am going to talk several times while I am here; so now I will do a little singing. I have not heard any singing since I came here.

Source: Stanton, Anthony, and Gage, *HWS*, 2: 193–194.

DOCUMENT 53: The Fourteenth Amendment (1868)

In July 1868 the Fourteenth Amendment to the Constitution was ratified. That ratification marks the first and only time the word "male" was inserted into the Constitution, in reference to the right to vote in federal elections. It would take some fifty-two years and the herculean efforts of women to reverse the wrong visited on them by that amendment. As will be seen in Part V of this volume, the equal protection and due process clauses of the Fourteenth Amendment have been instrumental in furthering women's rights. But that result was never contemplated in 1868 (see Document 60).

Section 1. All persons born or naturalized in the United States, and subject to the jurisdiction thereof, are citizens of the United States and of the state wherein they reside. No state shall make or enforce any law which shall abridge the privileges or immunities of citizens of the United States; nor shall any state deprive any person of life, liberty, or property without due process of law; nor deny to any person within its jurisdiction the equal protection of the law.

Section 2. Representatives shall be apportioned among the several states according to their respective numbers, counting the whole number of persons in each state, *excluding Indians not taxed*. But when the right to vote at any election for the choice of electors for President and Vice

President of the United States, representatives in Congress, the executive and judicial officers of a state, or the members of the legislature thereof, is denied to any of the male inhabitants of such state being of twenty-one years of age, and citizens of the United States, or in any way abridged, except for participation in rebellion or other crime, the basis of representation therein shall be reduced in the proportion which the number of such male citizens shall bear to the whole number of male citizens twenty-one years of age in such state. . . .

DOCUMENT 54: Statement by Frederick Douglass (1869)

Frederick Douglass (1817–1895) was one of the most forceful supporters of women's rights at the Seneca Falls convention. In 1869, however, this promoter of "the Negro hour" must have provoked dismay among many women's rights advocates when in a speech he gave his reasons for bypassing women to give priority to suffrage for freedmen.

When women, because they are women, are dragged from their homes and hung upon lamp-posts; when their children are torn from their arms and their brains dashed to the pavement; when they are objects of insults and outrage at every turn; when they are in danger of having their homes burnt down over their heads; when their children are not allowed to enter schools; then they will have an urgency to obtain the ballot.

Source: Eleanor Flexner, Century of Struggle (New York: Atheneum, 1972), 144.

DOCUMENT 55: An Act to Grant to the Women of Wyoming the Right of Suffrage, and to Hold Office (1869)

The first actual victory for women's suffrage in the United States came in 1869. In December of that year, the territory of Wyoming granted women the right to vote in that territory and to hold public office as well. Other developments flowed from those rights, among them a woman's right to control her own property and to become a juror. Once women were enrolled as voters, their names began to appear on lists of prospective jurors.

Be it enacted by the Council and House of Representatives of the Territory of Wyoming:

Section 1. That every woman of the age of twenty-one years, residing in this Territory, may at every election to be holden under the law thereof, cast her vote. And her rights to the elective franchise and to hold office shall be the same under the election laws of the Territory, as those of electors.

Section 2. This act shall take effect and be in force from and after its passage.

Approved December 10, 1869.
Signed by Governor John A. Campbell

Source: Beverly Beeton, *Women Vote in the West* (New York: Garland, 1986), 157.

DOCUMENT 56: The Fifteenth Amendment (1870)

The year 1870 was a time of both victory and defeat for women's rights in the United States. In that year, the Fifteenth Amendment to the Constitution was ratified, giving black men the right to vote. All Congress had to do in order to enfranchise women was to have added "sex" to the enumerated categories of citizens whose right to vote could not be denied or abridged; it failed to do so. On the other hand, the territory of Utah recognized women's right to vote. In Wyoming (see Document 55) women fought for the right, while in Utah it was granted to them for political purposes. Late in 1869 Congress had introduced a bill to outlaw polygamy. Mormon men, expediently seeking to secure the help of women to protest against this federal intrusion, gave them the right to vote in the territory. In 1887, by way of the Edmonds-Tucker Act, Congress outlawed polygamy, and women's right to vote in the territory of Utah was revoked.

Section 1. The right of the citizens of the United States to vote shall not be denied or abridged by the United States or by any state, on account of race, color, or previous condition of servitude.

DOCUMENT 57: Address of Victoria C. Woodhull to the Judiciary Committee of the House of Representatives (1871)

Victoria Claffin Woodhull (1838–1927), a strong and controversial advocate of women's rights as well as of fundamental reform of American society, was born in Ohio. In the 1860s, she and her sister, Tennessee Claffin, became the first women brokers on Wall Street. From 1870 to 1876 they collaborated in editing *Woodhull and Claffin's Weekly*, a journal that promoted a variety of causes, from free love and unionism to socialism and women's suffrage. In 1872, after working actively to shape the platform of the Equal Rights Party convention, she was nominated as its presidential candidate, becoming the first woman in U.S. history to achieve that distinction. She was also the first woman to address a congressional committee. An excerpt from her address to Congress in 1871 is reprinted below. She incisively points to the legal, moral, and political contradictions associated with denying women the right to vote.

The public law of the world is founded upon the conceded fact that sovereignty can not be forfeited or renounced. The sovereign power of this country is perpetually in the politically organized people of the United States, and can neither be relinquished nor abandoned by any portion of them. The people in this republic who confer sovereignty are its citizens; in a monarchy the people are the subjects of sovereignty. All citizens of a republic by rightful act or implication confer sovereign power. . . .

As sovereignty can not be forfeited, relinquished, or abandoned, those from whom it flows—the citizens—are equal in conferring the power, and should be equal in the enjoyment of its benefits and in the exercise of its rights and privileges. One portion of citizens have no power to deprive another portion of rights and privileges such as are possessed and exercised by themselves. The male citizen has no more right to deprive the female citizen of the free, public, political, expression of opinion than the female citizen has to deprive the male citizen thereof.

The sovereign will of the people is expressed in our written Constitution, which is the supreme law of the land. The Constitution makes no distinction of sex. The Constitution defines a woman born or naturalized in the United States, and subject to the jurisdiction thereof, to be a citizen. It recognizes the right of citizens to vote. It declares that the right of citizens of the United States to vote shall not be denied or abridged by the United States or by any State on account of "race, color, or previous condition of servitude."

Women, white and black, belong to races, although to different races. A race of people comprises all the people, male and female. The right to vote can not be denied on account of race. All people included in the term race have the right to vote, unless otherwise prohibited. Women of all races are white, black, or some intermediate color. Color comprises all people, of all races and both sexes. The right to vote can not be denied on account of color. All people included in the term color have the right to vote unless otherwise prohibited. . . .

The citizen who is taxed should also have a voice in the subject matter of taxation. "No taxation without representation" is a right which was fundamentally established at the very birth of our country's independence; and by what ethics does any free government impose taxes on women without giving them a voice upon the subject or a participation in the public declaration as to how and by whom these taxes shall be applied for common public use? . . . .

. . . The American nation, in its march onward and upward, can not publicly choke the intellectual and political activity of half its citizens by narrow statutes. The will of the entire people is the true basis of republican government, and a free expression of that will by the public vote of all citizens, without distinctions of race, color, occupation, or sex, is the only means by which that will can be ascertained. As the world has advanced into civilization and culture; as mind has risen in its dominion over matter; as the principle of justice and moral right has gained sway, and merely physical organized power has yielded thereto; as the might of right has supplanted the right of might, so have the rights of women become more fully recognized, and that recognition is the result of the development of the minds of men, which through the ages she has polished, and thereby heightened the lustre of civilization. . . .

Therefore, Believing firmly in the right of citizens to freely approach those in whose hands their destiny is placed under the Providence of God, your memorialist has frankly, but humbly, appealed to you, and prays that the wisdom of Congress may be moved to action in this matter for the benefit and the increased happiness of our beloved country.

Source: Stanton, Anthony, and Gage, *HWS*, 2: 444–448.

DOCUMENT 58: The Comstock Law (1873)

The Act for the Suppression of Trade in, and Circulation of, Obscene Literature and Articles of Immoral Use was passed by Congress as a result of political pressure. That pressure came largely from a fierce anti-obscenity campaign, led by Anthony Comstock (1844–1915), which was launched in the United States during the 1870s. With many states emulating the federal example, the Comstock law became a national limitation on access to birth control information and the use of what were considered pornographic materials. But it stood for much more.

It expressed the then widespread belief that the substantial increase in the incidence of abortion since the 1840s threatened to impair the demographic balance between the socially established who were seeking to limit child-bearing and newly arriving immigrants, who had many children. Likewise, it reflected the view that abortion interfered with God's will and the natural order as well as women's natural function as mothers and homemakers. Finally, it manifested an attempt by men to gain control of the abortion practice, which was then dominated by women. As long as that domination continued, men could neither prevent nor control abortion. It is noteworthy that no distinction was made between drugs for abortion and other materials employed as contraceptives—all were labeled as pornographic. It would take exactly a century (1973 in *Miller v. California*, 413 U.S. 15) for the Supreme Court to agree on a definition of obscenity.

Be it enacted . . . That whoever, within . . . the jurisdiction of the United States . . . shall sell, . . . or shall offer to sell, or lend, or give away, or in any manner to exhibit, or shall otherwise publish or offer to publish in any manner, or shall have in his possession, for any such purpose or purposes, an obscene book, pamphlet, paper, writing, advertisement, circular, print, picture, drawing . . . or other article of an immoral nature, or any drug or medicine, or any article, whatever, for the prevention of conception, or for causing unlawful abortion, or shall advertise the same for sale, or shall write or print, or cause to be written or printed, any card, circular, book, pamphlet, advertisement, or notice of any kind, stating when, where, how, or of whom, or by what means, any of these articles in this section . . . can be purchased or obtained, or shall manufacture, draw, or print, or in any wise make any of such articles, shall be deemed guilty of a misdemeanor, and, on conviction thereof . . . shall be imprisoned at hard labor in the penitentiary for not less than six months nor more than five years for each offense, or fined not less than one hundred dollars nor more than two thousand dollars, with costs of court.

Source: "An Act for the Suppression of Trade in, and Circulation of, Obscene Literature and Articles of Immoral Use," in *Acts and Resolutions of the United States of America Passed at the Third Session of the Forty-Second Congress, December 2,*

1872–*March 3, 1873* (Washington, D.C.: Government Printing Office, 1873), 234–236.

DOCUMENT 59: *U.S. v. Susan B. Anthony* (1873)

A leader in the women's rights movement, Susan B. Anthony (see Document 37), like other feminists, employed increasingly militant tactics after the Civil War to promote women's rights, including nonpayment of taxes, sit-ins at polling places, and tax payment under protest.

In 1872 she was one of a group of women who voted in Rochester, New York, in violation of the law. They were arrested and charged with voting illegally under the relevant statute, which carried a potential jail term of three years. Anthony's defense was that under the Fourteenth Amendment, all *"persons* born and naturalized in the United States ... are citizens of the United States," which made women eligible to vote. The presiding judge did not allow her to testify. After her attorney had presented her defense, Judge Hunt drew from his pocket a written opinion prepared before the trial and read it to the all-male jury. It instructed them to bring back a guilty verdict. When Anthony's lawyer protested the judge's procedure as unconstitutional and asked that the jury be polled, Judge Hunt dismissed the jurors. What follows is the scene in court the next day, when Anthony was sentenced (It should be observed that Anthony never paid the imposed fine.) Three years later, in the case of *Minor v. Happersett* (88 U.S. 162), the Supreme Court decided that, while women are citizens and thus entitled to "the privileges and immunities of citizens" of the United States, the right to vote was not part of those privileges and immunities.

Judge Hunt. (Ordering the defendant to stand up.) Has the prisoner anything to say why sentence shall not be pronounced?

Miss Anthony. Yes, your honor, I have many things to say; for in your ordered verdict of guilty you have trampled under foot every vital principle of our government. My natural rights, my civil rights, my political rights, my judicial rights, are all alike ignored. Robbed of the fundamental privilege of citizenship, I am degraded from the status of a citizen to that of a subject; and not only myself individually but all of my sex are, by your honor's verdict, doomed to political subjection under this so-called republican form of government.

Judge Hunt. The Court can not listen to rehearsal of argument which the prisoner's counsel has already consumed three hours in presenting.

Miss Anthony. May it please your honor, I am not arguing the question, but simply stating the reasons why sentence can not, in justice, be pronounced against me. Your denial of my citizen's right to vote, is the denial of my right of consent as one of the governed, the denial of my right of representation as one of the taxed, the denial of my right to a trial by a jury of my peers as an offender against law; therefore, the denial of my sacred right to life, liberty, property and—

Judge Hunt. The Court can not allow the prisoner to go on.

Miss Anthony. But your honor will not deny me this one and only poor privilege of protest against this high-handed outrage upon my citizen's rights. May it please the Court to remember that, since the day of my arrest last November, this is the first time that either myself or any person of my disfranchised class has been allowed a word of defense before judge or jury—

Judge Hunt. The prisoner must sit down—the Court can not allow it.

Miss Anthony. Of all my prosecutors, from the corner grocery politicians who entered the complaint, to the United States marshal, commissioner, district-attorney, district-judge, your honor on the bench—not one is my peer, but each and all are my political sovereigns; and had your honor submitted my case to the jury, as was clearly your duty, even then I should have had just cause of protest, for not one of those men was my peer; but, native or foreign born, white or black, rich or poor, educated or ignorant, sober or drunk, each and every man of them was my political superior; hence, in no sense, my peer. Under such circumstances a commoner of England, tried before a jury of lords, would have far less cause to complain than have I, a woman, tried before a jury of men. Even my counsel, Hon. Henry R. Selden, who has argued my cause so ably, so earnestly, so unanswerably before your honor, is my political sovereign. Precisely as no disfranchised person is entitled to sit upon a jury, and no woman is entitled to the franchise, so none but a regularly admitted lawyer is allowed to practice in the courts, and no woman can gain admission to the bar—hence, jury, judge, counsel, all must be of the superior class.

Judge Hunt. The Court must insist—the prisoner has been tried according to the established forms of law.

Miss Anthony. Yes, your honor, but by forms of law all made by men, interpreted by men, administered by men, in favor of men and against women; and hence your honor's ordered verdict of guilty, against a United States citizen for the exercise of the "citizen's right to vote," simply because that citizen was a woman and not a man. But yesterday, the same man-made forms of law declared it a crime punishable with $1,000 fine and six months' imprisonment to give a cup of cold water, a crust of bread or a night's shelter to a panting fugitive tracking his way to Canada; and every man or woman in whose veins coursed a drop of human sympathy violated that wicked law, reckless of consequences, and was justified in so doing. As then the slaves who got their freedom had to take it over or under or through the unjust forms of law, precisely so now must women take it to get their right to a voice in this government; and I have taken mine, and mean to take it at every opportunity.

Judge Hunt. The Court orders the prisoner to sit down. It will not allow another word.

Miss Anthony. When I was brought before your honor for trial, I hoped for a broad and liberal interpretation of the Constitution and its recent amendments, which should declare all United States citizens under its protecting aegis—which should declare equality of rights the national guarantee to all persons born or naturalized in the United States. But failing to get this justice—failing, even, to get a trial by a jury *not* of my peers—I ask not leniency at your hands but rather the full rigor of the law.

Judge Hunt. The Court must insist—[Here the prisoner sat down.] The prisoner will stand up. [Here Miss Anthony rose again.] The sentence of the Court is that you pay a fine of $100 and the costs of the prosecution.

Miss Anthony. May it please your honor. I will never pay a dollar of your unjust penalty. All the stock in trade I possess is a debt of $10,000, incurred by publishing my paper—The Revolution—the sole object of which was to educate all women to do precisely as I have done, rebel against your man-made, unjust, unconstitutional forms of law, which tax, fine, imprison, and hang women, while denying them the right of representation in the government; and I will work on with might and main to pay every dollar of that honest debt, but not a penny shall go to this unjust claim. And I shall earnestly and persistently continue to urge all women to the practical recognition of the old Revolutionary maxim, "Resistance to tyranny is obedience to God."

Judge Hunt. Madam, the Court will not order you to stand committed until the fine is paid.

Source: Stanton, Anthony, and Gage, *HWS*, 2: 687–689.

DOCUMENT 60: *Bradwell v. Illinois* (1873)

On April 15, 1873, the U.S. Supreme Court handed down two decisions that had a profound effect on the cause of women's rights.

One is known as the *Slaughterhouse cases* (83 U.S. 36); the other, reproduced in part below, is *Bradwell v. Illinois.* The first entailed an attempt by Louisiana butchers to invalidate a state statute that created a monopoly in the slaughterhouse trade. The complaining butchers contended that the statute violated the Fourteenth Amendment, which provides that no state "shall make or enforce any law which shall abridge the privileges or immunities of citizens of the United States." The butchers argued that the statute was invalid because it deprived them (citizens of the United States) of an opportunity to practice their trade—a privilege and immunity of U.S. citizens. But the Supreme Court disagreed and held that the privileges and immunities provision pertained to *national* citizenship only (as distinct from that of the respective states). Those privileges included the right to petition government and the right to travel from state to state. The right to pursue an occupation free from governmental regulation, however, was not one of the privileges or immunities of national (U.S.) citizenship.

With this new interpretation, the feminist cause was further set back. But women also hoped to use the equal protection clause of the Fourteenth Amendment, which says that no state shall "deny to any person under its jurisdiction the equal protection of the law." The Court doubted very much whether any action of a state not directed by way of discrimination against the Negro as a class, on account of race, will ever be held to come within the purview of this provision" (83 U.S. 81). Myra Bradwell, a suffragist and a champion of women's rights, had passed the Illinois examination for admission to the bar in 1869, but was not permitted to practice law by the highest court of that state solely because of her sex. She appealed to the U.S. Supreme Court, which also denied her the right to practice, on the grounds that such a right was not one of the privileges or immunities of national citizenship. What follows is, in part, the concurring opinion of Justice Bradley.

The civil law, as well as nature herself, has always recognized a wide difference in the respective spheres and destinies of man and woman. Man is, or should be, women's protector and defender. The natural and proper timidity and delicacy which belongs to the female sex evidently unfits it for many of the occupations of civil life. The constitution of the family organization, which is founded in the divine ordinance, as well as in the nature of things, indicates the domestic sphere as that which properly belongs to the domain and functions of womanhood. The harmony, not to say identity, of interests and views which belong, or should belong, to the family institution is repugnant to the idea of a woman adopting a distinct and independent career from that of her husband. So firmly fixed was this sentiment in the founders of the common law that it became a maxim of that system of jurisprudence that a woman had no legal existence separate from her husband, who was regarded as her head and representative in the social state; and, notwithstanding some recent modifications of this civil status, many of the special rules of law flowing from and dependent upon this cardinal principle still exist in full force in most States. One of these is, that a married woman is incapable, without her husband's consent, of making contracts which shall be binding on her or him. This very incapacity was one circumstance which the Supreme Court of Illinois deemed important in rendering a married woman incompetent fully to perform the duties and trusts that belong to the office of an attorney and counsellor.

It is true that many women are unmarried and not affected by any of the duties, complications, and incapacities arising out of the married state, but these are exceptions to the general rule. The paramount destiny and mission of woman are to fulfill the noble and benign offices of wife and mother. This is the law of the Creator. And the rules of civil society must be adapted to the general constitution of things, and cannot be based upon the exceptional cases.

The humane movements of modern society, which have for their object the multiplication of avenues for woman's advancement, and of occupations adapted to her condition and sex, have my heartiest concurrence. But I am not prepared to say that it is one of her fundamental rights and privileges to be admitted into every office and position, including those which require highly special qualifications and demanding special responsibilities. In the nature of things it is not every citizen of every age, sex, and condition that is qualified for every calling and position. It is the prerogative of the legislator to prescribe regulations founded on nature, reason, and experience for the due admission of qualified persons to professions and callings demanding special skill and confidence. This fairly belongs to the police power of the State; and, in my opinion, in view of the peculiar characteristics, destiny, and mission of woman, it is within the province of the legislature to ordain what offices, positions, and callings shall be filled and discharged by men, and shall receive the benefit of those energies and responsibilities, and that decision and firmness which are presumed to predominate in the sterner sex.

Source: 83 U.S. 130 (1873).

DOCUMENT 61: "Social Purity" (Susan B. Anthony, 1875)

Intemperance and its social consequences for women were a serious concern of the women's rights movement. Susan B. Anthony (see Document 37), who considered the disenfranchisement of women the single most important cause of their socioeconomic inequality, here takes on the "roots of the great evil, intemperance." In an address entitled "Social Purity," delivered in Chicago in 1875, she argued that rampant wife abuse (including murder), sex crimes, and the prevalence of prostitution were testimonies to men's incapacity to deal with social problems caused mainly by women's dependence. The cure? Women's equality (the franchise) and economic independence.

Though women, as a class, are much less addicted to drunkenness and licentiousness than men, it is universally conceded that they are by far the greater sufferers from these evils. Compelled by their position in society to depend on men for subsistence, for food, clothes, shelter, for every chance even to earn a dollar, they have no way of escape from the besotted victims of appetite and passion with whom their lot is cast. They must endure, if not endorse, these twin vices, embodied, as they so often are, in the person of father, brother, husband, son, employer. No one can doubt that the sufferings of the sober, virtuous woman, in legal subjection to the mastership of a drunken, immoral husband and father over herself and children, not only from physical abuse, but from spiritual shame and humiliation, must be such as the man himself can not possibly comprehend. . . .

The roots of the giant evil, intemperance, are not merely moral and social; they extend deep and wide into the financial and political structure of the government; and whenever women, or men, shall intelligently set themselves about the work of uprooting the liquor traffic, they will find something more than tears and prayers needful to the task. Financial and political power must be combined with moral and social influence, all bound together in one earnest, energetic, persistent force. . . .

The prosecutions in our courts for breach of promise, divorce, adultery, bigamy, seduction, rape; the newspaper reports every day of every year of scandals and outrages, of wife murders and paramour shootings, of abortions and infanticides, are perpetual reminders of men's incapacity to cope successfully with this monster evil of society.

The statistics of New York show the number of professional prostitutes in that city to be over twenty thousand. Add to these the thousands and tens of thousands of Boston, Philadelphia, Washington, New Orleans, St. Louis, Chicago, San Francisco, and all our cities, great and small, from ocean to ocean, and what a holocaust of the womanhood of this nation is sacrificed to the insatiate Moloch of lust. And yet more: those myriads of wretched women, publicly known as prostitutes, constitute but a small portion of the numbers who actually tread the paths of vice and crime. For, as the oft-broken ranks of the vast army of common drunkards are steadily filled by the boasted moderate drinkers, so are the ranks of professional prostitution continually replenished by discouraged, seduced, deserted unfortunates, who can no longer hide the terrible secret of their lives. . . .

Nor is it womanhood alone that is thus fearfully sacrificed. For every betrayed woman, there is always the betrayer, man. For every abandoned woman, there is always *one* abandoned man and oftener many more. It is estimated that there are 50,000 professional prostitutes in London, and Dr. Ryan calculates that there are 400,000 men in that city directly or indirectly connected with them, and that this vice causes the city an annual expenditure of $40,000,000. . . .

Man's legislative attempts to set back this fearful tide of social corruption have proved even more futile and disastrous than have those for the suppression of intemperance—as witness the Contagious Diseases Acts of England and the St. Louis experiment. And yet efforts to establish similar laws are constantly made in our large cities, New York and Washington barely escaping last winter. . . .

The work of woman is not to lessen the severity or the certainty of the penalty for the violation of the moral law, but to prevent this violation by the removal of the causes which lead to it. These causes are said to be wholly different with the sexes. The acknowledged incentive to this vice on the part of man is his own abnormal passion; while on the part of women, in the great majority of cases, it is conceded to be destitution—absolute want of the necessaries of life. . . .

In the olden times, when the daughters of the family, as well as the wife, were occupied with useful and profitable work in the household, getting meals and washing the dishes three times in every day of every year, doing the baking, the brewing, the washing and the ironing, the whitewashing, the butter and cheese and soap making, the mending and the making of clothes for the entire family, the carding, spinning and weaving of the cloth—when everything to eat, to drink and to wear was manufactured in the home, almost no young women "went out to work." But now, when nearly all these handicrafts are turned over to men and to machinery, tens of thousands, nay, millions of the women of both hemispheres are thrust into the world's outer market of work to earn their own subsistence. Society, ever slow to change its conditions, presents to these millions but few and meager chances. Only the barest necessaries, and oftentimes not even those, can be purchased with the proceeds of the most excessive and exhausting labor. . . .

Clearly, then, the first step toward solving this problem is to lift this vast army of poverty-stricken women who now crowd our cities, above the temptation, the necessity, to sell themselves, in marriage or out, for bread and shelter. To do that, girls, like boys, must be educated to some lucrative employment; women, like men, must have equal chances to earn a living. If the plea that poverty is the cause of woman's prostitution be not true, perfect equality of chances to earn honest bread will demonstrate the falsehood by removing that pretext and placing her on the same plane with man. Then, if she is found in the ranks of vice and crime, she will be there for the same reason that man is and, from an object of pity, she, like him, will become a fit subject of contempt. From being the party sinned against, she will become an equal sinner, if not the greater of the two. Women, like men, must not only have "fair play" in the world of work and self-support, but, like men, must be eligible to all the honors and emoluments of society and government. Marriage, to women as to men, must be a luxury, not a necessity; an incident of life, not all of it. And the only possible way to accomplish this great change is to accord to women equal power in the making, shaping and controlling of the circumstances of life. That equality of rights and privileges is vested in the ballot, the symbol of power in a republic. Hence, our first and most urgent demand—that women shall be protected in the exercise of their inherent, personal, citizens' rights to a voice in the government, municipal, state, national.

Alexander Hamilton said one hundred years ago, "Give to a man the right over my subsistence, and he has power over my whole moral being." No one doubts the truth of this assertion as between man and man; while, as between man and woman, not only does almost no one believe it, but the masses of people deny it. And yet it is the fact of man's possession of this right over woman's subsistence which gives to him the power to dictate to her a moral code vastly higher and purer than the one he chooses for himself. Not less true is it, that the fact of woman's dependence on man for her subsistence renders her utterly powerless to exact from him the same high moral code she chooses for herself. . . .

Whoever controls work and wages, controls morals. Therefore, we must have women employers, superintendents, committees, legislators; whenever girls go to seek the means of subsistence, there must be some woman. Nay, more; we must have women preachers, lawyers, doctors— that wherever women go to seek counsel—spiritual, legal, physical— there, too, they will be sure to find the best and noblest of their own sex to minister to them. . . .

Fathers should be most particular about the men who visit their daughters, and, to further this reform, pure women not only must refuse to meet intimately and to marry impure men, but, finding themselves deceived in their husband, they must refuse to continue in the marriage relation with them. We have had quite enough of the sickly sentimentalism which counts the woman a heroine and a saint for remaining the wife of a drunken, immoral husband, incurring the risk of her own health and poisoning the life-blood of the young beings that result from this unholy alliance. Such company as ye keep, such ye are! must be the maxim of married, as well as unmarried, women. . . .

In a western city the wives conspired to burn down a house of ill-fame in which their husbands had placed a half-dozen of the demi-monde. Would it not have shown much more womanly wisdom and virtue for those legal wives to have refused to recognize their husbands, instead of wreaking their vengeance on the heads of those wretched women? But how could they without finding themselves, as a result, penniless and homeless? The person, the services, the children, the sub-sistence, of each and every one of those women belonged by law, not to herself, but to her unfaithful husband. . . .

It is worse than folly, it is madness, for women to delude themselves with the idea that their children will escape the terrible penalty of the law. The taint of their birth will surely follow them. For pure women to continue to devote themselves to their man-appointed mission of visiting the dark purlieus of society and struggling to reclaim the myriads of badly-born human beings swarming there, is as hopeless as would be an attempt to ladle the ocean with a teaspoon; as unphilosophical as was the undertaking of the old American Colonization Society, which, with great labor and pains and money, redeemed from slavery and trans-ported to Liberia annually 400 negroes, or the Fugitive Slave Societies, which succeeded in running off to Canada, on their "under-ground rail-roads," some 40,000 in a whole quarter of a century. While those good men were thus toiling to rescue the 400 or the 40,000 individual victims of slavery, each day saw hundreds and each year thousands of human beings born into the terrible condition of chattelism. All see and admit now what none but the Abolitionists saw then, that the only effectual work was the entire overthrow of the system of slavery; the abrogation of the law which sanctioned the right of property in man. . . .

. . . [W]herever you go, you find the best women, in and out of the churches, all absorbed in establishing or maintaining benevolent or re-form institutions; charitable societies, soup-houses, ragged schools, in-dustrial schools, mite societies, mission schools—at home and abroad—homes and hospitals for the sick, the aged, the friendless, the foundling, the fallen; asylums for the orphans, the blind, the deaf and dumb, the insane, the inebriate, the idiot. The women of this century are neither idle nor indifferent. They are working with might and main to mitigate the evils which stare them in the face on every side, but much of their work is without knowledge. It is aimed at the effects, not the cause. . . .

The tap-root of our social upas lies deep down at the very foundations of society. It is woman's dependence. It is woman's subjection. Hence, the first and only efficient work must be to emancipate woman from her enslavement. The wife must no longer echo the poet Milton's ideal Eve, when she adoringly said to Adam, "God thy law; thou, mine!" She must feel herself accountable to God alone for every act, fearing and obeying no man, save where his will is in line with her own highest idea of divine law. . . .

I am a full and firm believer in the revelation that it is through woman that the race is to be redeemed. And it is because of this faith that I ask for her immediate and unconditional emancipation from all political, industrial, social and religious subjection.

. . . Ralph Waldo Emerson says, "Men are what their mothers made them." But I say, to hold mothers responsible for the character of their sons while you deny them any control over the surroundings of their lives, is worse than mockery, it is cruelty! Responsibilities grow out of rights and powers. Therefore, before mothers can be held responsible for the vices and crimes, the wholesale demoralization of men, they must possess all possible rights and powers to control the conditions and circumstances of their own and their children's lives.

Source: Ida Husted Harper, *The Life and Work of Susan B. Anthony*, vols. (Indianapolis: Hollenback Press, 1898), 2: 1004–1012.

DOCUMENT 62: Testimony on Prostitution (1876)

The socioeconomic dependence of women and the political oppression they faced caused many of their social problems, especially prostitution, as Susan B. Anthony points out (see Document 61). Women who had no economic support from men—widows, deserted wives, orphaned daughters—were usually poor. To be female and self-supporting often meant being indigent or constantly faced with destitution. Prostitution was a means of last resort. Men often exploited prostitutes and even enslaved them. The following testimony about the slave trade was given by a minister from San Francisco before California legislators who were investigating prostitution.

The women, as a general thing, are held as slaves. They are bought or stolen in China and brought here. They have a sort of agreement to cover up the slavery business, but it is all a sham . . . after the term of prostitution service is up, the owners so manage as to have the women in debt more than ever, so that their slavery becomes life-long. There is no release from it. . . . Sometimes women take opium to kill themselves. They do not know they have any rights, but think they must keep their contracts and believe themselves under obligations to serve in prostitution. . . . They have come to the asylum all bruises. They are beaten and punished cruelly if they fail to make any money. When they become worn out and unable to make any more money, they are turned out to die.

Source: Catherine Clinton, *The Other Civil War: American Women in the Nineteenth Century* (New York: Hill and Wang, 1984), 118.

DOCUMENT 63: Socialist Statement on Women's Rights (The First International, 1876)

As early as the 1850s, controversies had developed within the ranks of American socialists about the nature of their commitment to women's rights. Some members saw the agitation for women's rights as being led by "bad" wives; others, especially union members, sought to eliminate competition for jobs by excluding or seeking to exclude women from unions; and still others, who saw the unrelieved misery and increased prostitution that resulted from the low wages paid women, called for equal wages for equal work. These differences led socialists to fear a split in their ranks. At the historic conference of 1876, which sought to bury old differences, unify factions, and ensure a permanent socialist movement in the United States, the delegates turned down a demand for a pledge of equality for women. Instead, they adopted the statement below on women's economic and political status as well as an oft-repeated promise—that socialism would emancipate both men and women. (The Workingmen's Party of the United States—the Socialist party—lasted only another year, but the position statement lived on.)

The emancipation of Labor is a social problem, a problem concerning the whole human race and embracing both sexes. The emancipation of women will be accomplished with the emancipation of *men*, and the so-called woman's rights question will be solved with the labor question. All evils and wrongs of the present society can be abolished only when economical freedom is conquered for men as well as for women.

It is the duty therefore of the wives and daughters of workingmen to organize themselves and take their places within the ranks of struggling labor. To aid and support them in this work is the duty of the *men*. By uniting their efforts they will succeed in breaking the economic fetters, and a new and free race of men and women will arise recognizing each other as peers.

We acknowledge the perfect equality of rights of both sexes and in the Workingmen's Party of the United States this equality of rights is a principle and is strictly observed.

Source: Mari Jo Buhle, *Women and American Socialism, 1870–1920* (Urbana: University of Illinois Press, 1981), 13.

DOCUMENT 64: 1876 Declaration of Rights

During the summer of 1876, as the American public prepared to celebrate the centennial at a huge exposition in Philadelphia, the National Woman Suffrage Association plotted its strategy to commemorate the U.S. democratic tradition. At a large Fourth of July celebration in Independence Hall, where no woman was scheduled to speak, Susan B. Anthony, representing the association, dramatically handed the Declaration of Rights for Women to the chairperson of the program, Thomas W. Ferry, president pro tempore of the U.S. Senate. Later, outside, she read the declaration to a growing throng of listeners. From a clear and forceful voice, they heard about democracy for men and despotism for women.

While this nation is buoyant with patriotism, and all hearts are attuned to praise, it is with sorrow we come to strike the one discordant note, on this one-hundredth anniversary of our country's birth. When subjects of kings, emperors, and czars, from the old world join in our national jubilee, shall the women of the republic refuse to lay their hands with benedictions on the nation's head? Surveying America's exposition, surpassing in magnificence those of London, Paris, and Vienna, shall we not rejoice at the success of the youngest rival among the nations of the earth? May not our hearts, in unison with all, swell with pride at our great achievements as a people; our free speech, free press, free schools, free church, and the rapid progress we have made in material wealth, trade, commerce and the inventive arts? And we do rejoice in the success, thus far, of our experiment of self-government. Our faith is firm and unwavering in the broad principles of human rights proclaimed in 1776, not only as abstract truths, but as the corner stones of a republic. Yet we cannot forget, even in this glad hour, that while all men of every race, and clime, and condition, have been invested with the full rights of citizenship under our hospitable flag, all women still suffer the degradation of disfranchisement.

The history of our country the past hundred years has been a series of assumptions and usurpations of power over woman, in direct opposition to the principles of just government, acknowledged by the United States as its foundation, which are:

First—The natural rights of each individual.

Second—The equality of these rights.

Third—That rights not delegated are retained by the individual.

Fourth—That no person can exercise the rights of others without delegated authority.

Fifth—That the non-use of rights does not destroy them.

And for the violation of these fundamental principles of our government, we arraign our rulers on this Fourth day of July, 1876,—and these are our articles of impeachment:

Bills of attainder have been passed by the introduction of the word "male" into all the State constitutions, denying to women the right of suffrage, and thereby making sex a crime—an exercise of power clearly forbidden in article I, sections 9, 10, of the United States constitution.

The writ of habeas corpus, the only protection against *lettres de cachet* and all forms of unjust imprisonment, which the constitution declares "shall not be suspended, except when in cases of rebellion or invasion the public safety demands it," is held inoperative in every State of the Union, in case of a married woman against her husband—the marital rights of the husband being in all cases primary, and the rights of the wife secondary.

The right of trial by a jury of one's peers was so jealously guarded that States refused to ratify the original constitution until it was guaranteed by the sixth amendment. And yet the women of this nation have never been allowed a jury of their peers—being tried in all cases by men, native and foreign, educated and ignorant, virtuous and vicious. Young girls have been arraigned in our courts for the crime of infanticide; tried, convicted, hanged—victims, perchance, of judge, jurors, advocates—while no woman's voice could be heard in their defense. And not only are women denied a jury of their peers, but in some cases, jury trial altogether. During the war, a woman was tried and hanged by military law, in defiance of the fifth amendment, which specifically declares: "No person shall be held to answer for a capital or otherwise infamous crime, unless on a presentment or indictment of a grand jury, except in cases ... of persons in actual service in time of war." During the last presidential campaign, a woman, arrested for voting, was denied the protection of a jury, tried, convicted, and sentenced to a fine and costs of prosecution, by the absolute power of a judge of the Supreme Court of the United States.

Taxation without representation, the immediate cause of the rebellion of the colonies against Great Britain, is one of the grievous wrongs the women of this country have suffered during the century. Deploring war, with all the demoralization that follows in its train, we have been taxed to support standing armies, with their waste of life and wealth. Believing in temperance, we have been taxed to support the vice, crime and pauperism of the liquor traffic. While we suffer its wrongs and abuses infinitely more than man, we have no power to protect our sons against this giant evil. During the temperance crusade, mothers were arrested, fined, imprisoned, for even praying and singing in the streets, while men blockade the sidewalks with impunity, even on Sunday, with their military parades and political processions. Believing in honesty, we are taxed to support a dangerous army of civilians, buying and selling the offices of government and sacrificing the best interests of the people. And, moreover, we are taxed to support the very legislators and judges who make laws, and render decisions adverse to woman. And for refusing to pay such unjust taxation, the houses, lands, bonds, and stock of women have been seized and sold within the present year, thus proving Lord Coke's assertion, that "The very act of taxing a man's property without his consent is, in effect, disfranchising him of every civil right."

Unequal codes for men and women. Held by law a perpetual minor, deemed incapable of self-protection, even in the industries of the world, woman is denied equality of rights. The fact of sex, not the quantity or quality of work, in most cases, decides the pay and position; and because of this injustice thousands of fatherless girls are compelled to choose between a life of shame and starvation. Laws catering to man's vices have created two codes of morals in which penalties are graded according to the political status of the offender. Under such laws, women are fined and imprisoned if found alone in the streets, or in public places of resort, at certain hours. Under the pretense of regulating public morals, police officers seizing the occupants of disreputable houses, march the women in platoons to prison, while the men, partners in their guilt, go free. While making a show of virtue in forbidding the importation of Chinese women on the Pacific coast for immoral purposes, our rulers, in many States, and even under the shadow of the national capitol, are now proposing to legalize the sale of American womanhood for the same vile purposes.

Special legislation for woman has placed us in a most anomalous position. Women invested with the rights of citizens in one section—voters, jurors, office-holders—crossing an imaginary line, are subjects in the next. In some States, a married woman may hold property and transact business in her own name; in others, her earnings belong to her husband. In some States, a woman may testify against her husband, sue and be sued in the courts; in others, she has no redress in case of damage to person, property, or character. In case of divorce on account of adultery in the husband, the innocent wife is held to possess no right to children or property, unless by special decree of the court. But in no State of the Union has the wife the right to her own person, or to any part of the joint earnings of the co-partnership during the life of her husband. In some States women may enter the law schools and practice in the courts; in others they are forbidden. In some universities girls enjoy equal educational advantages with boys, while many of the proudest institutions in the land deny them admittance, though the sons of China, Japan and Africa are welcomed there. But the privileges already granted in the several States are by no means secure. The right of suffrage once exercised by women in certain States and territories has been denied by subsequent legislation. A bill is now pending in congress to disfranchise the women of Utah, thus interfering to deprive United States citizens of the same rights which the Supreme Court has declared the national government powerless to protect anywhere. Laws passed after years of untiring effort, guaranteeing married women certain rights of property, and mothers the custody of their children, have been repealed in States where we supposed all was safe. Thus have our most sacred rights been made the football of legislative caprice, proving that a power which grants as a privilege what by nature is a right, may withhold the same as a penalty when deeming it necessary for its own perpetuation.

Representation of woman has had no place in the nation's thought. Since the incorporation of the thirteen original States, twenty-four have been admitted to the Union, not one of which has recognized woman's right of self-government. On this birthday of our national liberties, July Fourth, 1876, Colorado, like all her elder sisters, comes into the Union with the invidious word "male" in her constitution.

Universal manhood suffrage, by establishing an aristocracy of sex, imposes upon the women of this nation a more absolute and cruel despotism than monarchy; in that, woman finds a political master in her father, husband, brother, son. The aristocracies of the old world are based upon birth, wealth, refinement, education, nobility, brave deeds of chivalry; in this nation, on sex alone; exalting brute force above moral power, vice above virtue, ignorance above education, and the son above the mother who bore him.

The judiciary above the nation has proved itself but the echo of the party in power, by upholding and enforcing laws that are opposed to the spirit and letter of the constitution. When the slave power was dominant, the Supreme Court decided that a black man was not a citizen, because he had not the right to vote; and when the constitution was so amended as to make all persons citizens, the same high tribunal decided that a woman, though a citizen, had not the right to vote. Such vacillating interpretations of constitutional law unsettle our faith in judicial authority, and undermine the liberties of the whole people. . . .

And now, at the close of a hundred years, as the hour-hand of the great clock that marks the centuries points to 1876, we declare our faith in the principles of self-government; our full equality with man in natural rights; that woman was made first for her own happiness, with the absolute right to herself—to all the opportunities and advantages life affords for her complete development; and we deny that dogma of the centuries, incorporated in the codes of all nations—that woman was made for man—her best interests, in all cases, to be sacrificed to his will. We ask of our rulers, at this hour, no special favors, no special privileges, no special legislation. We ask justice, we ask equality, we ask that all the civil and political rights that belong to citizens of the United States, be guaranteed to us and our daughters forever.

Source: Stanton, Anthony, and Gage, HWS, 3: 31–34.

DOCUMENT 65: Letter to Susan B. Anthony (1881)

In the struggle for women's rights, American women have encountered many disappointments. Few documents express their disappointment, pain, and sadness, their sense of betrayal by former friends (liberals, socialists, equal rights groups, and others), better than the following letter to Susan B. Anthony. This letter also exhibits a spirit of determination, conviction about woman's capacity for self-determination, and a resolution to depend on no one but women in the search for equality.

After the question of a free State seemed settled, we who had thought and talked on woman's rights before we came to Kansas, concluded that now was the woman's hour. We determined to strive to obtain Constitutional rights, as they would be more secure than Legislative enactments. On the 13th of February, 1858, we organized the Moneka Woman's Rights Society. There were only twelve of us, but we went to work circulating petitions and writing to every one in the Territory whom we thought would aid us. Our number was afterwards increased to forty; fourteen of them were men. We sent petitions to Territorial Legislatures, Constitutional Conventions, State Legislatures, and Congress. Many of the leading men were advocates of women's rights. Governor Robinson, S. N. Wood, and Erastus Heath, with their wives, were constant and efficient workers. . . .

When the question was submitted in 1867, and the men were to decide whether women should be allowed to vote, we felt very anxious about the result. We strongly desired to make Kansas the banner State for Freedom. We did all we could to secure it, and some of the best speakers from the East came to our aid. Their speeches were excellent, and were listened to by large audiences, who seemed to believe what they heard; but when voting day came, they voted according to their prejudices, and our cause was defeated. . . .

So utterly had the women been deserted in the Kansas campaign by those they had the strongest reason to look to for help, that at times all effort seemed hopeless. The editors of the New York *Tribune* and the *Independent* can never know how wistfully, from day to day, their papers were searched for some inspiring editorials on the woman's amendment, but naught was there; there were no words of hope and encouragement, no eloquent letters from an Eastern man that could be read to the people; all were silent. Yet these two papers, extensively taken all over Kansas, had they been as true to woman as to the negro, could have revolutionized the State. But with arms folded, Greeley, Curtis, Tilton, Beecher, Higginson, Phillips, Garrison, Frederick Douglass, all calmly watched the struggle from afar, and when defeat came to both propositions, no consoling words were offered for woman's loss, but the women who spoke in the campaign were reproached for having "killed negro suffrage."

We wondered then at the general indifference to that first opportunity of realizing what all those gentlemen had advocated so long; and, in looking back over the many intervening years, we still wonder at the stolid incapacity of all men to understand that woman feels the invidious distinctions of sex exactly as the black man does those of color, or the white man the more transient distinctions of wealth, family, position, place, and power; that she feels as keenly as man the injustice of disfranchisement. Of the old abolitionists who stood true to woman's cause in this crisis, Robert Purvis, Parker Pillsbury, and Rev. Samuel J. May were the only Eastern men. Through all the hot debates during the period of reconstruction, again and again, Mr. Purvis arose and declared, that he would rather his son should never be enfranchised, unless his daughter could be also, that, as she bore the double curse of sex and color, on every principle of justice she should first be protected. These were the only men who felt and understood as women themselves do the degradation of disfranchisement. . . .

And here is the secret of the infinite sadness of women of genius; of their dissatisfaction with life, in exact proportion to their development. A woman who occupies the same realm of thought with man, who can explore with him the depths of science, comprehend the steps of progress through the long past and prophesy those of the momentous future, must ever be surprised and aggravated with his assumptions of leadership and superiority, a superiority she never concedes, an authority she

utterly repudiates. Words can not describe the indignation, the humiliation a proud woman feels for her sex in disfranchisement. . . .

It was not from ignorance of the unequal laws, and false public sentiment against woman, that our best men stood silent in this Kansas
campaign; it was not from lack of chivalry that they thundered forth no
protests, when they saw noble women, who had been foremost in every
reform, hounded through the State by foul mouthed politicians; it was
not from lack of money and power, of eloquence of pen and tongue, nor
of an intellectual conviction that our cause was just, that they came not
to the rescue, but because in their heart of hearts they did not grasp the
imperative necessity of woman's demand for that protection which the
ballot alone can give; they did not feel for *her* the degradation of disfranchisement.

The fact of their silence deeply grieved us, but the philosophy of their
indifference we thoroughly comprehended for the first time and saw as
never before, that only from woman's standpoint could the battle be
successfully fought, and victory secured. "It is wonderful," says Swift,
"with what patience some folks can endure the sufferings of others."
Our liberal men counseled us to silence during the war, and we were
silent on our own wrongs; they counseled us again to silence in Kansas
and New York, lest we should defeat "negro suffrage," and threatened
if we were not, we might fight the battle alone. We chose the latter, and
were defeated. But standing alone we learned our power; we repudiated
man's counsels forevermore; and solemnly vowed that there should
never be another season of silence until woman had the same rights
everywhere on this green earth, as man. . . .

We would point for them the moral of our experiences: that woman
must lead the way to her own enfranchisement, and work out her own
salvation with a hopeful courage and determination that knows no fear
nor trembling. She must not put her trust in man in this transition period,
since, while regarded as his subject, his inferior, his slave, their interests
must be antagonistic. . . .

Source: Stanton, Anthony, and Gage, *HWS*, 2: 451.

DOCUMENT 66: "The Relation of the Sexes to Government" (Edward D. Cope, 1888)

Edward D. Cope (1840–1897), an American zoologist and pale-
ontologist, was one of the most accomplished scholars of the nine-

teenth century and published more than 600 works. In this selection he attempts to bring his scientific knowledge and mode of inquiry to bear on the question of gender equality. Reproduced below is his definition of what a scientifically based relationship between government and the sexes ought to be. He argues that women should be excluded from suffrage because their moral development has not evolved to the level of men's. Therefore they cannot impartially enact and apply the law.

As is well known, the diversity of sex is of very ancient origin. It appeared in the history of life before the rise of any but the most rudimental mentality, and has at various points in the line of development of living things displayed itself in the most profound manner. Great peculiarities of sex structure are witnessed in the higher forms of life, as in birds and mammalia. The greatest peculiarity of mental sex character can only be seen where mind is most developed—that is, in man. . . .

In comparing male and female minds, we should take them at their best, and not at their worst. We should take real livers, and not pretenders; that is, persons who exercise their higher faculties, or who live up to their capacities. . . . We find in man a greater *capacity* for rational processes, a capacity which is not always exercised to its full. We find in men a greater capacity for endurance of the activity of the rational faculty. We find in men a greater capacity for work in those departments of intelligence which require mechanical skill of a high order. In the esthetic department we find incapacity more general than in women—certainly in the department of the esthetics of the person. In women we find that the deficiency of endurance of the rational faculty is associated with a general incapacity for mental strain, and, as her emotional nature is stronger, that strain is more severe than it is in man under similar circumstances. Hence the easy breakdown under stress, which is probably the most distinctive feature of the female mind. This peculiarity, when pronounced, becomes the hysterical temperament. But in all departments of mental action that depend on affection or emotion for their excellence, woman is the superior of man; in those departments where affection should not enter, she is his inferior. I think that most of the peculiarities of mind of the sexes may be traced to these first principles. The origin of these leading differences is not difficult to trace to the different functions of the sexes in the family relation, emphasized by repetition throughout the long ages of vertebrate, mammalian, and human history. Beginning with the material instinct, woman has become by constant exercise, a being of affections. . . . We inquire, then, in the first place, Is government a function adapted to the female character, or within the scope of her natural powers? We then endeavor to discover whether her occupation of this field of action is calculated to promote the mutual sex interest which has been referred to above, and thus to subserve the natural evolution of humanity.

In endeavoring to answer the first question we are at once met by the undoubted fact that woman is physically incapable of carrying into execution any law she may enact. She cannot, therefore, be called on to serve in any executive capacity where law is to be executed on adults. Now, service in the support of laws enacted by those who "rule by the consent of the governed" is a *sine qua non* of the right to elect governors. It is a common necessity which all of the male sex are, during most of their lives, liable to be called on to sustain. This consideration alone, it appears to me, puts the propriety of female suffrage out of the question. The situation is such that the sexes cannot take an equal share of governmental responsibilities even if they should desire to do so. . . .

Immunity from service in executing the law would make most women irresponsible voters. But there are other reasons why the questions involved in government are foreign to the thoughts of most women. The characteristics of the female mind have been already described. Most men who have associated much with girls and women remember how many needed lessons they have learned from them in refinement and benevolence; and how they have had, on the other hand, to steel their minds against their aimlessness and pettiness. And from youth to later years they have observed one peculiarity for which no remedy has been yet found, and that is, a pronounced frailty of the rational faculty in thought or action. . . .

On account of their stronger sympathies girls always thinks themselves the moral superiors of boys, who are often singularly devoid of benevolence, especially toward the lower animals. Some women imagine, for this reason, that their entire sex is morally the superior of the male. But a good many women learn to correct this opinion. In departments of morals which depend on the emotional nature, women are the superior; for those which depend on the rational nature, man is the superior. When the balance is struck, I can see no inferiority on either side. But the quality of justice remains with the male. It is on this that men and women must alike depend, and hence it is that women so often prefer to be judged by men rather than by their own sex. They will not gain anything, I believe, by assuming the right of suffrage that they cannot gain without it, and they might meet with serious loss. In serving the principle of "the greatest good of the greatest number," man is constantly called on to disregard the feelings of particular persons, and even to outrage their dearest ties of home and family. Women cannot do this judicially. . . .

In the practical working of woman suffrage, women would either vote in accordance with the views of their husbands and lovers or they would not. Should they do the former habitually, such suffrage becomes a farce, and the only result would be to increase the aggregate number of votes cast. Should women vote in opposition to the men to whom they are bound by ties sentimental or material, unpleasant consequences would sooner or later arise. No man would view with equanimity the spectacle of his wife or daughters nullifying his vote at the polls, or contributing their influence to sustain a policy of government which he should think injurious to his own well-being or that of the community. . . .

Source: M. G. Van Rensselear, ed., *Why Women Do Not Want the Ballot* (N.p.: Privately printed, n.d.), 1–20.

DOCUMENT 67: "Solitude of Self" (Elizabeth Cady Stanton, 1892)

Elizabeth Cady Stanton (see Document 46), in her January 18, 1892, address before the U.S. House Judiciary Committee, eloquently spoke of the essential isolation of the human soul and its need for self-sovereignty to ensure human development and human dignity. This argument supports the spiritual and moral *need* (as distinct from mere desire) for women's equality. The claims of Professor Cope (see Document 66) and others notwithstanding, it is one of the most significant statements of nineteenth century political theory.

Mr. Chairman and gentlemen of the committee:

The point I wish plainly to bring before you on this occasion is the individuality of each human soul; our Protestant idea, the right of individual conscience and judgment—our republican idea, individual citizenship. In discussing the rights of woman, we are to consider, first what belongs to her as an individual, in a world of her own, the arbiter of her own destiny, an imaginary Robinson Crusoe with her woman Friday on a solitary island. Her rights under such circumstances are to use all her faculties for her own safety and happiness.

Secondly, if we consider her as a citizen, as a member of a great nation, she must have the same rights as all other members, according to the fundamental principles of our Government.

Thirdly, viewed as a woman, an equal factor in civilization, her rights and duties are still the same—individual happiness and development.

Fourthly, it is only the incidental relations of life, such as mother, wife, sister, daughter, that may involve some special duties and training. In the usual discussion in regard to woman's sphere, such men as Herbert Spencer, Frederic Harrison, and Grant Allen uniformly subordinate her rights and duties as an individual, as a citizen, as a woman, to the necessities of these incidental relations some of which a large class of women may never assume. In discussing the sphere of man we do not decide his rights as an individual, as a citizen, as a man by his duties as a father, a husband, a brother, or a son, relations some of which he may never fill. Moreover, he would be better fitted for these very relations, and whatever special work he might choose to do to earn his bread, by the complete development of all his faculties as an individual.

Just so with woman. The education that will fit her to discharge the duties in the largest sphere of human usefulness, will best fit her for whatever special work she may be compelled to do.

The isolation of every human soul and the necessity of self-dependence must give each individual the right to choose his own surroundings. The strongest reason for giving woman all the opportunities for higher education, for the full development of her faculties, forces of mind and body; for giving her the most enlarged freedom of thought and action; a complete emancipation from all forms of bondage, of custom, dependence, superstition; from all the crippling influences of fear, is the solitude and personal responsibility of her own individual life. The strongest reason why we ask for woman a voice in the government under which she lives; in the religion she is asked to believe; equality in social life, where she is the chief factor; a place in the trades and professions, where she may earn her bread, is because of her birthright to self-sovereignty; because, as an individual, she must rely on herself. No matter how much women prefer to lean, to be protected and supported, nor how much men desire to have them do so, they must make the voyage of life alone, and for safety in an emergency they must know something of the laws of navigation. To guide our own craft, we must be captain, pilot, engineer; with chart and compass stand at the wheel; watch the wind and waves and know when to take in sail, and read the signs in the firmament over all. It matters not whether the solitary voyager is man or woman. . . .

To appreciate the importance of fitting every human soul for independent action, think for a moment of the immeasurable solitude of self. We come into the world alone, unlike all who have gone before us; we leave it alone under circumstances peculiar to ourselves. No mortal ever has been, no mortal ever will be like the soul just launched on the sea of life. There can never again be just such environments as make up the infancy, youth and manhood of this one. Nature never repeats herself, and the possibilities of one human soul will never be found in another. No one has ever found two blades of grass alike, and no one will ever find two human beings alike. . . .

To throw obstacles in the way of a complete education is like putting out the eyes; to deny the rights of property, like cutting off the hands. To deny political equality is to rob the ostracised of all self-respect; of credit in the market place; of recompense in the world of work; of a voice among those who make and administer the law; a choice in the jury before whom they are tried, and in the judge who decides their punishment. Shakespeare's play of Titus and Andronicus [sic] contains a terrible satire on woman's position in the nineteenth century—"Rude men" (the play tell[s] us) "seized the king's daughter, cut out her tongue, cut off her hands, and then bade her go call for water and wash her hands." What a picture of woman's position. Robbed of her natural rights, handicapped by law and custom at every turn, yet compelled to fight her own battles, and in the emergencies of life to fall back on herself for protection. . . .

How the little courtesies of life on the surface of society, deemed so important from man towards woman, fade into utter insignificance in view of the deeper tragedies in which she must play her part alone, where no human aid is possible. . . .

Nothing strengthens the judgment and quickens the conscience like individual responsibility. Nothing adds such dignity to character as the recognition of one's self-sovereignty; the right to an equal place, every-where conceded; a place earned by personal merit, not an artificial at-tainment, by inheritance, wealth, family, and position. Seeing, then, that the responsibilities of life rest equally on man and woman, that their destiny is the same, they need the same preparation for time and eter-nity. The talk of sheltering woman from the fierce storms of life is the sheerest mockery, for they beat on her from every point of the compass, just as they do on man, and with more fatal results, for he has been trained to protect himself, to resist, to conquer. . . .

Source: Address Delivered Before the United States Congressional Committee on the Judiciary, Monday, January 18, 1892.

DOCUMENT 68: "A Letter on Woman Suffrage from One Woman to Another" (1894)

"A Letter on Woman Suffrage from One Woman to Another" was written to one "M" and signed "H. De K. G." This letter re-peats many of the traditional arguments against women securing the right to vote—their alleged intellectual inferiority, their claimed

difference in habits, mind, and methods of action, and their supposed failure to prove that securing the right to vote will contribute
to their betterment. There is one particular argument that antici-
pates the position of contemporary cultural feminists that the wom-
en's movement should not seek to make women into men; women
may want to be "other."

I began by listening to the old arguments with a sort of dreamy acquiescence. Men and women must be "equal"—it sounds so encouraging! Why should not women have a voice in what concerns them as
much as it does men, and in some things that concern them more than
men? Why indeed? . . .

Men have deliberately taken upon themselves the duties of the state,
finding that by giving every man a voice, without distinction of persons
or property, they got, as they believed, a more just administration of the
laws. Such duties women were exempted from; because the duties imposed on woman by nature kept her secluded part of her life, and were
most burdensome when she was in her prime. . . .

If men have burdened themselves with the state, they have left women
free to be their critics, their intelligent advisors. They have kept them
from all that is coarse and vulgar in politics. How is it that if they have
a real sense of government they have not been more felt?

Educate them so far as you can afford, but not as *men*, not to take the
field shoulder to shoulder with the harder nature, lest, as in the fable of
the earthen and iron pot floating on the stream, the least rough jolting
break the weaker material. The stronger must protect the weaker vessel,
for she is the promise of the future and the precious yet frail vessel in
which the flame of life is carried. Take away from men the task of protection and you cast them back two thousand years,—you make them sav-
ages. Men love the struggle for mastery with one another: it makes them
better, stronger, wiser; if they struggle with women it brutalizes them and
degrades them while it robs women of their especial superiority.

I have not mentioned what as an artist I personally feel to be the
strongest argument of all—to make little men of women is so ugly; to
unsex them, so intensely inartistic. I know all my socialistic friends who
have gone over to this woman-suffrage movement will scoff at the word
art. To them it is a great impertinence that one bud should take it upon
itself to say, "I will not develop into green leaves; I will draw double
nourishment from my stem, and the air, and the sunshine, and I will
become a flower, a lovely, perishable, delicate bloom that all who see
me will love and protect and cherish, and go on their way thanking God
for my blooming." . . .

Source: M. G. Van Rensselaer, ed., *Why Women Do Not Want the Ballot* (N.p.: Privately printed, n.d.), 2–9.

DOCUMENT 69: *The Woman's Bible* (Elizabeth Cady Stanton, 1895)

The spiritual and intellectual genius of Elizabeth Cady Stanton is generally well catalogued. Nowhere was the expression of that genius more insightfully manifested than in her decision to issue a woman's Bible. Because of the traditional Bible's general authority, its pervading influence in civil society, including the family, the school, the church, unions, and political parties, and its abiding impact on the law, the courts, and the executive arm of government, she knew that women would never have a full chance for "self-sovereignty" if the very source of that authority and influence were not changed to reflect the experience of women. Rejecting the view that the Bible is an objective and scientific exegesis, *The Woman's Bible* (1895) is a worthy forerunner of *The Women's Bible Commentary* (1992), edited by Carol A. Newsom and Sharon H. Ringe. Although *The Woman's Bible* was the work of a committee, Stanton wrote the introduction, reproduced below. The National American Woman Suffrage Association, at its twenty-eighth annual convention, held in Washington, D.C., in 1896, passed a resolution disassociating itself from any official connection with *The Woman's Bible*.

From the inauguration of the movement for woman's emancipation the Bible has been used to hold her in the "divinely ordained sphere," prescribed in the Old and New Testaments.

The canon and civil law; church and state; priests and legislators; all political parties and religious denominations have alike taught that woman was made after man, of man, and for man, an inferior being, subject to man. Creeds, codes, Scriptures and statutes, are all based on this ideas. The fashions, forms, ceremonies and customs of society, church ordinances and discipline all grow out of this idea. . . .

The Bible teaches that woman brought sin and death into the world, that she precipitated the fall of the race, that she was arraigned before the judgment seat of Heaven, tried, condemned and sentenced. Marriage for her was to be a condition of bondage, maternity a period of suffering and anguish, and in silence and subjection, she was to play the role of a dependent on man's bounty for all her material wants, and for all the information she might desire on the vital questions of the hour, she was commanded to ask her husband at home. Here is the Bible position of woman summed up.

Those who have the divine insight to translate, transpose and transfigure this mournful object of pity into an exalted, dignified personage, worthy our worship as the mother of the race, are to be congratulated as having a share of the occult mystic power of the eastern Mahatmas.

The plain English to the ordinary mind admits of no such liberal interpretation. The unvarnished texts speak for themselves. The canon law, church ordinances and Scriptures, are homogeneous, and all reflect the same spirit and sentiments.

These familiar texts are quoted by clergymen in their pulpits, by statesmen in the halls of legislation, by lawyers in the courts, and are echoed by the press of all civilized nations, and accepted by woman herself as "The Word of God." So perverted is the religious element in her nature, that with faith and works she is the chief support of the church and clergy; the very powers that make her emancipation impossible. When, in the early part of the Nineteenth Century, women began to protest against their civil and political degradation, they were referred to the Bible for an answer. When they protested against their unequal position in the church, they were referred to the Bible for an answer.

This led to a general and critical study of the Scriptures. Some, having made a fetish of these books and believing them to be the veritable "Word of God," with liberal translations, interpretations, allegories and symbols, glossed over the most objectionable features of the various books and clung to them as divinely inspired. Others, seeing the family resemblance between the Mosaic code, the canon law, and the old English common law, came to the conclusion that all alike emanated from the same source; wholly human in their origin and inspired by the natural love of domination in the historians. Others, bewildered with their doubts and fears, came to no conclusions. While their clergymen told them on the one hand, that they owed all the blessings and freedom, they enjoyed to the Bible, on the other, they said it clearly marked out their circumscribed sphere of action: that the demands for political and civil rights were irreligious, dangerous to the stability of the home, the state and the church. Clerical appeals were circulated from time to time conjuring members of their churches to take no part in the anti-slavery or woman suffrage movements, as they were infidel in their tendencies, undermining the very foundations of society. No wonder the majority of women stood still, and with bowed heads, accepted the situation.

Listening to the varied opinions of women, I have long thought it would be interesting and profitable to get them clearly stated in book form. To this end six years ago I proposed to a committee of women to issue a Woman's Bible, that we might have women's commentaries on women's position in the Old and New Testaments. It was agreed on by several leading women in England and America and the work was begun, but from various causes it has been delayed, until now the idea is received with renewed enthusiasm, and a large committee has been formed, and we hope to complete the work within a year.

Those who have undertaken the labor are desirous to have some Hebrew and Greek scholars, versed in Biblical criticism, to gild our pages with their learning. Several distinguished women have been urged to do so, but they are afraid that their high reputation and scholarly attainments might be compromised by taking part in an enterprise that for a time may prove very unpopular. Hence we may not be able to get help from that class.

Others fear that they might compromise their evangelical faith by affiliating with those of more liberal views, who do not regard the Bible as the "Word of God," but like any other book, to be judged by its merits. If the Bible teaches the equality of Woman, why does the church refuse to ordain women to preach the gospel, to fill the offices of deacons and elders, and to administer the Sacraments, or to admit them as delegates to the Synods, General Assemblies and Conferences of the different denominations? They have never yet invited a woman to join one of their Revising Committees, not tried to mitigate the sentence pronounced on her by changing one count in the indictment served on her in Paradise.

The large number of letters received, highly appreciative of the undertaking, is very encouraging to those who have inaugurated the movement, and indicate a growing self-respect and self-assertion in the women of this generation. But we have the usual array of objectors to meet and answer. One correspondent conjures us to suspend the work, as it is "ridiculous" for "women to attempt the revision of the Scriptures." I wonder if any man wrote to the late revising committee of Divines to stop their work on the ground that it was ridiculous for men to revise the Bible. . . . Others say it is not *politic* to rouse religious opposition. This much-lauded policy is but another word for *cowardice*. How can woman's position be changed from that of a subordinate to an equal, without opposition, without the broadest discussion of all the questions involved in her present degradation? For so far-reaching and momentous a reform as her complete independence, an entire revolution in all existing institutions is inevitable. . . .

To women still believing in the plenary inspiration of the Scriptures, we say give us by all means your exegesis in the light of the higher criticism learned men are now making, and illumine the Woman's Bible, with your inspiration.

Bible historians claim special inspiration for the Old and New Testaments containing most contradictory records of the same events, of miracles opposed to all known laws, of customs that degrade the female sex of all human and animal life, stated in most questionable language that could not be read in a promiscuous assembly, and call all this "The Word of God."

The only points in which I differ from all ecclesiastical teaching is that I do not believe that any man ever saw or talked with God, I do not believe that God inspired the Mosaic code, or told the historians what they say he did about woman, for all the religions on the face of the earth degrade her, and so long as woman accepts the position that they assign her, her emancipation is impossible. Whatever the Bible may be made to do in Hebrew or Greek, in plain English it does not exalt and dignify woman. My standpoint for criticism is the revised edition of 1888. . . .

But the verbal criticism in regard to woman's position amounts to little. The spirit is the same in all periods and languages, hostile to her as an equal. . . .

The canon law, the Scriptures, the creeds and codes and church discipline of the leading religions bear the impress of fallible man, and not of our ideal great first cause, "the Spirit of all Good," that set the universe of matter and mind in motion, and by immutable law holds the land, the sea, the planets, revolving round the great centre of light and heat, each in its own elliptic, with millions of stars in harmony all singing together, the glory of creation forever and ever.

ELIZABETH CADY STANTON

Source: *The Woman's Bible* (New York: European Publishing Co., 1895), 7–13.

DOCUMENT 70: Black and White Women's Clubs— Some Goals (1895)

Club women played an important role and made a significant contribution to women's rights. They espoused domestic feminism, which pursued the extension of what are considered women's natural and domestically nurtured traits into the public sphere. In so doing, they represented a middle ground between those women who were committed or resigned to remaining in the home and those who, like the suffragists, sought the "radical" goal of equality with men. Women's clubs (and clubwomen) did more than provide a middle ground for women. Indeed, in 1914 they endorsed the suffrage movement. The first club, Sorosis, was founded in 1868 in New York, in reaction to the exclusion of women from a New York

Press Club dinner given in honor of Charles Dickens. Angry at this humiliation, women established their own clubs so that they could pursue cultural activities otherwise denied them. While these clubs were initially linked primarily to states, by the 1890s regional and national federations had been formed with a range of activities far beyond what was originally contemplated. Even in areas such as the Midwest where such clubs were late in forming or were unknown, the influence of women's clubs was felt in popular movements such as the Patrons of Husbandry or the Grange.

Women's clubs nurtured the development of art programs and libraries, supported social reforms in child labor and juvenile courts, fought for improvements in wages and factory conditions, and became one of the most forceful advocates of coeducation and academic scholarships for the needy. In addition, the clubs were for many an instrument of formal education, an outlet from the confines of home, and a source from which women gained confidence in their intellectual and other abilities. Document 70A is the statement of purpose adopted by the National Association of Colored Women's Clubs in 1895. Document 70B is an example of a typical program organized by a middle-class white women's club.

A. STATEMENT OF PURPOSE

The reasons why we should confer are so apparent that it would seem hardly necessary to enumerate them, and yet there are none of them but demand our serious consideration. In the first place we need to feel the cheer and inspiration of meeting each other; we need to gain the courage and fresh life that comes from the mingling of congenial souls, of those working for the same end. Next, we need to talk over those things that are of special interest to us as colored women, the training of our children, openings for our boys and girls, how they can be prepared for occupations and occupations may be found that are open for them, what we especially can do in moral education and physical development, the home training that is necessary to give our children in order to prepare them to meet the peculiar conditions in which they shall find themselves, how to make the most of our own, to some extent, limited opportunities. These are some of our own peculiar questions to be discussed. Besides these are the general questions of the day, which we cannot afford to be indifferent to: temperance, morality, the higher education, hygenic and domestic questions. If these things need the serious consideration of women more advantageously placed by reason of all the aid to right thinking and living with which they are surrounded, surely we, with everything to pull us back, to hinder us in developing, need to take every opportunity and means for the thoughtful consideration which shall lead to wise action.

I have left the strongest reason for our conferring together until the last. All over America there is to be found a large and growing class of earnest, intelligent, progressive colored women who, if not leading full, useful lives, are only waiting for the opportunity to do so, many of them still warped and cramped for lack of opportunity, not only to do more, but to be more. . . .

Source: Charles H. Welsley, ed., *The History of the National Association of Colored Women's Clubs: A Legacy of Service* (Washington, D.C.: National Association of Colored Women's Clubs, 1984), 33.

B. SUGGESTED PROGRAMS

OCTOBER	American Citizenship
	1st week—Responsibilities of a Citizen in a Democracy.
	2nd week—Equal Rights for Women Citizens.
	3rd week—Civic Responsibility.
	4th week—World Citizenship.
NOVEMBER	Education
	1st week—Vocational Training.
	2nd week—Religion in Educational Institutions.
	3rd week—Adult Education—Public Forum
	(Stage a forum on public affairs).
	4th week—Character Education in the Schools.
DECEMBER	Fine Arts
	1st week—American Folk Lore—Antiques.
	2nd week—Why Religious Music at This Time?
	3rd week—Latin American Art and Music.
	4th week—Drama in Pageantry depicting American History. Pageants in each club.
JANUARY	American Home
	1st week—Religious Forum—"Why Youth Turns from Religion."
	2nd week—Character Building.
	3rd week—Consumer Problems and Taxation.
	4th week—American Home and Citizenship.

FEBRUARY	International Relations
	1st week—Peace in the New World.
	2nd week—Comparative Governments of the World.
	3rd week—Why a Democracy?
	4th week—Current International Affairs.
MARCH	Public Welfare
	1st week—Public Welfare Institutions. (Have meeting in one of your public institutions.)
	2nd week—Housing Problems.
	3rd week—Killing Diseases—symposium. (Have prominent doctors speak.) Cancer, tuberculosis, syphilis, heart disease, pneumonia.
	4th week—Crime Control and Prevention.
APRIL	Political Science
	1st week—History of Politics in This Country.
	2nd week—Study of Party Set-Up in This Country. (Heads of political parties to speak.)
	3rd week—Issues Before Us—County, City, State, Nation.
	4th week—Departments of the Government— County, City, State, Nation. (Speakers on each subject.)
MAY	Summary
	1st week—Citizenship and International Relations.
	2nd week—Education and American Home.
	3rd week—Fine Arts.
	4th week—Election of Officers and Annual Reports.

Source: Sara A. Whitehurst, *The Twentieth Century Clubwoman: A Handbook for Organization Leaders* (General Federation of Women's Clubs, 1942), 42–43.

DOCUMENT 71: Women's Constitution and Health— Some Interpretations (1870, 1895)

Collaborating in the societal oppression of women was one of the most respected male-dominated professional groups—physicians.

Indeed, much of the evidence that claimed to prove women's physical inferiority came from that group. First, in pursuit of their pecuniary interests, physicians sought to support the claim that women were of a weak, sickly, and delicate nature. Second, by substantiating their claim, physicians sought to advance their professional interests: if women are indeed sickly and delicate, then they cannot compete as professionals in medicine. In Document 71A Dr. W. W. Bliss propounds the widely accepted view of women's feebleness and what we label the "ovarian theory of woman's vocation." Document 71B gives the views of Dr. Mary P. Jacobi (1842–1906), the foremost woman physician in the United States during her day and an intellectual match for any male in her profession.

A. DR. W. W. BLISS

Accepting, then these views of the gigantic power and influence of the ovaries over the whole animal economy of woman,—that they are the most powerful agents in all the commotions of her system; that on them rest her intellectual standing in society, her physical perfection, and all that lends beauty to those fine and delicate contours which are constant objects of admiration, all that is great, noble and beautiful, all that is voluptuous, tender, and endearing; that her fidelity, her devotedness, her perpetual vigilance, forecast, and all those qualities of mind and disposition which inspire respect and love and fit her as the safest counsellor and friend of man, spring from the ovaries,—*what must be their influence and power over the great vocation of woman and the august purposes of her existence when these organs have become compromised through disease!* Can the record of woman's mission on earth be otherwise than filled with tales of sorrow, sufferings, and manifold infirmities, all through the influence of these important organs?

B. DR. MARY P. JACOBI

... it is considered natural and almost laudable to break down under all conceivable varieties of strain—a winter dissipation, a houseful of servants, a quarrel with a female friend, not to speak of more legitimate reasons. ... Women who expect to go to bed every menstrual period expect to collapse if by chance they find themselves on their feet for a few hours during such a crisis. Constantly considering their nerves, urged to consider them by well-intentioned but short-sighted advisors, they pretty soon become nothing but a bundle of nerves.

... I think, finally, it is in the increased attention paid to women, and especially in their new function as lucrative patients, scarcely imagined a hundred years ago, that we find explanation for much of the ill-health among women, freshly discovered today.

Source: Barbara Ehrenreich and Deidre English, *Complaints and Disorders: The Sexual Politics of Sickness* (Old Westbury, N.Y.: Feminist Press, 1974), 19, 25, 29.

DOCUMENT 72: *Women and Economics* (Charlotte Perkins Gilman, 1898)

Charlotte Perkins Gilman (1860–1935), one of the most widely read women of her day, preferred to be known as a sociologist or a human rights advocate rather than as a feminist. Her commitment to equal rights for women, however, was unmistakable. In her book, *Women and Economics*, published in 1898, she argued with exemplary originality that the main barrier to women's social progress was not political—as many suffragists contended—but economic. In so doing, she focused on a fundamental theme in Western political tradition: the exclusion of women from political initiatives because they were defined, like children and slaves, as dependent. The character of that dependence, said Gilman, was economic. She went further, joining those who called for the "right to labor"— meaning that women had a right to have their labor recognized and *diversified*. For Gilman, diversification, in all spheres of human possibilities, was critical for the growth and development of women, whom she saw as stunted in their overspecialized role of sex partners and mothers.

The economic status of the human race in any nation, at any time, is governed mainly by the activities of the male: the female obtains her share in the racial advance only through him.

Studied individually, the facts are even more plainly visible, more open and familiar. From the day laborer to the millionaire, the wife's worn dress or flashing jewels, her low roof or her lordly one, her weary feet or her rich equipage,—these speak of the economic ability of the husband. The comfort, the luxury, the necessities of life itself, which the woman receives, are obtained by the husband, and given her by him.

And, when the woman, left alone with no man to "support" her, tries to meet her own economic necessities, the difficulties which confront her prove conclusively what the general economic status of the woman is. None can deny these patent facts,—that the economic status of women generally depends upon that of men generally, and that the economic status of women individually depends upon that of men individually, those men to whom they are related. But we are instantly confronted by the commonly received opinion that, although it must be admitted that men make and distribute the wealth of the world, yet women earn their share of it as wives. This assumes either that the husband is in the position of employer and the wife as employee, or that marriage is a "partnership," and the wife an equal factor with the husband in producing wealth.

Economic independence is a relative condition at best. In the broadest sense, all living things are economically dependent upon others,—the animals upon the vegetables, and man upon both. In a narrower sense, all social life is economically interdependent, man producing collectively what he could by no possibility produce separately. But, in the closest interpretation, individual economic independence among human beings means that the individual pays for what he gets, works for what he gets, gives to the other an equivalent for what the other gives him. I depend on the shoemaker for shoes, and the tailor for coats; but, if I give the shoemaker and the tailor enough of my own labor as a house-builder to pay for the shoes and coats they give me, I retain my personal independence. I have not taken of their product, and given nothing of mine. As long as what I get is obtained by what I give, I am economically independent.

Women consume economic goods. What economic product do they give in exchange for what they consume? The claim that marriage is a partnership, in which the two persons married produce wealth which neither of them, separately, could produce, will not bear examination. A man happy and comfortable can produce more than one unhappy and uncomfortable, but this is as true of a father or son as of a husband. To take from a man any of the conditions which make him happy and strong is to cripple his industry, generally speaking. But those relatives who make him happy are not therefore his business partners, and entitled to share his income.

Grateful return for happiness conferred is not the method of exchange in a partnership. The comfort a man takes with his wife is not in the nature of a business partnership, nor are her frugality and industry. A housekeeper, in her place, might be as frugal, as industrious, but would not therefore be a partner. Man and wife are partners truly in their mutual obligation to their children,—their common love, duty, and service. But a manufacturer who marries, or a doctor, or a lawyer, does not take a partner in his business, when he takes a partner in parenthood, unless his wife is also a manufacturer, a doctor, or a lawyer. In his business, she cannot even advise wisely without training and experience. To love her husband, the composer, does not enable her to compose; and the loss of a man's wife, though it may break his heart, does not cripple his business, unless his mind is affected by grief. She is in no sense a business partner, unless she contributes capital or experience or labor, as a man would in like relation. Most men would hesitate very seriously before entering a business partnership with any woman, wife or not.

If the wife is not, then, truly a business partner, in what way does she earn from her husband the food, clothing, and shelter she receives at his hands? By house service, it will be instantly replied. This is the general misty idea upon the subject,—that women earn all they get, and more, by house service. Here we come to a very practical and definite economic ground. Although not producers of wealth, women serve in the final processes of preparation and distribution. Their labor in the household has a genuine economic value.

For a certain percentage of persons to serve other persons, in order that the ones so served may produce more, is a contribution not to be overlooked. The labor of women in the house, certainly, enables men to produce more wealth than they otherwise could; and in this way women are economic factors in society. But so are horses. The labor of horses enables men to produce more wealth than they otherwise could. The horse is an economic factor in society. But the horse is not economically independent, nor is the woman. If a man plus a valet can perform more useful service than he could minus a valet, then the valet is performing useful service. But, if the valet is the property of the man, is obliged to perform this service, and is not paid for it, he is not economically independent.

The labor which the wife performs in the household is given as part of her functional duty, not as employment. The wife of the poor man, who works hard in a small house, doing all the work for the family, or the wife of the rich man, who wisely and gracefully manages a large house and administers its functions, each is entitled to fair pay for services rendered. . . .

But the salient fact in this discussion is that, whatever the economic value of the domestic industry of women is, they do not get it. The women who do the most work get the least money, and the women who have the most money do the least work. Their labor is neither given nor taken as a factor in economic exchange. It is held to be their duty as women to do this work; and their economic status bears no relation to their domestic labors, unless an inverse one. Moreover, if they were thus fairly paid,—given what they earned, and no more,—all women working in this way would be reduced to the economic status of the house servant. Few women—or men either—care to face this condition. The ground that women earn their living by domestic labor is instantly forsaken, and we are told that they obtain their livelihood as mothers. This is a peculiar position. We speak of it commonly enough, and often with deep feeling, but without due analysis.

In treating of an economic exchange, asking what return in goods or labor women make for the goods and labor given them,—either to the race collectively or to their husbands individually,—what payment women make for their clothes and shoes and furniture and food and shelter, we are told that the duties and services of the mother entitle her to support.

If this is so, if motherhood is an exchangeable commodity given by women in payment for clothes and food, then we must of course find some relation between the quantity or quality of the motherhood and the quantity and quality of the pay. This being true, then the women who are not mothers have no economic status at all; and the economic status of those who are must be shown to be relative to their motherhood. This is obviously absurd. The childless wife has as much money as the mother of many,—more; for the children of the latter consume what would otherwise be hers; and the inefficient mother is no less provided for than the efficient one. Visibly, and upon the face of it, women are not maintained in economic prosperity proportioned to their motherhood. Motherhood bears no relation to their economic status. . . .

Driven off these alleged grounds of women's economic independence; shown that women, as a class, neither produce nor distribute wealth; that women, as individuals, labor mainly as house servants, are not paid as such, and would not be satisfied with such an economic status if they were so paid; that wives are not business partners or co-producers of wealth with their husbands, unless they actually practice the same profession; that they are not salaried as mothers, and that it would be unspeakably degrading if they were,—what remains to those who deny that women are supported by men? This (and a most amusing position it is),—that the function of maternity unfits a woman for economic production, and, therefore, it is right that she should be supported by her husband. . . .

Is this the condition of human motherhood? Does the human mother, by her motherhood, thereby lose control of brain and body, lose power and skill and desire for any other work? Do we see before us the human race, with all its females segregated entirely to the uses of motherhood, consecrated, set apart, specially developed, spending every power of their nature on the service of their children?

We do not. We see the human mother worked far harder than a mare, laboring her life long in the service not of her children only, but of men;

husbands, brothers, fathers, whatever male relatives she has; for mother and sister also; for the church a little, if she is allowed; for society, if she is able; for charity and education and reform,—working in many ways that are not the ways of motherhood.

It is not motherhood that keeps the housewife on her feet from dawn till dark; it is house service not child service. Women work longer and harder than most men, and not solely in maternal duties. . . .

In spite of her supposed segregation to maternal duties, the human female, the world over, works at extra-maternal duties for hours enough to provide her with an independent living, and the is denied independence on the ground that motherhood prevents her working! . . .

The human animal manifests an excess in sex-attraction which not only injures the race through its morbid action on the natural processes of reproduction, but which injures the happiness of the individual through its morbid reaction on his own desires.

What is the cause of this excessive sex-attraction in the human species? The immediately acting cause of sex-attracting is sex-distinction. . . .

When, then, it can be shown that sex-distinction in the human race is so excessive as not only to affect injuriously its own purposes, but to check and pervert the progress of the race, it becomes a matter for most serious consideration. Nothing could be more inevitable, however, under our sexuo-economic relation. By the economic dependence of the human female upon the male, the balance of forces is altered. Natural selection no longer checks the action of sexual selection, but co-operates with it. Where both sexes obtain their food through the same exertions, from the same sources, under the same conditions, both sexes are acted upon alike, and developed alike by their environment. Where the two sexes obtain their food under different conditions, and where that difference consists in one of them being fed by the other, then the feeding sex becomes the environment of the fed. Man, in supporting woman, has become her economic environment. Under natural selection, every creature is modified to its environment, developing perforce the qualities needed to obtain its livelihood under that environment. Man, as the feeder of woman, becomes the strongest modifying force in her economic condition. Under sexual selection the human creature is of course modified to its mate, as with all creatures. When the mate becomes also the master, when economic necessity is added to sex-attraction, we have the two great evolutionary forces acting together to the same end; namely, to develope [sic] sex-distinction in the human female. For, in her position of economic dependence in the sex-relation, sex-distinction is with her not only a means of attracting a mate, as with all creatures, but a means of getting her livelihood, as is the case with no other creature under heaven. Because of the economic dependence of the human female on her mate, she is modified to sex to an excessive degree. This excessive modification she transmits to her children; and so is steadily implanted in the human constitution the morbid tendency to excess in this relation, which has acted so universally upon us in all ages, in spite of our best efforts to restrain it. It is not the normal sex-tendency, common to all creatures, but an abnormal sex-tendency, produced and maintained by the abnormal economic relation which makes one sex get its living from the other by the exercise of sex-functions. This is the immediate effect upon individuals of the peculiar sexuo-economic relation which obtains among us.

The evolution of organic life goes on in geometrical progression: cells combine, and form organs; organs combine, and form organisms; organisms combine, and form organizations. Society is an organization. Society is the fourth power of the cell. . . .

In the industrial evolution of the human race, that marvellous and subtle drawing out and interlocking of special functions which constitute the organic life of society, we find that production and consumption go hand in hand; and production comes first. One cannot consume what has not been produced. Economic production is the natural expression of human energy,—not sex-energy at all, but race-energy,—the unconscious functioning of the social organism. Socially organized human beings tend to produce, as a gland to secrete: it is the essential nature of the relation. The creative impulse, the desire to make, to express the inner thought in outer form, "just for the work's sake, no use at all i' the work!" this is the distinguishing character of humanity. "I want to mark!" cries the child, demanding the pencil. He does not want to eat. He wants to mark. He is not seeking to get something into himself, but to put something out of himself. He generally wants to do whatever he sees done,—to make pie-crust or to make shavings, as it happens. The pie he may eat, the shavings not; but he likes to make both. This is the natural process of production, and is followed by the natural process of consumption, where practicable. But consumption is not the main end, the governing force. Under this organic social law, working naturally, we have the evolution of those arts and crafts in the exercise of which consists our human living, and on the product of which we live. So does society evolve within itself—secrete as it were—the social structure with all its complex machinery; and we function therein as naturally as so many glands, other things being equal.

But other things are not equal. Half the human race is denied free productive expression, is forced to confine its productive human energies to the same channels as its reproductive sex-energies. Its creative skill is confined to the level of immediate personal bodily service, to the making of clothes and preparing of food for individuals. No social service is possible. While its power of production is checked, its power of consumption is inordinately increased by the showering upon it of the "unearned increment" of masculine gifts. For the woman there is, first, no free production allowed; and, second, no relation maintained between what she does produce and what she consumes. She is forbidden to make, but encouraged to take. Her industry is not the natural output of creative energy, not the work she does because she has the inner power and strength to do it; nor is her industry even the measure of her gain. She has, of course, the natural desire to consume; and to that is set no bar save the capacity or the will of her husband.

Source: Charlotte P. Gilman, *Women and Economics*, ed. Carl Degler (New York: Harper and Row, 1966), 1–145.

DOCUMENT 73: *Muller v. Oregon* (1908)

In *Lockner v. New York* (1905), the Supreme Court ruled unconstitutional a New York law that set at ten the maximum number of hours individuals—both men and women—could work per day in bakeries. (The law also set a maximum of sixty hours per week.) The Court held that the law violated the liberty of contract. Three years later, in *Muller v. Oregon* (1908), the Court examined the constitutionality of an Oregon law that prohibited employment of women in any mechanical establishment, factory, or laundry. Muller, a laundry owner convicted for violating the law, appealed. In spite of the Lockner precedent, the Supreme Court, reflecting the then prevalent ideology about women's physical weakness and inferiority, upheld the Oregon law. Following is an excerpt from the Court's decision.

That woman's physical structure and the performance of maternal functions place her at a disadvantage in the struggle for subsistence is obvious. This is especially true when the burdens of motherhood are upon her. Even when they are not, by abundant testimony of the medical fraternity continuance for a long time on her feet at work, repeating this from day to day, tends to injurious effects upon the body, and as healthy mothers are essential to vigorous offspring, the physical well-being of woman becomes an object of public interest and care in order to preserve the strength and vigor of the race.

Still again, history discloses the fact that woman has always been dependent upon man. He established his control at the outset by superior physical strength, and this control in various forms, with diminishing intensity, has continued to the present. As minors, though not to the same extent, she has been looked upon in the courts as needing especial care that her rights may be preserved. Education was long denied her, and while now the doors of the school room are opened and her opportunities for acquiring knowledge are great, yet even with that and the consequent increase of capacity for business affairs it is still true that in the struggle for subsistence she is not an equal competitor with her brother. Though limitations upon personal and contractual rights may be removed by legislation, there is that in her disposition and habits of life which will operate against a full assertion of those rights. She will still be where some legislation to protect her seems necessary to secure a real equality of right. Doubtless there are individual exceptions, and there are many respects in which she has an advantage over him; but looking at it from the viewpoint of the effort to maintain an independent position in life, she is not upon an equality. Differentiated by these matters from the other sex, she is properly placed in a class by herself, and legislation designed for her protection may be sustained, even when like legislation is not necessary for men and could not be sustained. It is impossible to close one's eyes to the fact that she still looks to her brother and depends upon him. Even though all restrictions on political, personal and contractual rights were taken away, and she stood, so far as statutes are concerned, upon an absolutely equal plane with him, it would still be true that she is so constituted that she will rest upon and look to him for protection; that her physical structure and a proper discharge of her maternal functions—having in view not merely her own health, but the well-being of the race—justify legislation to protect her from the greed as well as the passion of man. The limitations which this statute places upon her contractual powers, upon her right to agree with her employer as to the time she shall labor, are not imposed solely for her benefit, but also largely for the benefit of all. Many words cannot make this plainer. The two sexes differ in structure of body, in the functions to be performed by each, in the amount of physical strength, in the capacity for long-continued labor, particularly when done standing, the influence of vigorous health upon the future well-being of the race, the self-reliance which enables one to assert full rights, and in the capacity to maintain the struggle for subsistence. This difference justifies a difference in legislation and upholds that which is designed to compensate for some of the burdens which rest upon her.

We have not referred in this discussion to the denial of the elective franchise in the State of Oregon, for while it may disclose a lack of political equality in all things with her brother, that is not of itself decisive. The reason runs deeper, and rests in the inherent difference between the two sexes, and in the different functions in life which they perform.

Source: 208 U.S. 421 (1908).

DOCUMENT 74: Reactions to Socialists' Position on Women's Rights (1907)

Conflicts within the American socialist movement over women's suffrage (see Document 63) became more vocal at the beginning of the twentieth century. Some factions wanted women to cast their lot with the socialists, in the belief that revolutionary victory for the working class would automatically liberate women. Others wanted more specific commitment to the rights of women. At the Stuttgart Congress of the Second International in 1907, a resolution was passed explicitly instructing socialist women not to make common cause with suffragists. Two resolutions to the conflict by leaders in the American women's rights movement follow: "The Socialist and the Suffragist," by Charlotte P. Gilman (see Document 74A), and comments by Carrie Chapman Catt (1859–1947), who accepted the appropriateness of women pursuing different approaches to their liberation. She was suspicious, however, about subordinating the cause of women's rights to any other.

A. CHARLOTTE P. GILMAN

The Socialist and the Suffragist

Said the Socialist to the Suffragist:
"My cause is greater than yours!
You only work for a Special Class,
We for the gain of the General Mass.
Which every good ensures!"

Said the Suffragist to the Socialist:
"You underrate my Cause!
While women remain a Subject Class,
You never can move the General Mass.
With your Economic Laws!"

The world awoke, and tartly spoke:
"Your work is all the same;
Work together or work apart,
Work, each of you, with all your heart—
Just get into the game!"

B. CARRIE CHAPMAN CATT

Others parties before now have invited women to withdraw from regular suffrage organizations and to labor for the party only. Women have listened and followed the command only to find that they have been employed as mere catspaws to pull appetizing chestnuts from the fire, which others ate, while burnt fingers were their only reward. In the United States, Greenback, Populist, Prohibition and Socialist parties furnish good examples of this proceeding. History has so often repeated itself along this line that I, for one, have grown skeptical. . . . Our movement is destined to end in victory, but we are not permitted to know the agencies which may be employed to bring it about.

Source: Mari Jo Buhle, *Women and American Socialism, 1870–1920* (Urbana: University of Illinois Press, 1981), 71.

DOCUMENT 75: *The Lady* (Emily James Putnam, 1910)

Emily James Putnam (1865–1944) was a beneficiary of the fruits of earlier feminist activism. A classics scholar specializing in ancient Greek, she was a member of the first graduating class of Bryn Mawr (opened in 1885), did postgraduate work at Cambridge University in England, and became the first dean of Barnard College in New York City. In 1910 she published *The Lady*, which analyzes the special position of upper-class women from early Greek civilization to nineteenth century America, focusing on their important cultural contributions to the West but also on their dependence and, hence, on their disturbing complicity in the oppression of other women. In her conclusion, she saw the lady, a social construct, as becoming obsolete. An excerpt from the Introduction to *The Lady* follows.

The lady is proverbial for her skill in eluding definition, and it is far from the intention of the writer to profess to say what she is in essence. For the purpose of the present discussion she may be described merely as the female of the favoured social class. The sketches in this volume aim to suggest in outline the theories that various typical societies have entertained of the lady; to note the changing ideals that she has from time to time proposed to herself; to show in some measure what her daily life has been like, what sort of education she has had, what sort of man she has preferred to marry; in short, what manner of terms she has contrived to make with the very special conditions of her existence. Such an attempt, like every other inquiry into the history of European ideas, must begin with an examination of the Greeks. The lover of Greek literature knows it to be full of the portraits of strong and graceful women who were also great ladies. On the other hand the student of Greek history is aware that during the great period of the bloom of Athens the women of the upper classes were in eclipse. . . .

The difference between the feminism of the Greek in literature, art and social science, and his anti-feminist practice cannot be explained away, but a near view of some of its aspects throws light both forward and backward upon the history of the lady. At Rome she becomes thoroughly intelligible to us. The society in which she lived there is very similar in essentials to that of our own day. We see the Roman lady helping to evolve a manner of life so familiar now that it is difficult to think it began so relatively late in the history of Europe and is not the way people have always lived. But if it is hard to realise the novelty in Roman times of a free, luxurious, mixed society in a great centre, it is even harder to picture its eclipse. The dark age put the lady back where Homer knew her; instead of a social creature she became again a lonely one, supported by the strong hand, kept safe from her enemies behind thick walls, and as the price of safety, having but few friends. We have glimpses in Greek tradition of the lady in insurrection, refusing the restraint of the patriarchal family. In the dark age the insurgent Germanic lady makes her appearance, and by the oddest of paradoxes finds freedom in the cloister. The lady abbess is in some sort the descendant of the amazon.

The dying-out of violence and the consequent increase of comfort in private life, brought the lady once more into the stream of human intercourse. The movement called the Renaissance valued her as the most precious object of art, the chosen vessel of that visible beauty which men deemed divine. As conventional social life was organised in the sixteenth, the seventeenth and the eighteenth centuries, the lady's position became one of very great strength, reaching its climax in the career of the salonière. The great social changes that began to prevail at the end of the eighteenth century had a corresponding effect on the status of the lady and their work is not yet complete. In the United States during the two generations preceding the war for the union, the Slave States furnished the background for perhaps the last example the world will see on a large scale of the feudal lady. But the typical lady everywhere tends to the feudal habit of mind. In contemporary society she is an archaism, and can hardly understand herself unless she knows her own history.

Every discussion of the status of woman is complicated by the existence of the lady. She overshadows the rest of her sex. The gentleman has never been an analogous phenomenon, for even in countries and times where he has occupied the centre of the stage he has done so chiefly by virtue of his qualities as a man. A line of gentlemen always implies a man as its origin, and cannot indeed perpetuate itself for long without at least occasional lapses into manhood. Moreover the gentleman, in the worst sense of the term, is numerically negligible. The lady, on the other hand, has until lately very nearly covered the surface of womanhood. She even occurs in great numbers in societies where the gentleman is an exception; and in societies like the feudal where ladies and gentlemen are usually found in pairs, she soars so far above her mate in the development of the qualities they have in common that he sinks back relatively into the plane of ordinary humanity. She is immediately recognized by everyone when any social spectrum is analysed. She is an anomaly to which the western nations of this planet have grown accustomed but which would require a great deal of explanation before a Martian could understand her. Economically she is supported by the toil of others; but while this is equally true of other classes of society, the oddity in her case consists in the acquiescence of those most concerned. The lady herself feels no uneasiness in her equivocal situation, and the toilers who support her do so with enthusiasm. She is not a producer; in most communities productive labour is by consent unladylike. On the other hand she is the heaviest of consumers, and theorists have not been wanting to maintain that the more she spends the better off society is. In aristocratic societies she is required for dynastic reasons to produce offspring, but in democratic societies even this demand is often waived. Under the law she is a privileged character. If it is difficult to hang a gentleman-murderer, it is virtually impossible to hang a lady. Plays like The Doll's House and The Thief show how clearly the lady-forger or burglar should be differentiated from other criminals. Socially she is in general the product and the beneficiary of monogamy. ... The true lady is in theory either a virgin or a lawful wife. Religion has given the lady perhaps her strongest hold. Historically it is the source of much of her prestige, and it has at times helped her to break her tabu and revert to womanhood. Her roots are nourished by its good soil and its bad. Enthusiasm, mysticism, renunciation, find her ready. On the other hand the anti-social forces of religion are embodied in her; she can renounce the world more easily than she can identify herself with it. A lady may become a nun in the strictest and poorest order without altering her view of life, without the moral convulsion, the destruction of false ideas, the birth of character that would be the preliminary steps toward becoming an efficient stenographer. Sentimentally the lady has established herself as the criterion of a community's civilisation. Very dear to her is the observance that hedges her about. In some subtle way it is so bound up with her self-respect and with her respect for the man who maintains it, that life would hardly be sweet to her without it. When it is flatly put to her that she cannot become a human being and yet retain her privileges as a non-combatant, she often enough decides for etiquette.

The product of many cross-impulses, exempt apparently in many cases from the action of economic law, of natural law and of the law of the land, the lady is almost the only picturesque survival in a social order which tends less and less to tolerate the exceptional. Her history is distinct from that of woman though sometimes advancing by means of it, as a railway may help itself from one point to another by leasing an independent line. At all striking periods of social development her status has its significance. In the age-long war between men and women, she is a hostage in the enemy's camp. Her fortunes do not rise and fall with those of women but with those of men. . . .

It would be interesting to note if we could the stages by which, through the accumulation of property and through the man's aesthetic development and his snobbish impulses acting in harmony, he came to feel that it was more desirable to have an idle than a working wife. The idle wife ranked with the ornamentally wrought weapon and with the splendid offering to the gods as a measure of the man's power to waste, and therefore his superiority over other men. Her idleness did not come all at once. One by one the more arduous tasks were dropped that made her less constant or less agreeable in unremitting personal attendance on her lord. The work that remained was generally such as could be performed within the house. Here we find her when history dawns, a complete lady, presiding over inferior wives and slaves, performing work herself, for the spirit of workmanship is ineradicable within her, but tending to produce by preference the useless for the sake of its social and economic significance. As is the case with any other object of art, her uselessness is her use.

Source: Emily James Putnam, *The Lady*, with foreword by Jeannette Misrky (Chicago: University of Chicago Press, 1970), xxvii–xli.

DOCUMENT 76: *History of Women in Industry in the United States* (1910)

By the first decade of the twentieth century, many feminists had begun to argue that economic dependence was the root of women's powerlessness and oppression (see Document 72). Industrial work was seen to offer some degree of economic independence and to promise a cure for social ills affecting women. But in actuality industry enslaved women further: long and exhausting hours of labor, low wages, unstable economic conditions, the absence of job benefits, and changes in technology—especially for those with limited skills—generally reduced women to material poverty. Far from conferring economic independence, industrial labor induced further dependence and humiliation. Prostitution and physical abuse grew in proportion to that dependence. In 1908 Congress authorized an investigation into the conditions of working women. That study, *Women and Child Wage-Earners in the United States* (19 volumes) was completed in 1911. Reproduced below are excerpts from Volume 9, entitled *History of Women in Industry in the United States.*

The history of women in industry in the United States is the story of a great industrial readjustment, which has not only carried woman's work from the home to the factory, but has changed its economic character from unpaid production for home consumption to gainful employment in the manufacture of articles for sale. Women have always worked, and their work has probably always been quite as important a factor in the total economy of society as it is to-day. But during the nineteenth century a transformation occurred in their economic position and in the character and conditions of their work. Their unpaid services have been transformed into paid services, their work has been removed from the home to the factory and workshop, their range of possible employment has been increased and at the same time their monopoly of their traditional occupations has been destroyed. The individuality of their work has been lost in a standardized product.

The story of woman's work in gainful employments is a story of constant changes or shiftings of work and workshop, accompanied by long hours, low wages, unsanitary conditions, overwork, and the want on the part of the woman of training, skill, and vital interest in her work. It is a story of monotonous machine labor, of division and subdivision of tasks until the woman, like the traditional tailor who is called the ninth part of a man, is merely a fraction, and that rarely as much even as a tenth part, of an artisan. It is a story, moreover, of underbidding, of strike breaking, of the lowering of standards for men breadwinners.

In certain industries and certain localities women's unions have raised the standard of wages. The opening of industrial schools and business colleges, too, though affecting almost exclusively the occupations entered by the daughters of middle-class families who have only recently begun to pass from home work to the industrial field, has at least enabled these few girls to keep from further swelling the vast numbers of the unskilled. The evil of long hours and in certain cases other conditions which lead to overstrain, such as the constant standing of saleswomen, have been made the subject of legislation. The decrease of strain due to shorter hours has, however, been in part nullified by increased speed of machinery and other devices designed to obtain the greatest possible amount of labor from each woman. Nevertheless, the history of woman's work in this country shows that legislation has been the only force which has improved the working conditions of any large number of women wage-earners. Aside from the little improvement that has been effected in the lot of working women, the most surprising fact brought out in this study is the long period of time through which large numbers of women have worked under conditions which have involved not only great hardships to themselves but shocking waste to the community.

Changes in Occupations of Women

The transfer of women from nonwage-earning home work to gainful occupations is evident to the most superficial observer, and it is well known that most of this transfer has been effected since the beginning of the nineteenth century. In 1870 it was found that 14.7 per cent of the female population 16 years of age and over were breadwinners, and by 1900 the percentage was 20.6 per cent. During the period for which statistics exist, moreover, the movement toward the increased employment of women in gainful pursuits was clear and distinct in all sections of the country and was even more marked among the native-born than among the foreign-born. It must be borne in mind, however, that even in colonial days there were many women who worked for wages, especially at spinning, weaving, the sewing trades, and domestic service. Many women, too, carried on business on their own account in the textile and sewing trades and also in such industries as the making of blackberry brandy. The wage labor of women is as old as the country itself and has merely increased in importance. The amount, however, of unremunerated home work performed by women must still be considerably larger than the amount of gainful labor, for even in 1900 only about one-fifth of the women 16 years of age and over were breadwinners.

Along with the decrease in the importance of unremunerated home labor and the increase in the importance of wage labor has gone a considerable amount of shifting of occupations. Under the old domestic system the work of the woman was to spin, to do a large part of the weaving, to sew, to knit; in general, to make most of the clothing worn by the family, to embroider tapestry in the days and regions where there was time for art, to cook, to brew ale and wine, to clean, and to perform the other duties of the domestic servant. These things women have always done. But machines have now come in to aid in all these industries—machines which in some cases have brought in their train men operatives and in other cases have enormously increased the productive power of the individual and have made it necessary for many women, who under the old régime, like Priscilla, would have calmly sat by the window spinning, to hunt other work. One kind of spinning is now done by men only. Men tailors make every year thousands of women's suits. Men dressmakers and even milliners are common. . . .

Before the introduction of spinning machinery and the sewing machine the supply of female labor appears never to have been excessive. But the spinning jenny threw out of employment thousands of "spinsters," who were obliged to resort to sewing as the only other occupation to which they were in any way trained. This accounts for the terrible pressure in the clothing trades during the early decades of the nineteenth century. Later on, before any readjustment of women's work had been effected, the sewing machine was introduced, which enormously increased the pressure of competition among women workers. Shortly after the substitution of machinery for the spinning wheel the women of certain localities in Massachusetts found an outlet in binding shoes—an opportunity opened to them by the division of labor and by the development of the ready-made trade. But when the sewing machine was introduced this field, at least for a time, was again contracted. Under this pressure, combined with the rapid development of wholesale industry and division of labor, women have been pressed into other industries, almost invariably in the first instance into the least skilled and most poorly paid occupations. This has gone on until there is now scarcely an industry which does not employ women. Thus woman's sphere has expanded, and its former boundaries can now be determined only by observing the degree of popular condemnation which follows their employment in particular industries.

Attitude of the Public Toward the Employment of Women

The attitude of the public toward the employment of women has, indeed, made their progress into gainful occupations slow and difficult, and has greatly aggravated the adjustment pains which the industrial revolution has forced upon woman as compared with those of man, whose traditional sphere is bounded only by the humanly possible. This attitude has, moreover, been an important factor in determining the woman's choice of occupations. . . .

Causes of the Entrance of Women into Industry

Machinery, combined with division of labor and the substitution of water, steam, and electric power for human muscles, has certainly made it possible to employ the unskilled labor of women in occupations formerly carried on wholly by men. Machinery, however, has as yet affected only slightly the broad lines of division between woman's work and man's work. And especially upon its first introduction the sex of the employees is rarely at once changed to any considerable extent. Thus when spinning machinery was first introduced women and children were employed to operate it. Later women became the power-loom weavers. The sewing machine, too, has always been operated largely by women. On the other hand, most of the machinery of the iron and steel industry is operated by men. . . .

Division of labor, indeed, which has always accompanied and frequently preceded machinery, is probably even more responsible than the latter for the introduction of women into new occupations. The most striking single tendency in manufacturing industries has been toward the division and the subdivision of processes, thereby making possible the use of woman's work, as well as of unskilled man's work, in larger proportion to that of skilled operatives. A more recent tendency toward the combination of several machines into one has even been checked, in some cases, because a competent machinist would have to be hired. Unless the advantage of the complicated mechanism is very great, in many industries simpler machinery, which can be easily run by women, is preferred.

As a result, both of machinery and of division of labor, the actual occupations of women, within industries, do not differ so widely as do the occupations of men within the same industries. It frequently happens, indeed, that the work of a woman in one industry is almost precisely the same as that of another woman in an entirely different industry.

Other historical forces have brought about changes in the occupations of women. Often, especially in the printing trades and in cigar making, women have been introduced as strike breakers. On the other hand trade unions have in some places been strong enough to prevent the introduction of women in industries to which they were well adapted. Usually, however, this has been only for a short period.

The scarcity of labor supply in particular places or at particular times has often been responsible for the use of women's work. Thus during the early years of the Republic the employment of women in manufacturing industries was doubtless greatly accelerated by the scarcity and high price of other labor. This, too, was doubtless largely responsible for the fact that, in the early years of the cotton industry, a larger proportion of women was employed in the cotton mills of Massachusetts and New Hampshire than in those of Rhode Island, New Jersey, and Pennsylvania. One of the remedies frequently suggested in the thirties and forties for the evils under which working women suffered was that "the excess of spinsters" should be transported to the places where "there is a deficiency of women."

The Civil War was another force which not only drove into gainful occupations a large number of women, but compelled many changes in their employments. In 1869 it was estimated that there were 25,000 working women in Boston who had been forced by the war to earn their living. The war, too, caused a large number of cotton factories to shut down, and thousands of women thus thrown out of employment were obliged to seek other occupations.

Similar to war in its influence, and in some ways more direful, has been the influence of industrial depressions. The industrial depression which began in 1837, for example, temporarily destroyed the newly-arisen wholesale clothing manufacture, and caused untold hardships to the tailoresses and seamstresses of New York and Philadelphia. These women turned, naturally, to any occupation in which it was possible for them to engage. Industrial depressions, too, like war, have taken away from thousands of women the support of the men upon whom they were dependent and have forced them to snatch at any occupation which promised them a pittance.

Expansion of Woman's Sphere

As a result of these factors and forces and in many cases of others less general in their operation, woman's sphere of employment has been greatly expanded during the past hundred years. . . .

When, however, the occupations in which women are engaged are considered with reference to the relative number of women employed in each, at different periods, it is evident that the vast majority of working women have remained within the limits of their traditional field. . . . in every census year considerably more than half of all the women employed in manufacturing industries have been in the first two groups, textile and clothing industries. These industries . . . have as household industries been theirs from time immemorial. But women have been driven, by the industrial forces already in part analyzed, into many occupations formerly considered as belonging exclusively to man's sphere. . . .

Home and Factory Work

. . . Home workers have become sweat-shop workers and sweat-shop workers are gradually becoming factory workers. So long ago as now to be almost forgotten a similar transformation took place in the textile industries. Indeed, this is the general tendency of the employment of both men and women in manufacturing industries. Independent domestic production has practically become a thing of the past. But the history of woman's work shows that their wage labor under the domestic system has often been under worse conditions than their wage labor under the factory system. The hours of home workers have been longer, their wages lower, and the sanitary conditions surrounding them more unwholesome than has generally been the case with factory workers. The movement away from home work can hardly, then, be regretted.

General Conditions of Life and Labor

The conditions under which the working women of this country have toiled have long made them the object of commiseration. Mathew Carey devoted a large part of the last years of his life, from 1828 to 1839, to agitation in their behalf. Again and again he pointed out in newspaper articles, pamphlets, and speeches that the wages of working women in New York, Philadelphia, Baltimore and Boston were utterly insufficient for their support; that their food and lodging were miserably poor and unwholesome; and that the hours they were obliged to work were almost beyond human endurance. . . .

In 1845 an investigation of "female labor" in New York, used as the basis of a series of articles in the New York Tribune, developed "a most deplorable degree of servitude, privation, and misery among this helpless and dependent class of people," including "hundreds and thousands" of shoe binders, type rubbers, artificial-flower makers, matchbox makers, straw braiders, etc., who "drudge away, heartbroken in want, disease and wretchedness." . . .

Again in 1869 the working women of Boston, in a petition to the Massachusetts legislature . . . asserted that they were insufficiently paid, scantily clothed, poorly fed, and badly lodged, that their physical health, if not already undermined by long hours and bad conditions of work, was rapidly becoming so, and that their moral natures were being undermined by lack of proper society and by their inability to attend church on account of the want of proper clothing and the necessity, being constantly occupied throughout the week, "to bring up the arrears of our household duties by working on the Lord's Day."

Wages and Unemployment

The low wages paid to women and the inequality of men's and women's wages have always been the chief causes of complaint. . . .

The average wages paid to women in New York in 1863, taking all the trades together, were said to have been about $2 a week and in many instances only 20 cents a day, while the hours ranged from 11 to 16 a day. The price of board, which before the war had been about $1.50 a week, had been raised by 1864 to from $2.50 to $3.

During the war period, indeed, . . . the wages of women increased less, on the whole, than the wages of men, while their cost of living increased out of all proportion to their wages. This fact was recognized, at least, by the labor papers of that period. "While the wages of workingmen have been increased more than 100 per cent," said the Daily Evening Voice, in commenting upon the report for 1864 of the New York Working Women's Protection Union, "and complaint is still made that this is not sufficient to cover the increased cost of food and fuel, the average rate of wages for female labor has not been raised more than 20 per cent since the war was inaugurated; and yet the poor widow is obliged to pay as much for a loaf of bread or a pail of coal as the woman who has a husband or a stalwart son to assist her. In many trades the rate of wages has been lowered during the year, until it has become a mere pittance, while in other occupations the prices paid to females are generally insufficient to maintain them comfortably." . . .

History teaches that working women have suffered fully as much and perhaps more than workingmen from unemployment. Especially is this true in the sewing trades, nearly all of which are seasonal in character. Domestic servants, who have always been in great demand, have long had employment agencies to aid them in their search for work, but little aid has been given the women engaged in manufacturing industries, except by wholly or partially charitable societies, which have given them work, often at starvation prices. . . .

In the sewing trades, since the early part of the nineteenth century, the proportion of workers who have been without steady employment has always been large. Piecework and a fluctuating demand for labor, combined with a constant oversupply, have been largely responsible. Even in other trades, however, women, partly because of their lack of training and skill, have continually suffered from unemployment. In 1890, according to the census figures, 12.7 per cent, and in 1900, 23.3 per cent of all the females engaged in gainful occupations were unemployed during some portion of the census year. . . .

That working women should receive the same pay as men for the same work has long been the desire of trade-unionists. Though not expressly stated, it was implied in the resolution of the National Trades' Union in 1835, which complained that "the extreme low prices given for female labor, afford scarcely sufficient to satisfy the necessary wants of life, and create a destructive competition with the male laborer." . . . A generation later the National Labor Union, moreover, repeatedly passed resolutions expressing sympathy for the "sewing women and daughters of toil," urging them to unite in trade-unions, and demanding for them "equal pay for equal work." . . .

Again in 1868 the president of the National Labor Union, in his opening address to the congress, referred to "the extent to which female labor is introduced into many trades" as "a serious question," and stated that "the effect of introducing female labor is to undermine prices, that character of labor being usually employed, unjustly to the women, at a lower rate than is paid for male labor on the same kind of work." . . .

Scope and Sources of the Report

In this report on the history of women in industry, wage-earning occupations alone are considered. The unremunerated home work of women, which has probably dovetailed in with their wage labor in such a way that at all periods approximately the same proportion of the work of the world has been done by them, is necessarily neglected. Women engaged in professions, in independent business, and in agriculture, too, are considered only in their relation to the wage-earning women in industry. . . .

The character and conditions of woman's work within recent years have been fully described in reports, books, magazines, and newspapers which can be easily obtained, but the history of the formative period of woman's work has long been buried away in rare old books and papers, many of them until recently unknown even to close students of the labor question. The history of the wage labor of women during and shortly after this formative period, moreover, is not only comparatively unknown, but furnishes the only possible basis for any historical interpretation of women in industry.

Source: Helen L. Sumner, *Senate Report—History of Women in Industry in the United States* (Washington, D.C.: Government Printing Office, 1910: 7–51; reprinted by Arno Press, 1974).

DOCUMENT 77: *The Traffic in Women* and *Marriage and Love* (Emma Goldman, 1910)

Emma Goldman (1869–1940), born of Russian parents, migrated to the United States when she was a teenager. Throughout her life, she supported causes incompatible with American society—anarchism, free love, birth control, communism, feminism, lesbianism, and the working class. Her choices were consistent with her principles. She was passionately committed to liberty as a first principle, because she saw individual liberty as indispensable for human growth and development—two values she saw as being undermined by the society in which she lived. While other feminists generally sought to reform society, she sought to recreate it; and where most sought to work within the law, she advocated moving outside of the law. Reproduced below are excerpts from two works she published in 1910. In *The Traffic in Women* she focuses on the exploitation of the prostitute and links that exploitation to the degradation of all women. In *Marriage and Love* she argues that the institution of marriage is but an economic arrangement and, in some respects, a form of prostitution.

A. TRAFFIC IN WOMEN

Our reformers have suddenly made a great discovery—the white slave traffic. The papers are full of these "unheard-of conditions," and lawmakers are already planning a new set of laws to check the horror.

It is significant that whenever the public mind is to be diverted from a great social wrong, a crusade is inaugurated against indecency, gambling, saloons, etc. And what is the result of such crusades? Gambling is increasing, saloons are doing a lively business through back entrances, prostitution is at its height, and the system of pimps and cadets is but aggravated. . . .

What is really the cause of the trade in women? Not merely white women, but yellow and black women as well. Exploitation, of course; the merciless Moloch of capitalism that fattens on underpaid labor, thus driving thousands of women and girls into prostitution. With Mrs. Warren these girls feel, "Why waste your life working for a few shillings a week in a scullery, eighteen hours a day?"

Naturally our reformers say nothing about this cause. They know it well enough, but it doesn't pay to say anything about it. It is much more profitable to play the Pharisee, to pretend an outraged morality, than to go to the bottom of things. . . .

Nowhere is woman treated according to the merit of her work, but rather as a sex. It is therefore almost inevitable that she should pay for her right to exist, to keep a position in whatever line, with sex favors. Thus it is merely a question of degree whether she sells herself to one man, in or out of marriage, or to many men. Whether our reformers admit it or not, the economic and social inferiority of woman is responsible for prostitution.

Just at present our good people are shocked by the disclosures that in New York City alone, one out of every ten women works in a factory, that the average wage received by women is six dollars per week for forty-eight to sixty hours of work, and that the majority of female wage workers face many months of idleness which leaves the average wage about $280 a year. In view of these economic horrors, is it to be wondered at that prostitution and the white slave trade have become such dominant factors? ...

Dr. Alfred Blaschko, in *Prostitution in the Nineteenth Century*, is even more emphatic in characterising economic conditions as one of the most vital factors of prostitution.

"Although prostitution has existed in all ages, it was left to the nineteenth century to develop it into a gigantic social institution. The development of industry with vast masses of people in the competitive market, the growth and congestion of large cities, the insecurity and uncertainty of employment, has given prostitution an impetus never dreamed of at any period in human history." ...

The most amusing side of the question now before the public is the indignation of our "good, respectable people," especially the various Christian gentlemen, who are always to be found in the front ranks of every crusade. Is it that they are absolutely ignorant of the history of religion, and especially of the Christian religion? Or is it that they hope to blind the present generation to the part played in the past by the Church in relation to prostitution? Whatever their reason, they should be the last to cry out against the unfortunate victims of today, since it is known to every intelligent student that prostitution is of religious origin, maintained, and fostered for many centuries, not as a shame but as a virtue, hailed as such by the Gods themselves. ...

It would be one-sided and extremely superficial to maintain that the economic factor is the only cause of prostitution. There are others no less important and vital. That, too, our reformers know, but dare discuss even less than the institution that saps the very life out of both men and women. I refer to the sex question, the very mention of which causes most people moral spasms.

It is a conceded fact that woman is being reared as a sex commodity, and yet she is kept in absolute ignorance of the meaning and importance of sex. Everything dealing with that subject is suppressed, and persons who attempt to bring light into this terrible darkness are persecuted and thrown into prison. Yet it is nevertheless true that so long as a girl is not to know how to take care of herself, not to know the function of the most important part of her life, we need not be surprised if she becomes an easy prey to prostitution, or to any form of a relationship which degrades her to the position of an object for mere sex gratification.

It is due to this ignorance that the entire life and nature of the girl is thwarted and crippled. We have long ago taken it as a self-evident fact that the boy may follow the call of the wild; that is to say, that the boy may, as soon as his sex nature asserts itself, satisfy that nature; but our moralists are scandalized at the very thought that the nature of a girl should assert itself. To the moralist prostitution does not consist so much in the fact that the woman sells her body, but rather that she sells it out of wedlock. That this is no mere statement is proved by the fact that marriage for monetary considerations is perfectly legitimate, sanctified by law and public opinion, while any other union is condemned and repudiated. Yet a prostitute, if properly defined, means nothing else than "any person for whom sexual relationships are subordinated to gain."

"Those women are prostitutes who sell their bodies for the exercise of the sexual act and make of this a profession." . . .

Of course, marriage is the goal of every girl, but as thousands of girls cannot marry, our stupid social customs condemn them either to a life of celibacy or prostitution. Human nature asserts itself regardless of all laws, nor is there any plausible reason why nature should adapt itself to a perverted conception of morality. . . .

Girls, mere children, work in crowded, over-heated rooms ten to twelve hours daily at a machine, which tends to keep them in a constant over-excited sex state. Many of these girls have no home or comforts of any kind; therefore the street or some place of cheap amusement is the only means of forgetting their daily routine. This naturally brings them into close proximity with the other sex. It is hard to say which of the two factors brings the girl's over-sexed condition to a climax, but it is certainly the most natural thing that a climax should result. That is the first step toward prostitution. Nor is the girl to be held responsible for it. On the contrary, it is altogether the fault of society, the fault of our lack of understanding, of our lack of appreciation of life in the making; especially is it the criminal fault of our moralists, who condemn a girl for all eternity, because she has gone from the "path of virtue"; that is, because her first sex experience has taken place without the sanction of the Church.

The girl feels herself a complete outcast, with the doors of home and society closed in her face. Her entire training and tradition is such that the girl herself feels depraved and fallen, and therefore has no ground to stand upon, or any hold that will lift her up, instead of dragging her down. Thus society creates the victims that it afterwards vainly attempts to get rid of. The meanest, most depraved and decrepit man still considers himself too good to take as his wife the woman whose grace he was quite willing to buy, even though he might thereby save her from a life of horror. Nor can she turn to her own sister for help. In her stupidity the latter deems herself too pure and chaste, not realizing that her own position is in many respects even more deplorable than her sister's of the street.

"The wife who married for money, compared with the prostitute," says Havelock Ellis, "is the true scab. She is paid less, gives much more in return in labor and care, and is absolutely bound to her master. The prostitute never signs away the right over her own person, she retains her freedom and personal rights, nor is she always compelled to submit to man's embrace." . . .

Moralists are ever ready to sacrifice one-half of the human race for the sake of some miserable institution which they can not outgrow. As a matter of fact, prostitution is no more a safeguard for the purity of the home than rigid laws are a safeguard against prostitution. Fully fifty per cent of married men are patrons of brothels. It is through this virtuous element that the married women—nay, even the children—are infected with venereal diseases. Yet society has not a word of condemnation for the man, while no law is too monstrous to be set in motion against the helpless victim. She is not only preyed upon by those who use her, but she is also absolutely at the mercy of every policeman and miserable detective on the beat, the officials at the station house, the authorities in every prison.

In a recent book by a woman who was for twelve years the mistress of a "house," are to be found the following figures: "The authorities compelled me to pay every month fines between $14.70 to $29.70, the girls would pay from $5.70 to $9.70 to the police." Considering that the writer did her business in a small city, that the amounts she gives do not include extra bribes and fines, one can readily see the tremendous revenue the police department derives from the blood money of its victims, whom it will not even protect. Woe to those who refuse to pay their toll; they would be rounded up like cattle, "if only to make a favorable impression upon the good citizens of the city, or if the powers needed extra money on the side. For the warped mind who believes that a fallen woman is incapable of human emotion it would be impossible to realize the grief, the disgrace, the tears, the wounded pride that was ours every time we were pulled in."

Strange, isn't it, that a woman who has kept a "house" should be able to feel that way? But stranger still that a good Christian world should bleed and fleece such women, and give them nothing in return except obloquy and persecution. Oh, for the charity of a Christian world!

Source: Emma Goldman, *The Traffic in Women* (New York: Mother Earth Publishing, 1910), 2–27.

B. MARRIAGE AND LOVE

Marriage is primarily an economic arrangement, an insurance pact. It differs from the ordinary life insurance agreement only in that it is more binding, more exacting. Its returns are insignificantly small compared with the investments. In taking out an insurance policy one pays for it in dollars and cents, always at liberty to discontinue payments. If, however, woman's premium is a husband, she pays for it with her name, her privacy, her self-respect, her very life, "until death doth part." Moreover, the marriage insurance condemns her to life-long dependency, to parasitism, to complete uselessness, individual as well as social. Man, too, pays his toll, but as his sphere is wider, marriage does not limit him as much as woman. He feels his chains more in an economic sense. . . .

[B]ehind every marriage stands the life-long environment of the two sexes; an environment so different from each other that man and woman must remain strangers. Separated by an insurmountable wall of superstition, custom, and habit, marriage has not the potentiality of developing knowledge of, and respect for, each other, without which every union is doomed to failure.

Henrik Ibsen, the hater of all social shams, was probably the first to realize this great truth. Nora leaves her husband, not—as the stupid critic would have it—because she is tired of her responsibilities or feels the need of woman's rights, but because she has come to know that for eight years she had lived with a stranger and borne him children. Can there by anything more humiliating, more degrading than a lifelong proximity between two strangers? No need for the woman to know anything of the man, save his income. As to the knowledge of the woman—what is there to know except that she has a pleasing appearance? We have not yet outgrown the theologic myth that woman has no soul, that she is a mere appendix to man, made out of his rib just for the convenience of the gentleman who was so strong that he was afraid of his own shadow.

Perchance the poor quality of the material whence woman comes is responsible for the inferiority. At any rate, woman has no soul—what is there to know about her? Besides, the less soul a woman has the greater her asset as a wife, the more readily will she absorb herself in her husband. It is this slavish acquiescence to man's superiority that has kept the marriage institution seemingly intact for so long a period. Now that woman is coming into her own, now that she is actually growing aware of herself as a being outside of the master's grace, the sacred institution of marriage is gradually being undermined, and no amount of sentimental lamentation can stay it.

From infancy, almost, the average girl is told that marriage is her ultimate goal; therefore her training and education must be directed towards that end. Like the mute beast fattened for slaughter, she is prepared for that. Yet, strange to say, she is allowed to know much less about her function as wife and mother than the ordinary artisan of his trade. It is indecent and filthy for a respectable girl to know anything of the marital relation. Oh, for the inconsistency of respectability, that needs the marriage vow to turn something which is filthy into the purest and most sacred arrangement that none dare question or criticize. Yet that is exactly the attitude of the average upholder of marriage. The prospective wife and mother is kept in complete ignorance of her only asset in the competitive field—sex. Thus she enters into life-long relations with a man only to find herself shocked, repelled, outraged beyond measure by the most natural and healthy instinct, sex. It is safe to say that a large percentage of the unhappiness, misery, distress, and physical suffering of matrimony is due to the criminal ignorance in sex matters that is being extolled as a great virtue. Nor is it at all an exaggeration when I say that more than one home has been broken up because of this deplorable fact.

If, however, woman is free and big enough to learn the mystery of sex without the sanction of State or Church, she will stand condemned as utterly unfit to become the wife of a "good" man, his goodness consisting of an empty head and plenty of money. Can there be anything more outrageous than the idea that a healthy, grown woman, full of life and passion, must deny nature's demand, must subdue her most intense craving, undermine her health and break her spirit, must stunt her vision, abstain from the depth and glory of sex experience until a "good" man comes along to take her unto himself as a wife? That is precisely what marriage means. How can such an arrangement end except in failure? This is one, though not the least important, factor of marriage, which differentiates it from love. . . .

The moral lesson instilled in the girl is not whether the man has aroused her love, but rather is it, "How much?" The important and only God of practical American life: Can the man make a living? Can he support a wife? That is the only thing that justifies marriage. Gradually this saturates every thought of the girl; her dreams are not of moonlight and kisses, of laughter and tears; she dreams of shopping tours and bargain counters. This soul-poverty and sordidness are the elements inherent in the marriage institution. The State and the Church approve of no other ideal, simply because it is the one that necessitates the State and Church control of men and women.

Doubtless there are people who continue to consider love above dollars and cents. Particularly is this true of that class whom economic necessity has forced to become self-supporting. The tremendous change in woman's position, wrought by that mighty factor, is indeed phenomenal when we reflect that it is but a short time since she has entered the industrial arena. Six million women wage workers; six million women, who have the equal right with men to be exploited, to be robbed, to go on strike; aye, to starve even. Anything more, my lord? Yes, six million wage workers in every walk of life, from the highest brain work to the mines and the railroad tracks; yes, even detectives and policemen. Surely the emancipation is complete.

Yet with all that, but a very small number of the vast army of women wage workers look upon work as a permanent issue, in the same light as does man. No matter how decrepit the latter, he has been taught to be independent, self-supporting. Oh, I know that no one is really independent in our economic treadmill; still, the poorest specimen of a man hates to be a parasite; to be known as such, at any rate.

The woman considers her position as worker transitory, to be thrown aside for the first bidder. That is why it is infinitely harder to organize women than men. "Why should I join a union? I am going to get married, to have a home." Has she not been taught from infancy to look upon that as her ultimate calling? She learns soon enough that the home, though not so large a prison as the factory, has more solid doors and bars. It has a keeper so faithful that naught can escape him. The most tragic part, however, is that the home no longer frees her from wage slavery; it only increases her task.

According to the latest statistics submitted before a Committee "on labor and wages, and congestion of population," ten per cent of the wage workers in New York City alone are married, yet they must continue to work at the most poorly paid labor in the world. Add to this horrible aspect the drudgery of housework, and what remains of the protection and glory of the home? As a matter of fact, even the middle-class girl in marriage can not speak of her home, since it is the man who creates her sphere. It is not important whether the husband is a brute or a darling. What I wish to prove is that marriage guarantees woman a home only by the grace of her husband. There she moves about in *his* home, year after year, until her aspect of life and human affairs becomes as flat, narrow, and drab as her surroundings. Small wonder if she becomes a nag, petty, quarrelsome, gossipy, unbearable, thus driving the man from the house. She could not go, if she wanted to; there is no place to go. Besides, a short period of married life, of complete surrender of all faculties, absolutely incapacitates the average woman for the outside world. She becomes reckless in appearance, clumsy in her movements, dependent in her decisions, cowardly in her judgment, a weight and a bore, which most men grow to hate and despise. . . .

The institution of marriage makes a parasite of woman, an absolute dependent. It incapacitates her for life's struggle, annihilates her social consciousness, paralyzes her imagination, and then imposes its gracious protection, which is in reality a snare, a travesty on human character. . . .

Some day, some day men and women will rise, they will reach the mountain peak, they will meet big and strong and free, ready to receive, to partake, and to bask in the golden rays of love. What fancy, what imagination, what poetic genius can foresee even approximately the potentialities of such a force in the life of men and women. If the world is ever to give birth to true companionship and oneness, not marriage, but love will be the parent.

Source: Emma Goldman, *Marriage and Love* (New York: Mother Earth Publishing, 1910), 5–18.

DOCUMENT 78: Hearings on Women's Suffrage Before the House Committee on the Judiciary (1912)

In 1912 the House of Representatives held hearings on women's suffrage. During the debates, views were entertained for and against a constitutional amendment granting suffrage to women. Although by then five states—Wyoming in 1869, Colorado in 1893, Utah in 1896, Washington in 1910, and California in 1911—had granted full suffrage to women, only three had had enough experience with it to serve as a basis for appraising its impact on social and political life. Included below are portions of two letters, one by a woman and the other by a man, to the House of Representatives. They advance another reason for not granting women the right to vote— that the quality of life had not improved in states that had granted women suffrage.

Woman Suffrage in Colorado

I have voted since 1893. I have been a delegate to the city and State conventions, and a member of the Republican State committee from my county. I have been a deputy sheriff and a watcher at the pools. For 23 years I have been in the midst of the woman suffrage movement in Colorado. For years I believed in woman suffrage and have worked day in and day out for it. I now see my mistake and would abolish it to-morrow if I could.

No law has been put on the statute books of Colorado for the benefit of women and children that has been put there by the women. The child-labor law went through independently of the women's vote. The hours of the working women have not been shortened; the wages of school-teachers have not been raised; the type of men that got into office has not improved a bit.

Frankly, the experiment is a failure. It has done Colorado no good. It has done woman no good. The best thing for both would be if to-morrow the ballot for women could be abolished.

Mrs. Francis W. Goddard,
President of the Colonial Dames of Colorado.

December, 1910

Our State has tried the female suffrage plan a sufficiently long time to form a fair idea of its workings. I am not prejudiced in any way, but honestly do not see where the experiment has proved of benefit.***It has produced no special reforms, and it has had no particular purifying effect upon politics. There is a growing tendency on the part of most of the better and more intelligent of the female voters of Colorado to cease exercising the ballot.*** If it were to be done over again, the people of Colorado would defeat woman suffrage by an overwhelming majority.

Hon. Moses Hallett,
United States District Judge for Colorado.

Source: *Woman Suffrage, Hearings Before the Committee on the Judiciary, House of Representatives, Sixty-Second Congress, Second Session, March 13, 1912* (Washington, D.C.: Government Printing Office, 1912), 100.

DOCUMENT 79: *Woman's Share in Social Culture* (Anna Garlin Spencer, 1912)

Anna Garlin Spencer (1851–1931), a successful teacher in Rhode Island public schools, a journalist for the Providence *Daily Journal*, and an ordained minister in an independent church in Providence, understood and appreciated the development and contribution of genius in women. For her, society had, to paraphrase the words of the English poet Thomas Gray, "repressed the noble rage" of many women of genius, and ensured the waste of that of others through artificial obstacles. Her comments below eloquently convey her thinking.

"Talent," says Lowell, "is that which is in a man's power; genius is that in whose power a man is." If genius, even in its lesser ranges, be this irresistible pressure toward some unique self-expression, then women cannot be left out of the charmed circle; especially when we remember Helen Hunt with her solitary but wide approach to love and life, and Emily Dickinson, that hermit thrush among poets. Nor can those unique interpreters of art and literature among women whose vital expression has so enhanced the works of genius as to make them seem new creations, be left out of the count. In modern times, the growing company of musicians, some of them composers, and the artists of pen and brush, and the sculptors among women who swell the secondary ranks of genius in numbers and in power, must have increasing recognition.

All this, however, does not reach the deepest considerations involved in taking account of the intellectual contribution of women to art, science, philosophy and affairs. Whatever may be the reasons in nature for the lower level of women along these lines of man's greatest achievement, there are the gravest reasons in circumstance for the comparatively meagre showing. In addition to the handicap of lack of education, a handicap which no exceptional success of the self-made man or woman can offset for the majority of the talented, there is no less important deprivation which all women have suffered in the past and most women now suffer. This deprivation is that of the informal but highly stimulating training which the good fellowship of their chosen guild of study and of service gives to men, but which is denied for the most part even to professional women. For example, women have been in the medical profession for a considerable time, and have obtained high distinction in it. They have won just recognition from many influential doctors of the other sex. Yet they can hardly be said to have entered the inner circle of their clan. They may stop to dinner at medical conventions, it is true, provided they make no fuss about smoking and do not mind being in the minority; but there are few men, even in that enlightened group, who can so sink sex-consciousness in professional comradeship as either to give or get the full social value that might be gained from a mixed company of like vocation. The women lawyers and members of the clergy are in even smaller minority, and hence suffer still more from the embarrassment of the "exception" which prevents easy and familiar association. In the teaching profession, where the relative numbers of the sexes are reversed, there is often more adequate professional intercourse; but the woman college professor, or college president, is still that one among many whose reception into her special class, even if courteous and friendly, is too formal and occasional for real guild fellowship.

To this negative deprivation must be added the positive opposition of men to the entrance of women into that professional life and work from which the genius arises as the race flower from a vast field. The whole course of evolution in industry, and in the achievements of higher education and exceptional talent, has shown man's invariable tendency to shut women out when their activities have reached a highly specialized period of growth. The primitive woman-worker, as Jack-at-all-trades, does not develop any one employment to its height of perfection. Gradually initiating old men and boys, not fitted for war and the chase, into these varied forms of effort, women start the other sex toward that concentration of effort upon one process-activity which finally develops separate arts, sciences and professions. When this point is reached, the "woman's work" usually becomes "man's work"; and when that time comes, men turn round and shut out women from the labor which women themselves have initiated. This monopolistic tendency of men is shown most clearly in the history of the learned professions. Women were seldom, if ever, priests but they participated in religious services when religion was a family affair. When a priestly caste arose and became the symbol of peculiar authority, only men entered its ranks. . . .

Again, women developed law and its application to life in the germs of family rule and tribal custom quite as much as did men; but when statutes took the place of tradition, and courts superseded personal judgeship, and when a special class of lawyers was needed to define and administer laws, which grew more difficult to understand with growing complexity of social relationship, men alone entered that profession. . . .

This process of differentiating and perfecting intellectual labor, the process in which at most acute periods of specialization and advance, women were wholly shut out of their own ancient work, finds its most complete and its most dramatic illustration in the history of the medical profession. Some phases of the healing art have always been connected in primitive society with the priestly office and, hence, in the hands of man. Three great branches, however, were always, in all forms of social organization of which we have knowledge, in the hands exclusively of women, namely, midwifery, the treatment of diseases of women so far as those were cared for at all, and the diseases of children. . . . The result of this sex-segregation in the care of the sick in these important branches has been that women doctors, unschooled but often not unskilled, have served all the past of human experience in childbirth, in child-care, and in the special illnesses of women. This has been true in our own, as well as in older civilizations up to the 18th century. In our own country, in colonial times, only women ushered into a bleak New England the potential citizens of the new world. We read of Mrs. Wiat, who died in 1705 at the age of 94 years, having assisted as midwife at the birth of more than 1,100 children. And in Rehoboth, one of the oldest communities in Massachusetts, the Town Meeting itself "called" from England, "Dr. Sam Fuller and his mother," he to practise medicine and she "as midwife to answer to the town's necessity, which was great." Busied with other matters, the Colonies paid little attention to medical science until the war of the American Revolution betrayed the awful results of ignorance in the slaughter of soldiers by preventable disease. When the healing art began to become a true science and took great strides toward better training and facilities of practice for the student, attention was at once drawn to the need for better service in the fields wholly occupied by women. The opening and improvement of the medical schools, however, was a new opportunity for men alone and the new demand for more scientific care of women in childbirth and for higher medical service to childhood and for the women suffering from special diseases, resulted in the greatest of innovations, namely, the assumption by men of the office of midwife and their entrance into the most intimate relationships with women patients. Dr. James Lloyd, after two years' study in England, began to practise "obstetrics" (the new name that disguised in some degree the daring change in medical practice) in Boston, in 1762. Dr. Shippen, similarly trained abroad, took up the same practice in Philadelphia and added lectures upon the subject. Thus began in our own country the elevation of this important branch of the healing art to a professional standard and the consequent exclusion of women from their immortal rights in the sickroom. It was a poor recognition of the debt the race owed to the mother-sex, both as suffering the pangs of childbirth and as helping to assuage them and in caring for the infants and children of all time! After men entered upon the task of perfecting the medical profession, and incidentially shutting women out of it, it did not take long, however, for the thoughtful to see the propriety of allowing women those advantages of training which would put them back again into their rightful place on the higher plane of science now demanded. What gave sharp point to this feeling was the common opposition to men engaging in these ancient prerogatives of women. This was at first as intense and as bitter as the later opposition to the entrance of women in the coeducational medical schools. . . . The first women who tried to secure training in medical schools in order to reënter those branches of the healing art from which they had so recently been driven, and on the higher plane of science now properly demanded, endured such hardships as made them veritable martyrs. In 1847 Harriot K. Hunt knocked at the door of Harvard Medical School to be persistently refused admission. In 1849 Elizabeth Blackwell graduated from Geneva Medical School, having secured instruction as a special favor, and began her great career, devoted equally to securing the best possible medical training for women, and to elevating to higher standards than had as yet been attained by men the whole area of medical training. Among the heroic figures of these early days are to be found many married women whose husbands, often themselves physicians, helped them to obtain their training. . . . The attitude of the men of the medical profession generally, however, was one of the utmost hostility, showing every form of monopolistic selfishness and injustice. . . . All this was without reference to the intellectual standing or practical efficiency of the women graduates. The mere fact of women entering the profession meant, in the minds of these protestants, degradation to the men already in it! Earlier than this, in 1859, the Medical Society of the County of Philadelphia passed "resolutions of excommunication" against every physician who should "teach in a medical school for women" and every one who should "consult with a woman physician or with a man teaching a woman medical student." . . . Nevertheless, the women did reënter their ancient profession of healing after a brief exclusion. So far from permanently lowering the standards of training newly established, their chief pioneer leader, Elizabeth Blackwell, was instrumental in inaugurating modern preventive medicine, by the establishment in the New York Medical College for Women, opened in 1865, of the first chair of Hygiene ever set apart in a medical college in the United States. In 1882 this pioneer medical college for women set forth the bravest and truest of philosophies respecting women's work in the following words: "We call upon all those who believe in the higher education of women to help set the highest possible standards for their medical education; and we call upon those who do not believe in such higher education to help in making such requirements as shall turn aside the incompetent;—not by any exercise of arbitrary power, but by a demonstration of incapacity, which is the only logical, manly reason for refusing to allow women to pursue an honorable calling in an honorable way."

This brief allusion to the heroic struggle of woman to reënter the healing art against the positive opposition of men already entrenched in all the coigns of vantage in professional training and organized professional guilds, furnishes a flashlight picture of the whole course of woman's entrance into the more modern types of differentiated labor. . . .

In addition to these handicaps must be named the well-known but scarcely adequately measured interruptions to both study and self-expression which the women of talent and specialized power have always experienced. Anyone can see that to write *Uncle Tom's Cabin* on the knee in the kitchen, with constant calls to cooking and other details of housework to punctuate the paragraphs, was a more difficult achievement than to write it at leisure in a quiet room. . . .

. . . When we read of Charles Darwin's wife not only relieving him from financial cares but seeing that he had his breakfast in his room, with "nothing to disturb the freshness of his morning," we do not find the explanation of Darwin's genius, but we do see how he was helped to express it. Men geniuses, even of second grade, have usually had at least one woman to smooth their way, and often several women to make sure that little things, often even self-support itself, did not interfere with the development and expression of their talent. On the other hand, the obligation of all the earlier women writers to prepare a useful cook-book in order to buy their way into literature, is a fitting symbol of the compulsion laid upon women, however gifted, to do all the things that women in general accomplish before entering upon their special tasks. . . .

Added to all this, the woman of talent and of special gifts has had until very lately, and in most countries has still, to go against the massed social pressure of her time in order to devote herself to any particular intellectual task. The expectation of society has long pushed men toward some special work; the expectation of society has until recently been wholly against women's choosing any vocation beside their functional service in the family. This is a far more intense and all-pervading influence in deterring women from success in intellectual work than is usually understood. . . . No book has yet been written in praise of a woman who let her husband and children starve or suffer while she invented even the most useful things, or wrote books, or expressed herself in art, or evolved philosophic systems. On the contrary, the mildest approach on the part of a wife and mother, or even of a daughter or sister, to that intense interest in self-expression which has always characterized genius has been met with social disapproval and until very recent times with ostracism fit only for the criminal. Hence her inner impulsion has needed to be strong indeed to make any woman devote herself to ideas.

In view of these tremendous obstacles, it is fair to assume that when women in the past have achieved even a second or third place in the ranks of genius they have shown far more native ability than men have needed to reach the same eminence. Not excused from the more general duties that constitute the cement of society, most women of talent have had but one hand free with which to work out their ideal conceptions. . . .

The genius is at once the most self-centered and the most universal of human beings. He sees only himself and the world of thought or of affairs he would master for his special work. All that lies between, family, friends, social groups, is but material for his elect service. Delight in his own personality, absorbed attention to the processes of his own mind, have made him generally the master shirker in respect to the ordinary duties of life. He has been often "ill to live with," and greedy in demand upon the support and care of others. He is so rare and precious, however, that "with all his faults we love him still." . . . to suppress in wholesale fashion, and at the outset, all troublesome "variations" in women, while leaving men free to show what they can become and giving them besides a good chance to prove their quality, is to make that discipline too one-sided. The universal social pressure upon women to be all alike, and do all the same things, and to be content with identical restrictions, has resulted not only in terrible suffering in the lives of exceptional women, but also in the loss of unmeasured feminine values in special gifts. The Drama of the Woman of Genius has been too often a tragedy of misshapen and perverted power. . . .

Source: Anna Garlin Spencer, *Woman's Share in Social Culture* (New York: J. B. Lippincott, 1912), 45–88.

DOCUMENT 80: From a Drunkard's Wife (1894)

Victorian social and sexual attitudes made sharp distinctions between the sexual nature of men and women. Women were characterized as (and expected to be) sexually pure, while men were viewed as more animal-like and lacking in self-control. Women were supposed to help men gain or maintain control of themselves and to preserve the moral integrity of the home and society. Women were charged with responsibility for the moral instruction of the young. Although society benefited from women's assumption of the role of moral standard bearer, women were not allowed to voice their moral concerns publicly. Even in the face of the continuing temperance movement, women often bore the physical and emotional abuse of their husbands silently. The song below captures aspects of that abuse which have frequently gone unmentioned.

Then I fell to the floor and was born from the room,
A wreck since that night I've been.
And the boy that was left had a passion for drink,
The sad mark of his father's sin.
It claimed him, though young a hopeless slave,
And early he filled a drunkard's grave.

I beg of you girls, as you value your lives
From the drunker to turn aside,
And give heed to no plea, whatever it be
Of a drinker to be the bride.
To save from such sorrow as wrecked my life,
Oh never become a drunkard's wife.

Source: "The Drunkard's Wife," music by L. L. Tickett and lyrics by M. M. Knapt (1894), in Donald M. Scott and Bernard Wishy, eds., *American Families: A Documentary History* (New York: Harper and Row, 1982), 357–358.

DOCUMENT 81: Sex Education and Contraception (1913)

Margaret Sanger (1883–1966) was one of the most prominent pioneers in the fight for birth control. She believed, as did others such as Emma Goldman (see Document 77), that contraceptives freed women by restoring to them greater control of their bodies and thus lessening their economic dependence on men. Sanger's efforts on behalf of birth control also contributed to a shift in thinking about sexual matters. The notion of "passionless woman," for example, was disabused; and the view that sexual experience, separated from considerations of reproduction and birth control, could be an instrument of improved sexual relationship, was debated.

Arrested under the Comstock law (see Document 58), Sanger escaped to the United Kingdom in 1914, but she returned to New York and in 1916 opened a birth control clinic in Brooklyn to help poor women. Authorities closed the clinic and she was convicted of obscenity. On appeal, her conviction was upheld, but the court ruled that physicians could distribute birth control information as part of the process of preventing disease. This exception formed the core of a strategy adopted by the American Birth Control League, founded by Sanger in 1921. In a later case, *Eisenstadt v. Baird* (1972), the U.S. Supreme Court overturned a Massachusetts law under which Baird had been convicted for distributing contraceptives to unmarried persons. The law said that unmarried persons could obtain contraceptives only to prevent the spread of disease, not to prevent pregnancy. The excerpts that follow voice the pain of some of the women who motivated Sanger's fight for birth control.

The excerpts contained in this chapter are typical of the letters which come to me by the thousands. They tell their own story, simply—sometimes ungrammatically and illiterately, but nevertheless irresistibly. It is the story of slow murder of the helpless by a society that shields itself behind ancient, inhuman moral creeds—which dares to weigh those dead creeds against the agony of the living who pray for the "mercy of death."

Can a mother who would "rather die" than bear more children serve society by bearing still others? Can children carried through nine months of dread and unspeakable mental anguish and born into an atmosphere of fear and anger, to grow up uneducated and in want, be a benefit to the world? Here is what the mother says:

I have read in the paper about you and am very interested in Birth Control. I am a mother of four living children and one dead the oldest 10 and baby 22 months old. I am very nervous and sickly after my children. I would like you to advise me what to do to prevent from having any more as I would rather die than have another. I am keeping away from my husband as much as I can, but it causes quarrels and almost separation. All my babies have had marasmus in the first year of their lives and I almost lost my baby last summer. I always worry about my children so much. My husband works in a brass foundry it is not a very good job and living is so high that we have to live as cheap as possible. I've only got 2 rooms and kitchen and I do all my work and sewing which is very hard for me.

... Here is a letter from a paralytic mother, whose days and nights are tortured by the thought of another child, and whose reason is tottering at the prospect of leaving her children without her care:

I sent for a copy of your magazine and now feel I must write you to see if you can help me.

I was a high school girl who married a day laborer seven years ago. In a few months, I will again be a mother, the fourth child in less than six years. While carrying my babies am always partly paralyzed on one side. Do not know the cause but the doctor said at last birth we must be "more careful," as I could not stand having so many children. Am always very sick for a long time and have to have chloroform.

We can afford help only about 3 weeks, until I am on my feet again, after confinement. I work as hard as I can but my work and my children are always neglected. I wonder if my body does survive this next birth if my reason will.

It is terrible to think of bringing these little bodies and souls into the world without means or strength to care for them. And I can see no relief unless you give it to me or tell me where to get it. I am weaker each time and I know that this must be the last one, for it would be better for me to go, than to bring more neglected babies into the world. I can hardly sleep at night for worrying. Is there an answer for women like me?

In another chapter, we have gotten a glimpse of the menace of the feebleminded. Here is a woman who is praying for help to avoid adding to the number of mentally helpless:

My baby is only 10 months old and the oldest one of four is 7, and more care than a baby, has always been helpless. We do not own a roof over our heads and I am so discouraged I want to die if nothing can be done. Can't you help me just this time and then I know I can take care of myself. Ignorance on this all important subject has put me where I am. I don't know how to be sure of bringing myself around. I beg of you to help me and anything I can do to help further your wonderful work I will do. Only help me this once, no one will know only I will be blessed.

I not only have a terrible time when I am confined but caring for the oldest child it preys so on my mind that I fear more defective children. Help me please!

Not even the blindest of all dogmatists can ignore the danger to the community of to-day and the race of to-morrow in permitting an insane woman to go on bearing children. Here is a letter which tells a two-sided story—how mother instinct, even when clouded by periodic insanity, seeks to protect itself and society; and how society prevents her from attaining that end:

> There is a woman in this town who has six children and is expecting another. Directly after the birth of a child, she goes insane, a raving maniac, and they send her to the insane asylum. While she is gone, her home and children are cared for by neighbors. After about six months, they discharge her and she comes home and is in a family way again in a few months. Still the doctors will do nothing for her.
>
> She is a well-educated woman and says if she would not have any more children, she is sure she could be entirely free from these insane spells.
>
> If you will send me one of your pamphlets, I will give it to her and several others equally deserving.
>
> Hoping you will see fit to grant my request, I remain, etc.

The very word "syphilis" brings a shudder to anyone who is familiar with the horrors of the malady. Not only in the suffering brought to the victim himself and in the danger of infecting others, but in the dire legacy of helplessness and disease which is left to the offspring of the syphilitic, is this the most destructive socially, of all "plagues." Here is a letter, which as a criticism to national waste and to contraceptives, defies comment:

> I was left without a father when a girl of fourteen years old. I was the oldest child of five. My mother had no means of support except her two hands, so we worked at anything we could, my job being nurse girl at home while mother worked most of the time, as she could earn more money than I could, for she could do harder work.
>
> I wasn't very strong and finally after two years my mother got so tired and worn out trying to make a living for so many, she married again, and as she married a poor man, we children were not much better off. At the age of seventeen I married a man, a brakeman on the——Railroad, who was eleven years older than I. He drank some and was a very frail-looking man, but I was very ignorant of the world and did not think of anything but making a home for myself and husband. After eleven months I had a little girl born to me. I did not want more children, but my mother-in-law told me it was a terrible sin to do anything to keep from having children and that the Lord only sent just what I could take care of and if I heard of anything to do I was told it was injurious, so I did not try.
>
> In eleven months again, October 25, I had another little puny girl. In twenty-three months, Sept. 25th, I had a seven-lb. boy. In ten months, July 15, I had a seven-months baby that lived five hours. In eleven months, June 20, I had another little girl. In seventeen months, Nov. 30, another boy. In nine months a four months' miscarriage. In twelve months another girl, and in three and a half years another girl.

All of these children were born into poverty; the father's health was always poor, and when the third girl was born he was discharged from the road because of his disability, yet he was still able to put children into the world. When the oldest child was twelve years old the father died of concussion of the brain while the youngest child was born two months after his death.

Now, Mrs. Sanger, I did not want those children, because even in my ignorance I had sense enough to know that I had no right to bring those children into such a world where they could not have decent care, for I was not able to do it myself nor hire it done. I prayed and I prayed that they would die when they were born. Praying did no good and to-day I have read and studied enough to know that I am the mother of seven living children and that I committed a crime by bringing them into the world, their father was syphilitic (I did not know about such things when I was a girl). One son is to be sent to Mexico, while one of my girls is a victim of the white slave traffic.

Source: Margaret Sanger, *Women and the New Race* (New York: Brentano's, 1920), 74–82.

DOCUMENT 82: The Nineteenth Amendment (1920)

The federal women's suffrage amendment was first introduced into Congress in 1868. It failed to pass. Between 1868 and 1896, the Anthony amendment, as it came to be called (after Susan B. Anthony), continued to be introduced, but with the same negative results. In the meantime, the American Woman Suffrage Association, which had followed a strategy of seeking amendments to state constitutions, had had but meager success. Between 1870 and 1910, seventeen state referenda were held, but only two proved victorious. By 1912 some residents who had supported their states' granting of full suffrage to women began to express reservations about that decision (see Document 78).

But a number of developments improved the rather bleak prospects for women's rights, including the merger of women's organizations (the NWSA and the AWSA), the work of Alice Paul (a Quaker social worker who brought to the struggle for women's rights an accentuated degree of militancy, including hunger strikes), the work of women during World War I, the embarrassment caused by the apparent rights granted women by the Communist regime in the newly established Soviet Union, and the improved organizational skills of a new generation of women who benefited from their sisters' earlier efforts. So after forty-two years of continuous campaigns—56 referenda to male voters, 480 to legislatures to submit suffrage amendments to votes; and 47 to get state constitutional conventions to write women's suffrage into state constitutions—the Nineteenth Amendment to the Constitution was approved in the spring of 1919 and ratified by the necessary thirty-six states in August 1920. Its wording was essentially the same as that introduced to Congress more than fifty years earlier.

Section 1. The right of the citizens of the United States to vote shall not be denied or abridged by the United States or by any state on account of sex.

Part IV

A Woman Is a Woman Is a Woman: The Struggle Continues, 1920–1963

By the 1920s women had made sufficient gains in education and work to offset what appeared to be temporary ideological setbacks in women's rights. Feminist issues continued to be raised, although less forcefully than in earlier periods.

Postwar America gave the appearance of being an optimistic and lively place. With World War I over and the vote won, women had many new opportunities to develop their potential, especially in the cities, which experienced a surge in economic growth. By the second decade of the twentieth century, half the population lived in urban settings, surrounded by technological advances such as the telephone, radio, and movies.

In the 1920s flappers (see Document 83) seemed to be in pursuit of immediate pleasure, which they expressed by their emancipation from Victorian sexual, social, and dress codes. These "new women" promoted the feminist cause by claiming equality with men and demonstrating this claim by their behavior. They rejected corsets and long dresses, which they claimed symbolized servility to men, and they advocated free love.

This shift in social attitudes is reflected in statistical studies done by Alfred Kinsey, who found that about twice as many women had had premarital sex during the early 1920s as in earlier decades. This behavior indicates a decline in the double standard.

At about the same time that flappers sought sexual and social equality with men, another group of women outlined their post-suffrage plans to achieve equality with men. Organized by Alice Paul, these women broke with the NAWSA, the major suffrage organization, even before the passage of the Nineteenth Amendment (see introduction to Part III). By 1920 they had established them-

selves as the New Woman's Party (NWP)—really the old National
Woman's Party. The choice of name was important, for it at once
signaled its exclusive female membership and drew attention to its
new post-suffrage agenda. Its goal was complete political equality
for women in the form of a constitutional amendment, called the
Equal Rights Amendment (ERA) (Document 85). If enacted, ERA
would have removed all legal distinctions between the sexes.

During the 1920s, while Alice Paul's group vigorously advocated
ERA, other major women's organizations stood in opposition. They
believed that its passage would invalidate protective legislation,
one of women's few tangible achievements, and one they were unwilling to give up. One opposition group was the League of
Women Voters (LWV), which had evolved from the NAWSA after
1920, while another was the Women's Bureau, formed during the
war. Emotions ran strong on both sides, making the ERA debate
the most important women's right issue of the decade. It was, moreover, taken up by many other interested parties. The pros and cons
were argued in the pages of the austere journal of the American
Bar Association (see Documents 87 and 88), and women union
members who feared removal of protective legislation also voiced
their objections (Document 89). Some opponents of ERA believed
that protective legislation, which limited working hours for women
and barred certain forms of strenuous activity would be forfeited.
Others stressed that physical differences between men and women
required protection of females (Document 87). Women reformers,
on the other hand, contended that the legal equality promised by
ERA was a myth and that equality was possible only when economic parity between the sexes was achieved. To some extent this
latter view was supported by the court's opinion in *Adkins v. Children's Hospital* (Document 84), which stated that women's wages,
like men's, should be subject to the marketplace. Although some
said that this decision gave women the opportunity to achieve
equality with men, others suggested otherwise, such as Blanche
Grozier who did not favor protection (see Document 90), because,
she believed, among other things, it was men based on a lie that
women are weak. However it is not hard to understand why some
women's rights advocates could not support ERA.

The LWV did not oppose ERA (which it later came to support)
because it was unaware of women's legal disabilities. On the contrary. During the early twenties, both the LWV and the NWP undertook an analysis of women's legal status in each state
(Document 85). Both groups reached the same conclusion: that in
every state and in all areas of the law women suffered legal disabilities. Nevertheless, they supported different remedies. The NWP

claimed that ERA would promote efforts to educate women regarding their disabilities and that they would, in turn, influence
state legislatures to pass laws to end them. Notwithstanding the
vigorous campaign by the NWP, ERA proved too controversial to
pass Congress during this period. Nevertheless, the issue was kept
alive for forty years. In 1972 ERA passed both houses of Congress
but fell three states short of the constitutionally required ratification
by two-thirds of the states.

Apart from ERA debates and the flapper phenomenon, women's
rights advanced on other fronts. Large numbers of women, particularly married women, went to work outside the home. Employment opportunities improved in clerical and sales jobs, raising their
standard of living. Many more women graduated from high school
(surpassing the number of male high school graduates), and many
continued their education in college. This accounts for the increase
in the number of professional women in teaching, nursing, and
librarianship, and for the erosion of the traditional image of women
only as nurturers within the home.

Despite these advances, however, traditionally male professions
such as law, medicine, and university teaching were still largely
closed to women (Document 91). And the few women who entered
these professions did not receive equal pay. Outside the professions
pay disparities were gender linked, minimized slightly by sex-
typed protective legislation.

Few women reformers expected that suffrage would immediately
produce the promised land. Rather, the NWP, the LWV, and other
organizations continued in their own way to keep their goal of
equality alive. They were joined by feminists such as Suzanne
LaFollette, whose book *Concerning Women* (1926) states that equality
between the sexes would occur only when women achieved economic independence. She believed this goal to be possible as more
women entered the labor force, creating what she called "the great
unconscious and unorganized women's movement."

But the Depression years proved to be anomalous. Poll after poll
recorded that Americans believed that married women should stay
at home. In 1936, Gallup asked people if wives should work when
their husbands had a job; 82 percent said no. A 1936 *Fortune* magazine poll showed that 85 percent of the men and 79 percent of the
women agreed. In addition, the powerful American Federation of
Labor (AFL) proclaimed that a married woman should not work if
her husband had a job. A further blow to women's economic independence was struck by the passage of the National Economy
Act (1933), which stipulated that no more than one member of a
family could work in the federal civil service. In passing this act,

Congress ignored the objections of the LWV, the NWP, and First Lady Eleanor Roosevelt. Once the act was passed, three-quarters of the women in the federal service had to resign.

Finally, many school boards voted not to hire married women as teachers, and many women who already had teaching jobs were dismissed. Between 1920 and 1940 the percentage of women teachers dropped from 85 to 78. Loss of professional work did not stop with teaching, either. In all professional areas, women were negatively affected.[1]

On the other hand, in the work force during the Depression working wives suffered fewer job losses than men, and their numbers continued to increase (Document 92) (with the exception of black women, who always endured double discrimination as women and as blacks). While jobs for men declined in heavy industry, jobs for white women increased in gender-typed sales, service, and clerical areas. More women sought such work to compensate for jobs lost by male family members—and the number of working women increased by 25 percent. In 1930 married women comprised 29 percent of the work force, and by 1940, 35 percent. During the Depression years women's access to employment continued to improve.[2]

The proliferation of working women joined other "unconscious" forces—to borrow LaFollette's term—during the Depression years. Although Roosevelt did not have the women's movement in mind when he established the minimum wage and restricted hours of work as part of the New Deal legislation, this course of action had been urged by the NWP in 1920. And although his reform program excluded women from agencies such as the Civilian Conservation Corps and denied them assistance in some work relief programs targeted only to heads of households, nevertheless, women benefited when protection was mandated by law, and from the pro-union New Deal legislation. As a result their participation in unions tripled between 1930 and 1940 and led to improved working conditions.

In 1935 another goal of women's rights activists was fulfilled with the passage of the Social Security Act, which provided women with maternal and child welfare assistance. Their champion was Eleanor Roosevelt, who had long fought for women's causes. They could point to her all-night vigil in 1924 outside the room of the platform committee at the Democratic National Convention (which still excluded women) in order to give the committee a list of demands from Democratic women. According to Bess Furman, a newspaper reporter and friend of Eleanor, the list "practically forecast the New Deal" by demanding "the eight-hour day, collective bargaining, a federal employment agency, equal pay for equal work, [and] federal aid for maternal health and child welfare." Continuing her feminist efforts in the early days of the Roosevelt administration, Eleanor influenced Franklin to reward those women who had labored for his victory. One notable success was the appointment of Frances Perkins as secretary of labor (1933), the first woman ever to receive a cabinet position. Perkins paid homage to her sex when she said, "I have always felt that it was not I alone who was appointed to the Cabinet, but that it was all the women in America." (Toward the end of her life Eleanor Roosevelt's association with women's causes was appropriately recognized by President Kennedy when he appointed her the first chairperson of his newly created Commission on the Status of Women, the first federal commission to study the status and rights of women.)

The Roosevelt administration recognized early on that women needed to work. This led to the establishment of child care centers for poor working mothers (Document 93).

Although World War II fundamentally influenced women's lives, it did not usher in a reinvigorated women's right movement. One gain was a reversal of the federal policy that excluded married women from working and which finally allowed black women in significant numbers to enter the factory (Documents 92 and 94), but the reason for the change in policy was an acute labor shortage, not rights. Nevertheless, the war years saw over 6 million women enter the labor force for the first time, especially married, older, and unionized women. And despite being used as a "reserve army" (Document 92), women appeared ready to perform whenever needed. They were absorbed mostly in the war industry, manufacturing airplanes, artillery, and rivet guns. They learned these specialties in a short period of time. At the end of 1943 half the workers at the Boeing plant in Seattle were women, and by the end of the war women had infiltrated every part of the work force. They even entered the armed forces, breaking a traditional sex barrier by becoming test pilots.

Even as wartime needs led the government to offer men's jobs to women, traditional ideology remained. Women were told that once the war was over men would reclaim their jobs. Propaganda posters portrayed women as temporarily sacrificing their duties at home for patriotic reasons. Meanwhile, the government failed to provide enough child care centers until 1943; even then the centers were so poorly run that only 10 percent of defense workers used them (Document 93).

When the war was over women were encouraged to make room for the returning G.I.s. A Gallup poll taken soon after the war revealed that 86 percent of Americans believed that married women should remain at home (Document 96). Studies of the postwar period show that people married at a younger age and had more children than in previous generations. During the 1950s traditional family values and separate-sphere ideology received widespread support from the popular media and the world of ideas. In *Generation of Vipers* (1942) Philip Wylie portrayed women who were other than docile as emasculating their husbands and sons. Many sociologists and psychologists declared women's destiny to be strictly domestic. Child care expert Dr. Benjamin Spock urged mothers not to work, claiming that children fared best in the care of a full-time mother. Married mothers who continued to work often felt guilty for making that choice (Document 96).

The return to separate-sphere ideology after the war is reflected in a decline in female enrollment in college, in the decrease in support for the major women's rights organizations, and in important court decisions of the period limiting women's constitutional rights (Documents 95 and 99). But this was also a generation that benefited from Planned Parenthood, the successor to Margaret Sanger's organization, the American Birth Control League. Planned Parenthood clinics instructed women in birth control and educated them about their bodies (Document 97). The number of marriages rose in the 1950s, but unhappily married women increasingly filed for divorce.

After the war the number of women working outside the home nevertheless continued to climb. During the 1890s women comprised only 18 percent of the work force as compared to 30 percent in the 1950s. More women joined unions: in 1930 there were 800,000 women union members; by 1960 there were well over three million. By the 1960s more women attended college, while the number of professional women increased.[3]

Black women always had to work. They profited from the opportunity to perform more desirable, better paying jobs during World War II, but they were the first to lose those jobs to the returning men after the war. Minority women had little choice but to continue to look for work (see Document 94). The postwar boom in the 1950s and the civil rights and feminist movements of the 1950s and 1960s (see introduction to Part V) enabled more black women to improve their working conditions or receive a better education.

NOTES

1. D'Ann Campbell, *Women at War with America: Private Lives in a Patriotic Era* (Cambridge, Mass.: Harvard University Press, 1984).

2. Peter G. Filene, *Him/Her/Self: Sex Roles in Modern America*, 2nd ed. (Baltimore: Johns Hopkins University Press, 1986), esp. chaps. 1 and 2.

3. Nancy Woloch, *Women and the American Experience* (New York: Alfred A. Knopf, 1984), chaps. 17 and 18.

DOCUMENT 83: "The Flapper and Her Critics" (Gerald E. Critoph, early 1920s)

During the decade or so after the end of World War I and the passage of the Nineteenth Amendment, which granted suffrage to women, a youth movement emerged that challenged the moral order known as Victorianism. The young women who participated in this rebellion were called flappers or "New Women" and could be identified by the way they dressed, danced, and did their hair. Not since the introduction of bloomer, in the mid-nineteenth century had middle-class women dared act against the constraints of their costume. Rejecting the traditional dress code of the "womanly woman"—ankle-length skirt, high collar, corseted waist—flappers inched up the skirt to mid-calf, lowered the neckline, cast off the corset, and even dispensed with the brassiere. Furthermore, they altered what some considered the feminine crown by bobbing their hair. Some flappers played sports, drank, smoked, and danced the fox-trot.

In the following document Gerald E. Critoph describes various reactions to the unconventional behavior of flappers. Critics blamed the decline of the social order on the flapper, particularly since women were identified as the moral nurturers of family life and hence of society. Others, however, recognized that the flapper represented a positive response to the sociopolitical changes of the war and suffrage, reflecting women's attempt to free themselves from the unnatural restrictions imposed on them, but not on men.

A Flapper was commonly understood to be a girl or young woman who demonstrated a rebellious, or at least unconventional, attitude through her appearance, behavior, and speech....

... The Flapper and her male counterparts were in rebellion against the Victorian code of manners and morals which had developed over several generations in Great Britain and the United States. One of the essential elements of this code, as it applied to middle- and upper-class Americans, was based on the widespread assumption that women were morally superior to men. Therefore, they were to be "guardians of morality" and were expected to act accordingly. "Proper" young ladies refrained from all physical contact with men before they married. They were supposed to wait until the "right man" came along, then marry, and presumably "live happily ever after." Most Americans felt that it was wrong for respectable women to smoke or drink, although among some families, it was acceptable to sip an occasional glass of wine.

The so-called Victorian code also drew upon the most universal conviction that women were weaker than men physically, emotionally, and perhaps intellectually, and were dependent on male relatives for social position, security, and direction. Therefore, women's greatest aspiration should be to be dutiful daughters, sisters, wives, and mothers. As Rheta Childe Dorr described the role of women in 1910, "women . . . have been engaged in the rearing, as well as the bearing of children. They have made the home, they have cared for the sick, ministered to the aged, and given to the poor. . . . They lived lives of constant service, within the narrow confines of a home. Their labor was given to those they loved, and the reward they looked for was purely a spiritual reward." Because they were supposed to be dependent upon men, proper young ladies restrained any temptations to be aggressive or authoritative. Men must make the decisions and women must accommodate themselves obediently to those decisions.

This code had been under strain before World War I. Forces generated by the industrial developments of the late nineteenth century had opened up new job opportunities for women and had increased middle-class affluence sufficiently to encourage some women to go beyond the well-established patterns of behavior. . . .

As Flapperism became more and more in vogue among young women and girls, its characteristics were more specifically identified. In looking back on her recent Flapper experiences, Ruth Hooper explained: "Of course a flapper is proud of her nerve . . . She is shameless, selfish and honest, but at the same time she considers these three attributes virtues. Why not? She takes a man's point of view as her mother never could, and when she loses she is not afraid to admit defeat, whether it be a prime lover or $20 at auction. . . . She can take a man—the man of the hour—at his face value, with no foolish promises that will need a disturbing and disagreeable breaking." Except for the heavy application of bright cosmetics, the Flapper was acquiring traits and behavioral practices hitherto belonging exclusively to men, and this ex-Flapper did not repent of her actions one bit.

Attitudes of this sort were bound to cause controversy between the generations, and they did. They drew special attention from clergymen, educators, and other arbiters of manners and morals. The *Literary Digest* inquired in its issue for May 14, 1921: "Is the Younger Generation in Peril? Is the 'old-fashioned girl,' with all that she stands for in sweetness, modesty, and innocence, in danger of becoming extinct? Or was she really no better nor worse than the 'up-to-date' girl—who, in turn, will become 'the old-fashioned girl' to a later generation? Is it even possible, as a small but impressive minority would have us believe, that the girl of today has certain new virtues of 'frankness, sincerity, seriousness of purpose,' lives on 'a higher level of morality,' and is on the whole 'more-clean-minded and clean-lived' than her predecessors?" The *Digest* asked the opinions of church newspaper editors, presidents of colleges and universities, and editors of college newspapers, and in so doing laid the groundwork for a literary debate on the Flapper that was to continue throughout the decade. The responses to the *Digest* inquiry showed a surprisingly even division of opinion between those who believed that conditions were unusually bad and those who believed that they were not. . . .

. . . The *Digest* reported that Catholics were joining Protestants in decrying Flapperism. In an encyclical letter, Pope Benedict admonished the many women, "who, infatuated with the ambition of charming others," wore dresses that "not only excite the disapproval of honest people, but, what is worse, offend Our Lord." He also reprimanded those who indulged in the "barbarous and exotic dances which . . . tear away the shreds of modesty." Reactions from many Catholic publications expanded on the Pope's theme. . . .

While the critics of Flapperism outnumbered its defenders in 1921, there was a substantial group that felt compelled to point out its positive qualities. Supporters suggested that Flapper dress fashions were more sensible and even more healthful than those worn by previous generations of women. President Ray Lyman Wilbur of Stanford University, who thought the new style afforded women "greater freedom of action and better health," was seconded by the mother of a growing girl who said, "the short, not too narrow skirt, and the throat freed from the stiff, uncomfortable collar are a decided improvement in women's dress." Mrs. H. Fletcher Brown, a forty-year-old matron from Wilmington, Delaware, approved the Flapper dress style for older women. She wrote in the *Literary Digest*, July 9, 1921: "Skirts can't be too short for me, now that at this age I am climbing in and out of automobiles, and gardening in the mud, and playing golf in all weather." She also complained about corsets, "with bones digging in and garters pulling at every move. No wonder the modern athletic girl wants them off."

Other defenders of the Flapper in 1921 denied that the morals of the young women, or their male companions, had degenerated. President Kenneth C. M. Sills of Bowdoin College suggested that the new dances and dress styles represented changes in manners rather than morals, and President Henry Lewis Smith of Washington and Lee University concurred. In Smith's opinion "the level of sexual morality is higher today than formerly" among college students, and the Dean of Women at Northwestern University supported these views by declaring in the *Lit-*

erary Digest, May 14, 1921: "There is nothing wrong with the girl of to-day." . . .

The crucial issue in the Flapper controversy centered on whether her actions and attire constituted a basic change in the moral code or simply a shift in style. Those who believed that she was threatening the moral code condemned her. Most of those who considered her a pace-setter in style cheered her on. The debate in 1921 set the tone of the arguments for the rest of the decade. . . .

. . . The Flapper gave the women who followed her an important leg-acy. She created a breach in the wall of tradition and convention that was never quite closed, despite continuing efforts to keep women in "their place"—the home. She reduced the bulk of clothing that the tra-ditional code has insisted was necessary for modesty. She established woman's equal claim to such previously male-only privileges as drink-ing, smoking, swearing, sexual aggressiveness, and even disturbing the peace. As each crop of Flappers came of age, they helped to undercut the strength of the old social values, but this would not have been pos-sible if those values had been constructively relevant to the times.

Source: Gerald E. Critoph, "The Flapper and Her Critics," in *Remember the Ladies: New Perspectives in Women in American History: Essays in Honor of Nelson Manfred Blake,* ed. Carol V. R. George (Syracuse: Syracuse University Press, 1975), 145–160.

DOCUMENT 84: *Adkins v. Children's Hospital* (1923)

In 1918 Congress authorized the Wage Board of the District of Columbia to establish minimum wages for women and children in order to protect them from "conditions detrimental to their health and morals, resulting from wages" deemed "inadequate to main-tain a decent standard of living." Children's Hospital, operating in the District of Columbia, employed in various capacities a number of women with whom it had agreed on wages satisfactory to em-ployees which, in some instances, were lower than the minimum wage fixed by the board. The suit was brought by the hospital to restrain the board from enforcing its order for a minimum wage, arguing that the order, as well as the congressional authorization, as an unconstitutional interference with the right of employer and employee to contract freely.

The Supreme Court supported the hospital, using the Nineteenth Amendment, among other grounds, to argue against special pro-tective legislation for women. It distinguished between maximum hours legislation (see Document 82)—which it saw as associated with concerns of health—and minimum wage legislation, which it viewed as "exclusively ... price-fixing." The opinion of the Court, as delivered by Justice Sutherland, appears in part below. That opinion not only frustrated the efforts of the Consumers' League to show that a ceiling on hours without a floor for wages left women peculiarly unprotected, but it arrested, until the Equal Pay Act of 1963, all progress toward pay equity for women.

The ancient inequality of the sexes, otherwise than physical, as suggested in the *Muller Case* has continued "with diminishing intensity." In view of the great—not to say revolutionary—changes which have taken place since that utterance, in the contractual, political, and civil status of women, culminating in the Nineteenth Amendment, it is not unreasonable to say that these differences have now come almost, if not quite, to the vanishing point. . . . we cannot accept the doctrine that women of mature age . . . require or may be subjected to restrictions upon their liberty of contract which could not lawfully be imposed in the case of men under similar circumstances. To do so would be to ignore all the implications to be drawn from the present day trend of legislation, as well as that of common thought and usage, by which woman is accorded emancipation from the old doctrine that she must be given special protection or be subjected to special restraint in her contractual and civil relationships. . . .
. . . What is sufficient to supply the necessary cost of living for a woman worker and maintain her in good health and protect her morals is obviously not a precise or unvarying sum—not even approximately so. The amount will depend upon a variety of circumstances. . . . The relation between earnings and morals is not capable of standardization. It cannot be shown that well-paid women safeguard their morals more carefully than those who are poorly paid. Morality rests upon other considerations than wages, and there is certainly no such prevalent connection between the two as to justify a broad attempt to adjust the latter with reference to the former. . . .

Source: 261 U.S. 525 (1923).

DOCUMENT 85: Proposed Equal Rights Amendment (1923)

Even before the Nineteenth Amendment was ratified, a militant section of the National American Woman Suffrage Association (NASWA) broke away and in 1920 became the National Woman's

Party (NWP). The NWP saw suffrage as only the first step in the achievement of women's rights. Under the leadership of Alice Paul, the NWP articulated its new mission. The agenda they established had one goal, the civic equality of men and women, which they hoped to achieve by an Equal Rights Amendment (ERA) to the Constitution. In July 1923, the NWP held a convention in Seneca Falls where Alice Paul's draft of the ERA—also known as the Lucretia Mott Amendment—was unanimously accepted.

The NWP's legal research department undertook a state by state analysis of legal discrimination against women. They recognized that eliminating such discrimination in each of the states would be a long, formidable process; by contrast, this discrimination could be ended in one blow with enactment of ERA. Accordingly, the amendment was introduced into both houses of Congress in 1923 and in each successive congressional term thereafter until 1972. (See Part V, Document 107.)

Men and Women shall have equal rights throughout the United States and every place subject to its jurisdiction.

Source: Senate Joint Resolution 21, 68th Cong., 1st Sess., 65 *Congressional Record*, p. 150 (1923).

DOCUMENT 86: A League of Women Voters Survey of the Legal Status of Women (1924)

One year after the National Woman's Party (NWP) introduced the ERA, a survey undertaken by the League of Women Voters documented that women's rights were far from equal to those of men, and that the remnants of English common law still affected women negatively in such areas as contractual and property rights and guardianship of their children. The 1920 suffrage amendment notwithstanding women's legal status in 1924 remained unsatisfactory in many states, lending credence to the arguments of Alice Paul and the NWP that a constitutional amendment was needed.

CONTRACTUAL RIGHTS

There are sixteen states in which married women have an absolute right of contract, without any restrictions. There are four more states where the only restriction is as to her right to convey real estate without her husband joining, and in three of these there is a similar restriction against the husband. There are eight community property states, in which the married woman may make contracts freely as to community property, which is under the control of the husband. In four of the community property states, the wife must join in the conveyance of any real estate which constitutes a part of the community property. In four states, in which her general right to contract has been asserted, her right to convey her real estate without her husband joining in the deed is denied without any reciprocal requirement concerning the husband's real estate. In eight states, a married woman is specifically denied the right to become a surety. This is also true of those states in which there has been no statute giving the general right of contract, and there are nine such states. There are several states in which a decree in court is required before she can become a free trader. There are two states in which women are now living practically under the common law.

PROPERTY RIGHTS

There are eight community property states in which the husband has control of the community property during his lifetime, but in four of these states the wife must join in a conveyance of real estate. In these states, husband and wife have no interest whatever in each other's separate estates. Of the remaining forty states, the laws of twenty-five provide for an equal interest by married persons in each other's real estate. In four states, a married woman has a right to a certain interest in her husband's real estate, where no reciprocal right is granted to the husband.

In seven states, the common law rights of dower and curtesy still subsist.

In fifteen states, there are differences which cannot well be summarized, but which are set out in the body of this pamphlet.

No state by law accords to wives any portion of the family income, except such as they may have earned outside the home, and in six states the husband also takes her wages. In no state may a wife collect for services performed in the home.

In nineteen states, the wife is given the family clothing after the husband's death, and in seven others it may be awarded to her as a part of the special allowance made to the husband's estate.

In forty-three states, parents inherit equally from a deceased child. In only seventeen states, does a wife share equally with the husband in the children's earnings, and there is no state in which the wife is entitled to

a voice in the choice of a family home or in which there is a joint head-
ship in husband and wife.

EQUAL GUARDIANSHIP OF CHILDREN

In thirty-seven states, an equal guardianship law has been passed.
Some of these laws are not so broad as that which has been suggested
by the League Committee, and in other states, interpretations have not
been wholly satisfactory, but in most of the states, where laws have been
passed, interpretations are satisfactory. In one state there is added a proviso that in case of dispute the father's authority shall prevail.

In one, and possibly two states, a father may will a child, born or
unborn, away from the custody of the mother, and in one more state,
may do so in case of the insanity of the mother. Another state permits
the father to appoint a guardian, by his will for a child over fourteen. In
nine states, such a will is recognized where the consent of the mother
has been obtained.

MARRIAGE AND DIVORCE

In fourteen states, common law marriages have been abolished by statute. In five states, some form of provision for a health certificate is made.
In six states, a law has been passed prohibiting the evasion of marriage
laws.

In thirty-eight states, men must be 21 years of age before they may
marry without the consent of parents or guardian, while only nine states
have the same requirement for women. In seven states men are required
to be 18 years of age before they can marry without the consent of parents or guardian, in one state 20 years, one at 17, and one at 16. In thirty-
one states, women must be 18 years of age before they may marry
without consent of the parents or guardian, three at 16, one at 15, and
one at 14.

With consent, there are five states where boys marry as young as 16
and six states in which they may marry at 14. As to girls, with consent
of parents and guardians, in six states they may marry at 12, in seven at
14, in five at 15, and in ten at 16. The other states maintain a higher
standard.

In twenty-one states women are received as jurors.

Source: *Women in American Law*, Vol. 1: *From Colonial Times to the New Deal*, ed.
Marlene Stein Worthman (London: Holmes and Meier, 1985), 376–378.

DOCUMENT 87: "Shall Women Throw Away Their Privileges?" (Edward C. Lukens, 1925)

Discussion as to whether the Equal Rights Amendment (ERA) would help or harm women entered the more important journals of the legal profession. Edward C. Lukens, a practicing attorney, believed that women who supported ERA were either ignorant or irrational. Basing his views on the irreconcilable "physical handicap which nature places upon women," Lukens found it beyond comprehension that women should want to give up their work place protections or the right to receive support if deserted by a spouse, or that they should desire to enter military service.

Until recently popular and even scientific opinion regarded women's reproductive organs as "causing" them to be physically weaker than men, and viewed the condition of child-bearing as a form of illness. Consequently, chivalrous men understood that women—black and immigrant women were not included—needed "easier" working conditions than men as well as other kinds of protection. In Lukens's view, biology determined the destiny of each gender. No wonder he thought that women who wanted ERA were either ignorant or irrational.

It is amazing to anyone familiar with legislation for the protection of women that an effort the success of which would mean the end of all such protection should be made by women. A resolution to amend the Constitution has been introduced in Congress which provides that "Men and women shall have equal rights throughout the United States and every place subject to its jurisdiction." The author and sponsor of this proposed amendment is the National Woman's Party, which announces as its object the "removal of all discriminations in the law." Whether the group that is conducting the campaign in favor of this measure understands its import matters not. The danger is that the great mass of voters, especially the women, will favor it because they do not understand it.

"Equality" is a pleasing word, and we have come to regard "discrimination" as a displeasing word. But equality may involve reduction as well as addition, and the removal of discriminations means the loss of privileges as well as the removal of handicaps. It must not be assumed that equal rights for women in all respects means greater rights for them, nor that the discriminations which the amendment would remove would all be discriminations against them. . . .

... When ... a group of women asks us at one stroke to render it impossible for the rights of women to be either greater or less than the rights of men in any subject whatsoever, it behooves us to look carefully at the possible results. Those who would benefit women must use care lest in removing restrictions they rob them of privileges. Let us therefore look at a few situations in which the equalization process would work in the opposite way to the one chiefly intended. To list completely the existing Federal and State statutes under which women have some right or privilege not granted to men would be tedious. It will suffice to point out a few of them in order to illustrate the danger.

First and foremost, we have the great mass of legislation protecting the working conditions of women. These statutes vary greatly in detail, but there are only four states in the Union that do not have some law limiting the hours of work for women. Nine states have an eight hour limit, while in the majority the limit is nine or ten hours. Eighteen states also have statutory regulations providing for a day of rest, time for meals, or rest periods for women laborers. Sixteen states prohibit night work for women in certain industries or occupations. Thirteen states have laws establishing a minimum wage for women workers.

These statutes apply to women only, treating the question of their working conditions as a subject apart from other labor legislation. To apply the same limits to men would be possible neither constitutionally nor practically. Such laws are restrictions not only upon the employer's right to employ, but also upon the woman's right to work. From a legal standpoint they are restrictions upon the employees, though from an economic and social viewpoint they are for their protection. Equality in legislation, compelled by constitutional amendment, would sweep away this entire body of protective law and bring back the woman worker to her former position which made such laws necessary and caused them to be enacted.

Next in importance come the desertion and nonsupport laws. Most of the states have laws either making it a penal offense for a man to desert and fail to support his wife and children, or enabling the court to compel such a husband or father to make periodical payments for their support, or both. The courts having jurisdiction in this matter are exceedingly busy, and thousands of dollars are collected for destitute families from deserting husbands through their process. There is no provision in these statutes for compelling a deserted wife to contribute to the support of her husband, and the statutory basis for these "support orders" would fall, under the equality amendment. The unfortunate wives who bring their petitions to these courts come asking for support and not for equality. In the large cities they come in great numbers. They ask for bread, and shall we give them a stone by telling them that their husbands can desert them with impunity because women have been granted equality? ...

... There are many ways in which the position of women has improved that are economic and social. The most effective efforts of those who have sincerely and intelligently desired to help women, whether in the field of legislation or in other fields, have been directed toward the solution of problems and the alleviation of hardships which are peculiar to women. The legislation cited represents an attempt to make women more nearly equal to men in the competitive struggle than nature has made them, by allowing them privileges and immunities not given to men. The physical handicap which nature places upon women cannot be removed even by constitutional amendment, and the laws and customs of civilization recognize this handicap and seek to protect women from dangers and hardships that may result from it. The kind of legislation that assists in this beneficent purposes [sic] rests upon the difference between women and men, and a system of law which refused to recognize this difference would be cruel to women. There are various forms of protection that women need and that men do not need.

It is surprising indeed that women should seek to throw away these protections. Do they really want to be allowed to work at night in factories and mills? Would they rather not be able to compel deserting husbands to support them? Or is it the women who do not work in factories anyhow, and who do not need their husbands' support, who desire an empty equality at the expense of their less fortunate sisters' real welfare?

Let no woman nor man favor this amendment with closed eyes, and fail to see the ugly thing that lurks behind the alluring mask of equality. A few women favor the measure because they are out of touch with the real facts of life's struggle; the danger is that many will favor it because of ignorance of the results that it must bring. If women act in ignorance, and men follow them through stupid sentimentality, the efforts of a century of true liberalism may be sacrificed to a fetish based upon a falsehood. If women become awake to their own interests, and men temper their chivalry with common sense, the way will be left open for further progress toward the real safeguarding and elevation of womanhood.

Source: Edward C. Lukens, "Shall Women Throw Away Their Privileges?," *American Bar Association Journal* 11, no. 10 (October 1925), 645–646.

DOCUMENT 88: "Women Should Have Equal Rights with Men: A Reply" (Burnita S. Matthews, 1926)

The reply to Edward Lukens (Document 87) came from a lawyer, Burnita Shelton Matthews, who found his position unpersuasive.

Matthews contended that protective legislation did not protect women; rather, it benefited men, who profited from the limitations imposed on women workers.

Second, she argued Lukens was wrong on factual grounds regarding the dependency of women. She asserted that many women, including over half of those recently fired, supported children and other dependents. Further, as regards his claim that women were acting out of ignorance in supporting the proposed Equal Rights Amendment, she contended that various women's groups had done important research on the issue of such an amendment. They had formed their conclusions on the basis of these considered judgments.

Finally, although not included in the portion of the document which follows (but part of the reply to Lukens), she affirmed the need for an unequivocal constitutional position on equality, rather than a slow, piecemeal legislation, that could be altered by the next legislature.

In an article in the October issue of the American Bar Association Journal, Edward Clark Lukens, of the Philadelphia Bar, states that the Woman's Party is proposing an amendment to the National Constitution providing that "Men and women shall have equal rights throughout the United States and every place subject to its jurisdiction," and that it is amazing to find women thus seeking to end the "privileges" and "protection" of their sex. . . .

The Woman's Party believes that if labor legislation is desirable, or necessary, it should be enacted for all workers irrespective of sex. Protective legislation that includes women, but exempts men, handicaps women's economic advancement. It limits the woman worker's scope of activity and increases that of the man by barring her from certain occupations, by excluding her from employments at night, and by "protecting" her to such an extent as to render her ineffective as a competitor. Moreover, to restrict the conditions of women's work, and not those of men, fortifies the harmful assumption that to labor for pay is primarily the prerogative of the male, and that women are a class apart who are only allowed to engage in paid work at special hours, under special supervision, and subject to special government regulations.

When there is an examination one by one of each of the "privileges" women are supposed to enjoy, it is found that in practically every case it is really the man, not the woman, who is protected. Take an instance from Wisconsin. Several years ago that state gave to women "the same rights and privileges under the law as men," except that they were not to be denied "the special protection and privileges" which they then enjoyed "for the general welfare." Of course, it was supposed that by the passage of this law, women were eligible for employment by the legislature, and that an old statute limiting legislative employees to men had been superseded. But the positions were not opened to women. The ruling was that the "legislative service necessitates work during very long and often unseasonable hours," and that it is for the special protection of women to be excluded from such service. So women still retain the "privilege" of having all positions under the Wisconsin legislature closed to them, and open only to men.

And if another instance is needed, witness the women employees of the New York Transportation companies who lost the actual protection of well-paid jobs when the legislature in 1919 imposed upon them the theoretical protection of a labor law for women only. It will be remembered that this law limited the working day of women employed as ticket agents, guards and conductors, to nine hours, and prohibited night work between 10 p. m. and 6 a. m. At the request of the Industrial Commission, an examination of the books of the transportation companies in Greater New York was made to show how nearly the new law was in harmony with women's employment at the time the law was passed. What this examination really revealed was that 83 per cent of the employments of women were not in accord with the new statute. Nor could adjustments to the law be made. For example, the women could not take any of the night shifts, and hence could not conform to the established seniority rule whereby those employees who had been the longest in the service had the preference in shifts and easy runs. The Brooklyn Rapid Transit discharged more than 300 women. The New York Railways Company dropped 203. These eliminations are typical of those of other companies. Yet the women and their employers were very anxious that they retain their positions. More than half of the women were supporting children or other dependents. The work was much easier than domestic service, and the hours fewer and more regular. The rate of pay was higher. The health of the women was improved. Notwithstanding this, the "protection" of the law ousted the women from their jobs. Men, many of whom opposed the employment of women in the transportation service, were in reality the law's beneficiaries. . . .

Mr. Lukens intimates that in favoring the proposed Equal Rights Amendment, women act in ignorance. The Woman's Party had a staff of attorneys examine and tabulate all the constitutional and statutory provisions and court decisions in the United States relative to the existing status of women. In addition, Councils composed of different economic and professional groups of women, such as industrial workers, home makers, teachers, students and federal employees, conducted studies as to the desirability of equality, and the best way of establishing it in their particular fields. The Woman's Party did all this before proposing the Equal Rights Amendment, and in order determine the wisest method to pursue. So any charge that the proponents of the amendment are not well informed is without foundation.

Source: Burnita S. Matthews, "Women Should Have Equal Rights with Men: A Reply," *American Bar Association Journal* 12, no. 2 (February 1926), 117–120.

DOCUMENT 89: Working Women Respond to the Equal Rights Amendment (1920–1940)

It is a testimony to the complexity of the issues surrounding the proposed Equal Rights Amendment that some working women sided with conservatives like Lukens (see Document 87)—but not because they thought themselves physically weaker than men. Rather, they saw themselves as lacking other protections that men had, including a legal system that supported men over women (see Document 86) and unions that favored men. Fearing that ERA would remove their only tangible protection, they refused to support it.

WHAT DO WORKING WOMEN SAY?

The Woman's Party Amendment Would Endanger
Labor Laws Now Affecting 4,000,000 of Them

Would you say that, in order to give women in Ohio the right to be taxi-drivers or open a shoe-shining parlor, you ought to take away the 48-hour law for women in Massachusetts and the hour laws of 42 other states?

Would you say that in order to give the right to jury service to women in twenty states, you ought to throw into court the mother's pension laws of 39 states?

Would you go so far as to say that you would be justified in even taking the risk of such consequences to the millions of wage earning women and mothers, for the sake of a few prospective women taxi-drivers, bootblacks, and jurors?

Especially when you could get what you want without taking such risk?

Where the Risk Lies

Yet it is just exactly those risks—and many more—that the National Woman's Party proposes to take in its constitutional amendment which reads:

"Men and women shall have equal rights throughout the United States and every place subject to its jurisdiction."

The risk is due to the fact, first, that this is an amendment to the United States Constitution and would invalidate automatically all laws in conflict with it, without automatically replacing most of them.

It is due, second, to the fact that blanket provisions in law, whether in the constitution or in statutes, require court interpretation in each case, and the term[s] "rights" and "equal rights" are subject to diverse construction.

Legal Rights vs. Economic Rights

And, last but not least, the risk is due to the fact that legal rights and other rights are not by any means identical. Legal equality is not necessarily the same as economic equality. It may actually defeat economic equality.

For instance, a state may give the wife a right to sue her husband for non-support. The husband has not the same right to sue her. The proposed amendment would probably, lawyers say, give this man and this woman equal rights by taking away, automatically, the woman's right to sue.

Having thus achieved **legal equality**, however, the wife, whose best years have been spent caring for her home and children, now finds herself confronted with the necessity of earning her living and also of contributing to the support of her children. Untrained for business or industry, her life's experience totally different from her husband's, she is now faced with identical responsibilities and a handicap which only a superhuman could overcome.

Legal equality it may be.

Economic equality it is not.

Reality vs. Theory

Or consider the woman in industry. She is working, say, in a state with an 8-hour law for women, passed because women had been working much longer hours. The man-employing industries of that state, however, are probably on an 8-hour schedule established by their unions. The 8-hour law and the 8-hour trade agreement both limit the worker's freedom of contract. But the law would probably be destroyed by the so-called "equal rights" amendment, because the **legal** rights of women are restricted thereunder but not the **legal** rights of men. In other words, to give the women legal equality with the men, the amendment would take away the 8-hour day from the women but not from the men.

This may be legal equality.

Economic equality, decidedly not.

The Sensible Course

The risk involved in the National Woman's Party amendment is, moreover, a wholly gratuitous risk. The amendment is altogether unnecessary, because the things it purports to do can all be done, right now, exactly as most of them would have to be done in any case by Acts of Congress and the states, which already have the power the amendment would confer.

Not only **can** those things all be done, but they are actually being done—86 new laws or amendments to laws in 30 states since the federal woman suffrage amendment was passed.

Why take a gratuitous risk?

Elisabeth Christman
Secretary International Glove Workers Union,
Secretary-Treasurer National Women's League of America

Source: *America's Working Women*, comp. and ed. Rosalyn Baxandall, Linda Gordon, and Susan Reverby (New York: Random House, 1976), 253–255.

DOCUMENT 90: Regulation of Employment for Women (1933)

In this document Blanche Grozier takes issue with protective laws that are grounded on the view that work produces, "as a matter of fact," physical harm to women, their children, and "the race in the indefinite future"; and that, given these self-evident effects, government should regulate women's working conditions.

In advancing her argument, she uses *Muller v. Oregon* (Document 73), which maintained that because of their delicate nature, women required protective legislation limiting their working hours and types of employment. As a background to her thinking was the decision in *Adkins v. Children's Hospital* (Document 84), that argued that since "revolutionary changes" such as the Nineteenth Amendment had almost erased the differences between the sexes, there was no need for protective legislation.

For Grozier, women are not delicate—no more so than men; and the so-called protective legislation such as that examined in *Muller v. Oregon*, simply interfere with women's capacity to compete equally with men.

In so arguing, she was expressing the views of some women who saw both *Muller* and *Adkins* (and these two decisions should be read together, if one wishes to understand their meaning in full) as poor decisions. *Muller* because it placed limitations on women's work hours, and *Adkins* because it did not remove *all* protections, only the legislation that placed a floor on women's salaries. The consequences? Because of *Adkins*, women could continue to receive lower wages than men—there was no floor on what women could be paid; and on account of *Muller*, they would not be able to work more hours to make up the difference—a classic double bind.

Courts have upheld "protective" laws on the ground that (1) the work produces, as a matter of fact, actual physical harm to (a) women, (b) their children, or (c) the race in the indefinite future; or that (2) there is such a general belief to that effect that proof of its correctness is not required. Both of these positions are unjustified. There are in these cases judicial allusions to women's "delicate organism" which would have done credit to the historic talent of a Victorian lady, or to an advertising writer for Lydia Pinkham. Such phrases occur over and over in all the decisions on this subject, in the same words or with slight modifications, and they present a strange contrast with the well-known facts of the situation.

Women live longer than men, boy babies have a higher mortality that girls, and the women of primitive races have always been the heavy workers—a condition by no means confined to primitive races. The male sex has its full share of physical weaklings, whether that refers to stature and weight or to illness or general predilection to illness upon slight provocation. Since Victorian times, when an appearance of ill health was a practical advantage to a woman, it has not even been contended that women are less healthy than men. Their endurance is generally considered high. The idea of the physical superiority of men, from which has come a long train of consequences which are still with us, is practically reduced to the single point of muscular strength—lifting power—which in ordinary occupations is of no significance whatever. Even that has to be bolstered up by a policy of selecting always for comparison the largest men and the smallest women. A recent automobile advertisement was a perfect example of this tendency; it said that the brakes worked as well under the feather-like touch of a ninety-pound woman as under the heavy tread of a two-hundred-pound man. If it is a question of physical superiority, there should be laws limiting the physical exertion of small or unhealthy men, and large women should step into the freedom from such restriction now enjoyed by small men.

The court said in *Muller* v. *Oregon* that the physical inferiority of women placed them at a disadvantage in the struggle for existence. That seems very doubtful. A muscular superiority alone, even if uniformly present, is not much of an advantage in the struggle for existence now, and it probably never was. There are too many other and more potent factors. "She is not an equal competitor," said the court as a reason for upholding legislation which is the reason why she is not an equal competitor. "From the standpoint of the effort to maintain an independent position in life, she is not upon an equality." She has at least an equality in that respect, except when she encounters laws which put her at a disadvantage. Even where the maintaining of an independent position in life is a matter of an isolated and hand-to-hand encounter with a little piece of stony land, many women have managed to get a living, and probably easier than a man could get along without a woman's assistance in the same situation. Women even enter such a life voluntarily, as is shown by the fact that almost one-third of the homesteads taken up in Alberta, since the new regulations permitting it early in 1931, have been secured by women. Much more in cities, where work is more specialized, and small individuals of either sex do not have any particular difficulties, it would seem that women are very well equipped with natural resources with which to make their own way....

... From all this it would be suspected, even if it were not plain on the face of it, that this latter-day "protection" is not very different from the method of the common law, which gave a woman's property to her husband in order to protect her. Certainly the conservative courts unhesitatingly recognized the old principle in spite of its new guise.

Source: Blanche Grozier, "Regulation of Conditions of Employment of Women," *Boston University Law Review* 13 (1933): 280–292.

DOCUMENT 91: "Challenging Sexual Discrimination in the Historical Profession" (Jacqueline Goggin, circa 1930s)

Throughout the nineteenth and twentieth centuries women's struggle to attain professional status was arduous and unending. The history profession was no exception. From 1893, when Kate Ernest Levi became the first woman to earn a Ph.D., from the University of Wisconsin, to 1993, only two women became president of the American Historical Society, the leading professional organization. In addition, only relatively recently have women historians been considered able enough to teach in coeducational institutions.

Even today they are rarely found in all-male institutions, although men have taught in all-women's institutions from their inception.

The following document demonstrates the obstacles placed in the path of women who strove to achieve professional status in history and sought work in their field of interest. Men were regarded as the guardians of the profession: they defined the important fields of historical study and what was considered historical reality, and they determined whose papers would be published and who would be hired. It should come as no surprise, therefore, that only in the last five to ten years have the leading professional journals published articles on women's history, even though earlier historians, such as Julia Cherry Spruill and Elizabeth Anthony Dexter, wrote important doctoral dissertations on the subject.

Feeling excluded by men from all regional historical groups, women historians, mainly from the seven sister colleges (see introduction to Part III), organized a conference in Lakeville, Connecticut, which later became known as the Berkshire Conference. The Berkshire Conference now exercises strong influence on the policy of the American Historical Association and has played a leading role in defining women's history as a significant scholarly activity.

Almost from its inception, the historical profession has been dominated by white male practitioners. There is little evidence that, prior to 1940, white male historians collectively offered encouragement or support to female colleagues. In fact, the records of the American Historical Association and history departments, and the personal papers of male and female historians reveal that discrimination against women deterred them from realizing fully their scholarly and professional potential as historians.

Women confronted many difficulties as they attempted to gain scholarly credibility and respect from male historians. The intellectual and social isolation imposed by sexual discrimination was a powerful deterrent to sustained scholarly and professional activity. Viewed as intellectually inferior, women had difficulty finding employment commensurate with their education and training. They had difficulty obtaining positions on historical association committees and governing boards, publishing articles in the major historical journals, and presenting papers at meetings of the major historical organizations. When they did attend professional meetings, they were frequently confronted with segregated social functions, such as smokers for men and teas for women. Yet women historians published, served on committees, were elected to office, and presented papers at historical meetings. They also actively protested against sexual discrimination and formed support groups and networks to promote scholarly and professional advancement. They formed alliances with and received support from women outside the historical profession and were active members of women's organizations such as the American Association of University Women, the General Federation of Women's Clubs, the League of Women Voters, the National Woman's Party, and the Women's International League for Peace and Freedom. . . .

Although female historians had by 1940 acquired an organization in the Berkshire Conference and a small measure of recognition from their male colleagues, these gains were fragile, part of what sociologist Jesse Bernard termed the "flowing and ebbing tides" of professional women's status. Female historians, like women in other professions, were increasingly marginalized in the 1940s and 1950s. Only in the 1960s did large numbers of women reenter the profession. Many turned to and developed women's history as a means of advancing the position of women. Women historians and women's history are now well integrated into the profession. Less certain is whether the increasing presence of women and women's history will produce full equality for female historians.

Source: Jacqueline Goggin, "Challenging Sexual Discrimination in the Historical Profession: Women Historians and the American Historical Association, 1890–1940," *American Historical Review* 97 no.3 (June 1992): 770–802.

DOCUMENT 92: Gender at Work: The Depression and World War II (1933)

Ruth Milkman's essay discusses how women workers were affected by the Great Depression and World War II. Her analysis examines the Marxist-feminist theory that women functioned as a "reserve army," discarded when employment needs were low and called into use when the demand for labor was high.

In her discussion of the Great Depression, Milkman uses Labor Department statistics (not included in the document below) to demonstrate that the reserve army hypothesis does not accurately describe how women were affected, for the statistics reveal a far lower percentage of unemployment among women than among men. (See Document 94 for the exception among black women workers.)

In order to explain this phenomenon, Milkman examined the different kinds of jobs held by men and women and the conditions of their employment. She concluded that women's sex-typed work, which was mainly service oriented, was less affected by the Depression than were men's jobs in the manufacturing area. Furthermore, many women managed to retain their part-time jobs during the Depression, and those who lost part-time jobs were not accounted for statistically. Statistics also reveal that a greater number of women sought and obtained work than ever before, to compensate for the unemployment of their husbands and fathers.

But from Milkman's perspective, the biggest blow to the reserve army thesis was the great need for women's work in the home. The Depression required women to become more resourceful at home, taking on more duties perhaps by running rooming houses or washing clothes, and extending greater support to husbands who had lost their jobs. The reserve army theory therefore bore no resemblance to Depression reality, which, however, deepened gender roles.

The war years increased the demand for female labor. In this instance, the reserve army thesis worked. Women replaced men who entered the armed forces and were even given opportunities to earn men's wages—not without reminders, however, of the temporary nature of the work. These work experiences were important, for women discovered that they had untapped capabilities. After the war many refused to give up their jobs, or when forced to, looked for other work. They joined the growing number of female professionals, setting the stage for the feminist movements that emerged in the sixties and seventies, especially after the publication of Betty Friedan's *The Feminine Mystique* (see Document 100).

Marxist-feminists have argued that women function as a "reserve army" of labor power, to be drawn on in periods when labor is scarce and expelled in periods of labor surplus. Ideology, in this view, plays a crucial role, both perpetuating women's lack of class consciousness over the long term, and propelling them in and out of the labor force in response to changing economic conditions. . . .

The Great Depression of the 1930s was the most severe economic contraction Americans have experienced in the twentieth century to date. The official estimate of unemployment for 1933 is 25 percent (and the actual proportion of people who experienced economic deprivation was probably much larger). Unfortunately, the only national unemployment data available for this period which are disaggregated by sex are those collected by the U.S. Census Bureau in 1930, when the percentage of all workers who had been laid off or fired and were seeking work was only 6.5. These early data are in several respects highly problematic, and can by no means be assumed to be an accurate representation of the extent to which the nation's available labor power was unutilized in 1930. Nevertheless, for our purposes they are quite instructive.

The April 1930 census found an unemployment rate of 4.7 percent for women, while that enumerated for men was 7.1 percent. . . . There is some evidence that as the Depression deepened the relative position of women grew somewhat worse, but the available data clearly indicate that, *insofar as their paid labor force participation was concerned, women were less affected than men by the contraction.*

This is precisely the opposite of what the "reserve army" theory about the relationship of women to economic fluctuations would lead one to expect. One might turn to an alternative hypothesis . . . that the increasing participation of women in the "male" sphere of paid work outside the home has been carefully delimited by an ideology linking that activity to their sex. The vast majority of women work in "women's jobs," occupations which frequently have some structural resemblance to their family role. They work in industries which produce commodities formerly manufactured by women in the home, such as clothing and processed food. In white collar occupations, [they worked] as secretaries, teachers, waitresses, nurses, and so forth. . . .

. . . Even in occupational groups sex-typed male, the unemployment rates of women are lower than those of men in the same occupation. This suggests that the overall gap between the male and female rates may have been somewhat less wide in actuality. . . . One reason for this is that women were probably undercounted in the Census of Unemployment. To be counted as "unemployed" one must either have been temporarily laid off or have lost her/his job and be actively seeking another one. Young single women and, even more so, widows and divorced women would be those most likely to be self-supporting, and therefore most likely to continue seeking work in spite of any difficulties. This would also be true of the majority of men in the labor force. Married women, in contrast, might be more easily discouraged if their husbands were employed, and as a result undercounted in the official unemployment statistics. Indeed . . . women under twenty suffered the highest unemployment rates, and . . . there was a general decrease in frequency of unemployment with increasing age. Furthermore, the recorded unemployment rate of married women was slightly lower than that of single women, while that of widowed and divorced women was highest of all.

There are other factors as well which suggest that the gap in male and female unemployment rates may have been somewhat less wide than the data indicate. Women workers, both in hard times and in the best of times, suffer various forms of discrimination which increase the likelihood that they will be underemployed. They frequently work in highly seasonal industries, and therefore have only irregular employment, being hired and fired in response to *short-term* industrial fluctuations. Also, women work part-time more frequently than men. Thus there is characteristically a substantial amount of unrecorded underemployment among women, even in good times, and under depressed industrial conditions one would expect some increase in its frequency. To the extent that this was true in the 1930s, one might conclude that the "reserve army" theory is applicable to some sectors of the female labor market, but this was the case only because the "women's jobs" involved were volatile, *not because men replaced women in them.*

. . . One explanation for the deterioration of women's relative position in the unemployment rolls might be that large numbers of women previously engaged only in unpaid housework were forced to seek paid work during the depression, in efforts to compensate for the decline in family income resulting from the unemployment of male family members. Indeed, total female labor force participation rose in the period from 1930 to 1940 more than in any previous decade in the twentieth century. . . .

. . . Perhaps the most important reason for the inadequacy of the "reserve army" theory is its failure to comprehend the primary importance of women's economic role in the family. Indeed, it is the economic need for their unpaid work in the home from which the caste-like structure of the female labor force, which is so basic to the experience of women during a crisis in their role as paid workers, first emerges. Even for this reason alone, it would be foolhardy to overlook the impact of economic crises on women's family role.

The productive activity of women in the home is accorded lower social status than any other occupation: housework is a "labor of love" in a society whose universal standard of value is money. Because it is not remunerated with a wage, housework does not directly produce surplus value. However, it does maintain and reproduce the ability of family members to work productively, their labor power, which they sell in the labor market for a wage. . . .

. . . People who were unemployed naturally turned to their families for support. The work of women in physically and psychologically maintaining their families became tremendously difficult as family incomes declined and the psychological stresses attending unemployment took their toll. Women showed amazing resourcefulness in coping with the crisis on the family level. They used a wide variety of strategies, generally turning back toward "traditional" forms of family organization.

The most immediate problem facing the family struck by unemployment was the material hardship created by their lowered income. Women cut back family expenditures in many areas. Typical strategies were moving to quarters with lower rent, having telephones removed, and denying themselves many purchased goods and services to which they had become accustomed in the prosperity of earlier years. Clothing, prepared meals, domestic service, automobiles, magazine subscriptions and amusements were among the many products and services which suffered declines in sales as optimists heralded the "live at home movement." . . .

. . . Since his role as wage-earner is often the basis of the father's status within the family, that status tends to be lowered by his unemployment. The man without a job in the 1930s often felt superfluous and frustrated, "because in his own estimation he fails to fulfill what is the central duty of his life, the very touchstone of his manhood—the role of family provider." The strain attending unemployment was exacerbated in cases where other family members were earning money. . . .

To say that the unemployed father lost status in the family would seem to imply that women who assumed the role of "provider" gained somehow. But such a role reversal was not a simple exchange of power. Women's responsibility for providing emotional support to family members was not diminished during this period. On the contrary, the reversal roles made this task much more difficult, for an unemployed husband demanded more support than ever before. If there was any increased recognition of woman's economic role in the family, it did not represent a gain in status, for no one was comfortable with the new state of affairs, and the reversal of roles was resented by everyone involved . . . .

Women in families affected by unemployment, then, were under incredible pressure from all sides. Their responsibility to maintain their families materially and psychologically became much more difficult to fulfill. Sociologists who studied the impact of the depression on families at the time noted that these strains generally resulted in an initial period of disorientation, which was ultimately resolved either through adjustment or "disintegration" of the family. Whether or not a family was able to adjust to the new situation depended on a variety of factors, but on the whole, these studies showed that the impact of the crisis was to exaggerate previous family patterns. "Well-organized" families became more unified, while the problems of unstable families were accentuated. . . .

[As regards WW II] Even where the beginning wages for women and men were equal, however, women rarely had equal opportunities for advancement. Similarly, although women war workers often became members of unions, they frequently experienced differential treatment within the union structure. Many contracts provided that women and men be listed on separate seniority lists, and some stated outright that women's tenure in jobs previously held by men would be theirs "for the duration" only.

This definition of women's war employment as temporary was not limited to unions, but had been explicit in all of the propaganda issued by government and industry urging women to enter the paid labor force. The thrust of the appeal, indeed, was that women could do "their part" in the war effort by taking industrial jobs. The expectation that they would gracefully withdraw from "men's jobs" when the war ended and the rightful owners reappeared on the scene was clear from the first.

Moreover, during World War II, suddenly jobs which had previously had all the attributes of "men's work" acquired a new femininity and glamour. There was an unrelenting effort to reconcile the traditional image of women with their new role. . . .

Women were laid off in huge numbers immediately after the war ended. As industrial plants reconverted to consumer-oriented production they returned to their pre-war male work force. In January 1946 the number of women in the labor force was 4 million less than at the 1944 peak, and only 2 million more than in 1940. And yet, the material fact of "reconversion" to peacetime production would force the withdrawal of many women from the labor force. They were eventually reintegrated into it, not in the heavy industry "war jobs" but rather in the white collar and service occupations which had been part of the female labor force before the war and which continued to expand in the postwar years. While women's penetration into "men's jobs" with high status and pay during the war years proved ephemeral, then, their increased presence in the paid labor force would be duplicated in later years.

Source: Ruth Milkman, "Women's Work and the Economic Crisis: Some Lessons from the Great Depression," in *A Heritage of Her Own: Towards a New Social History of American Women*, ed. Nancy F. Cott and Elizabeth H. Pleck (New York: Simon and Schuster, 1979), 507–539.

DOCUMENT 93: Employed Mothers and Child Care During the Depression and World War II (circa 1940)

One of the most unchanging, ubiquitous issues facing working mothers is child care. Prior to World War II, however, few middle-class women considered working after childbirth, leaving the issue largely unattended, with one exception. During the Depression years, the administration of Franklin Roosevelt created some jobs for the unemployed by opening nursery schools for the children of working mothers. The Federal Emergency Relief Administration authorized the establishment of the nursery schools in 1933, and the Works Progress Administration (WPA) estimated that by 1938 about 200,000 children from low-income families had attended the schools. As prosperity and family incomes increased, fewer children were eligible to attend.

The involvement of the federal government in day care was revived during World War II. But many working mothers did not resort to using the day care centers, largely because the government did not make them sufficiently attractive; inconvenient location, high charges, and concern over the care given to sick children were some factors. Many preferred to make their own arrangements, often using other family members. At the end of the war the government withdrew its participation despite the increased number of women who continued to work.

When the economic depression of the 1930's impelled the Government to make plans to increase employment, nursery schools were among the types of educational work organized. They were specifically authorized by the Federal Emergency Relief Administration in October 1933. They enabled many children to attend nursery schools whose families otherwise could not have given them this experience, even though the primary objective had been to give useful work to unemployed persons and though these services had to be fitted in among other work projects.

In 1931–35, the Works Progress Administration reported some 1,900 nursery schools in which 75,000 children were enrolled. Early in 1938 the Administrator estimated that more than 200,000 children of low-income families had benefited from these schools. As the country moved toward greater prosperity, fewer families were eligible to send children to the WPA schools, but the value of nursery schools had been so fully shown that public demand for them continued.

During World War II women were drawn into the labor force more extensively than at any previous time in this country's history. . . .

In June 1941, Congress passed Public Law 137 (the Lanham Act) assigning responsibility to the Federal Works Agency "to provide for the acquisition and equipment of public works (community facilities) made necessary by the defense program." The language contained no specific provision that child-care facilities would come within the meaning of public works.

The liberalization of this law, sought by the Federal Works Agency, was granted in August 1942 by the Committee on Buildings and Grounds, whose members recognized the imperative need and specified that child-care centers were public works within the meaning of the act. . . . The number of child-care centers receiving financial assistance from the Federal Government varied from month to month. The first regular report, August 1943, showed 19,197 children enrolled in 1,726 centers operating with an average daily attendance of 36,923. Enrollments, attendance, and number of units in operation continued to increase, with few exceptions, every month until the peak in July 1944, when 3,102 units were in operation servicing 129,357 children, with an average daily attendance of 109,202. About 60 percent of the children served throughout the program were of preschool age....

It is difficult to establish the total number of different children cared for during the life of the Lanham Act program, since there was considerable turnover throughout the period as families moved from one area to another, changed employment, or withdrew their children from centers for various reasons. However, it has been estimated that roughly 550,000 to 600,000 different children received care at one time or another during the period of time Lanham Act funds were dispensed for these purposes.... After the war, the number of centers decreased gradually, then more rapidly. Federal funds finally were discontinued at the end of February 1946....

Source: America's Working Women, comp. and ed. Rosalyn Baxandall, Linda Gordon, and Susan Reverby (New York: Random House, 1976), 272–275.

DOCUMENT 94: Puerto Rican and Black Women's Paid Labor (1940s)

Women have always suffered from wage discrimination, although during the early years of the American Industrial Revolution the gender gap in wages lessened because of the decreased importance of muscle power and the increased participation of women in factory work. But between 1950 and 1980 the gap stabilized. In Puerto Rico, as well as in the continental United States, the postwar economy brought an increase in the number of women factory and service sector workers. Gender wage discrimination, as the following document demonstrates, is prevalent in Puerto Rico.

Black American women suffered in competition with Caucasian women entering the service sector during the Depression. The experience of Florence Rice in the following document reveals the precariousness of their position. They were and are subject to two widespread prejudices, being African American and female.

A. SOME EXPERIENCES OF PUERTO RICAN WOMEN

Industrialization and economic growth in Puerto Rico . . . resulted in increasing participation of women in the labor force. In 1970, women constituted 27.1% of the total labor force, up from 22% in 1962, an increase due totally to non-agricultural employment. This difference would appear to be due to the fact that, at least in this early phase of industrialization in Puerto Rico, which emphasized light manufacturing, women were employed at a rate nearly equal to men. Thus, in 1970, women constituted 48.6% or nearly half of the labor force in manufacturing. They also constituted 44.8% of the persons employed in public administration, and 47.2% of those in service jobs, two other fast-growing employment sectors.

Women provided a cheap labor force for the start of industrialization in Puerto Rico. In the industries established through the Office of Economic Development, the salary differential was as high as 30.3% in industries where women predominated as compared to those employing mostly men. This reflected the fact that women were concentrated in the manufacture of nondurable consumer goods such as textiles, clothing, leather goods, and tobacco, where pay is considerably lower than in durable goods such as metal, stone, or glass products, where men predominate. The average salary for all women working full-time in 1970 was $3,006, compared to $3,382 for men. However, women were also concentrated in the lower-paid jobs, with 42.2% receiving less than $2,000 a year (compared to 26.7% of the men).

The recent concentration upon heavy capital-intensive industry in Puerto Rico as well as in other developing areas also threatens female employment. In these capital-intensive industries, labor tends to be reduced to a minimum and to be highly skilled, favoring the creation of a labor aristocracy in which men predominate.

Source: *America's Working Women*, comp. and ed. Rosalyn Baxandall, Linda Gordon, and Susan Reverby (New York: Random House, 1976), 313.

B. THE EXPERIENCE OF FLORENCE RICE

I know the Bronx slave market. We used to stand there and people would come and give you any kind of work. At that time it was at 174th street and Sedgwick Avenue. We used to go up there for domestic work. You were competing against each other, because you went out there and you was looking for a dollar a day.

Many times you got a dollar and a half. I always remember my domestic days. Some of the women, when they didn't want to pay, they'd accuse you of stealing. I remember a couple of times the woman said that I had stole something, which I know I hadn't—I just walked out and left that money. It was like intimidation. In those days a white woman says something about a black person, that was it. And what you were subjected to if you'd go in domestic work, the men—I encountered it one time. This man picked me up and said his wife was ill and then when I got there his wife wasn't there and he wanted to have an affair. It seems like I just had enough sense not to let myself get involved with anything like that and I started crying and he didn't force me and I was able to get out. When maids would get together, they'd talk of it. Some of them was very attractive and good-looking. They always had to fight off the woman's husband.

I got out of domestic and went into the laundry. In fact, it was quite interesting. I got my first laundry job on the slave market. This man came to recruit. If you got there early enough they were recruiting for the laundry. They'd pick you up for a day's work or they'd just pick you up for regular work. I think I got regular work from that time on. I went to work in the Bonn Laundry, which is at 175th street. It was better than domestic work, certainly. You were getting twelve dollars and whatever the change was at that time. This was in '36, I think. I was in the laundry before the unions were organizing there. Twelve dollars—oh God, you had to be there at seven and I know you didn't get off at five. I think you got off at six and you were forced to work Saturdays. I wasn't in there too long before the unions came about. The Laundry Workers Union. It was like the salvation. It certainly got better after the union came in. We got better wages, worked a certain amount of hours.

During the war I worked for Wright Aeronautical. They claim that people can't be trained, that you've got to go through seven, eight weeks of training, when during the war we trained in two weeks. I was an internal grinder. You grind with a great big machine and use a micrometer. And we knew how to use a micrometer and we read blueprints and we read the outline. I think I was making anywhere eighty-five, ninety-five dollars a week, which was utopia. I don't think I belonged to the union. There was a lot of black people in the plant. One of the things, there was no black personnel that I can remember. Our heads was white.

At the end of the war we were turned out into the street. The factory didn't close at that time. The factory continued on. They laid us off. This is no more than I think mostly all of us expected.

I had made up my mind that I wasn't going back into the laundry. I didn't go back to the employment service. What the employment agencies did to the blacks was always direct you back into all the servitude jobs. They never tried to encourage you to get something better. And I had a daughter, but I was just determined I wasn't going to the laundry. At that time in the black community the factory was much better than the laundry, like the laundry was better than domestic work.

It was the same with welfare. I always remember when I went to apply for welfare one time, and the woman said, well she needed someone to clean up her house—the welfare investigator, the intake woman, when they sent me to the investigator. She wanted me to do domestic work, and because I refused to do domestic work, I didn't get welfare at that time.

At that time you found lots of black women coming into the garment area. In the cheap shops you found all black women, black and Puerto Rican. A friend of mine heard of a job that was available in her shop. I never saw the kind of a machine I was supposed to work on, and I lied and I said that I knew that machine. She showed me how, she taught me that machine. She said, "All you have to do is sit down and run the machine, if anything happens I'll come up and thread it."

I worked on leggings as a piece worker in Feldman's shop. It was Local 105, International Ladies Garment Workers Union (ILGWU). It was an integrated local. One of the things, they took care of the whites, you didn't have to worry about that. In other words, the white women, white Jewish women, they did always get the work there. Yet I must say with Feldman, he was a pretty fair guy. You would automatically assume this. He was a pretty good boss compared to many of the other bosses. When I say he was fair, I remember that he wanted me to work two machines. When you finished one you got on another machine, and I refused to do it. And I brought the complaint to the union, and the union man came in there, and was very nasty to me, and told me if I didn't want to do it he would get someone else. Well, the union wasn't for us blacks, that's one of the things you recognize. What happened, instead of the union fighting for me, what I did, I got up, put on my clothes, and left. And Feldman, he came to the door and said, "Florence, you and I can talk this out." He said, "I'll tell you what I'll do. I'll guarantee you a salary, that you'll never make less than that." And we worked it out. But as far as the union, the union never stood up for us.

Source: Black Women in White America: A Documentary History, ed. Gerda Lerner (New York: Vintage Books, 1973), 275–281.

DOCUMENT 95: *Goesaert v. Cleary* (1948)

At issue in this case was a 1945 Michigan law that allowed women to work as waitresses in taverns, but barred them, unless they were the wives or daughters of male tavern owners, from the more financially rewarding job of bartender. Other states had enacted comparable legislation (usually after the lobbying efforts of bartenders' associations that excluded women), so license to engage in bartending was denied women in many jurisdictions.

The complaining party, Goesaert, argued that, contrary to conventional belief, women employees in taverns had not experienced any significant safety risks; that, rather, their presence introduced a "civilizing" influence on patrons; and that the law imposed arbitrary and damaging hardships on women, who could serve drinks but could not mix them, unlike the higher-paid bartenders. Thus the law violated the equal protection clause of the Constitution. The opinion of the Court, delivered by Justice Frankfurter, supported the state of Michigan. Frankfurter spoke of the "grave social problems" created by female bartenders, in contrast to the "wholesome atmosphere" male owners could maintain if their wives or daughters tended bars. So he concluded that exceptions for wives and daughters were "not without reason." A dissenting group of three justices, however, saw that the essential issue was not between wives and daughters of tavern owners and all other women, as the majority had ruled, but rather between male and female tavern owners. We have included both the opinion of the Court and that of the dissenters.

Since bartending by women may, in the allowable legislative judgment, give rise to moral and social problems against which it may devise preventive measures, the legislature need not go to the full length of prohibition if it believes that as to a defined group of females other factors are operating which either eliminate or reduce the moral and social problems otherwise calling for prohibition. Michigan evidently believes that the oversight assured through ownership of a bar by a barmaid's husband or father minimizes hazards that may confront a barmaid without such protecting oversight. This Court is certainly not in a position to gainsay such belief by the Michigan legislature.

The dissent:

The statute arbitrarily discriminates between male and female owners of liquor establishments. A male owner, although he himself is always absent from his bar, may employ his wife and daughter as barmaids. A female owner may neither work as a barmaid herself nor employ her daughter in that position, even if a man is always present in the establishment to keep order. This inevitable result of the classification belies the assumption that the statute was motivated by a legislative solicitude for the moral and physical well-being of women who, but for the law, would be employed as barmaids. Since there could be no other conceivable justification for such discrimination against women owners of liquor establishments, the statute should be held invalid as a denial of equal protection.

Source: 335 U.S. 464 (1948).

DOCUMENT 96: "Why I Quit Working" (1951)

Bombarded by views that women's place is in the home, especially after childbirth, many women felt guilty about working. The article below, from *Good Housekeeping* magazine, whose readership was predominantly middle- and working-class women, reflects the ambivalence and tensions of a working mother who was exposed to antiwork propaganda. Although today many more mothers continue to work, studies reveal that they experience the same tensions and ambivalence.

Just over a year ago, I was suffering from that feeling of guilt and despondency familiar to most working mothers who have small children. During the hours I spent in the office, an accusing voice charged continuously, "You should be home with the children." I couldn't have agreed more, which only created an additional tension: the frustrated anger of one who knows what is right but sees no way of doing it. Children need clothes as well as attention; they must be nourished with food as well as love. . . .

One day in 1950, I finally worked out a compromise: a way to be at home with the children and still do some work for which I'd be paid. . . .

A year has passed, and I've had time to judge the advantages and disadvantages of leaving my office job. How they will total up ten years from now, I don't know. But here is my balance sheet of the results to date.

LOST

The great alibi: work. My job, and the demands it made on me, were my always accepted excuses for everything and anything: for spoiled children, neglected husband, mediocre food; for being late, tired, preoccupied, conversationally limited, bored, and boring.

The weekly check. And with that went many extravagances and self-indulgences. I no longer had the pleasure of giving showy gifts (the huge doll, the monogrammed pajamas) and the luxury of saying "My treat." . . .

The special camaraderie and the common language. The warm but impersonal and unprying relationship among working people is one of the most rewarding things about having a job. . . .

One pretty fallacy. For some reason, most working mothers seem to think they could retire with perfect ease; that they could readily adjust themselves to their new role. I don't think so. When you start to devote all your time to homemaking, you run into a whole *new* set of problems. The transition from part-time and full-time mother is difficult to make.

One baseless vanity. I realize now (and still blush over it) that during my working days I felt that my ability to earn was an additional flower in my wreath of accomplishments. Unconsciously—and sometimes consciously—I thought how nice it was for my husband to have a wife who could *also* bring in money. But one day I realized that my office job was only a substitution for the real job I've been "hired" for: that of being purely a wife and mother.

The sense of personal achievement. A working woman is someone in her own right, doing work that disinterested parties consider valuable enough to pay for. The satisfactions of housekeeping are many, but they are not quite the same.

The discipline of an office. The demands made on you by business are much easier to fulfill than the demands you make on yourself. Self-discipline is hard to achieve.

Praise for a good piece of work. No one can expect her husband to tell her how beautifully clean she keeps the house or how well she makes the beds. . . .

FOUND
A role. At first I found it hard to believe that being a woman is something in itself. . . . Later, when I understood the role better, it took on unexpected glamour. Though I still wince a little at the phrase "wife and mother," I feel quite sure that these words soon will sound as satisfying to me as "actress" or "buyer" or "secretary" or "president."

New friends and a wider conversational range. It was sad to drift apart from my office colleagues, but their hours and, alas, their interests were now different from mine. So I began to make friends with people whose problems, hours, and responsibilities were the same as mine. I gratefully record that my friendship with them is even deeper than it was with business associates. . . . As for conversation, I had been brought up on the satirical tales of the housewife who bored her husband with tiresome narratives about the grocer and the broken stove. Maybe it was true in those days. But not any more. I've had to exercise my mind to keep up with these new friends of mine. . . .

Normalcy. The psychiatrists say there is no such thing, but that's what it *feels* like. My relationship with my children is sounder, for instance. I have fewer illusions about them. I have found I can get bored with them. Exhausted by them. Irritated to the point of sharp words. At first I was shocked, and then I realized that when I worked and we had so little time together, we had all played our "Sunday best." . . . Now I'm not so interesting to them as I was. I'm not so attentive and full of fun, because

I'm myself. I scold, I snap, I listen when I have time. I laugh, I praise, I read to them when I have time. In fact, I'm giving a pretty good representation of a human being, and as the children are going to spend most of their lives trying to get along with human beings, they might as well learn right now that people's behavior is variable.

The luxury of free time. This is one of the crown jewels of retirement. The morning or afternoon that occasionally stretches before me, happily blank, to be filled with a visit to a museum or a movie, a chat with a friend, an unscheduled visit to the zoo with the children, the production of the elaborate dish I'd always meant to try, or simply doing nothing, is a great boon.

Leisure. The pleasure of dawdling over a second cup of coffee in the morning can be understood only by those who have, sometime in their lives, gulped the first cup, seized gloves and bag, and rushed out of the house to go to work.

Source: *American Working Women*, comp. and ed. Rosalyn Baxandall, Linda Gordon, and Susan Reverby (New York: Random House, 1976), 299–301.

DOCUMENT 97: Planned Parenthood (early 1950s)

In 1940 Francis Hand Ferguson joined the Birth Control Federation of America (BCFA), prompted by her sense of the injustice suffered by poor women unable to afford contraception.

In 1942, much to the chagrin of Margaret Sanger (see Document 81), BCFA changed its name to Planned Parenthood Federation of America (PPFA) due to the influence of D. Kenneth Rose, a fundraiser and public relations expert who believed the new name would be less provocative. Nevertheless, ardent Sanger supporter Ferguson remained loyal and active. Between 1953 and 1956 she was president of PPFA and between 1959 and 1962 was vice-president of International Planned Parenthood as the original organization expanded beyond America's borders.

The name change also ushered in small but important shifts in policy. Planned Parenthood strove to highlight family stability by concentrating almost solely on the poor rather than on all families, a distinction Sanger would not make. PPFA began to expand its educational functions through family counseling about sexual matters and provided advice in a scientific manner, by describing sexual activity in matter-of-fact, anatomical terms. However, PPFA left untouched emotional issues related to women's traditional

homebound role. Some have argued that these educational programs failed to remain neutral and acquired political overtones.
Nevertheless women not only gained greater knowledge about
their sexual functions, but were instilled with the belief that they
were entitled to sexual pleasure. PPFA prepared the way for the
more broadly based contraceptive movement of the late 1960s and
the 1970s, for women's greater enjoyment of sex, and ultimately,
some would suggest, for women's sexual liberation.

The way I got interested in this movement . . . in Planned Parenthood . . .
was when I was a child, in the teens. My mother had . . . on her desk . . .
little pamphlets . . . that Margaret Sanger sent out for fund raising. . . .
They have photo offsets of the begging mothers asking for help to stop
having children; and it always seemed to me terribly, terribly unjust that
the rich had . . . birth control means which the poor did not.

Source: Schlesinger-Rockefeller Oral History Project, Francis Hand Ferguson, June
1974 interview with James W. Reed, 8–9.

DOCUMENT 98: "Women Are People" (1952)

In 1952 fifteen American women formed the Committee of Correspondence to share knowledge with and gain the support of other
women throughout the world. Members came from ninety-two
countries and territories and represented such areas of activity as
trade unions, radio, and women's organizations.

In order to profit from the knowledge and experience of these
women, the committee sponsored an essay contest. Entrants were
invited to write on issues of concern to them. Below is a summary
of the issues gleaned from the essays. The work of this committee
shows women's awareness of their common ties with one another
and with humanity in general.

In response to the Committee of Correspondence contest, one hundred
and eighty-four essays were received. They came from the Far and Near
East, from Europe, Africa, Latin America and the South Pacific. They
represent earnest and dedicated efforts by women from all parts of the
world. From these essays has emerged a comprehensive picture of wom-
en's "willing work" throughout the free world.

Now the question arises: What has been gained by this far-reaching
look? This we hope:

That there will be a deepening realization of our interdependence, our common humanity, our similar goals. Specifically, we hope that this sampling of thought from so many different countries and cultures will be an impetus to us all. For example, it has been suggested:

- that, in order for more work to be done in our communities, women of many social and economic groups be recruited as volunteers;
- that organizations work more closely together to relate their program to developing needs;
- that more women work together with men in legislative bodies and governmental councils;
- that the many training materials, studies, pamphlets and other aids offered by international volunteer organizations, by the U.N., UNESCO, UNICEF and various Technical Assistance Programs be more widely used;
- that greater advantage be taken of contacts between students, travelers, government and business officials from different countries (and their husbands or wives) as a means of broadening international understanding. International letter-writing, foreign language courses, studies of other cultures in school and adult education curriculums should also be promoted.
- that attention be focused on the growing body of international ethical codes for behavior between person and person, and between nation and nation—the United Nations Charter, the Universal Declaration of Human Rights, the Declaration on the Rights of the Child, the International Convention on Genocide, on Civil and Political Rights for Women, and many others.

Speaking for the Committee of Correspondence, it is our sincere hope that we may contribute to the end suggested by Dr. Arnold Toynbee, when he wrote: "The twentieth century will be chiefly remembered by future generations as an age in which human society dared to think of the welfare of the whole human race as a practical objective."

Source: "Women Are People . . . ": Selections from Essays Submitted to the Committee of Correspondence, comp. and ed. Marion Bijur (New York: Committee of Correspondence, 1960).

DOCUMENT 99: *Hoyt v. Florida* (1961)

A state of Florida statute *automatically* exempted women from jury duty, unless they expressed an affirmative desire to serve. Hoyt, who was convicted by an all-male jury on a second degree murder charge, contested the legality of the statute by arguing that it violated the equal protection clause of the Constitution. She had assaulted and killed her husband with a baseball bat during a quarrel in which, she said, he had humiliated her to the point of emotional and mental breakdown. She felt that a jury that included women might have better understood her state of being and her defense of temporary insanity. But a unanimous Supreme Court, relying largely on a line of reasoning that has been used since the founding of the country to undermine the rights of women, disagreed.

In neither respect can we conclude that Florida's statute is not "based on some reasonable classification", and that it is thus infected with unconstitutionality. Despite the enlightened emancipation of women from the restrictions and protections of bygone years, and their entry into many parts of community life formerly considered to be reserved to men, woman is still regarded as the center of home and family life. We cannot say that it is constitutionally impermissible for a State, acting in pursuit of the general welfare, to conclude that a woman should be relieved from the civil duty of jury service unless she herself determines that such service is consistent with her own special responsibilities.

Source: 368 U.S. 57 (1961).

DOCUMENT 100: *The Feminine Mystique* (Betty Friedan, 1963)

After four long years of war (1941–1945), with its accompanying deprivation and dislocation, men and women were anxious to return to a normal life. This they interpreted as settling into family life, with men as the providers and women as homemakers taking care of the children. This traditional polarized image of the roles of middle-class men and women, failed, however, to take into account some of the important changes in the lives of women, among them the acquisition of the vote, their improved education, their successful performance, although often temporary, in men's work, and their increased work in all other areas including the professions. But the pressure to restore "the American way of life" was strong. As a consequence the postwar years saw an unprecedented decline in the age at which women married and a propaganda blitz idealizing the perfect woman.

Not all women accepted Madison Avenue's stereotype. Many refused to give up working. And in less than a generation strong signs of discontent among middle-class suburban women became apparent. Instead of experiencing bliss, some of them developed drinking problems and depression, and feelings of isolation. Many began to consult psychiatrists when their lives failed to conform to the images of women projected on television, in the movies, and in women's magazines.

From her own personal experiences, a talented suburban housewife, Betty Friedan, a graduate of Smith College with a degree in psychology, identified what she called "the problem that has no name" as "the feminine mystique" in her book of that title. The pressure to conform to the mystique of woman as sex object/friend/intellectual companion to her husband, mother who raised and nurtured children, and housewife who cooked, baked, and cleaned, came from many sources. In particular, Friedan identified as sources psychiatrist Sigmund Freud and anthropologist Margaret Mead. Friedan also believed that women's depression resulted from their homebound status, which deprived them of the self-fulfillment of work. Her book was read by millions of women and became a clarion call for action.

In 1966 at a convention in Washington, D.C., a group of reformers unhappy with women's work opportunities, particularly in regard to discrimination in the workplaces, decided to organize a group that would pressure the Equal Employment Opportunity Commission (EEOC), a government agency, to do something about discrimination against women. In October of that year the National Organization for Women (NOW) was officially established, with Friedan as its first president. Its 300 charter members, one-quarter of whom were men, asked to have women included in all parts of American society in a "truly equal partnership." Seven years later NOW had 40,000 members.

The problem lay buried, unspoken, for many years in the minds of American women. It was a strange stirring, a sense of dissatisfaction, a yearning that women suffered in the middle of the twentieth century in the United States. Each suburban wife struggled with it alone. As she made the beds, shopped for groceries, matched slipcover material, ate peanut butter sandwiches with her children, chauffeured Cub Scouts and Brownies, lay beside her husband at night—she was afraid to ask even of herself the silent question—"Is this all?"

For over fifteen years there was no word of this yearning in the millions of words written about women, for women, in all the columns, books and articles by experts telling women their role was to seek fulfillment as wives and mothers. Over and over women heard in voices of tradition and of Freudian sophistication that they could desire no greater destiny than to glory in their own femininity. Experts told them how to catch a man and keep him, how to breastfeed children and handle their toilet training, how to cope with sibling rivalry and adolescent rebellion; how to buy a dishwasher, bake bread, cook gourmet snails, and build a swimming pool with their own hands; how to dress, look, and act more feminine and make marriage more exciting; how to keep their husbands from dying young and their sons from growing into delinquents. They were taught to pity the neurotic, unfeminine, unhappy women who wanted to be poets or physicists or presidents. They learned that truly feminine women do not want careers, higher education, political rights—the independence and the opportunities that the old-fashioned feminists fought for. Some women, in their forties and fifties, still remembered painfully giving up those dreams, but most of the younger women no longer even thought about them. A thousand expert voices applauded their femininity, their adjustment, their new maturity. All they had to do was devote their lives from earliest girlhood to finding a husband and bearing children.

By the end of the nineteen-fifties, the average marriage age of women in America dropped to 20, and was still dropping, into the teens. Fourteen million girls were engaged by 17. The proportion of women attending college in comparison with men dropped from 47 per cent in 1920 to 35 per cent in 1958. A century earlier, women had fought for higher education; now girls went to college to get a husband. By the mid-fifties, 60 per cent dropped out of college to marry, or because they were afraid too much education would be a marriage bar. Colleges built dormitories for "married students," but the students were almost always the husbands. A new degree was instituted for the wives—"Ph.T." (Putting Husband Through).

Then American girls began getting married in high school. And the women's magazines, deploring the unhappy statistics about these young marriages, urged that courses on marriage, and marriage counselors, be installed in the high schools. Girls started going steady at twelve and thirteen, in junior high. Manufacturers put out brassieres with false bosoms of foam rubber for little girls of ten. And an advertisement for a child's dress, sizes 3–6x, in the *New York Times* in the fall of 1960, said: "She Too Can Join the Man-Trap Set." . . .

The suburban housewife—she was the dream image of the young American women and the envy, it was said, of women all over the world. The American housewife—freed by science and labor-saving appliances from the drudgery, the dangers of childbirth and the illnesses of her grandmother. She was healthy, beautiful, educated, concerned only about her husband, her children, her home. She had found true feminine fulfillment. As a housewife and mother, she was respected as a full and equal partner to man in his world. She was free to choose automobiles, clothes, appliances, supermarkets; she had everything that women ever dreamed of.

In the fifteen years after World War II, this mystique of feminine fulfillment became the cherished and self-perpetuating core of contemporary American culture. Millions of women lived their lives in the image of those pretty pictures of the American suburban housewife, kissing their husbands goodbye in front of the picture window, depositing their stationwagonsful of children at school, and smiling as they ran the new electric waxer over the spotless kitchen floor. They baked their own bread, sewed their own and their children's clothes, kept their new washing machines and dryers running all day. They changed the sheets on the beds twice a week instead of once, took the rug-hooking class in adult education, and pitied their poor frustrated mothers, who had dreamed of having a career. Their only dream was to be perfect wives and mothers; their highest ambition to have five children and a beautiful house, their only fight to get and keep their husbands. They had no thought for the unfeminine problems of the world outside the home; they wanted the men to make the major decisions. They gloried in their role as women, and wrote proudly on the census blank: "Occupation: housewife." . . .

If a woman had a problem in the 1950's and 1960's, she knew that something must be wrong with her marriage, or with herself. Other women were satisfied with their lives, she thought. What kind of a woman was she if she did not feel this mysterious fulfillment waxing the kitchen floor? She was so ashamed to admit her dissatisfaction that she never knew how many other women shared it. If she tried to tell her husband, he didn't understand what she was talking about. She did not really understand it herself. For over fifteen years women in America found it harder to talk about this problem than about sex. Even the psychoanalysts had no name for it. When a woman went to a psychiatrist for help, as many women did, she would say, "I'm so ashamed," or "I must be hopelessly neurotic." "I don't know what's wrong with women today," a suburban psychiatrist said uneasily. "I only know something is wrong because most of my patients happen to be women. And their problem isn't sexual." Most women with this problem did not go to see a psychoanalyst, however. "There's nothing wrong really," they kept telling themselves. "There isn't any problem." . . .

It is easy to see the concrete details that trap the suburban housewife, the continual demands on her time. But the chains that bind her in her trap are chains in her own mind and spirit. They are chains made up of mistaken ideas and misinterpreted facts, of incomplete truths and unreal choices. They are not easily seen and not easily shaken off.

How can any woman see the whole truth within the bounds of her own life? How can she believe that voice inside herself, when it denies the conventional, accepted truths by which she has been living? And yet the women I have talked to, who are finally listening to that inner voice, seem in some incredible way to be groping through to a truth that has defied the experts.

I think the experts in a great many fields have been holding pieces of that truth under their microscopes for a long time without realizing it. I found pieces of it in certain new research and theoretical developments in psychological, social and biological science whose implications for women seem never to have been examined. I found many clues by talking to suburban doctors, gynecologists, obstetricians, child-guidance clinicians, pediatricians, high-school guidance counselors, college professors, marriage counselors, psychiatrists and ministers—questioning them not on their theories, but on their actual experience in treating American women. I became aware of a growing body of evidence, much of which has not been reported publicly because it does not fit current modes of thought about women—evidence which throws into question the standards of feminine normality, feminine adjustment, feminine fulfillment, and feminine maturity by which most women are still trying to live. . . .

If I am right, the problem that has no name stirring in the minds of so many American women today is not a matter of loss of femininity or too much education, or the demands of domesticity. It is far more important than anyone recognizes. It is the key to these other new and old problems which have been torturing women and their husbands and children, and puzzling their doctors and educators for years. It may well be the key to our future as a nation and a culture. We can no longer ignore that voice within women that says: "I want something more than my husband and my children and my home."

Source: Betty Friedan, *The Feminine Mystique,* twentieth anniversary ed. (New York: W. W. Norton, 1983), 15–32.

Part V

At the Crossroads,
1963–1993

The final section covers a period during which the women's rights movement experienced a number of important victories as well as anxieties and questions about its nature and direction. Areas of victory included women's right to control their own bodies, equal employment opportunities (including compensation for labor), assignment in the armed forces, citizenship issues, and consciousness-raising.

As discussed in Part III, control of women's bodies—especially as it affects reproductive rights—has been an area of intense struggle for feminists. For over a century states and the national government passed laws that limited access to birth control information and criminalized abortion. Through the efforts of people like Margaret Sanger in the area of birth control (see Document 81), and the overwhelming questioning of values and institutions during the 1960s, legislative and judicial organs of government became susceptible to political pressure. Some of that pressure was exerted by the women's rights movement, especially by the National Organization for Women (NOW), after 1945 the most powerful national women's organization. Because of NOW's efforts a number of states modified their abortion laws. NOW also pressured many political leaders to take public positions on matters affecting women, including reproductive rights. Those positions helped women to gain a broader social and political legitimacy on other issues as well.

It is within this political context that one should view the Supreme Court decision in *Roe v. Wade* (see Document 110), which recognized a woman's right to abort a fetus during the first three months of pregnancy, based on her private decision in consultation with her physician. But the decision, along with *Griswold v. Con-*

necticut, which recognized the private right of married couples to have access to and to use contraceptives, is significant for reasons broader than a constitutionally recognized right to privacy; it ratified a woman's right to reproductive freedom, to autonomy of her person.

One area in which women have faced a serious material disadvantage has been that of compensation for their labor. From their limited success in forming and joining labor unions and in organizing strikes during the 1840s to their failure to secure a minimum wage in the 1920s (see Document 84), women had vainly struggled to win equitable compensation for their labor. During World War II, in order to assure servicemen that temporary femininization of the workplace would not destroy the existing wage structure for them when they returned, the War Labor Board ruled that people whose production was substantially the same should have equal pay. But the board did little to enforce its own ruling. In 1963 Congress enacted the Equal Pay Act (Document 101), which prohibits sex-based discrimination in wages. Combined with Title VII of the 1964 Civil Rights Act, which outlaws sex-based discrimination in hiring and other associated terms of employment (Document 102), it represents a significant legal victory.

That victory can be better appreciated from the larger perspective of the issue of equal employment opportunity. Title VII improves the chances of pay equity by increasing the number of women in the work force and having them as part of teams that negotiate wages. But it does more. Employers are now required to employ, train, promote, and retain women on the same terms as men. Of course, if women are not technically and otherwise qualified, the chances for equal employment are nil. Title IX of the Civil Rights Act (1972), which prohibits discrimination based on sex in educational programs receiving federal funds, seeks to ensure that women are qualified. The work of women's colleges (and here one must note that with the exception of Spelman in Atlanta and Bennett in Greensboro, black women's colleges have had little support), plus the general acceptance of coeducation by the 1970s, contributed to women's advancement in the workplace. The 1991 Civil Rights Act (see Document 119) makes sexual harassment a form of sex-based discrimination and provides compensatory and punitive damages for victims.

The issue of women in the armed forces entails more than employment benefits, although *Frontiero v. Richardson* (see Document 109), the most far-reaching Supreme Court decision affecting women's rights, dealt with benefits discrimination in the armed forces. With the passing of property holding as a major prerequisite for full citizenship, military service became the last area of false distinction between men and women and the *symbolic* justification for all the social disadvantages women have had to face in and out of the armed forces. Men fought (engaged in combat), women did not, and institutions, including the Supreme Court in *Rostker v. Goldberg* (see Document 114), made that claim. Feminists have understood the importance of this cultural symbol and have fought for women's inclusion in all armed forces activities. Due partly to those battles and the Vietnam War, some restrictions were lifted in the 1970s. In 1976 women were admitted to the U.S. Military Academy of West Point, the Air Force Academy, and the Naval Academy at Annapolis. This was a very important step to equal status for women in command position, in which not a single female served as late as 1967. Today there are twenty-one female generals, and the 1993 policy statement by the secretary of defense respecting assignment of women in the armed forces (see Document 125) could result in some modifications of the restrictions on land combat—the sole remaining area of combat from which women are excluded.

The women's rights movement has also had measurable success in the area of citizenship rights. Women serve on juries, are administrators of estates (see Document 106), have the right to privacy (see Document 110), and hold public office at all levels of political life. President Clinton's appointment of Ruth B. Ginsburg to the Supreme Court increased the female representation on that body to two. Clinton has stated his commitment to appoint to high administrative positions in proportion to their representation in the population.

Perhaps the most important achievement of the period under discussion is that of consciousness-raising. The women's movement in the United States succeeded in making citizens aware of gender discrimination, although few have understood how much change is required to remedy it. Political leaders at every level of society must now appear to be sensitive to sex-based discrimination.

Notwithstanding the victories gained by the women's movement, uneasiness has developed about some of those victories and the very nature of the movement's emphases. For example, while NOW and other women's groups succeeded in helping many women move from the confinement of the home to the industrial marketplace, that move did not in most cases ensure factual equality for women. The focus on *legal* changes such as the Equal Pay Act and ERA has obscured the need for wider and deeper cultural transformation. So, while women have worked more hours outside the home, with some achieving positions of authority, more and more women live in poverty, finding themselves less socially secure and increasingly stressed psychologically and spiritually. Such concerns are expressed by Mary Ann Mason in *The Equality Trap* (see Document 117). Mason finds that legal entitlements such as those provided by the Family and Medical Leave Act (see Document 122) do not even begin to grapple with the differences between women and men on matters such as pregnancy.

A related but broader concern has been posed by cultural or relational feminists who celebrate the differences between women and men. They claim that women have distinct values—values that emphasize mutual aid, relationships, nurturing, and moral commitment to the group; and that gender inequalities arise more from the devaluation of the functions and qualities associated with women than from the denial of opportunities open to men. Carol Gilligan's book *In a Different Voice* gives scholarly support to some of these concerns by challenging Lawrence Kohlberg's influential six-stage theory of moral development. Kohlberg's theory, based on the study of males only, contends that the highest levels of moral growth demand the deemphasizing and even the subordination of relationships to rules (stage four) and of rules to universal principles of right and justice (stages five and six). Gilligan, in a study that included both females and males, found that females conducted themselves in a "different voice"—one that emphasized mutual aid, duties (as distinct from rights), and relationships. With other cultural feminists, she has argued that, from curricular development in schools to the policies of government, the women's movement should emphasize the ethic of caring, cooperation, and responsibility, values that define women.

Gilligan's conclusion is reflected, in part, in Betty Friedan's *The Second Stage* (see Document 115), which calls for a restructuring of institutions to accommodate women's needs and to transform the very nature of power. Likewise, that conclusion reflects the concern of other feminists about pornography—indeed, the entire area of violence against women.

In *Miller v. California* (1973) the Supreme Court defined obscenity (pornography) for the first time, using a three-part test: whether the average person, using contemporary community standards, would find a work in question one that appealed to "prurient interest"; whether it depicted sexual conduct in a "patently offensive" manner; and whether, taken as a whole, it lacked serious literary, artistic, or scientific value. Published materials falling within the above definition have been prohibited, since 1973.

To feminists like Catherine MacKinnon, using these abstract rules to evaluate sexual material cannot adequately deal with the relationship of pornography to violence against women (see Document 118). That relationship must be considered and understood within the context of a wider culture of inequality for women. Pornography, which objectifies, humiliates, brutalizes, and subordinates women, not only links their sexuality to that subordination but eroticizes women's supposed inferiority, associates it with male pleasure, and, most important, shapes the *social construction* of gender.

A final question raised by this collection asks, Can women gain equality, absent a social revolution? Shulamith Firestone answers no (see Document 105). To her the current social and political culture is largely constructed on the biological difference between women and men, and that construction favors males. That basic difference must be acknowledged if women are to be fully equal, since it is the foundation—though not the entire source—of women's inequality. Acceptance of that basic cause of women's social subordination to men may then be used by women to take control of their reproductive faculties and the institutions associated with them in order to transform society. Instead of asking, Why can't a woman be more like a man?, such a society will ask, How can women and men, given their biological differences, fashion a society that authentically represents human beings, female and male?

bell hooks thinks revolution may be necessary. Equal rights for women is not a question of gender only, but of race and class as well. She feels that the contemporary women's movement has largely overlooked the plight of non–middle-class women and racial minorities. Finally, the Convention on the Elimination of All Forms of Discrimination Against Women (Document 125) promises to do what ERA might have done, but also symbolizes the fact that in an evolving global society the struggle for rights will take on more of a transnational dimension.

DOCUMENT 101: The Equal Pay Act of 1963

In 1961, a newly elected President Kennedy created a national Commission on the Status of Women (CSW) for the stated purpose of combatting "the prejudices and outmoded customs" that serve as "barriers to the realization of women's basic rights." CSW was also to serve purposes other than that stated. Among them was that of giving greater satisfaction to women, an important political constituency which had received no executive post apart from the Labor Department's Women's Bureau. Equally important, the Kennedy administration hoped that the commission would help it deal tactfully with the politically controversial issue of the proposed Equal Rights Amendment to the Constitution.

The CSW (fulfilling the hope of the administration) rejected the idea of an ERA, claiming that the rights of women could be adequately protected through the Fifth and Fourteenth Amendments— a claim that was hardly persuasive, given the recent rulings of the Supreme Court (see Documents 95 and 99). But the commission recommended a number of antidiscrimination measures, including the Equal Pay Act, which was enacted by Congress in 1963. That act, the first piece of national legislation in U.S. history to prohibit discrimination on the basis of sex, requires equal compensation for women and men who perform equal work.

Sec. 206

(d)(1) No employer having employees subject to any provisions of this section shall discriminate, within any establishment in which such employees are employed, between employees on the basis of sex by paying wages to employees in such establishment at a rate less than the rate at which he pays wages to employees of the opposite sex in such establishment for equal work on jobs the performance of which requires equal skill, effort, and responsibility, and which are performed under similar working conditions, except where such payment is made pursuant to (i) a seniority system; (ii) a merit system; (iii) a system which measures earnings by quantity or quality of production; or (iv) a differential based on any other factor other than sex: *Provided,* That an employer who is paying a wage rate differential in violation of this subsection shall not, in order to comply with the provisions of this subsection, reduce the wage rate of any employee.

(2) No labor organization, or its agents, representing employees of an employer having employees subject to any provisions of this section shall cause or attempt to cause such an employer to discriminate against an employee in violation of paragraph (1) of this subsection.

(3) For purposes of administration and enforcement, any amounts owing to any employee which have been withheld in violation of this subsection shall be deemed to be unpaid minimum wages or unpaid overtime compensation under this Act.

(4) As used in this subsection, the term "labor organization" means any organization of any kind, or any agency or employee representation committee or plan, in which employees participate and which exists for the purpose, in whole or in part, of dealing with employers concerning grievances, labor disputes, wages, rates of pay, hours of employment, or conditions of work.

Source: 29 U.S.C.

DOCUMENT 102: The Civil Rights Act of 1964

The very year of the Equal Pay Act witnessed an increasingly militant civil rights movement in the United States on behalf of blacks. And with the preoccupation of the Kennedy and Johnson administrations with black civil rights, the women's movement was overshadowed. But that movement got some support from an unexpected source: Congress.

In an effort to make passage of the pending civil rights legislation protecting the rights of racial minorities more difficult, Congressman Howard Smith of Virginia proposed the inclusion of women among the protected groups. The political ploy backfired. A coalition of labor, civil rights, and women's groups, emboldened by support from the Johnson administration, won the day. Title VII of the act, which prohibits discrimination on the grounds of sex, color, race, religion, and national origin, also established the Equal Employment Opportunity Commission (EEOC) to conciliate complaints and recommend cases for federal litigation. The act, though slow to gain the required enforcement, is perhaps the single most significant piece of federal legislation in the area of women's rights.

§2000e-2. Unlawful Employment Practices

(a) Employer practices

It shall be an unlawful employment practice for an employer—

(1) to fail or refuse to hire or to discharge any individual, or otherwise to discriminate against any individual with respect to his compensation, terms, conditions, or privileges of employment, because of such individual's race, color, religion, sex, or national origin; or

(2) to limit, segregate, or classify his employees or applicants for employment in any way which would deprive or tend to deprive any individual of employment opportunities or otherwise adversely affect his status as an employee, because of such individual's race, color, religion, sex, or national origin.

(b) Employment agency practices

It shall be an unlawful employment practice for an employment agency to fail or refuse to refer for employment, or otherwise to discriminate against, any individual because of his race, color, religion, sex, or national origin, or to classify or refer for employment any individual on the basis of his race, color, religion, sex, or national origin.

(c) Labor organization practices

It shall be an unlawful employment practice for a labor organization—

(1) to exclude or to expel from its membership, or otherwise to discriminate against, any individual because of his race, color, religion, sex, or national origin;

(2) to limit, segregate, or classify its membership or applicants for membership, or to classify or fail or refuse to refer for employment any individual, in any way which would deprive or tend to deprive any individual of employment opportunities, or would limit such employment opportunities or otherwise adversely affect his status as an employee or as an applicant for employment, because of such individual's race, color, religion, sex, or national origin; or

(3) to cause or attempt to cause an employer to discriminate against an individual in violation of this section.

(d) Training programs

It shall be an unlawful employment practice for any employer, labor organization, or joint labor-management committee controlling apprenticeship or other training or retraining, including on-the-job training programs to discriminate against any individual because of his race, color, religion, sex, or national origin in admission to, or employment in, any program established to provide apprenticeship or other training.

(e) Businesses or enterprises with personnel qualified on basis of religion, sex, or national origin; educational institutions with personnel of particular religion

Notwithstanding any other provision of this subchapter, (1) it shall not be an unlawful employment practice for an employer to hire and employ employees, for an employment agency to classify, or refer for employment any individual, for a labor organization to classify its membership or to classify or refer for employment any individual, or for an employer, labor organization, or joint labor-management committee controlling apprenticeship or other training or retraining programs to admit or employ any individual in any such program, on the basis of his religion, sex, or national origin in those certain instances where religion, sex, or national origin is a bona fide occupational qualification reasonably necessary to the normal operation of that particular business or enterprise. . . .

§2000e-3. Other Unlawful Employment Practices

(a) Discrimination for making charges, testifying, assisting, or participating in enforcement proceedings

It shall be an unlawful employment practice for an employer to discriminate against any of his employees or applicants for employment, for an employment agency, or joint labor-management committee controlling apprenticeship or other training or retraining, including on-the-job training programs, to discriminate against any individual, or for a labor organization to discriminate against any member thereof or applicant for membership, because he has opposed any practice made an unlawful employment practice by this subchapter, or because he has made a charge, testified, assisted, or participated in any manner in an investigation, proceeding, or hearing under this subchapter . . . .

§2000e-4. Equal Employment Opportunity Commission

(a) Creation; composition; political representation; appointment; term; vacancies; Chairman and Vice Chairman; duties of Chairman; appointment of personnel; compensation of personnel

There is hereby created a Commission to be known as the Equal Employment Opportunity Commission, which shall be composed of five members, not more than three of whom shall be members of the same political party. Members of the Commission shall be appointed by the President by and with the advice and consent of the Senate. . . .

(b) General Counsel; appointment; term; duties; representation by attorneys and Attorney General

(1) There shall be a General Counsel of the Commission appointed by the President, by and with the advice and consent of the Senate, for a

term of four years. The General Counsel shall have responsibility for the conduct of litigation . . . .

(g) Powers of Commission
The Commission shall have power—

(1) to cooperate with and, with their consent, utilize regional, State, local, and other agencies, both public and private, and individuals;

(2) to pay to witnesses whose depositions are taken or who are summoned before the Commission or any of its agents the same witness and mileage fees as are paid to witnesses in the courts of the United States;

(3) to furnish to persons subject to this subchapter such technical assistance as they may required to further their compliance with this subchapter or an order issued thereunder;

(4) upon the request of (i) any employer, whose employees or some of them, or (ii) any labor organization, whose members or some of them, refuse or threaten to refuse to cooperate in effectuating the provisions of this subchapter, to assist in such effectuation by conciliation or such other remedial action as is provided by this subchapter.

(5) to make such technical studies as are appropriate to effectuate the purposes and policies of this subchapter and to make the results of such studies available to the public;

(6) to intervene in a civil action brought under section 2000e-5 of this title by an aggrieved party against a respondent other than a government, governmental agency or political subdivision.

Source: 42 U.S.C.

DOCUMENT 103: "Notes of a Radical Lesbian" (Martha Shelly, 1969)

In the late 1960s, when feminism became increasingly diverse and the demand for women's rights more vociferous, groups heretofore silent and largely underground became more public. One of these groups was the radical lesbians, who, like the Society to Cut Up Men (SCUM), for example, saw men as the enemy. To radical lesbians, depending on the "enemy" was incompatible with the struggle for liberation. The solution was to break the dependency hold totally. The deliberations of radical lesbian Martha Shelly in the following excerpt reflect an understanding of all women's dilemmas, heterosexual or lesbian.

For women, as for other groups, there are several American norms. All of them have their rewards, and their penalties. The nice girl next door, virginal until her marriage—the Miss America type—is rewarded with community respect and respectability. She loses her individuality and her freedom, to become a toothpaste smile and a chastity belt. The career woman gains independence and a large margin of freedom—if she is willing to work twice as hard as a man for less pay, and if she can cope with emotional strains similar to those that beset the black intellectual surrounded by white colleagues. The starlet, call girl, or bunny, whose source of income is directly related to her image as a sex object, gains some financial independence and freedom from housework. She doesn't have to work as hard as the career woman, but she pays through psychological degradation as a sex object, and through the insecurity of knowing that her career, based on youthful good looks, is short-lived.

The Lesbian, through her ability to obtain love and sexual satisfaction from other women, is freed of dependence on men for love, sex, and money. She does not have to do menial chores for them (at least at home), nor cater to their egos, nor submit to hasty and inept sexual encounters. She is freed from fear of unwanted pregnancy and the pains of childbirth, and from the drudgery of child raising.

On the other hand, she pays three penalties. The rewards of child raising are denied her. This is a great loss for some women, but not for others. Few women abandon their children, as compared with the multitudes of men who abandon both wives and children. Few men take much interest in the process of child raising. One suspects that it might not be much fun for the average person, and so the men leave it to the women.

The Lesbian still must compete with men in the job market, facing the same job and salary discrimination as her straight sister.

Finally, she faces the most severe contempt and ridicule that society can heap on a woman.

When members of the Women's Liberation Movement picketed the 1968 Miss America pageant, the most terrible epithet heaped on our straight sisters was "Lesbian." The sisters faced hostile audiences who called them "commies," and "tramps," but some of them broke into tears when they were called Lesbians. When a woman showed up at a feminist meeting and announced that she was a Lesbian, many women avoided her. Others told her to keep her mouth shut, for fear that she would endanger the cause. They felt that men could be persuaded to accept some measure of equality for women—as long as these women would parade their devotion to heterosexuality and motherhood.

A woman who is totally independent of men—who obtains, love, sex, and self-esteem from other women—is a terrible threat to male supremacy. She doesn't need them, and therefore they have less power over her.

Source: Martha Shelly, "Notes of a Radical Lesbian," in *Sisterhood Is Powerful: An Anthology of Writings from the Women's Liberation Movement*, ed. Robin Morgan (New York: Vintage Books, 1970), 344–345.

DOCUMENT 104: "The Secretarial Proletariat" (Judith Ann, 1970)

The secretarial proletariat could be most women in the 1970s and—with increasing exceptions—most women today. The work world, then as now, was essentially polarized along gender lines, with women placed in the more menial jobs and receiving less pay than men for the same or comparable work.

Judith Ann's vibrant, angry spirit reaches out as she describes the drudgery of all her makeshift jobs. As she explains, employers assumed that women would not remain at work long, so it was best not to train them for more interesting work with future opportunities. Yet even today, as women remain in the workplace after they become mothers, their jobs are still largely sex-typed, often boring, and still underpaid.

Although we work at desks instead of on assembly lines, female clerical work is very much like factory labor in its exploitative nature. But unlike factory workers, we don't even have unions. The Bosses make a false separation between "blue collar" and "white collar" workers, because it's in their interest to keep us clerical workers from organizing to demand better wages, better working conditions, day-care for our children—or maybe even a revolution. And the unions which now exist don't do much good for the workers either; in fact, many of them are racist and sexist institutions in themselves.

Another thing that has kept women workers from organizing is that we are prevented from finding an identity through our work. There are several reasons for this. First of all, the work we are assigned, as women, is the lowest level, most meaningless and degrading work available in the society—who wants to identify as a file clerk. Second, all work in a capitalist society is alienating to the workers because the workers do not benefit from the fruits of their own labor—we sell our labor, while management reaps the profits and makes the identification with what we have produced. Third (and perhaps most important), as women we are allowed to identify not through production, achievement, and action, but through men. When you're bored and miserable all day at work, flirtation and role-playing with men begins to sound like fun. Marriage and staying at home with the children seem like liberating alternatives to the kind of jobs we can get. But we soon find out that that's a myth. When we marry, we only exchange our status as a worker for status as domestic slave labor—we do the cooking, cleaning, child-rearing (all important productive tasks) and we get no wages at all, only patronizing security and protection and perhaps a weekly allowance from a benevolent master. And we don't always even get to stay at home. Many working women *are* married (I was married during my last job; since my husband was sick at the time, I was the sole support of the household, on a salary that was half what my husband could make with the same qualifications). Then we have *two* full-time jobs instead of just one— underpaid clerical worker and unpaid housekeeper. In this way, they keep us just too damn *busy* to organize!

Maybe some readers of this article will think that I was unusual among clerical workers because I knew that I was being exploited and rebelled against it. Maybe some of you think that most clerical workers accept and even like their lot and don't care about changing it. But it's not true. Everywhere I worked the women at the bottom knew that they were underpaid and overworked, denied job security and the possibility of advancement, exploited by male supremacy and a class system. And everywhere we rebelled in a thousand small ways—taking extra time in the ladies' room, misfiling important letters, "forgetting" to correct typos.

What we must do now is resist collectively instead of in isolation. We have feared that by speaking out against our oppression we might lose our lousy jobs and thus our livelihood, which does happen if we speak out alone. We have feared that maybe our present conditions are just the way things are and can't be changed. But these and other fears can be overcome through collective actions and solidarity. We can pool our financial resources to reduce the danger of summary findings; we can share our child-rearing responsibilities to free each other's time for action. We can support each other emotionally and become sisters in oppression and, finally, in victory.

Source: Judith Ann, "The Secretarial Proletariat," in *Sisterhood Is Powerful: An Anthology of Writings from the Women's Liberation Movement*, ed. Robin Morgan (New York: Vintage Books, 1970), 108–110.

DOCUMENT 105: *The Dialectics of Sex* (Shulamith Firestone, 1970)

The women's rights movement in the United States was defined by the widest variety of views and subgroups during the 1960s and

1970s. Among those views were some expressed by Shulamith Firestone, a pioneer radical feminist. Below, in part, is her daring and admirably argued case for a feminist revolution to eradicate what she considered the deepest source of social and cultural oppression: the sexual class system and the political, economic, and technical machinery on which that system has been grounded.

The *biological family*—the basic reproductive unit of male/female/ infant, in whatever form of social organization—is characterized by these fundamental—if not immutable—facts:

1) That women throughout history before the advent of birth control were at the continual mercy of their biology—menstruation, menopause, and "female ills," constant painful childbirth, wetnursing and care of infants, all of which made them dependent on males (whether brother, father, husband, lover, or clan, government, community-at-large) for physical survival.

2) That human infants take an even longer time to grow up than animals, and thus are helpless and, for some short period at least, dependent on adults for physical survival.

3) That a basic mother/child interdependency has existed in some form in every society, past or present, and thus has shaped the psychology of every mature female and every infant.

4) That the natural reproductive difference between the sexes led directly to the first division of labor at the origins of class, as well as furnishing the paradigm of caste (discrimination based on biological characteristics).

These biological contingencies of the human family cannot be covered over with anthropological sophistries. Anyone observing animals mating, reproducing, and caring for their young will have a hard time accepting the "cultural relativity" line. For no matter how many tribes in Oceania you can find where the connection of the father to fertility is not known, no matter how many matrilineages, no matter how many cases of sex-role reversal, male housewifery, or even empathic labor pains, these facts prove only one thing: the amazing *flexibility* of human nature. But human nature is adaptable *to* something, it is, yes, determined by its environmental conditions. And the biological family that we have described has existed everywhere throughout time. Even in matriarchies where woman's fertility is worshipped, and the father's role is unknown or unimportant, if perhaps not on the genetic father, there is still some dependence of the female and the infant on the male. And though it is true that the nuclear family is only a recent development, one which, as I shall attempt to show, only intensifies the psychological penalties of the biological family, though it is true that throughout history there have been many variations on this biological family, the contingencies I have described existed in all of them, causing specific psychosexual distortions in the human personality.

But to grant that the sexual imbalance of power is biologically based is not to lose our case. We are no longer just animals. And the Kingdom of Nature does not reign absolute. . . . Thus, the "natural" is not necessarily a "human" value. Humanity has begun to outgrow nature: we can no longer justify the maintenance of a discriminatory sex class system on grounds of its origins in Nature. Indeed, for pragmatic reasons alone it is beginning to look as if we *must* get rid of it. . . .

The problem becomes political, demanding more than a comprehensive historical analysis, when one realizes that, though man is increasingly capable of freeing himself from the biological conditions that created his tyranny over women and children, he has little reason to want to give this tyranny up. . . . Though the sex class system may have originated in fundamental biological conditions, this does not guarantee once the biological basis of their oppression has been swept away that women and children will be freed. On the contrary, the new technology, especially fertility control, may be used against them to reinforce the entrenched system of exploitation.

So that just as to assure elimination of economic classes requires the revolt of the underclass (the proletariat) and, in a temporary dictatorship, their seizure of the means of *production*, so to assure the elimination of sexual classes requires the revolt of the underclass (women) and the seizure of control of *reproduction*: not only the full restoration to women of ownership of their own bodies, but also their (temporary) seizure of control of human fertility—the new population biology as well as all the social institutions of childbearing and childrearing. And just as the end goal of socialist revolution was not only the elimination of the economic class *privilege* but of the economic class *distinction* itself, so the end goal of feminist revolution must be, unlike that of the first feminist movement, not just the elimination of male *privilege* but of the sex *distinction* itself: genital differences between human beings would no longer matter culturally. (A reversion to an unobstructed *pansexuality*—Freud's "polymorphous perversity"—would probably supersede hetero/homo/bisexuality.) The reproduction of the species by one sex for the benefit of both would be replaced by (at least the option of) artificial reproduction: children would be born to both sexes equally, or independently of either, however one chooses to look at it; the dependence of the child on the mother (and vice versa) would give way to a greatly shortened dependence on a small group of others in general, and any remaining inferiority to adults in physical strength would be compensated for culturally. The division of labor would be ended by the elimination of labor altogether (cybernation). The tyranny of the biological family would be broken.

And with it the psychology of power. As Engels claimed for strictly socialist revolution:

> The existence of not simply this or that ruling class but of any ruling class at all [will have] become an obsolete anachronism.

That socialism has never come near achieving this predicated goal is not only the result of unfulfilled or misfired economic preconditions, but also because the Marxian analysis itself was insufficient: it did not dig deep enough to the psychosexual roots of class. Marx was onto something more profound than he knew when he observed that the family contained within itself in embryo all the antagonisms that later develop on a wide scale within the society and the state. For unless revolution uproots the basic social organization, the biological family—the vinculum through which the psychology of power can always be smuggled—the tapeworm of exploitation will never be annihilated. We shall need a sexual revolution much larger than—inclusive of—a socialist one to truly eradicate all class systems.

Source: Shulamith Firestone, *The Dialectics of Sex: The Case for Feminist Revolution* (New York: Bantam Books, 1970), 1–14.

DOCUMENT 106: *Reed v. Reed* (1971)

In this case, Sally Reed, the petitioner, challenged an Idaho statute which provided that when heirs were equally entitled to administer a decedent's estate, males should be given preference over females. One of the purposes of the statute was to reduce the workload of probate courts by eliminating one class of contestants. In invalidating the statute, the Supreme Court—though not using specifically the levels of analysis mentioned in *Frontiero v. Richardson* (see Document 109)—indicated that it would be less tolerant of legislative classifications based on sex. Thus, *Reed v. Reed* represents a major judicial departure in favor of women's rights.

Having examined the record and considered the briefs and the oral arguments of the parties, we have concluded that the preference established in favor of males by . . . the Idaho Code cannot stand in face of the Fourteenth Amendment's command that no State deny the equal protection of the laws to any person under its jurisdiction. . . .

In applying [the Equal Protection Clause], this Court has consistently recognized that the Fourteenth Amendment does not deny to States the power to treat different classes of persons in different ways.... The Equal Protection Clause of that Amendment does, however, deny to States the power to legislate that different treatment be accorded to persons placed by a statute into different classes on the basis of criteria wholly unrelated to the objective of that statute. A classification "must be reasonable, not arbitrary, and must rest upon some grounds of difference having a fair and substantial relation to the object of the legislation, so that all persons similarly circumstanced shall be treated alike." ... The question presented in this case, then, is whether a difference in the sex of competing applicants for letters of administration bears a rational relationship to a state objective that is sought to be advanced....

Clearly the objective of reducing the workload on the probate courts by eliminating one class of contestants is not without some legitimacy. The crucial question, however, is whether [the statute] advances that objective in a manner consistent with the command of the Equal Protection Clause. We hold that it does not. To give mandatory preference to members of either sex over members of the other, merely to accomplish the elimination of hearings on the merits, is to take the very arbitrary legislative choice forbidden by the Equal Protection Clause . . . and whatever may be said as to the positive values of avoiding intrafamily controversy, the choice in this context may not be lawfully mandated solely on the basis of sex.

Source: 404 U.S. 71 (1971).

DOCUMENT 107: The Equal Rights Amendment and Some Arguments Pro and Con (1972)

As seen in Document 85, feminists have sought to have an Equal Rights Amendment to the Constitution since the early 1920s. The pursuit of that goal has brought with it many controversies, including which of three distinct legal methods of effecting social and political changes can best assure equal rights for women. One of those methods, typified by *Reed v. Reed* (see Document 106), is through judicial review under the equal protection clause of the Constitution (the due process clause of the Fifth Amendment in the case of the federal government). Another is through piecemeal revision of existing federal and state law. The third is through a new constitutional amendment. In 1972 Congress, under strong pressure from the women's movement, especially NOW, embraced the third method and passed the Equal Rights Amendment, but imposed a seven-year deadline for its ratification. In 1979 that deadline was extended for another three years; nevertheless the proposed amendment fell short of ratification by three of the required thirty-eight states. The first section of the proposed ERA is included below, followed by some of the arguments advanced for and against it.

A. THE EQUAL RIGHTS AMENDMENT

Section 1. Equality of rights under the law shall not be denied or abridged by the United States or by any State on account of sex.

Source: Congressional Record 118 (March 22, 1971): 9568.

B. CON: "WHAT'S WRONG WITH EQUAL RIGHTS FOR WOMEN?"

The proposed Equal Rights Amendment states: "Equality of rights under the law shall not be denied or abridged by the United States or by any state on account of sex." So what's wrong with that? Well, here are a few examples of what's wrong with it.

This Amendment will absolutely and positively make women subject to the draft. Why any woman would support such a ridiculous and un-American proposal as this is beyond comprehension. Why any Congressman who had any regard for his wife, sister or daughter would support such a proposition is just as hard to understand. Foxholes are bad enough for men, but they certainly are *not* the place for women—and we should reject any proposal which would put them there in the name of "equal rights." . . .

Another bad effect of the Equal Rights Amendment is that it will abolish a woman's right to child support and alimony, and substitute what the women's libbers think is a more "equal" policy, that "such decisions should be within the discretion of the Court and should be made on the economic situation and need of the parties in the case."

Under present American laws, the man is *always* required to support his wife and each child he caused to be brought into the world. Why should women abandon these good laws—by trading them for something so nebulous and uncertain as the "discretion of the Court"?

The law now requires a husband to support his wife as best as his financial situation permits, but a wife is not required to support her husband (unless he is about to become a public charge). A husband cannot demand that his wife go to work to help pay for family expenses. He has the duty of financial support under our laws and customs. Why should we abandon these mandatory wife-support and child-support laws so that a wife would have an "equal" obligation to take a job?

By law and custom in America, in case of divorce, the mother always is given custody of her children unless there is overwhelming evidence of mistreatment, neglect or bad character. This is our special privilege because of the high rank that is placed on motherhood in our society. Do women really want to give up this special privilege and lower themselves to "equal rights", so that the mother gets one child and the father gets the other? I think not.

The Right NOT To Take A Job

Passage of the Equal Rights Amendment would open up a Pandora's box of trouble for women. It would deprive the American woman of many of the fundamental special privileges we now enjoy, and especially the greatest rights of all: (1) NOT to take a job, (2) to keep her baby, and (3) to be supported by her husband.

Source: Phyllis Schlafly, "What's Wrong with 'Equal Rights' for Women?" *Phyllis Schlafly Report* 5, no. 7 (February 1972).

C. PRO: WHAT THE EQUAL RIGHTS AMENDMENT WILL DO

WILL end the practice of imposing higher qualifications for women than for men in the military and thus extend the possibilities of G.I. benefits (learning skills, G.I. job preference, medical benefits, mortgage insurance, education) to a greater number of women.

WILL require tax supported public schools and State universities to admit men and women under the same standards, and to make all courses and extracurricular activities equally available.

WILL cause the Government to accept women and men on the same standards in the manpower training programs.

WILL support extension of laws banning employment discrimination on the basis of sex to all employers and employees.

WILL extend to men such employment benefits as are now applied only to women, such as minimum wages, rest periods, etc.

WILL extend to men the right to benefits from their wives' Social

Security contributions and equalize special disability and death benefits to include widowers as well as widows.

WILL provide that men may receive welfare payments under the same circumstances as women—the father would no longer have to run away from home.

WILL support inheritance rights in land to widowers, comparable to present dower rights to widows.

WILL support laws placing a recognized value upon the services of the homemaker not employed outside the home to support and ownership in the property acquired during the marriage.

WILL give the "homemaker" an individual credit rating and give constitutional status to the Equal Credit Opportunity Act.

WHAT THE EQUAL RIGHTS AMENDMENT WILL NOT DO

WILL NOT invalidate laws which punish rape.

WILL NOT invalidate State laws requiring separate public rest rooms for men and women in public institutions.

WILL NOT drag mothers from the cradle to serve on the combat line because of the drafting of women into military service. The same deferments and exemptions will apply to exempt women on grounds of motherhood (as for fatherhood) and because of hardship on dependents.

WILL NOT force women into the business world while their children are placed in Government controlled day care centers—one of the most heinous and irresponsible of charges thrown at susceptible uninformed women.

WILL NOT apply to laws directly concerned with physical differences found in only one sex, such as functioning as wet nurse or sperm donor where there can be no denial of equal rights to the other sex. For example, it WILL NOT apply to abortion; maternity leave; forcible rape as legally defined; homosexual relations; paternity legislation.

Source: Marguerite Rawalt, "What The Equal Rights Amendment Will Not Do" (Washington, D.C.: Women's Equity Action League, 1976).

DOCUMENT 108: The Second Revolution (1973)

In 1973 the prestigious Carnegie Commission on Higher Education of Berkeley, California, issued a report entitled *Opportunities for Women in Higher Education: Their Current Participation, Prospects for the Future, and Recommendations for Action.* Among its conclusions was that the most important need was for a "change in attitude" to bring about broader options and greater freedom of choice for women to make the maximum use of their abilities. That change has not taken place—in part because people have not acknowledged the scope of transformation represented by the women's movement. The following quotation from an anonymous source, found at the beginning of the report, captures the meaning and scope of that transformation.

The second most fundamental revolution in the affairs of mankind on earth is now occurring. The first came when man settled down from hunting, fishing, herding and gathering to sedentary agriculture and village life. The second is now occurring as women, no longer so concentrated on and sheltered for their child-bearing and child-rearing functions, are demanding equality of treatment in all aspects of life, are demanding a new sense of purpose.

Source: Carnegie Commission on Higher Education, *Opportunities for Women in Higher Education: Their Current Participation, Prospects for the Future, and Recommendations for Action* (New York: McGraw-Hill, 1973), n.p.

DOCUMENT 109: *Frontiero v. Richardson* (1973)

One of the legal approaches by which changes can be wrought to ensure equality for women is judicial review under the Equal Protection Clause (see Document 107). That clause prohibits states (and through the Due Process Clause of the Fifth Amendment, the federal government) from denying any person under its jurisdiction "the equal protection of the law." Over the years, the Supreme Court has developed differing "levels of scrutiny" in the examination of legislation seen as infringing on equal protection. At the lowest level of scrutiny is the so-called rational basis test. Here the Court requires only that a piece of legislation show a valid governmental purpose and a rational relationship between that purpose and the legal means selected to achieve it. The highest level of judicial scrutiny—the "strict scrutiny" test—is applied by the Court either when legislative classification is said to be inherently "suspect," as in the case of race and religion, or when legislation adversely affects what are called "fundamental rights" such as voting, interstate movement, and, of late, privacy. Under the "suspect" classification test, the Court requires not only that the legislative ends sought be *compelling* but that no other available means of a less intrusive nature could achieve those ends.

Frontiero v. Richardson challenged a federal statute that permitted any male in the armed forces to claim his wife as a dependent, regardless of whether she was in fact dependent on him, while permitting a female to claim her husband (and thus receive increased benefits) only if he were dependent on her for over one-half his support. Frontiero, a female lieutenant in the U.S. Air Force, sued, claiming that the statute discriminated on the basis of sex. In a groundbreaking opinion, the Court declared sex, like race, a "suspect classification." Since that decision, however, the Court has gradually backed away from its ruling, making arguments for an Equal Rights Amendment more persuasive—that is, with such an amendment, women's equality would not depend on shifts in the Court's opinions.

The question before us concerns the right of a female member of the uniformed services to claim her spouse as a "dependent" for purposes of obtaining increased quarters allowances and medical and dental benefits . . . on an equal footing with male members. . . .

At the outset, appellants contend that classifications based upon sex, like classifications based on race, alienage, and national origin, are inherently suspect and must therefore be subjected to close judicial scrutiny. We agree. . . .

There can be no doubt that our Nation has had a long and unfortunate history of sex discrimination. Traditionally, such discrimination was rationalized by an attitude of "romantic paternalism" which, in practical effect, put women, not on a pedestal, but in a cage. Indeed, this paternalistic attitude became so firmly rooted in our national consciousness that, 100 years ago, a distinguished Member of this Court was able to proclaim . . . "The natural and proper timidity and delicacy which belongs to the female sex evidently unfits it for many of the occupations of civil life. . . .

As a result of notions such as these, our statute books gradually became laden with gross, stereotypical distinctions between the sexes. . . .

It is true, of course, that the position of women in America has improved markedly in recent decades. Nevertheless, it can hardly be doubted that, in part because of the high visibility of the sex characteristic, women still face pervasive, although at times more subtle, discrimination in our educational institutions, in the job market, and perhaps most conspicuously, in the political arena. . . .

Moreover, since sex, like race and national origin, is an immutable characteristic determined solely by the accident of birth, the imposition of special disabilities upon the members of a particular sex because of their sex would seem to violate "the basic concept of our system that legal burdens should bear some relationship to individual responsibility...." And what differentiates sex from such nonsuspect statuses as intelligence or physical disability, and aligns it with the recognized suspect criteria, is that the sex characteristic frequently bears no relationship to ability to perform or contribute to society ....

We might also note that, over the past decade, Congress has itself manifested an increasing sensitivity to sex-based classifications. In Tit[le] VII of the Civil Rights Act of 1964, for example, Congress expressly declared that no employer, labor union, or other organization subject to the provisions of the Act shall discriminate against any individual on the basis of "race, color, religion, *sex*, or national origin." Similarly, the Equal Pay Act of 1963 provides that no employer covered by the Act "shall discriminate ... between employees on the basis of sex." ...

With these considerations in mind, we can only conclude that classifications based upon sex, like classifications based on race, alienage, or national origin, are inherently suspect, and must therefore be subjected to strict judicial scrutiny. Applying this analysis mandated by that stricter standard of review, it is clear that the statutory scheme now before us is constitutionally invalid.

Source: 411 U.S. 677 (1973).

DOCUMENT 110: *Roe v. Wade* (1973)

In *Griswold v. Connecticut* (381 U.S. 479, 1965), the Supreme Court supported the right to privacy and, by extension, the private use of contraceptives by married couples. (Later decisions extended the right to unmarried minors.) The right to privacy in matters generally related to procreation prepared the doctrinal foundation for the Court's most important decision to date affecting abortion, *Roe v. Wade*, in 1973. By the 1960s there was one abortion for every three or four live births, and it was obvious that many physicians were disregarding the anti-abortion laws. Because abortion was illegal, many women sought out unskilled practitioners, and many deaths were attributed to their unsafe procedures. Given the enormous physical, psychological, and socioeconomic consequences of an unwanted child, the growing concern for fetal deformities (as a result of drugs like Thalidomide), and the pressure of feminists, a number of states, including Alaska, Hawaii, New York, and Washington, legalized abortion.

With religious and other groups championing the sanctity of life, most states continued to prohibit abortion except for purposes of saving the mother's life. Texas was one of those states. In 1970 Norma McCorvey, a single pregnant woman, brought a class action suit (under the pseudonym Jane Roe, to protect her privacy) challenging the constitutionality of the Texas law. The following is an excerpt from the landmark decision legalizing abortion during the first three months of pregnancy, based on the right of privacy between a woman and her physician. Challenges to the decision have been many, including the 1989 *Webster v. Reproductive Services* (492 U.S. 490). In *Webster* the Court ruled that its decision in *Roe* remained unchanged, but it upheld a Missouri law which said that a woman was free to terminate her pregnancy so long as neither public funds nor facilities were used to effectuate it.

The principal thrust of the appellant's attack on the Texas statutes is that they improperly invade a right, said to be possessed by the pregnant woman, to choose to terminate her pregnancy. Appellant would discover this right in the concept of personal "liberty" embodied in the Fourteenth Amendment's Due Process Clause; or in personal, marital, familial and sexual privacy said to be protected by the Bill of Rights . . . or among those rights reserved to the people by the Ninth Amendment. . . .

It perhaps is not generally appreciated that the restrictive criminal abortion laws in effect in a majority of States today are of relatively recent vintage. Those laws, generally proscribing abortion or its attempt at any time during pregnancy except when necessary to preserve the pregnant woman's life, are not of ancient or even of common-law origin. Instead, they derive from statutory changes effected, for the most part, in the latter half of the nineteenth century. . . . At common law, at the time of the adoption of our Constitution, and throughout the major portion of the nineteenth century . . . a woman enjoyed a substantially broader right to terminate a pregnancy than she does in most states today. . . .

When most criminal abortion laws were first enacted, the procedure was a hazardous one for the woman. This was particularly true prior to the development of antisepsis. . . . Abortion mortality was high. . . . Modern medical techniques have altered this situation. Appellants . . . refer to medical data indicating that abortion in early pregnancy, that is, prior to the end of the first trimester, although not without its risk, is now relatively safe. Mortality rates for women undergoing early abortions, where the procedure is legal, appear to be as low as or lower than the rates for normal childbirth. Consequently, any interest of the State in protecting the woman from an inherently hazardous procedure . . . has largely disappeared. . . . The State has a legitimate interest in seeing to it that abortion, like any other medical procedure, is performed under circumstances that insure maximum safety for the patient. . . .

The Constitution does not explicitly mention any right of privacy. In a line of decisions, however . . . the Court has recognized that a right of personal privacy, or a guarantee of certain areas or zones of privacy, does exist under the Constitution. . . . This right . . . whether it be founded in the Fourteenth Amendment's concept of personal liberty . . . or . . . in the Ninth Amendment's reservation of rights to the people, is broad enough to encompass a woman's decision whether or not to terminate her pregnancy. . . . We . . . conclude that the right of personal privacy includes the abortion decision, but that this right is not unqualified and must be considered against important state interests in regulation.. . .

. . . the State does have an important and legitimate interest in preserving and protecting the health of the pregnant woman . . . and . . . it has still *another* important and legitimate interest in protecting the potentiality of human life. These interests are separate and distinct. Each grows in substantiality as the woman approaches term, and, at a point during pregnancy, each becomes "compelling."

With respect to the State's important and legitimate interest in the health of the mother, the "compelling" point, in the light of present medical knowledge, is at approximately the end of the first trimester. This is so because of the now-established medical fact . . . that until the end of the first trimester mortality in abortion may be less than mortality in normal childbirth. It follows that . . . for the period of pregnancy prior to this "compelling" point, the attending physician, in consultation with his patient, is free to determine, without regulation by the State, that in his medical judgment, the patient's pregnancy should be terminated.

. . . For the state subsequent to approximately the end of the first trimester, the State, in promoting its interest in the health of the mother, may, if it chooses, regulate the abortion procedure in ways that are reasonably related to maternal health.

For the state subsequent to viability, the State in promoting its interest in the potentiality of human life may, if it chooses, regulate, and even proscribe, abortion except where it is necessary, in appropriate medical judgment, for the preservation of the life or health of the mother.

Our conclusion . . . is . . . that the Texas abortion statutes, as a unit, must fall.

Source: 410 U.S. 113 (1973).

DOCUMENT 111: "Day Care in Connecticut: Problems and Perspectives" (1975)

Following the establishment of the National Commission on the Status of Women in 1961 (see note accompanying Document 101), many states established like organizations. In July 1975, the commission in Connecticut issued a report entitled "Day Care in Connecticut: Problems and Perspectives." Although it focused on Connecticut, its conclusions have had national significance. To date, those conclusions have not been reflected in national policy.

Day care is a vital issue in the pursuit of greater equality for women in this society. It is a prerequisite to the full participation of women at all levels of society—work, government, community—as well as to the realization of their individual capabilities. The issues, therefore, warrant careful analysis and the vigorous support of those believing in sexual equality. The freedom from total child rearing responsibilities is as basic to women's equality as is the freedom of equal opportunity in employment and education.

It is the belief of the Permanent Commission on the Status of Women that all elements of this society—male and female, government and business, family and community—share the responsibility of ensuring this freedom through the provision of day care facilities adequate to the needs of Connecticut women.

Source: Permanent Commission on the Status of Women, "Day Care in Connecticut: Problems and Perspectives" (Permanent Commission on the Status of Women, Hartford, Conn., 1975).

DOCUMENT 112: Diary of a Student–Mother–Housewife–Worker (mid-1970s)

As economic necessities and their human aspirations have combined to increase their participation in the marketplace, women have found themselves more and more saddled with work burdens that belie claims of increased gender equality. The following excerpt is from the diary of Marion Hudson, a mother, a student at SUNY–Old Westbury, and a part-time employee. Ms. Hudson, in fact, worked a "double day," although space allows the inclusion of a partial day here.

7 rooms
2 children (1 girl 1 year, 1 boy 3 years)
Husband   Monday

Clock starts playing loud noise

5:30	Henry wakes up to go work. "Trucking" by Marvin Gay can be heard all over the house at full volume. I'm awake.
5:35	Henry turns the radio down just a little.
5:40	Bathroom light is on. Kitchen light is on. Hallway light is on. (Why can't he turn off these lights when he's finished in a particular room!)
6:00	Monique and Tracey are awake. (Who isn't after the troops have just been called out—meaning Henry.)
6:05	Gave Monique a bottle and changed her diaper.
6:06	Told Tracey he could not have a peanut butter and jelly sandwich at this *ghastly* hour. (Didn't say ghastly.)
6:15	Henry is off to the post office.
6:16	Get up to cut off the lights.
6:17	Settle down for some *sleep*.
6:30	Tracey is up—walking around in the house—scares me half to death.
6:31	Tracey starts pounding me on my back to wake up. He didn't make it to the bathroom. His pajamas are wet.
6:32	I tell Tracey I am going to beat him half to death if he doesn't change those pajamas.
6:33	Tracey gets in my bed.
6:40	We both finally doze off.
6:41	Tracey is awake again. He wants some Bosco.
6:42	I threaten him with a severe beating.
7:00	Thoroughly exhausted from scolding Tracey, I get up and make him some delicious Bosco. (Actually I feel like dumping the whole glass on top of him.)
7:05	It's no use. I can't get back to sleep. Tell Tracey to go upstairs and play with his trucks. Nothing else to do but daydream and think of what I have to do and wear.

7:25	Tracey wants a piece of pie.
7:30	I get up and turn on Tracey's TV so he can watch *Little Rascals*.
8:00	Monique wants to get out of her crib. I let her yell till 8:30.
8:30	I'm up and ready. The wheels begin to move into motion.
8:35	Head for bathroom—wash.
8:45	Wash Monique and Tracey. Get them dressed. Fuss with Tracey about what shoes he is going to wear. He wants to wear his cowboy boots instead of the black ones.
9:00	Feed them breakfast. Eggs, Spam and toast. Turn on *Sesame Street*. Tracey doesn't want his eggs. More confrontation.
9:05	Pack the kids tote bag to take over to Grandma's. Tell Tracey he cannot take his new trucks. "Yes, I have to go to school today." Clean off kitchen table and stove after Henry and myself.
9:10	Get dressed. Make up Tracey's and Monique's beds. Go into my room and make up the bed.
9:20	Pack my schoolbooks and coat. Gather Monique's and Tracey's coats and hats.
9:25	Start towards day. Run to freezer—take something out for dinner.
9:30	Monique just messed in her pants. Back to the bedroom. Change her. Put her coat back on. Meanwhile Tracey is hollering—he wants to go.
9:40	Get in car—head for Grandma's.
9:55	Drop them off at Grandmother's.
10:00	Head for the expressway—another rat race.
10:30	School. . . .

Source: Marion Hudson "Diary of a Student–Mother–Housewife–Worker," in Rosalyn Baxandall, Linda Gordon, and Susan Reverby, eds., *America's Working Women* (New York: Random House, 1976), 337–340.

DOCUMENT 113: *The Battered Woman* (Lenore E. Walker, 1979)

Domestic violence has been an area of concern for feminists since the nineteenth century. Then, the emphasis was on temperance because it was felt that drunkenness was a principal cause of violence against women.

Contemporary women's rights advocates have sought to deal with domestic violence in a number of ways, including gaining support for battered women's shelters, economic independence for women, modification of self-defense law to recognize reactions by assault victims, and even support for what has come to be called "battered women's syndrome" (see *State v. Wanrow*, 81 Wash. 2nd 221, 1977). Battered women's syndrome has been defined as a condition in which the victim internalizes the blame for the violence she experiences, feeling—after repeated assaults—that escape is socially and economically ruinous, psychologically devastating, and physically impossible. So the victim often becomes passive, self-blaming, submissive, "forgiving," and even "helpless," until she reacts one day with fear, termbling, and unexpected force. Three battered women give their experiences here.

DENISE

After we got married, every little thing would set him right off. It seemed he needed extra special loving at all times, and I kept throwing hurdles because I wasn't doing that. Evidently, that was causing him to be very upset. I always got the impression that I wasn't loving enough, giving enough, that there was something defective in my character as far as giving love. That's basically the message he gave to me.

There was physical abuse right away. He would slap me a lot, and I would fight back. Sometimes I didn't, because I thought if I didn't, it might cure him. I never started the fights, I mean physically. I just wasn't inclined to strike out at anybody, ever. Then I tried striking back. I thought that might do it, that if I really fought back, he would straighten out; but that didn't solve it either. I think it made it worse.

I really saw red. I mean, when he hit me, it was like putting a cape in front of a bull. I could hardly see straight, just amazed. I just wanted to kill him. A couple of times, I got to the point where I would pull a knife on him. I don't think I ever would have stabbed him, but I just came darn close to it. I felt like . . . oh, I just had to.

In the beginning, I couldn't tell anyone what was happening; yet it was terrorizing me. I had one girl friend I told about it, and it tunred out she was being slapped, too. She could sympathize with me, but it was something that I couldn't and wouldn't talk to anyone else about. Every time I went to my parents, I wouldn't tell them. My brothers and sisters . . . I wouldn't tell anyone. It was very, very embarrassing to me. To them, he was still this gentle, kind, charming man.

JANET

The house was strangely quiet. Somehow, I just knew that tonight was going to be the night. It didn't matter what I did. I thought that perhaps I could stave it off. Maybe if I tried just a little bit harder, it would all work out. I cooked stew, one of his favorite dinners, and I set the table with his favorite tablecloth. I even put out some pretty candlesticks that he had bought me as a gift after one of the times that he had beaten me badly. I decided that I would wear something that he really enjoyed. I wasn't sure that I wanted to have sex with him, so I didn't do it too sexy. I just did it kind of pretty, a dress that he had bought me after another fight. It is interesting, isn't it, that I always picked the things that he gave me afterward, I knew that it made him feel good to see me using them, but I have to tell you that sometimes I didn't even want to have anything to do with them.

Sure enough, when Lew came in, I could tell that he had a couple of drinks with the guys after work. I decided not to say anything that might infuriate him even more. I went in and greeted him, gave him a big hello, a big hug and kiss, usually things that he liked. I told him what I had made for dinner and suggested that maybe he wanted to relax a little before we ate. He snapped back at me, "No, I'm hungry . . . I want food right now. Now, I want my food." I agreed to give it to him and suggested that he wash up and sit down, that I'd have dinner on the table in a few minutes.

I went into the kitchen and started serving out the dinner, and I heard Lew sit down at the table. All of a sudden, I heard a crashing sound on the floor and footsteps as he came running into the kitchen. I knew there was trouble ahead. "Why the hell did you put the goddamn candlesticks on the table?" he screamed. "What's the matter with you? You're so stupid. Don't you know that we save those only for good occasions? What's so good about tonight? Why do you always do things like that? Now your damned tablecloth is ruined. Why is it that you have to ruin everything? Don't you like anything that I give you? Can't you keep anything right? You're so stupid. You just can't do anything right." And on and on he went. I put my hands over my ears because I couldn't stand listening to it anymore. Immediately tears started welling in my eyes. I tried again to smooth things over, but it just didn't work. . . .

Lew lunged at me and grabbed me, holding me with his left hand, pushing the plate of stew in my face with his right hand. The scalding pain was more than I could bear. I screamed and screamed. He slapped me, kicked me, and pulled my hair until I just didn't know what was happening anymore. I started to run, and he grabbed me and ripped my dress as I was running. I didn't know what to do. I ran into our bedroom, instantly realizing I had made a mistake. I knew he'd follow me there and beat me more.

RENÉE

When we were married twenty-five years ago, we both came from extremely wealthy families. Both of our families were just delighted that we married. It was, as you would say, keeping up the family status. Three weeks after we were married, the abuse started, and continued pretty seriously while my children were little. I finally went back home to my parents. My father had a long talk with my husband, and he swore he would never do it again. My father also made sure that we had plenty of household help, so that if there were any more beatings, they would tell him about it. It's funny, because if they ever told my father, he never did anything anyhow.

The first five years of our marriage I really loved him, and I thought I could help him. I was going to be his psychiatrist. After a while, though, the fear of being killed took over. He would come home from cocktail parties and go to his gun collection and wave them and yell, "I'm no good and I'm going to kill myself! And I'm gonna kill you and the children, too." I really believed him. I was afraid he would kill himself, me, and the children. When we would go to bed at night, he would reach out and kick me out of bed for no reason at all. Many nights I would spend in motels, or in another part of the house, making sure one of the maids would sit up outside my room all night. I laugh now when I think about it, because I don't think she could have stopped him if he wanted to get into the room. But somehow it made me feel better then, like I really was protected.

I've always known that my husband was more powerful than the court. If I went to court or called the police, he would kill me. He's bigger than the law. When he would come home, he would batter down the doors if there was any room that had a closed door in it, so I used to make sure that all the maids left the doors open. Many nights he would come home and start banging on them, and I would wrap up the children and go to drive-in movies. I always knew it was going to be bad when he would go to see his mother. She had had lots of mental problems and had had a lobotomy when he was younger. Going to see her always seemed to set him off.

He's very good at what he does. If it weren't for him, this community wouldn't have a lot of the extra cultural things that his money has provided. Our relationship is so strong that it can't be broken. I know things

about him that he'd kill me before he'd let them out. When things get
so bad that I can't stand them anymore, I pack up and go to Europe,
and travel for a couple of months and then come back. That helps, even
though it's still very lonely. When my youngest child was twelve and
the others kids were in school, I packed her up and we lived in Europe
for a whole year. That was one of the best years that I can remember. I
don't know what I'm going to do. He'd kill me if I try to leave.

Source: Lenore E. Walker, *The Battered Woman* (New York: Harper and Row,
1979), 84–85, 101–105, 167–168.

DOCUMENT 114: *Rostker v. Goldberg* (1981)

At its founding the United States had two requirements for "full"
citizenship that outdistanced all others in a significance: property
holding (see Documents 9 and 47) and military obligation. Although women over the years have been employed by and rendered service to the armed forces (by 1990 women made up 11
percent of the armed forces), the combat emphasis on military service has been used to discriminate against them (men engage in combat, women do not). In 1977 Congress enacted a compulsory draft
registration system that excluded women. Four years later, the Supreme Court in *Rostker v. Goldberg* upheld that exclusion with little
analysis of the law's underlying justification. The Court reasoned
that the registration system was created to prepare for the draft of
combat-eligible troops. Women were not allowed in combat, hence
they could be treated differently in the registration system.

But why are women not permitted in combat? The very gender
stereotypes that were used to defeat the Equal Rights Amendment
are involved: women cannot fight effectively; mixed units would
undermine the effectiveness of men; a civilized society should not
place its daughters at such risk; and physical proximity of men and
women would induce sexual promiscuity. In the 1989 war with
Panama and the 1991 war with Iraq, women engaged in combat
support, and a 1993 Defense Department policy (see Document 123)
promised to reduce the discrimination against women in the armed
forces. There is considerable distance to go, however.

The question is whether the Military Selective Service Act . . . violates the
Fifth Amendment to the United States Constitution in authorizing the
. . . registration of males and not females.

Whenever called upon to judge the constitutionality of an Act of Congress—"the gravest and most delicate duty that this Court is called upon to perform," . . . the Court accords "great weight to the decisions of Congress."

. . . This case is quite different from several of the gender-based discrimination cases we have considered in that . . . Congress did not act "unthinkingly" or "reflexively and not for any considered reason." . . . The question of registering women for the draft not only received considerable national attention and was the subject of wide-ranging public debate, but also was extensively considered in hearings, floor debate, and in Committee. Hearings held by both Houses of Congress in response to the President's request for authorization to register women adduced extensive testimony and evidence concerning the issue. . . .

The foregoing clearly establishes that the decision to exempt women from registration was not the "accidental by-product of a traditional way of thinking about women. . . . "

Women as a group, however, unlike men as a group, are not eligible for combat. The restrictions on the participation of women in combat in the Navy and Air Force are statutory. . . . The Army and Marine Corps preclude the use of women in combat as a matter of established policy. . . . Congress specifically recognized and endorsed the exclusion of women from combat in exempting women from registration. . . . The purpose of registration was to prepare for a draft of combat troops. Since women are excluded from combat, Congress concluded that they would not be needed in the event of a draft, and therefore decided not to register them. . . .

. . . This is not a case of Congress arbitrarily choosing to burden one of two similarly situated groups, such as would be the case with an all-black or all-white, or all-Catholic or all-Lutheran, or All-Republican or all-Democratic registration. Men and women, because of the combat restrictions on women, are simply not similarly situated for purposes of a draft or registration for a draft. . . . The Constitution requries that Congress treat similarly situated persons similarly, not that it engage in gestures of superficial equality. . . .

In light of the foregoing, we conclude that Congress acted well within its constitutional authority when it authorized the registration of men, and not women. . . .

Justice Thurgood Marshall, Dissenting:

The Court today places its imprimatur on one of the most potent remaining public expressions of "ancient canards about the proper role of women". It upholds a statute that requires males but not females to register for the draft, and which thereby categorically excludes women from a fundamental civic obligation.

Source: 453 U.S. 57 (1981).

DOCUMENT 115: *The Second Stage* (Betty Friedan, 1981)

Betty Friedan's second feminist tract raises as many agonizing questions about the roles men and women play, and the ideological forces that define and drive their actions, as did *The Feminine Mystique*. Once again she senses a malaise among women. This time they are the daughters of her feminist generation. With so many battles fought and won, she asks, what is the quality of life that we have gained? Limited, she would answer.

There is no doubt in her mind that a new direction must be taken, because new conditions require new alternatives. Just as historical conditions in the 1960s dictated that women discard the feminist mystique, so the 1980s needs a new model.

American society, then, is in search of a second stage. This time Friedan urges that success be defined in terms of women's views and concerns. With this in mind, she urges that we take another look at the way family matters and work considerations are being handled.

In the first stage, our aim was full participation, power and voice in the mainstream, inside the party, the political process, the professions, the business world. Do women change, inevitably discard the radiant, inviolate, idealized feminist dream, once they get inside and begin to share that power, and do they then operate on the same terms as men? Can women, will women even try to, change the terms?

What are the limits and the true potential of women's power? I believe that the women's movement, in the political sense, is both less and more powerful than we realize. I believe that the personal is both more and less political than our own rhetoric ever implied. I believe that we have to break through our own *feminist* mystique now to come to terms with the new reality of our personal and political experience, and to move into the second stage. . . .

The second stage cannot be seen in terms of women alone, our separate personhood or equality with men.

The second stage involves coming to new terms with the family—new terms with love and with work.

The second stage may not even be a women's movement. Men may be at the cutting edge of the second stage.

The second stage has to transcend the battle for equal power in institutions. The second stage will restructure institutions and transform the nature of power itself.

The second stage may even now be evolving, out of or even aside from what we have thought of as our battle. . . .

The younger women have the most questions:

"How can I have it all? Do I *really* have to choose?"

"How can I have the career I want, and the kind of marriage I want, and be a good Mother?"

"How can I get him to share more responsibility at home? Why do I always have to be the one with the children, making the decisions at home?"

"I can't count on marriage for my security—look what happened to my mother—but can I get all my security from my career?"

"Can I make it in a man's world, doing it the man's way? What other way is there? But what is it doing to me? Do I want to be like men?"

"What do I have to give up? What are the tradeoffs?"

"Will the jobs open to me now still be there if I stop to have children?"

"Does it really work, that business of 'quality, not quantity' of time with the children? How much is enough?"

"How can I fill my loneliness, except with a man?"

"Do men really want an equal woman?"

"Why are men today so gray and lifeless, compared to women? How can I find a man I can really look up to?"

"How can I play the sex kitten now? Can I ever find a man who will let me be myself?"

"If I put off having a baby till I'm thirty-eight, and can call my own shots on the job, will I ever have kids?"

"How can I juggle it all?"

"How can I put it all together?"

"Can I risk losing myself in marriage?" . . .

This is the jumping-off point to the second stage, I believe: these conflicts and fears and compelling needs women feel about the choice to have children now and about success in the careers they now seek. . . .

There is no going back. The women's movement was necessary. But the liberation that began with the women's movement isn't finished. The equality we fought for isn't livable, isn't workable, isn't comfortable in the terms that structured our battle. The first stage, the women's movement, was fought within, and against, and defined by that old structure of unequal, polarized male and female sex roles. But to continue reacting against that structure is still to be defined and limited by its terms. What's needed now is to transcend those terms, transform the structure itself. . . .

How do we surmount the reaction that threatens to destroy the gains we thought we had already won in the first stage of the women's movement? How do we surmount our own reaction, which shadows our feminism and our femininity (we blush even to use that word now)? How do we transcend the polarization between women and women and between women and men, to achieve the new human wholeness that is the promise of feminism, and get on with solving the concrete, practical, everyday problems of living, working and loving as equal persons? This is the personal and political business of the second stage.

Source: Betty Friedan, *The Second Stage* (New York: Summit Books, 1981), 15–41.

DOCUMENT 116: Black Women and Feminism (bell hooks, 1981)

Unlike in the nineteenth century and the early twentieth century, black women did not give much active support to the women's rights movement from the 1920s to the 1960s. And even after the 1960s, when the struggle for the liberation of women gained its widest national support black women were reluctant to joint their white sisters. In the following document, bell hooks, a noted African-American scholar and feminist, furnishes some reasons for that reluctance.

In the forty years from the mid-1920s to the mid-1960s black female leaders no longer advocated women's rights. The struggle for black liberation and the struggle for women's liberation were seen as inimical largely because black civil rights leaders did not want the white American public to see their demands for full citizenship as synonymous with a radical demand for equality of the sexes. They made black liberation synonymous with gaining full participation in the existing patriarchal nation-state and their demands were for the elimination of racism, not capitalism or patriarchy. . . .

The tensions and conflicts that emerged in black male/female relationships were dramatized by the 1959 production of Lorraine Hansberry's award-winning play *A Raisin in the Sun*. Conflict prevails in the black male Walter Lee's relationship to his mother and wife. In one scene, as Walter tells his wife Ruth how he intends to spend his mother's insurance money, she refuses to listen; he becomes angry and yells:

Walter: That is just what is wrong with the colored woman in this world . . . don't understand about building their men up and making 'em feel like their somebody. Like they can do something.

Ruth: There are colored men who do things.

Walter: No thanks to the colored woman.

Ruth: Well, being a colored woman, I guess I can't help myself none.

Walter: We one group of men tied to a race of women with small minds.

Lorraine Hansberry's play was a foretelling of future conflicts between black women and men over the issue of sex-role patterns. This conflict was exaggerated and brought to public attention by the 1965 publication of Daniel Moynihan's report *The Negro Family: The Case for National Action*. In his report Moynihan argued that the black American family was being undermined by female dominance. He claimed that racist discrimination against black men in the work force caused black families to have a matriarchal structure which he asserted was out of line with the white American norm, the patriarchal family structure, and that this prevented the black race from being accepted into the mainstream of American life. Moynihan's message was similar to that of black women who admonished black men for not assuming the patriarchal role. The difference in the two perspectives was that Moynihan placed a measure of the responsibility for the black male's inability to assume a patriarchal role on black women, whereas black women felt that racism and black male indifference were the forces that caused black men to reject the role of sole economic provider.

By labeling black women matriarchs, Moynihan implied that those black women who worked and headed households were the enemies of black manhood. Even though Moynihan's supposition that the black family was matriarchal was based on data that showed that only one-fourth of all black families in America were female-headed households, he used this figure to make generalizations about black families as a whole. His generalizations about black family structure, though erroneous, had a tremendous impact upon the black male psyche. Like the American white male in the 50s and 60s, black men were concerned that all women were becoming too assertive and domineering. . . .

The extent to which black men absorbed this ideology was made evident in the 60s black liberation movement. Black male leaders of the movement made the liberation of black people from racist oppression synonymous with their gaining the right to assume the role of patriarch, of sexist oppressor. By allowing white men to dictate the terms by which they would define black liberation, black men chose to endorse sexist exploitation and oppression of black women. And in so doing they were compromised. They were not liberated from the system but liberated to serve the system. The movement ended and the system had not changed; it was no less racist or sexist.

Like black men, many black women believed black liberation could only be achieved by the formation of a strong black patriarchy. Many of the black women interviewed in Inez Smith Reid's book *Together Black Women*, published in 1972, openly stated that they felt the role of the female should be a supportive one and that the male ought to be the dominant figure in all black liberation struggles. . . .

When the movement toward feminism began in the late 60s, black women rarely participated as a group. Since the dominant white patriarchy and black male patriarchy conveyed to black women the message that to cast a vote in favor of social equality of the sexes, i.e. women's liberation, was to cast a vote against black liberation, they were initially suspicious of the white woman's call for a feminist movement. Many black women refused to participate in the movement because they had no desire to fight against sexism. . . .

Initially, black feminists approached the women's movement white women had organized eager to join the struggle to end sexist oppression. We were disappointed and disillusioned when we discovered that white women in the movement had little knowledge of or concern for the problems of lower class and poor women or the particular problems of non-white women from all classes. Those of us who were active in women's groups found that white feminists lamented the absence of large numbers of non-white participants but were unwilling to change the movement's focus so that it would better address the needs of women from all classes and races. Some white women even argued that groups not represented by a numerical majority could not expect their concerns to be given attention. Such a position reinforced the black female participants' suspicion that white participants wanted the movement to concentrate on the concerns not of women as a collective group, but on the individual concerns of the small minority who had organized the movement.

Black feminists found that sisterhood for most white women did not mean surrendering allegiance to race, class, and sexual preference, to bond on the basis of the shared political belief that a feminist revolution was necessary so that all people, especially women, could reclaim their rightful citizenship in the world. From our peripheral position in the movement we saw that the potential radicalism of feminist ideology was being undermined by women who, while paying lip service to revolutionary goals, were primarily concerned with gaining entrance into the capitalist patriarchal power structure.

Source: bell hooks, *Ain't I a Woman: Black Women and Feminism* (Boston: South End Press, 1981), 178–189.

DOCUMENT 117: *The Equality Trap* (Mary Ann Mason, 1988)

Much of the push for the ERA has been motivated by the feeling that the ad hoc legislative and judicial approaches to women's equality—approaches that purport to seek a balance between protective legislation for women and equality with men—have frustrated the march to full women's equality. Indeed, advocates of the ERA have argued that protective legislation for women has been necessary only because of systemic and historical discrimination against them. Where there is full equality, there will be no need for such protection. Mary Ann Mason, author of *The Equality Trap*, disagrees. She argues that "full equality" between men and women is a beguiling device that is leading women to greater inequality. Is Mason right? Or is she facing the nerve-filled "jumping off" transition to what Betty Friedan calls the second stage?

Something has gone very wrong with the lives of women. Women are working much harder than they have worked in recent history, they are growing steadily poorer, and they are suffering the brutality of divorce at an unprecedented rate. The greatly publicized success of a very few women in high positions has created the illusion that the equal-rights crusade has dramatically improved the lives of all women. The reality is that the everyday quality of women's lives has gravely deteriorated. . . .

At work, women can now expect to earn about seventy cents for every dollar earned by men, a slight rise since 1939, when they earned sixty-three cents on the dollar. The much heralded egalitarian legislation, Title VII of the 1964 Civil Rights Act, which prohibits discrimination against women in employment, and the Equal Pay Act of 1963, which mandates that men and women receive equal pay for the same task, have barely shaken this wage gap. And these figures do not tell the whole story. The shift from a manufacturing to a service economy has drastically reduced the paycheck brought home by the average worker. Between 1973 and 1985 the average weekly income of the typical worker fell by 13 percent. The majority of men no longer earn a wage which will support a family. Men and women alike must run faster to earn more to stay in place.

Most women are flooding the workplace, not driven by the desire to become a corporate executive, but struggling to maintain a decent lifestyle for their families, or simply to survive as a single parent. These women are "working to live." They are filling the same female-dominated occupations that they have always filled, secretaries, clerks, food service workers, only in greater numbers than ever before. Equal opportunity to compete with men in the workplace has done them no good, since they are mainly competing with other women. . . .

What about the woman corporate vice-president, or the first female law partner? They are the glamorous subjects of women's magazines, their stories are the fuel lighting the crusade toward equality, even though they represent a tiny percent of all working women. There is no doubt that the climate of egalitarian expectations has encouraged many women to try harder. These are the women who "live to work." . . .

The woman who "lives to work" does well until the baby arrives. The male working world has not changed its career clock to accommodate the needs of mothers; an executive or a lawyer is not expected to leave promptly at five to pick up a child at day care, or to stay home with a sick baby. And if the woman drops out of the career race even for a few years she will probably not be allowed to reenter. The egalitarian ideal of shared domestic chores inevitably falls apart at home. Even among couples who pledge an egalitarian union, women ultimately assume the vast bulk of what needs to be done. At best there is never enough help in this servantless era. Fatigue sets in, and the woman who "does it all" feels that she does it all badly. . . .

Laws that protected women and children following divorce have been replaced by laws that dictate that women can take care of themselves as well as men can, even when they are also taking care of the children. The result of this egalitarian approach in California, the pioneer of no-fault divorce, is that a woman can expect a 73 percent drop in disposable income one year after divorce, while her ex-husband experiences a 42 percent increase. Poor women get poorer, and comfortably middle-class women can suddenly fall into threadbare survival or even public dependency. A staggering 54 percent of single-parent families now live below the poverty line; more than 90 percent of these are headed by women. . . .

How did women get themselves into this fix? How can so many women sustain the illusion of progress if in fact their condition is deteriorating? Ironically, the failure to obtain passage of the Equal Rights Amendment, the capstone of the egalitarian crusade, delayed for more than a decade a realization of what was actually happening to women.

The real revolution in women's lives would have occurred whether or not there had been a feminist movement with its crusade for equal rights. The real revolution in the United States has been an economic revolution that requires women to work to maintain a family in the face of declining living wages. . . .

Beginning in the late sixties the American economy churned out more and more new jobs, twenty million between 1974 and 1984 alone, providing the illusion of a prosperous, expanding economy even though real wages were shrinking. The vast majority of these new jobs were in the amorphous service/information sector, which covers a wide range from fast-food attendant to word processor. What these new jobs almost all had in common were lower pay, fewer benefits, and less security than those in the declining manufacturing sector. They were also well suited to women, since they required less brawn and more communication skills. . . .

. . . The crusade for equal rights both glorified the experience of work and gave women equal responsibility for supporting the family. Men were conveniently relieved of the sole responsibility for supporting the family at a time when it became impossible for them to do so. Meanwhile, the hard-fought right to abortion freed women to hold jobs; a woman with four or five children has little energy left over for the marketplace.

But the concept of equality is a trap. Equal rights does not challenge the structure of the economy or the role of the government. Asking to be treated as men are treated is a fundamentally conservative position that asks for no special support from the government or special consideration from employers for working mothers. America lags behind all industrialized nations and many Third World countries in child care, maternity benefits, and health care for women and children. As the richest nation in the world, we rank an abysmal sixteenth in infant mortality. . . .

Our protracted, exhausting fight for the ERA narrowed our vision and obscured our understanding of the changes that were occurring in women's lives. We failed to see that most women were being marched out to work for low wages with no support for child care or housework, because our eyes were fixed on an ideal that would presumably solve all problems. We paid little attention to the drastic changes in divorce and custody laws, which had immediate punitive effects on women and children.

Expecting everything of the ERA, we did not consider that even if passed it had little to offer. The ERA campaign drained millions of dollars and millions of working hours into the attempt to pass an amendment which would have made little or no change in the fundamental conditions of women's lives. California, the golden progressive state, which passed a state equal-rights amendment in 1964 and has been the leader in sex-discrimination suits, has more poor women, more divorces, and a lower standard of living following divorce than the national average. In California women earn only 58.4 cents to every dollar earned by men . . . .

A bill written for the needs of working women would not have stressed equal competition, but would address the issues of government-subsidized child care, paid maternity leaves, a higher minimum wage (since 65 percent of all minimum-wage workers are women), medical care and pension rights for part-time workers, affirmative action, and reentry rights. It would also require some form of pay equity between male-dominated occupations and female-dominated occupations. Instead, women have trapped themselves into a competitive model that leaves no room for the special needs of women who are the primary child-rearers.

Many feminists claim that the solution to the problems of working mothers is not government involvement, but an egalitarian sharing of the child-care and domestic responsibilities between father and mother. Aside from the fact that many working women have no husband at home to share with, it is a truth that in all industrialized countries, including enlightened Sweden, women who work still bear the great majority of child-care responsibilities. . . .

The pregnancy issue is a serious snare in the skein of egalitarian logic. It has become popular in feminist circles and in Congress to advocate an *unpaid* parental leave which either partner can take. This egalitarian solution cleverly avoids the obvious truth that childbirth is not an equal situation. It is the woman who gives birth, and it is the woman who needs the leave in order to maintain her health before childbirth and to regain her strength following delivery. For many women following a difficult birth this can be weeks or months. How many families can survive if both breadwinners bring home far less than full pay? Surely the mother deserves first priority in taking time off. A parental leave will work only if at least one parent still receives full pay, otherwise it is simply egalitarian window-dressing. . . .

It is time for some hard rethinking and reevaluation of the direction of the women's movement. A return to the flexible, pragmatic concept of women's rights, rather than the rigid ideology of equal rights, is in order. This will require a change of heart as well as a change of mind. The idea of women's rights recognizes and promotes the role of motherhood and family in the lives of women, equal rights does not.

Source: Mary Ann Mason, *The Equality Trap* (New York: Simon and Schuster, 1988), 19–45.

DOCUMENT 118: Perspectives on Pornography (1991)

Matters relating to pornography have for years been defined by religious values, with religious conservatives exercising a dominant role in that definition. To those conservatives, pornography is wrong because it falsely teaches that sex is merely a physical act

and is separable from a meaningful emotional and spiritual relationship. Additionally, it appeals to libidinal impulses, which lead
to sexual promiscuity, because people are often unable to control
those impulses. Besides, they argue, it is addictive—its users become increasingly desensitized, finding what is shocking today routine tomorrow. Socially, it contributes to sex crimes and violence,
and undermines the family as well as the moral authority of society.
Increases in the consumption of pornographic materials triggered
national concern, which was addressed in 1967 when President
Johnson established a Commission on Obscenity and Pornography.
Its report, published in 1970, concluded that empirical evidence did
not show a causal connection between pornography and criminal
behavior, including sex crimes. Feminists disagreed with their conclusions. Indeed, radical—as distinct from libertarian—feminists,
felt that the commission did not even ask the right questions. The
following document compares the positions of these two group of
feminists.

The two sides of the feminist pornography debate began to crystallize
around the *radical* and *libertarian* feminist positions. . . .
The social theory of radical feminism asserts that the "social relations
of the sexes are organized so men may dominate and women must submit," and it holds that "the primary social sphere of male power" resides
in the area of sexuality. . . . Radical feminists believe that male-
dominated or patriarchal societies are hierarchically organized to expro-
priate women's sexuality (including their procreative capacities) for the
use of males, and that sexuality for women thus involves risks and abusive practices. Violence against women is maintained by the institution-
alization of a dichotomy between dominant masculine roles and
subordinate feminine roles in the patriarchal family and by sexual scripts
that promote sexual coercion as normal behavior and as a source of sexual pleasure for men and women. . . . Under condition of gender inequality, male dominance is normative and even eroticized, rendering the
notion of "consent" to sexual interaction problematic. . . .
Radical feminists emphasize the harm of pornography to *women*, in
contrast to the traditional (non-feminist) antipornography view that em-
phasizes the harm of pornography to the family and moral fabric of
society. Andrea Dworkin . . . and Catherine MacKinnon . . . articulate an
analysis of pornography that places it "at the center of a cycle of abuse"
and that views it as a "core constitutive practice" that helps to institutionalize and legitimate gender inequality. . . . Radical feminists assert
that pornography is both a form of misogyny and coercive sexuality and
a system of sexual exploitation and female sexual slavery, which involves
rape, incest, prostitution, and batterings. . . . It is a method of socializa-

tion that causes and perpetuates acts of violence against women, creates a social climate in which sexual assault and abuse are tolerated, and objectifies, dehumanizes, and degrades women.... Pornography constructs *who women are* since "men's power over women means that the way men see women defines who women can be."...

Pornography, from this perspective, is not mere fantasy or simulation. It is not a distortion or "artificial overlay upon an unalterable substratum of essential sexual being," but it is sexual reality itself.... Pornography is not an "idea" any more than racial segregation is an "idea." Like segregation, it is a concrete, discriminatory social practice that institutionalizes the inferiority and subordination of one group to another. Hence radical feminists favor remedies such as the antipornography civil rights ordinance that would enable women to redress this discrimination.

According to Kathleen Barry's ... analysis, pornography is the embodiment of "cultural sadism"—that ideology which depicts sexual violence as normative and pleasurable for women. By editing out "women's pain," ... pornography disguises the inequality of and coercion inherent in its creation and fuses male aggression with romantic love. Pornography is a principal medium through which cultural sadism is diffused into the mainstream culture and integrated into the sexual practices of individuals....

In contrast to radical feminists, who emphasize the problem of violence against women, libertarian feminists emphasize the sexual repression of women and sexual minorities (for example, lesbians and gays, sadomasochists, transsexuals). The objective of libertarian feminists is to advance women's sexual liberation, and according to their vision of liberation, the essential feature of sexuality should not be emotional intimacy per se, but the exchange of physical, especially genital, pleasure. ... Sexual freedom involves transgressing "socially respectable categories of sexuality and refusing to draw the line on ... politically correct sexuality." ... The ideal sexual relationship should take place between equal consenting partners who "negotiate to maximize one another's sexual pleasure and satisfaction by any means they choose." ... According to liberation feminists, women who only experience sexual feelings in a romantic or committed relationship are expressing "a hidden form of alienation rather than a superior ability to integrate sex and love." ... While conservatives and radical feminists may not agree on what the appropriate sexual norms should be, libertarian feminists are concerned that the "unfortunate result" of their antipornography stance "is a strengthening of the idea of sexual norms." ...

Although they do advance some criticisms of male-produced pornography, libertarian feminists' overriding desire to transcend sexual repression leads them to view pornography as a progressive cultural force ... [which] conveys messages other than the hatred of women. It "flout[s] conventional sexual mores, . . . ridicule[s] sexual hypocrisy and . . . underscore[s] the importance of sexual needs. . . . It advocates sexual adventure, sex outside marriage, sex for no other reason than pleasure, casual sex, anonymous sex, group sex, voyeuristic sex, illegal sex, [and] public sex." . . . These ideas are appealing to some women who may interpret them as legitimizing their feelings of "sexual urgency or desire to be sexually aggressive."

Libertarian feminists find the analysis of feminist film theorists valuable and believe pornographic representation can be a vehicle for women's sexual liberation. . . . They see it as providing an opportunity to investigate how sexuality is constructed, and believe it would be a mistake to leave this realm exclusively to men. Liberation feminists argue for the "possibility and desirability of women's active agency in relation to patriarchal cultural symbols" and encourage "the use of pornographic images for learning more about the workings of desire."

Source: Ronald J. Berger, Patricia Searles, and Charles Cottle, *Feminism and Pornography* (New York: Praeger, 1991), 33–43.

DOCUMENT 119: The Civil Rights Act of 1991

The refusal of unwelcome sexual advances by domestic servants and factory workers in other centuries bore with it the same consequences it bears now—ridicule, unfavorable references, job refusals, job dismissals, demotions, transfers, depression, loss of status and self-esteem. Yet, little was officially done, until recently, to confront the problem. With pressure from women's rights groups and the force of legal arguments by certain feminists, especially legal theorist Catherine MacKinnon, the Equal Employment Opportunity Commission (EEOC) in 1980 issued guidelines characterizing sexual harassment as a form of unlawful sex-based discrimination under Title VII (see Document 102). In 1986 the Supreme Court in *Meritor Savings Bank, FSB v. Vinson* (477 U.S. 57), adopted the above characterization and provided definitional grounds for two general types of liability, consistent with EEOC guidelines. The first deal with "quid pro harassments," where employment decisions are affected by responses to sexual advances; and the second with "work environment harassment," which entails conduct that creates an "intimidating, hostile or offensive" working environment or unreasonably interferes with the person's work performance.

Successful complainants of sexual harassment received little compensation beyond lawyers' fees and some back pay. Faced with enormous pressure as a result of the Anita Hill affair, Congress passed the Civil Rights Act of 1991. (Hill, a law professor at the University of Oklahoma, testified, during confirmation hearings for Supreme Court nominee Clarence Thomas, that Thomas had sexually harassed her when she worked for him.) The Civil Rights Act of 1991, an amendment to Title VII of the 1964 Civil Rights Act, provides substantial compensatory and punitive damages to one who can prove sexual harassment.

Sec. 102

(b) Compensatory and Punitive Damages.—

(1) Determination of punitive damages.—A complaining party may recover punitive damages under this section against a respondent (other than a government, government agency or political subdivision) if the complaining party demonstrates that the respondent engaged in a discriminatory practice or discriminatory practices with malice or with reckless indifference to the federally protected rights of an aggrieved individual.

(2) Exclusions from compensatory damages.—Compensatory damages awarded under this section shall not include backpay, interest on backpay, or any other type of relief authorized under section 706(g) of the Civil Rights Act of 1964.

(3) Limitations.—The sum of the amount of compensatory damages awarded under this section for future pecuniary losses, emotional pain, suffering, inconvenience, mental anguish, loss of enjoyment of life, and other nonpecuniary losses, and the amount of punitive damages awarded under this section, shall not exceed, for each complaining party—

> (A) in the case of a respondent who has more than 14 and fewer than 101 employees in each of 20 or more calendar weeks in the current or preceding calendar year, $50,000;

> (B) in the case of a respondent who has more than 100 and fewer than 201 employees in each of 20 or more calendar weeks in the current or preceding calendar year, $100,000; and

> (C) in the case of a respondent who has more than 200 and fewer than 501 employees in each of 20 or more calendar weeks in the current or preceding calendar year, $200,000; and

> (D) in the case of a respondent who has more than 500 employees in each of 20 or more calendar weeks in the current or preceding calendar year, $300,000.

Source: Public Law No. 102–166, 105 Stat. 1071 (1991).

DOCUMENT 120: U.S. Roman Catholic Bishops' Letter on Women (1992)

"The more things change, the more they remain the same," one could say, if one compares the responses of religious officials to Anne Hutchinson's attempt to be part of the public ministry of the seventeenth century (see Document 3) and the 1992 position of the U.S. Roman Catholic Bishops: "women must be seen but not be much heard." Faced with changes in women's status in almost every area of societal life, the nation's Roman Catholic bishops tried for some nine years to draft and approve a pastoral letter on the role of women in the church. In the end, the proposals, which would improve the status of women, were defeated in 1992. This document reaffirms the church's position on women in positions of church authority. Thus, even the lowly position of lector (one whose principal duty is to read the lessons in a church service) would be denied them, were the bishops' proposals adopted.

For nine years, the nation's Roman Catholic bishops have been trying to draft and approve a pastoral letter about the role of women in the church and in American society. Four drafts of the letter were prepared, as a committee of bishops struggled to reach closer compliance with Vatican teachings.

Although the issue of ordaining women to the priesthood played a central role in the letter, changes in the drafts can also be seen in the way the committee handled the question of opening other ministerial offices to women, ranging from the major ordained office of deacon to that of acolyte or altar server.

1988 The first draft urged a quick study of ordaining female deacons, indicated its positive attitude toward that change, and strongly recommended opening the other roles.

In particular, we recommend that the question of admission of women to the diaconal office . . . be submitted to thorough investigation. . . . We urge that this study be undertaken and brought to completion soon. Women serving in pastoral ministry accomplish, by virtue of some other title or commission, many of the functions performed by ordained deacons and are capable of accomplishing all of them. The question of women being formally installed in the permanent diaconate arises quite naturally, and pastoral reasons prompt its evaluation.

Even more compelling is the question of women being installed in the lay ministries of lector and acolyte. The exclusion of women and girls from certain aspects of service at the altar likewise raises concern. . . .

For this reason, we recommend that women participate in all liturgical ministries that do not require ordination.

1990   The second draft called for a study of ordaining female deacons but dropped the implied endorsement. It no longer called allowing women in other ministries "even more compelling."

> We recommend that the question of admission of women to the diaconal office . . . be submitted to thorough investigation. . . . We urge that this study be undertaken and brought to completion soon. We support further the study for admission of women to the lay ministries of lector and aco- lyte. The exclusion of women and girls from certain aspects of service at the altar likewise demands consideration. . . . For this reason, we encourage participation by women in all liturgical ministries that do not require or- dination.

April 1992   The third draft dropped the call for a study on the diaconate and contained only a reduced reference to the need for "continuing di- alogue and reflection."

> We also recognize the need for continuing dialogue and reflection on the meaning of ministry in the church, particularly in regard to the diaconate, to the offices of lector and acolyte, and to servers at the altar.

September 1992   The fourth draft repeated the third draft's language but added a caveat about respecting the official teaching of the church.

> We recognize the need also for continuing reflection on the meaning of ministry in the Church, particularly in regard to the diaconate and the offices of lector, acolyte, and servers at the altar. Such study should proceed with an objectivity and serenity whose necessary context is respect for the authority of the magisterium of the Church.

Source: "Struggling with Words: The Bishops' Letter on Women," *New York Times*, November 19, 1992.

DOCUMENT 121: "Science vs. the Female Scientist" (Shirley M. Tilghman, 1993)

Despite the academic advances that women have made in the United States—through women's and other colleges—women still

face great difficulties in the sciences. The document below by Dr.
Shirley Tilghman, professor of molecular biology at Princeton University, gives a glimpse of the difficulties women still face in the
field of science and some suggestions about how those difficulties
may be removed.

You can look at the last 20 years in two ways, depending on whether
you are an optimist or pessimist. The optimist sees that between 1966
and 1988, the percentage of women receiving science, medical or engineering degrees increased dramatically. In 1966, 23 percent of the bachelor's degrees in science were awarded to women; by 1988, that figure
had risen to 40 percent. Women now compose 38 percent of medical
school enrollments. As for science doctorates, women earned 9 percent
of the total in 1966 and 27 percent in 1988.

The first thing a pessimist would find in the same 20-year span is that
the increase in women in scientific and medical careers has not been
steady. Most of the increase came in the 1970's, with very little progress
after 1982. The second thing a pessimist would note is that the women
who have been trained are not in leadership positions in proportion to
their representation in the field. . . .

Finally, the pessimist would point out that the increases are the average of highly disparate disciplines and hide large differences between
fields. For example, in psychology women receive more than half of new
doctorates, while in engineering they earn just 7 percent. If you look
carefully, almost no progress has been made in increasing the number
of women practicing physics, mathematics and engineering in the last
50 years.

Physics and mathematics are clearly at one extreme. In the life sciences,
a slightly different dynamic is at work. Fifty percent of bachelor's degrees in biology are awarded to women. . . .

. . . By almost every measure, postgraduate women in the life sciences
are faring less well than their male colleagues. If one takes as a measure
of success those who have reached the status of principal investigator of
a National Institutes of Health grant, just 19 percent are women. Where
are the other 19 percent who received M.D.'s and Ph.D.'s? They are in
non-tenure-track positions in which they often cannot compete for research funds.

What the different experiences of women in the physical and life sciences tell us is that multiple forces are at work to retard the rate at which
women enter the scientific work force. Yet I believe that the common
thread is the role that culture plays in determining career choices for
women. . . .

Let's begin with education. A study by Joan Girgus for the Pew Charitable Trust Science Education Program revealed that differences in the

two sexes can be detected as early as 9 years of age, when girls report fewer science-related experiences, such as looking through a telescope. By 13, girls are less likely than boys to read science articles and books, watch science shows or have science hobbies. The cues girls receive in these formative years are not always subtle. Mattel Inc. recently marketed a Barbie doll that says, "I hate math!" when poked in the stomach. I shudder to think what Ken says back!

Another example comes from the experience of a young assistant professor at Princeton. In high school, she obtained the highest grades in science. Shortly before graduation, her principal called her in and asked if she would be willing to forgo the traditional science award so that the second-ranked student, a male, could receive it. The explanation was that he would be better able to use it, as he was headed for a career in science. To the principal, it was inconceivable that this young woman would also consider such a career.

These are shocking stories, the more so because they occurred in the 1980's and 1990's, not the 1950's. This failure of our society, particularly our educators, to equate women with careers in science, and the propensity to discount their achievements when they persist with this ambition lies at the heart of the problem. . . .

The problem of reconciling a scientific career with some semblance of a normal life is exacerbated by the tenure system. A woman is usually 30 years of age before assuming an assistant professorship at a university, which puts her tenure decision at age 35 to 36. Thus her critical scientific years, in which she is establishing her reputation, and her peak reproductive years coincide. This is a dirty trick. Many in my own generation chose to forgo child-bearing until the security of tenure had been granted, only to find that their biological clock had stopped ticking.

Institutions are beginning to grapple with this problem, with different solutions. Some have initiated programs allowing women to have one or more years before the tenure decision to compensate for the time lost in child-bearing. Others have adopted policies to allow both fathers and mothers to take this option.

I favor an even more radical solution: abolish tenure entirely, in favor of rolling appointments that are reviewed regularly. Tenure is no friend to women. It does not protect them from institutional discrimination. Rather it rigidifies their career path when they need maximum flexibility.

Ultimately we must solve this conflict between work and family if we hope to increase the participation of women in science. The alternative is to accept that women will never reach parity or continue to pay an unequal price for their success. . . .

I would suggest that the greatest change will come in institutions that focus in the short term on the senior faculty level. University faculties are extraordinarily hierarchical, and the graduate students and assistant professors at the bottom of the totem pole are very vulnerable. They are excluded from the most serious decisions on hiring and promotion, and often find it difficult to have their voices heard when they are included in decisions.

When women at the lowest level are vocal, they are too often dismissed as strident. Senior women, on the other hand, participate in all aspects of decision-making, and their presence in senior-level deliberations acts as a brake on the more egregious forms of discrimination. They provide the example of young students and faculty that women can have successful science careers. By acting as mentors, they can interpret not just the science, but the scientific culture.

Source: Shirley M. Tilghman, "Science vs. the Female Scientist," and "Science vs. Women—A Radical Solution," *New York Times*, January 25 and 26, 1993.

DOCUMENT 122: The Family and Medical Leave Act of 1993

As the cross-pressures of family and job have increasingly demonstrated their unfair impact on women (see Document 112), feminists have sought greater flexibility in the workplace. For years little happened. But in 1993 Congress passed the Family and Medical Leave Act, which requires companies with fifty or more employees to grant up to twelve weeks of unpaid leave annually for the birth or adoption of a child, to care for a spouse or immediate family member with a serious health condition, or when the employee is unable to work because of a serious health condition. Feminists and some employee advocates feel that the act should have gone further—at least as far as the European model, which extends paid leave. Not many workers, especially single parents, can afford to bypass a paycheck for twelve weeks.

SEC. 102.
(a) IN GENERAL.—
    (1) ENTITLEMENT TO LEAVE.—Subject to section 103, an eligible employee shall be entitled to a total of 12 workweeks of leave during any 12-month period for one or more of the following:
        (A) Because of the birth of a son or daughter of the employee and in order to care for such son or daughter.
        (B) Because of the placement of a son or daughter with the employee for adoption or foster care.
        (C) In order to care for the spouse, or a son, daughter, or parent,

of the employee, if such spouse, son, daughter, or parent has a serious health condition.

(D) Because of a serious health condition that makes the employee unable to perform the functions of the position of such employee.

(2) EXPIRATION OF ENTITLEMENT.—The entitlement to leave under subparagraphs (A) and (B) of paragraph (1) for a birth or placement of a son or daughter shall expire at the end of the 12-month period beginning on the date of such birth or placement. . . .

SEC. 104.

(a) RESTORATION TO POSITION.—

(1) IN GENERAL.—Except as provided in subsection (b), any eligible employee who takes leave under section 102 for the intended purpose of the leave shall be entitled, on return from such leave—

(A) to be restored by the employer to the position of employment held by the employee when the leave commenced; or

(B) to be restored to an equivalent position with equivalent employment benefits, pay, and other terms and conditions of employment.

(2) LOSS OF BENEFITS.—The taking of leave under section 102 shall not result in the loss of any employment benefit accrued prior to the date on which the leave commenced.

Source: Public Law No. 103–3, 107 Stat. 6 (1993).

DOCUMENT 123: Policy on the Assignment of Women in the Armed Forces (1993)

Throughout U.S. history, women have made significant contributions to the readiness and effectiveness of the armed forces. But their contribution, however, as seen even in the 1981 case *Rostker v. Goldberg* (see Document 114), has been restricted by laws and regulations that have excluded them from many privileges, positions, and functions. In 1991 Congress repealed the law that forbade the assignment of women to combat aircraft, but that repeal was not fully implemented. With women giving important combat support in the 1989 war with Panama and the 1991–92 war with Iraq, new pressures were brought to bear against the continued discrimination against women in the armed forces. Reproduced below is a 1993 directive by former Secretary of Defense Les Aspin designed to implement the congressional mandate respecting combat aircraft and to address some of the other remaining restrictions against women in the armed forces.

As we downsize the military to meet the conditions of the post-Cold War world, we must ensure that we have the most ready and effective force possible. In order to maintain readiness and effectiveness, we need to draw from the largest available talent pool and select the most qualified individual for each military job. . . .

Accordingly, I am directing the following actions, effective immediately.

A. The military services shall open up more specialties and assignments to women.

1. The services shall permit women to compete for assignments in aircraft, including aircraft engaged in combat missions.

2. The Navy shall open as many additional ships to women as is practicable within current law. The Navy also shall develop a legislative proposal, which I will forward to Congress, to repeal the existing combat exclusion law and permit the assignment of women to ships that are engaged in combat missions.

3. The Army and the Marine Corps shall study opportunities for women to serve in additional assignments, including, but not limited to, field artillery and air defense artillery.

4. Exceptions to the general policy of opening assignments to women shall include units engaged in direct combat on the ground, assignments where physical requirements are prohibitive and assignments where the costs of appropriate berthing and privacy arrangements are prohibitive. The services may propose additional exceptions, together with the justification for such exceptions, as they deem appropriate.

B. An implementation committee shall be established to ensure that the policy on the assignment of women is applied consistently across the services, including the reserve components.

Source: Secretary of Defense Les Aspin, Memorandum of April 28, 1993, concerning "Policy on the Assignment of Women in the Armed Forces."

DOCUMENT 124: "Special Versus Equal Treatment" (1993)

In July 1993, the U.S. Senate confirmed Judge Ruth Ginsburg as an Associate Justice of the Supreme Court. A product as well as a champion of women's rights—she was the one who so ably argued the case of *Frontiero v. Richardson* (see Document 109)—she will now have a chance to bring her considerable judicial experience to bear on the interpretation of the U.S. Constitution. The following excerpt is from a speech published in 1986.

Were I Queen, my principal affirmative action plan would have three legs. First, it would promote equal educational opportunity, and effective job training for women, so they would not be reduced to dependency on a man or the state. Second, my plan would give men encouragement and incentives to share more evenly with women the joys, responsibilities, worries, upsets, and sometimes tedium of raising children from infancy to adulthood. (This, I admit is the most challenging part of the plan to make concrete and implement). Third, the plan would make quality day care available from infancy on. Children in my ideal world would not be women's priorities, they would be human priorities.

Source: *New York Times*, June 27, 1993.

DOCUMENT 125: Convention on the Elimination of All Forms of Discrimination Against Women

Although the Equal Rights Amendment was defeated, there is a means available by which female citizens of the United States may secure the equality that proposed amendment promised: the international Convention on the Elimination of All Forms of Discrimination Against Women, which was adopted by the United Nations in 1979. The United States has signed the convention, but it will not become binding domestically until it has been ratified by the U.S. Senate. As of 1994 it is before the Senate Judiciary Committee, where it has been for the past few years. Were it to be ratified, there would be no need for an ERA.

The convention is divided into a preamble and six parts. Part I, which is included below, contains general provisions. The other parts, which deal with civil, political, economic, social, and cultural rights as well as civil and family rights, are more specific.

The States Parties to the present Convention, . . .
Convinced that the full and complete development of a country, the welfare of the world and the cause of peace require the maximum participation of women on equal terms with men in all fields,

Bearing in mind the great contribution of women to the welfare of the family and to the development of society, so far not fully recognized, the social significance of maternity and the role of both parents in the family and in the upbringing of children, and aware that the role of women in procreation should not be a basis for discrimination but that the upbringing of children requires a sharing of responsibility between men and women and society as a whole,

Aware that a change in the traditional role of men as well as the role of women in society and in the family is needed to achieve full equality between men and women, . . .

Have agreed on the following:

Part I

Article 1

For the purposes of the present Convention, the term "discrimination against women" shall mean any distinction, exclusion or restriction made on the basis of sex which has the effect or purpose of impairing or nullifying the recognition, enjoyment or exercise by women, irrespective of their marital status, on a basis of equality of men and women, of human rights and fundamental freedoms in the political, economic, social, cultural, civil or any other field.

Article 2

States Parties condemn discrimination against women in all its forms, agree to pursue by all appropriate means and without delay a policy of eliminating discrimination against women and, to this end, undertake:

(a) To embody the principle of the quality of men and women in their national constitutions or other appropriate legislation if not yet incorporated therein and to ensure, through law and other appropriate means, the practical realization of this principle;

(b) To adopt appropriate legislative and other measures, including sanctions where appropriate, prohibiting all discrimination against women;

(c) To establish legal protection of the rights of women on an equal basis with men and to ensure through competent national tribunals and other public institutions the effective protection of women against any act of discrimination;

(d) To refrain from engaging in any act or practice of discrimination against women and to ensure that public authorities and institutions shall act in conformity with this obligation;

(e) To take all appropriate measures to eliminate discrimination against women by any person, organization or enterprise;

(f) To take all appropriate measures, including legislation, to modify or abolish existing laws, regulations, customs and practices which constitute discrimination against women;

(g) To repeal all national penal provisions which constitute discrimination against women.

Article 3

States Parties shall take in all fields, in particular in the political, social, economic and cultural fields, all appropriate measures, including legislation, to ensure the full development and advancement of women, for the purpose of guaranteeing them the exercise and enjoyment of human rights and fundamental freedoms on a basis of equality with men.

Article 4

1. Adoption by States Parties of temporary special measures aimed at accelerating *de facto* equality between men and women shall not be considered discrimination as defined in the present Convention, but shall in no way entail as a consequence the maintenance of unequal or separate standards; these measures shall be discontinued when the objectives of equality of opportunity and treatment have been achieved.

2. Adoption by States Parties of special measures, including those measures contained in the present Convention, aimed at protecting maternity shall not be considered discriminatory.

Article 5

States Parties shall take all appropriate measures:

(a) To modify the social and cultural patterns of conduct of men and women, with a view to achieving the elimination of prejudices and customary and all other practices which are based on the idea of the inferiority or the superiority of either of the sexes or on stereotyped roles for men and women;

(b) To ensure that family education includes a proper understanding of maternity as a social function and the recognition of the common responsibility of men and women in the upbringing and development of their children, it being understood that the interest of the children is the primordial consideration in all cases.

Article 6

States Parties shall take all appropriate measures including legislation, to suppress all forms of traffic in women and exploitation of prostitution of women.

Source: U.N. General Assembly Resolution 34/180 (December 18, 1979).

Glossary

A mensa et thoro. A term which defines a judicial separation of spouses, who remain wife and husband without cohabitation.

Antinomianism. The belief among some Christians that salvation depends on the indwelling presence of the Holy Spirit, not obedience to a set of laws or specific deeds.

Appellant. The person or party in a legal action who appeals (takes to a higher level) the decision of a lower court.

Civil rights. Rights to legal and social equality that everyone is supposed to possess regardless of race, creed, age, national origin, gender, or disability. Civil rights differ from civil liberties in that the former are said to be positive in nature, while the latter are negative in that they are principally concerned with immunities from governmental interference. For example, the First Amendment to the Constitution prohibits Congress from making any law that may restrict the free exercise of one's religion.

Class action. A lawsuit brought by a representative member or by representative members of a large group of persons on behalf of all members of the group. The class (group) must be ascertainable; the members must demonstrably share a common interest in the issues of law and fact raised or to be raised by the plaintiff(s), and must satisfy a number of special requirements before a court will certify the suit as one that can be entertained as a class action.

Common law. A system of law that originated in England and was later applied in the United States (as well as in other former British colonies such as Australia and Canada). It is based on judicial precedent rather than on legislative enactments, and depends, for its vigor, on general principles that allow flexibility, in contrast to fixed rules.

Convention. A name given to certain written agreements concluded between states. A more general term is treaty.

Coverture. The condition of a woman during marriage at common law. See Part II of this volume.

Decedent. A term used to denote a deceased person.

Defendant. The person or party against whom a lawsuit has been instituted.

Domicile. The place where a person has her or his legal home or place of permanent residence.

Dower. The interest of a wife in her husband's real property. At common law it constituted a life interest in one-third of such property.

Due process of law. A judicial process which requires that, in the administration of justice, certain established rules and procedures be observed in order to protect the rights of individuals. The U.S. Constitution has two clauses dealing with due process. That in the Fifth Amendment protects persons from federal action. That in the Fourteenth Amendment protects them from state action.

Equal protection of the law. A guarantee under the U.S. Constitution that no person or class of persons shall be denied the same protection of the laws enjoyed by others belonging to the same class or similarly circumstanced. This guarantee is found in the Fourteenth Amendment.

Femme sole. An unmarried woman.

Indictment. A formal (usually written) statement charging a person with a criminal offense. The charge is based on the findings of a citizens' body called a grand jury.

Land grant college. A college founded by resources made available under the 1862 Morrill Land-Grant Act. That act allotted federally owned land to each state in proportion to the size of its congressional delegation, to be sold by the state for the purpose of establishing an agricultural college. These colleges were among the first to support coeducation.

Plaintiff. The person who institutes a lawsuit.

Sachem. A title (comparable to king, shah, or tsar) given to a paramount chief among some North American Indians.

Suffrage. The right to vote.

Temperance. The campaign against the nonmedical use of alcohol. That campaign, associated with an effort to mitigate the social and physical violence perpetrated against women as well as women's material dependence on men, was one of the largest reform movements in the United States during the nineteenth century and the early twentieth century.

Women's Organizations

Alice Paul Center for the Study of Women
University of Pennsylvania
106 Logan Hall, CN
Philadelphia, PA 19104

Black, Indian, Hispanic and Asian Women in Action
122 W. Franklin Ave., Suite 306
Minneapolis, MN 55404

Center for the American Woman and Politics
Rutgers University
Eagleton Institute of Politics
New Brunswick, NJ 08903

Center for Research on Women
Stanford University
Serra House, Serra St.
Stanford, CA 94305

Center for Research on Women in Higher Education and Professions
Wellesley College
828 Washington St.
Wellesley, MA 02181

Center for the Study, Education, and Advancement of Women
University of California, Berkeley
Building T-9; Room 112
Berkeley, CA 94720

Center for the Study of Women in Society
University of Oregon
Room 636 Prince Lucien Campell Hall
College of Arts and Sciences
Eugene, OR 97403

Center for Women's Studies and Services
2467 E Street
San Diego, CA 92102

Commission for Women's Equality
c/o American Jewish Congress
15 E. 84th St.
New York, NY 10028

Federation of Organizations for Professional Women
20001 S St. NW, Suite 500
Washington, DC 20009

Feminist Press
City University of New York
311 E. 94th St.
New York, NY 10128

Hispanic American Career Educational Resources, Inc.
115 W. 30 St., Room 900
New York, NY 10001

League of Women Voters
1730 M Street, NW
Washington, DC 20036

Mary Ingraham Bunting Institute
Radcliffe College
10 Garden St.
Cambridge, MA 02138

Mexican American National Association
1030 15th St. NW, Suite 468
Washington, DC 20005

Ms. Foundation for Women
141 5th Ave., Suite 6-S
New York, NY 10010

National Association of Commissions for Women
c/o DC Commission for Women
Room N-354, Reeves Center
2000 14th St. NW
Washington, DC 20009

National Association of Working Women
614 Superior Ave. NW, Room 852
Cleveland, OH 44113

National Council for Research on Women
Sara Delano Roosevelt Memorial House
47–49 E. 65th St.
New York, NY 10021

National Federation of Business and Professional
Women's Clubs, Inc. of USA
2012 Massachusetts Ave. NW
Washington, DC 20036

National Network of Minority Women in Science
Association for Advancement of Science
1776 Massachusetts Ave. NW
Washington, DC 20036

National Organization for Women
1000 16th St. NW, Suite 700
Washington, DC 20036

National Women's Health Network
224 Seventh St. SE
Washington, DC 20003

National Women's Law Center
1616 P St. NW
Washington, DC 20036

National Women's Studies Association
University of Maryland
203 Behavioral and Social Sciences Building
College Park, MD 20742

Nationwide Women's Program
American Friends Service Committee
Philadelphia, PA 19102

Organization of Chinese American Women
1300 N St. NW, Suite 100
Washington, DC 20005

Organization of Pan Asian Women
P.O. Box 39128
Washington, DC 20016

Radical Women
523-A Valencia St.
San Francisco, CA 94110

Rape Crisis Service
256 Main Street
Danbury, CT 06810

Religious Coalition for Abortion Rights
100 Maryland Ave. NE, Suite 307
Washington, DC 20002

Religious Network for Equality for Women
475 Riverside Drive, Room 812-A
New York, NY 10115

Southwest Institute for Research on Women
University of Arizona
Modern Languages 269
Tucson, AZ 85721

United Nations Development Fund for Women
304 E. 45th St., 6th Fl.
New York, NY 10017

Women Involved in Farm Economics
Box 191
Hingham, MT 59528

Women of Color Partnership Program
100 Maryland Ave. NE, Suite 307
Washington, DC 20002

Women's Alliance Against Pornography
P.O. Box 2027
Cambridge, MA 02238

Women's International Network
187 Grant St.
Lexington, MA 02173

Women's Project
2224 Main St.
Little Rock, AR 72206

Women's Rights Committee
c/o Human Rights Dept.
555 New Jersey Ave. NW
Washington, DC 20001

Women's Rights Project
c/o ACLU
132 W. 43rd St.
New York, NY 10036

Bibliography

GENERAL WORKS

Baker, Paula. "The Domestication of Politics: Women in American Society, 1780–1920." *American Historical Review* 89 (June 1984): 620–647.

Beard, Mary, ed. *America Through Women's Eyes.* Westport, Conn.: Greenwood Press, 1969.

Berkin, Carol Ruth, and Mary Beth Norton, eds. *Women of America: A History.* Boston: Houghton Mifflin, 1979.

Boylan, Anne M. "Growing Up Female in Young America." In Joseph Hawes and N. Ray Hiner, eds. *American Childhood: A Research Guide and Historical Handbook.* Westport, Conn.: Greenwood Press, 1988.

Chafe, William H. *The American Woman: Her Changing Social, Economic and Political Roles, 1920–1970.* New York: Oxford University Press, 1972.

Cott, Nancy F. *The Bonds of Womanhood: "Woman's Sphere" in New England, 1780–1835.* New Haven, Conn.: Yale University Press, 1977.

———. *The Grounding of Modern Feminism.* New Haven, Conn.: Yale University Press, 1987.

———, ed. *Root of Bitterness: Documents of the Social Heritage of American Women.* New York: E. P. Dutton, 1977.

Degler, Carl. *At Odds: Women and the Family in America from the Revolution to the Present.* New York: Oxford University Press, 1982.

Douglas, Ann. *The Feminization of American Culture.* New York: Alfred A. Knopf, 1977.

Etienne, Mona, and Eleanor Leacock, eds. *Women and Colonization: Anthropological Perspectives.* New York: Praeger, 1979.

Evans, Sara. *Personal Politics: The Roots of Women's Liberation in the Civil Rights Movement and the New Left.* New York: Vintage Books, 1979.

Fass, Paul S. *The Damned and the Beautiful: American Youth in the 1920's.* New York: Oxford University Press, 1979.

Filine, Peter G. *Him/Her Self: Sex Roles in Modern America*. New York: New American Library, 1976.

Kraditor, Aileen G., ed. *Up from the Pedestal: Selected Writings in the History of American Feminism*. Chicago: Quadrangle Books, 1968.

Leach, William. *True Love and Perfect Union: The Feminist Reform of Sex and Society*. New York: Basic Books, 1980.

Merrill, Marlene Deahl, ed. *Growing Up in Boston's Gilded Age: The Journal of Alice Stone Blackwell, 1872–1874*. New Haven, Conn.: Yale University Press, 1990.

Mohr, James. *Abortion in America: The Origins and Evolution of National Policy, 1855–1900*. New York: Oxford University Press, 1979.

Norton, Mary Beth. *Liberty's Daughters: The Revolutionary Experience of American Women, 1750–1800*. Boston: Little, Brown, 1980.

O'Neill, William L. *Everyone Was Brave: The Rise and Fall of Feminism in America*. Chicago: University of Chicago Press, 1969.

Rothman, Sheila M. *Women's Proper Place: A History of Changing Ideas and Practices 1870 to the Present*. New York: Basic Books, 1978.

Ryan, Mary. *Womanhood in America: From Colonial Times to the Present*. New York: New Viewpoints, 1979.

Smith-Rosenberg, Carol. *Disorderly Conduct: Visions of Gender in Victorian America*. New York: Alfred A. Knopf, 1985.

Solomon, Barbara Miller. *In the Company of Educated Women*. New Haven, Conn.: Yale University Press, 1985.

Tax, Meredith. *The Rising of Women: Feminist Solidarity and Class Conflict, 1880–1917*. New York: Monthly Review Press, 1980.

Tyack, David, and Elizabeth Hanset. *Learning Together: A History of Co-education in American Public Schools*. New Haven, Conn.: Yale University Press, 1990.

Ulrich, Laurel T. *Good Wives: Image and Reality in the Lives of Women in Northern New England, 1650–1750*. New York: Oxford University Press, 1982.

Ware, Susan. *Holding Their Own: American Women in the 1930's*. Boston: Twayne, 1982.

BIOGRAPHIES

Addams, Jane. *Twenty Years at Hull House, with Autobiographical Notes*. New York: Macmillan, 1910.

Barker-Benfield, G. J., and Catherine Clinton. *Portraits of American Women from Settlement to the Present*. New York: St. Martin's Press, 1991.

Duster, Alfreda M., ed. *Crusade for Justice: The Autobiography of Ida Wells*. Chicago: University of Chicago Press, 1970.

Flyn, Elizabeth C. *The Rebel Girl: An Autobiography*. New York: International Publishers, 1973.

Griffith, Elizabeth. *In Her Own Right: The Life of Elizabeth Cady Stanton*. New York: Oxford University Press, 1984.

Hill, Mary A. *Charlotte Perkins Gilman: The Making of a Radical Feminist, 1860–1896*. Philadelphia: Temple University Press, 1979.

Lerner, Gerda. *The Grimké Sisters from South Carolina: Rebels Against Slavery*. Boston: Houghton Mifflin, 1967.

Sanger, Margaret. *My Fight for Birth Control*. New York: Farrar, Reinhart, 1931.
Stanton, Elizabeth Cady. *Eighty Years or More: Reminiscences, 1815–1897*. New York: Schocken Books, 1971.
Steinem, Gloria. *Revolution from Within*. Boston: Little, Brown, 1993.

ETHNIC AMERICAN WOMEN

Acosta-Belen, Edna. *The Puerto Rican Woman*. New York: Praeger, 1970.
Albers, Patricia, and Beatrice Medicine, eds. *The Hidden Half: Studies of Plains Indian Women*. Washington, D.C.: University Press of America, 1983.
Antin, Mary. "The Promised Land" and "Initiation." Chapters 9 and 10 in *The Promised Land*. Boston: Houghton Mifflin, 1912.
Cade, Toni, ed. *The Black Woman: An Anthology*. New York: Signet Books, 1970.
Dener, Hasid. *Erin's Daughters in America: Irish Immigrant Women in the Nineteenth Century*. Baltimore: Johns Hopkins University Press, 1983.
Etter-Lewis, Gwendolyn. *My Soul Is My Own: Oral Narratives of African American Women in Professions*. New York: Rutledge, 1993.
Ewen, Elizabeth. *Immigrant Women in the Land of Dollars: Life and Culture on the Lower East Side, 1890–1925*. New York: Monthly Review Press, 1985.
Garcia, Mario T. "The Chicana in American History: The Mexican Women in El Paso, 1880–1920. A Case Study." *Pacific Historical Review* 49 (May 1980): 319–337.
Gutman, Herbert. *The Black Family in Slavery and Freedom, 1750–1925*. New York: Pantheon Books, 1976.
Hirata, Susie Cheng. "Free, Indentured, Enslaved: Chinese Prostitutes in Nineteenth-Century America." *Signs* 5 (Autumn 1979): 3–29.
Hull, Gloria, Patricia Bell Scott, and Barbara Smith, eds. *All the Women Are White, All the Blacks Are Men, but Some of Us Are Brave: Black Women's Studies*. New York: Feminist Press, 1982.
Ichiaka, Yugi. "Amerika Nadeshiko: Japanese Immigrant Women in the United States, 1900–1924." *Pacific Historical Review* 49 (May 1980): 339–357.
Jones, Jacquelyn. *Labor of Love, Labor of Sorrow: Black Women, Work and Family from Slavery to the Present*. New York: Vintage Books, 1985.
Neu, Irene D. "The Jewish Business Woman in America." *American Jewish Historical Quarterly* 66 (September 1976): 137–154.
Sterling, Dorothy, ed. *We Are Sisters: Black Women in the Nineteenth Century*. New York: W. W. Norton, 1984.
Zit Kala-Sa. "Impressions of an Indian Childhood" and "The School-Days of an Indian Girl." *Atlantic Monthly* 85 (January-February 1900): 45–47, 186–187.

THEORY

Bloch, Ruth. "The Gendered Meanings of Virtue in Revolutionary America." *Signs* 13 (Autumn 1987): 37–58.

Carroll, Bernice A., ed. *Liberating Women's History: Theoretical and Critical Essays.* Urbana: Illinois University Press, 1976.

Cott, Nancy F. "Passionless: An Interpretation of Victorian Sexual Ideology, 1790–1850." *Signs* 4 (1978): 219–236.

Daly, Mary. *The Church and the Second Sex.* New York: Harper and Row, 1975.

DuBois, Ellen Carol, and Linda Gordon. "Seeking Ecstasy in the Battlefield: Danger and Pleasure in Nineteenth Century Feminist Thought." *Feminist Studies* 9, no. 1 (1983): 7–25.

DyKeman, Therese Boos. *American Women Philosophers 1650–1930.* Lewiston, N.Y.: Edwin Mellea Press, 1993.

Erickson, Nancy S. "Women and the Supreme Court: Anatomy Is Destiny." *Brooklyn Law Review* 41 (Fall 1974): 209–282.

Gilligan, Carol. *In a Different Voice.* Cambridge, Mass.: Harvard University Press, 1982.

Goldstein, Leslie Friedman, ed. *Feminist Jurisprudence: The Difference Debate.* Lanham, Md.: University Press of America, 1992.

Harvey, Elizabeth D., and Kathleen O. Kruhlik, eds. *Women and Reason.* Ann Arbor: University of Michigan Press, 1992.

Kerber, Linda. *Women of the Republic: Interest and Ideology in Revolutionary America.* Chapel Hill: University of North Carolina Press, 1980.

Kittay, Eva Feder, and Diana T. Meyers, eds. *Women and Moral Theory.* Lanham, Md.: University Press of America, 1987.

MacKinnon, Catherine. *Feminism Unmodified.* Cambridge, Mass.: Harvard University Press, 1987.

———. *Only Words.* Cambridge, Mass.: Harvard University Press, 1993.

———. *Sexual Harassment of Working Women: A Case of Sex Discrimination.* New Haven, Conn.: Yale University Press, 1974.

Newson, Carol A., and Sharon H. Ringe, eds. *The Women's Bible Commentary.* London: John Knox Press, 1992.

Rosenberg, Rosalind. *Beyond Separate Spheres: Intellectual Roots of Modern Feminism.* New Haven, Conn.: Yale University Press, 1983.

Steinem, Gloria. *Revolution from Within.* Boston: Little, Brown, 1993.

Ulrich, Laurel T. *Good Wives: Image and Reality in the Lives of Women in Northern New England, 1650–1750.* New York: Oxford University Press, 1982.

Welter, Barbara. "The Cult of True Womanhood, 1800–1860." In *Dimity Convictions.* Athens: Ohio University Press, 1976, pp. 21–41.

SOCIAL AND POLITICAL ACTIVISM

Evans, Sara. *Personal Politics: The Roots of Women's Liberation in the Civil Rights Movement and the New Left.* New York: Vintage Books, 1979.

Flexner, Eleanor. *Century of Struggle: The Woman's Rights Movement in the United States.* New York: Atheneum, 1972.

Ginzberg, Lori D. *Women and the Work of Benevolence: Morality, Politics, and Class in the Nineteenth Century United States.* New Haven, Conn.: Yale University Press, 1990.

Hersh, Blanche G. *The Slavery of Sex: Feminist-Abolitionist in America.* Urbana: University of Illinois Press, 1968.

Hewitt, Nancy A. *Women's Activism and Social Change: Rochester, New York, 1822–1872*. Ithaca, N.Y.: Cornell University Press, 1984.

Hobson, Barbara M. *Uneasy Virtue: The Politics of Prostitution and the American Reform Tradition*. New York: Basic Books, 1987.

Melder, Keith. *Beginnings of Sisterhood: The American Women's Rights Movement, 1800–1850*. New York: Schocken Books, 1977.

O'Conner, Karen. *Women's Organizations' Use of the Courts*. New York: Lexington Books, 1980.

O'Neill, William L. *Everyone Was Brave: The Rise and Fall of Feminism in America*. Chicago: University of Chicago Press, 1969.

Reed, James. *From Private Vice to Public Virtue: The Birth Control Movement and American Society since 1830*. New York: Basic Books, 1978.

Sanger, Margaret. *My Fight for Birth Control*. New York: Farrar, Reinhart, 1931.

Scharf, Lois, and Joan M. Jensen, eds. *Decades of Discontent: The Woman's Movement, 1920–1940*. Westport, Conn.: Greenwood Press, 1983.

Tax, Meredith. *The Rising of Women: Feminist Solidarity and Class Conflict, 1880–1917*. New York: Monthly Review Press, 1980.

WOMEN'S BODIES AND HEALTH

Blake, John B. "Women and Medicine in Antebellum America." *Bulletin of History of Medicine* 39 (1965): 99–123.

Donegan, Jane B. *Women and Men Mid-wives: Medical Morality and Misogyny in Early America*. Westport, Conn.: Greenwood Press, 1978.

Ehrenreich, Barbara, and Deidre English. *Complaints and Disorders: The Sexual Politics of Sickness*. Old Westbury, N.Y.: Feminist Press, 1974.

Erickson, Nancy S. "Women and the Supreme Court: Anatomy Is Destiny." *Brooklyn Law Review* 41 (Fall 1974): 209–282.

Gordon, Linda. *Women's Body, Women's Right: A Social History of Birth Control in America*. New York: Penguin, 1979.

Leavitt, Judith W. *Brought to Bed: Child-Bearing in America, 1750–1950*. New York: Oxford University Press, 1984.

———, ed. *Women and Health in America: Historical Readings*. Madison: University of Wisconsin Press, 1984.

Mohr, James. *Abortion in America: The Origins and Evolution of National Policy, 1855–1900*. New York: Oxford University Press, 1979.

Reed, James. *From Private Vice to Public Virtue: The Birth Control Movement and American Society since 1830*. New York: Basic Books, 1978.

Smith, Daniel Scott, and Michael Henders. "Premarital Pregnancy in America, 1640–1671: An Overview and an Interpretation." *Journal of Interdisciplinary History* 5 (1975): 537–570.

WOMEN AND THE FAMILY

Burck, Frances Wells. *Mothers Talking: Sharing the Secret*. New York: St. Martin's Press, 1986.

Degler, Carl. *At Odds: Women and the Family in America from the Revolution to the Present.* New York: Oxford University Press, 1982.

Dudden, Fay. *Serving Women: Household Service in Nineteenth Century America.* Middletown, Conn.: Wesleyan University Press, 1983.

Eyer, Diane E. *Mother-Infant Bonding.* New Haven, Conn.: Yale University Press, 1992.

Gelles, Richard J. C. *Family Violence.* Beverly Hills: Sage Publications, 1979.

Gordon, Linda. *Heroes of Their Own Lives: The Politics of Family Violence, Boston, 1880–1960.* New York: Viking/Penguin, 1988.

Gutman, Herbert. *The Black Family in Slavery and Freedom, 1750–1925.* New York: Pantheon Books, 1976.

Pogrebin, Letty C. *Family Politics: Love and Power on an Intimate Frontier.* New York: McGraw-Hill, 1983.

Smith, Daniel Scott, and Michael Henders. "Premarital Pregnancy in America, 1640–1671: An Overview and an Interpretation." *Journal of Interdisciplinary History* 5 (1975): 537–570.

WOMEN AND THE LAW

Brown, Barbara et al. "The Equal Rights Amendment: A Constitutional Basis for Equal Rights for Women." *Yale Journal* 80, no. 5 (April 1971): 871–985.

Endlich, C. A., and Louis Richards. *The Rights and Liabilities of Married Women Concerning Property, Contracts and Torts under the Common and State Law of Pennsylvania.* Philadelphia, 1889.

Feinman, Clarice. *Women in the Criminal Justice System.* New York: Praeger, 1980.

Geidel, Peter. "The National Women's Party and the Origins of the Equal Rights Amendment, 1920–1923." *Historian* 42 (August 1980): 557–582.

Goldstein, Leslie Friedman, ed. *Feminist Jurisprudence: The Difference Debate.* Lanham, Md.: University Press of America, 1992.

Griswold, Robert L. "Apart but Not Adrift: Wives, Divorce, and Independence in California, 1850–1890." *Pacific Historical Review* 49 (May 1980): 265–284.

Grossberg, Michael. "Guarding the Altar: Physiological Restrictions and the Rise of State Intervention in Matrimony." *American Journal of Legal History* 26 (1982): 197–226.

Nicholas, Susan C., Alice M. Price, and Rachel Rubin. *Rights and Wrongs: Women's Struggle for Legal Equality.* Old Westbury, N.Y.: Feminist Press, 1979.

O'Conner, Karen. *Women's Organizations' Use of the Courts.* New York: Lexington Books, 1980.

O'Neill, William L. *Divorce in the Progressive Era.* New York: Franklin Watts, 1978.

Philbrook, Mary. "Women's Suffrage in New Jersey prior to 1807." *New Jersey Historical Society Proceedings* 57 (1939): 87–98.

Popiel, Marianne. "Sentencing Women: Equal Protection in the Context of Discretionary Decision Making." *Women's Rights Law Reporter* 6 (Fall/Winter 1989): 85–106.

Rabkin, Peggy A. *Fathers to Daughters: The Legal Foundations of Female Emancipation.* Westport, Conn.: Greenwood Press, 1980.

Salmon, Marylynn. *Women and the Law of Property in Early America*. Chapel Hill: University of North Carolina Press, 1986.

Tong, Rosemarie. *Women, Sex, and the Law*. Lanham, Md.: University Press of America, 1984.

WOMEN'S PROFESSIONS

Blake, John B. "Women and Medicine in Antebellum America." *Bulletin of History of Medicine* 39 (1965): 99–123.

Dahl, Linda. *Stormy Weather: The Music and Lives of a Century of Jazz Women*. New York: Limelight Editions, 1984.

Donegan, Jane B. *Women and Men Mid-wives: Medical Morality and Misogyny in Early America*. Westport, Conn.: Greenwood Press, 1978.

Drachman, Virginia. *Women Lawyers and the Origins of Professional Identity in America*. Ann Arbor: University of Michigan Press, 1993.

Epstein, Cynthia F. *Woman's Plans: Options and Limits in Professions and Careers*. Berkeley: University of California Press, 1970.

Etter-Lewis, Gwendolyn. *My Soul Is My Own: Oral Narratives of African American Women in Professions*. New York: Rutledge, 1993.

Graham, Patricia A. "Expansion or Exclusion: A History of Women in American Higher Education." *Signs* 3 (Summer 1978): 759–773.

Hummer, Patricia. *The Decade of Illusive Promise: Professional Women in the United States, 1920–1930*. Ann Arbor: UMI Research Press, 1979.

Leavitt, Judith W. *Brought to Bed: Child-Bearing in America, 1750–1950*. New York: Oxford University Press, 1984.

Litoff, Judy B. *American Midwives, 1860 to the Present*. Westport, Conn.: Greenwood Press, 1978.

WOMEN AND RELIGION

Dairdman, Lynn. *Traditions in a Rootless World: Women Turn to Orthodox Judaism*. Berkeley: University of California Press, 1991.

Daly, Mary. *The Church and the Second Sex*. New York: Harper and Row, 1975.

James, Janet W., ed. *Women in American Religion*. Philadelphia: University of Pennsylvania Press, 1980.

Karlsen, Carol F. *The Devil in the Shape of a Woman: Witchcraft in Colonial New England*. New York: W. W. Norton, 1987.

Keller, Rosemary S. "Creating a Sphere for Women in the Church: How Consequential an Accommodation." *Methodist History* 19 (January 1980): 83–91.

Newson, Carol A., and Sharon H. Ringe, eds. *The Women's Bible Commentary*. London: John Knox Press, 1992.

Pressler, Carolyn Jo. "The View of Women Found in the Deuteronomic Family Laws." Doctoral thesis, Princeton Theological Seminary, 1991.

Thurston, B. B. *The Widows: A Woman's Ministry in the Early Church*. Minneapolis: Fortress Press, 1989.

WOMEN AND THE SOUTH

Fox-Genovese, Elizabeth. *Within the Plantation Household: Black and White Women of the Old South*. Chapel Hill: University of North Carolina Press, 1988.

Hagood, Margaret. *Mothers of the South: Portraits of the White Tenant Farm Woman*. New York: W. W. Norton, 1977.

White, Deborah G. *Ain't I a Woman: Female Slaves in the Plantation South*. New York: W. W. Norton, 1985.

WOMEN AND THE WEST

Armitage, Susan, and Elizabeth Jameson, eds. *The Women's West*. Norman: University of Oklahoma Press, 1987.

Figber, Chriestiane, ed. *Let Them Speak for Themselves: Women in the American West, 1849–1900*. New York: E. P. Dutton, 1977.

Foster, Lawrence. "From Frontier Activism to Neo-Victorian Domesticity: Mormon Women in the Nineteenth and Twentieth Centuries." *Journal of Mormon History* 6 (1979): 3–21.

Jeffrey, Julie R. *Frontier Women: The Trans-Mississippi West*. New York: Hill and Wang, 1979.

Riley, Glenda. "Images of the Frontierswomen: Iowa as a Case Study." *Western Quarterly* 8 (April 1977): 189–200.

WOMEN AT WORK

Backhouse, Constance, and Leah Cohen. *Sexual Harassment on the Job*. New York: Prentice-Hall, 1981.

Baxandall, Rosalyn, Linda Gordon, and Susan Reverby, eds. *America's Working Women: A Documentary History*. New York: Simon and Schuster, 1979.

Benson, Susan Porter. *Counter Cultures: Saleswomen, Managers, and Customers in American Department Stores, 1890–1940*. Urbana: University of Illinois Press, 1986.

Blewett, Mary. *Men, Women, and Work: Class, Gender and Protest in the New England Shoe Industry, 1780–1910*. Urbana: University of Illinois Press, 1988.

Cantor, Milton, and Bruce Laurie, eds. *Class, Sex and the Woman Worker*. Westport, Conn.: Greenwood Press, 1977.

Dublin, Thomas. *Farm to Factory: Women's Letters, 1830–1860*. New York: Columbia University Press, 1981.

———. *Women at Work: The Transformation of Work and Community in Lowell, Massachusetts, 1826–1860*. New York: Columbia University Press, 1979.

Dudden, Fay. *Serving Women: Household Service in Nineteenth Century America.* Middletown, Conn.: Wesleyan University Press, 1983.

Foner, Philip. *Women and the American Labor Movement.* New York: Macmillan, 1979.

Greenwald, Maurine. *Women, War and Work: The Impact of World War I on Women Workers in the United States.* Westport, Conn.: Greenwood Press, 1980.

Hartmann, Heidi. "Capitalism, Patriarchy, and Job Segregation by Sex." In Zellah Eisenstein, ed., *Capitalist Patriarchy and the Case for Socialist Feminism.* New York: Monthly Review Press, 1979, pp. 206–247.

Jensen, Joan. *Loosening the Bonds: Mid-Atlantic Farm Women, 1750–1850.* New Haven, Conn.: Yale University Press, 1980.

Katzman, David. *Seven Days a Week: Women and Domestic Service in Industrial America.* Urbana: University of Illinois Press, 1978.

Kessler-Harris, Alice. *One of Work: A History of Wage-Earning Women in the United States.* New York: Oxford University Press, 1982.

———. "Where Are the Organized Women Workers?" *Feminist Studies* 3 (Fall 1975): 92–110.

———. *Women Have Always Worked: An Historical Overview.* Old Westbury, N.Y.: Feminist Press, 1981.

Milkman, Ruth, ed. *Women, Work and Protest: A Century of U.S. Women's Labor History.* Boston: Routledge and Kegan Paul, 1985.

Neu, Irene D. "The Jewish Business Woman in America." *American Jewish Historical Quarterly* 66 (September 1976): 137–154.

Strasser, Susan. *Never Done: A History of American Housework.* New York: Pantheon Books, 1982.

Tentler, Leslie W. *Wage-Earning Women: Industrial Work and Family Life in the U.S. 1900–1930.* New York: Oxford University Press, 1979.

Weiner, Lynn. *From Working Girl to Working Mother: The Female Labor Force in the United States, 1820–1920.* Chapel Hill: University of North Carolina Press, 1989.

Wertheiner, Barbara Mayer. *We Were There: The Story of Working Women in America.* New York: Pantheon Books, 1977.

WOMEN AND VIOLENCE

Backhouse, Constance, and Leah Cohen. *Sexual Harassment on the Job.* New York: Prentice-Hall, 1981.

Gordon, Linda. *Heroes of Their Own Lives: The Politics of Family Violence, Boston, 1880–1960.* New York: Viking/Penguin, 1988.

MacKinnon, Catherine. *Only Words.* Cambridge, Mass.: Harvard University Press, 1993.

Sanger, Margaret. *My Fight for Birth Control.* New York: Farrar, Reinhart, 1931.

Walker, Lenore E. *The Battered Woman.* New York: Harper and Row, 1979.

Index

About the Authors

WINSTON E. LANGLEY is Professor of Political Science and International Relations at the University of Massachusetts, Boston. He specializes in human rights and is the author of *Human Rights: The Major Global Instrument* (1992) and *Women's Rights in International Documents* (1991).

VIVIAN C. FOX is Professor of History at Worcester State College in Worcester, Massachusetts. A social historian whose speciality is family and women's history, she is the author of *Loving, Parenting and Dying: The Family Cycle in England and America Past and Present* (1981). She is working on a history of children's rights in England during the early modern period and a book about Lydia Ann Stow, the first Massachusetts state normal school teacher.

Recent Title in the New Series
Primary Documents in American History and Contemporary Issues

The Abortion Controversy: A Documentary History
Eva R. Rubin, editor